Swahili

by Seline Okeno and Asmaha Heddi

for dummies®
A Wiley Brand

Swahili For Dummies®

Published by: **John Wiley & Sons, Inc.**, 111 River Street, Hoboken, NJ 07030-5774, www.wiley.com

Copyright © 2024 by John Wiley & Sons, Inc., Hoboken, New Jersey

Published simultaneously in Canada.

For general information on our other products and services, please contact our Customer Care Department within the U.S. at 877-762-2974, outside the U.S. at 317-572-3993, or fax 317-572-4002. For technical support, please visit https://hub.wiley.com/community/support/dummies.

Wiley publishes in a variety of print and electronic formats and by print-on-demand. Some material included with standard print versions of this book may not be included in e-books or in print-on-demand. If this book refers to media such as a CD or DVD that is not included in the version you purchased, you may download this material at http://booksupport.wiley.com. For more information about Wiley products, visit www.wiley.com.

Library of Congress Control Number: 2023949262

ISBN: 978-1-394-19156-7 (pbk); 978-1-394-19158-1 (ebk); 978-1-394-19157-4 (ebk)

SKY10063309_122123

Contents at a Glance

Table of Contents

Introduction

According to UNESCO, Swahili, a Bantu language locally known as Kiswahili, is spoken by more than 100 million people. Swahili speakers are spread across East Africa, with other speakers found as far as Yemen and Oman in the Middle East. It is the national language of Kenya and Tanzania and serves as a lingua franca in the wider East African Community. The number of Swahili speakers is projected to grow significantly in the next few years following its adoption as an official working language of the African Union. (Did you know that July 7 is World Kiswahili Language Day? See? You've learned something already!)

Swahili For Dummies covers the basics of the language in a clear and easy-to-follow manner for complete beginners as well as for those with some prior exposure. These topics are presented in a utilitarian style to help users build their confidence in speaking about everyday situations. We also point out regional differences in language use, so you can comfortably switch between the Tanzanian and Kenyan variants of Swahili without difficulty.

Whether you are looking to learn a less commonly taught language, planning a trip to East Africa, or simply looking to explore a new African culture, this book offers the necessary tools for beginning to understand and use Swahili in common interactions, such as asking for and giving directions, placing a food order, and making small talk with people around you.

About This Book

This book is meant to be your companion on your journey to learn Swahili. Pick it up when you need to discover an aspect of the language and then put it away until you need to explore another topic again. This means you don't need to go through the units sequentially — feel free to skip over chapters that do not interest you at the moment. We do, however, strongly recommend starting with Chapter 1, especially if you're a complete beginner in the language and still not familiar with the pronunciation of Swahili sounds. You may also find it useful to familiarize yourself with verb formation and noun class rules in Chapters 3 and 4 for a good foundation of Swahili sentence structure.

Swahili For Dummies begins each unit by outlining the end goals so you can monitor your progress by assessing your ability to complete the communicative tasks in each topic. This book also revisits certain grammatical structures throughout the book so you can gradually grow more comfortable with different aspects of the language.

Conventions Used in This Book

To make the book easy to follow, we've set up a few stylistic rules:

>> Swahili words and phrases are set in **boldface** to make them stand out.

>> Pronunciations, which are shown in parentheses, follow the terms the first time they appear in a section.

>> Within the pronunciation, the part of the word that's stressed is shown in *italics*.

>> English translations, also in parentheses, appear in italics after the pronunciation.

In each chapter, you can also find the following sections:

>> **Talkin' the Talk:** These are short sample conversations designed to illustrate various language points in different contexts. You'll also find out how to pronounce the words plus their English translations. (As an added bonus, we have put some of these dialogues online to help you with your pronunciation; find them at www.dummies.com/go/swahilifd.)

>> **Words to Know:** You may study the grammar of a language all you want, but without a sizeable vocabulary, you'll still struggle to speak it confidently. After each "Talkin' the Talk" section, we have outlined key expressions from the dialogue and other related words and phrases that you may find useful in your own conversations.

>> **Fun & Games:** Practice your language skills at the end of each chapter with short activities in this part. This is not a test, so no need to sweat; use it as a chance to measure your understanding of the information in the topic. You can find answers to the Fun & Games activities in Appendix D of this book.

Foolish Assumptions

Writing this book was like having a conversation with you face-to-face. We had to imagine you seated across from us and picture what you were like. Here are some assumptions we had before starting our talk:

>> You have zero prior knowledge of Swahili or very little exposure to the language.

>> You do not live in an area with a lot of Swahili speakers.

>> You're curious about Swahili culture.

>> You want to travel and visit or conduct research/business in places where Swahili is spoken, so you need to be able to converse in it.

>> You would prefer to be able to use the language in everyday situations, rather than focusing mostly on grammar.

How This Book Is Organized

This book is divided into four parts and then into chapters. Chapters are further divided into digestible sections. The following sections tell you what types of information you can find in each part.

Part 1: Getting Started with Swahili

Explore the foundations of Swahili language in this part — learn how to pronounce different Swahili sounds, get started with basic expressions (stating your name, for example), start constructing simple sentences, and tackle counting in Swahili.

Part 2: Swahili in Action

This part focuses on speaking Swahili in different situations, thus building your repertoire of important vocabulary to use both in social situations and at work. We show you how to navigate topics for small talk and how to make a good impression on your Swahili-speaking friends or colleagues in various situations.

Part 3: Swahili on the Go

Get ready to explore East Africa with this part. Whether you're looking to use an agency or do your own bookings, this part prepares you to communicate your travel wish list, compare prices, understand contracts, and even take care of your health while on the move.

Part 4: The Part of Tens

Flip through three sections of important things to know about Swahili in this part. Learn ten common Swahili proverbs, ten ways to pick up Swahili quickly, and ten words to never say in Swahili unless you're looking for trouble.

Appendices

Use this part for quick reference when you need the following: a summary of Swahili noun classes, verb conjugation tables, a Swahili to English and English to Swahili mini-dictionary, and answers for the Fun & Games activities.

Icons Used in This Book

We have included a number of icons in this book to make it easier for you to access specific types of information. You can find them scattered across the left side of the page:

TIP

This icon shows tips and tricks that can help you grasp a concept quickly or save face in social situations.

REMEMBER

This icon reminds you of special information to pay extra attention to. This may involve an unexpected nuance in the language or important information about Swahili speakers.

WARNING

The Warning icon points out hidden dangers you may encounter as you journey through the deep forest of tangled words, slippery sentence structure, and the like.

CULTURAL WISDOM

This icon draws your attention to cultural nuances embedded within the Swahili language or explains some cultural aspects relevant to the topic.

AUDIO ONLINE

This icon marks those "Talkin' the Talk" conversations that are included online at www.dummies.com/go/swahilifd and reminds you that you can listen to the dialogue by Swahili speakers while you read it.

Beyond the Book

This book comes with a free online Cheat Sheet containing easy phrases to get you through simple conversations or understand your schedule. To get this Cheat Sheet, simply go to www.dummies.com and type **Swahili For Dummies Cheat Sheet** in the search box.

Where to Go from Here

This book is not a one-stop shop, so we recommend expanding your learning through other platforms such as listening to Swahili music and watching Swahili movies and news broadcasts. **Bahati njema!** (bah-*hah*-tee *njeh*-mah) (*good luck!*)

1

Getting Started with Swahili

IN THIS PART . . .

See the links between Swahili and English.

Master the basics of Swahili grammar.

Say "Hello" — and "Goodbye."

Work with numbers, time, and measurements.

Chapter **1**

The Swahili You Already Know

Welcome to Swahili! You're about to discover the most widely spoken African language and join 50 million other speakers of Swahili world-wide! Let's start by assuring you that it is a relatively easy language to learn, so settle in and enjoy this journey.

We begin this chapter by showing you some Swahili words and phrases that you might already know or recognize from pop culture and everyday usage, before introducing the Swahili alphabet and explaining the pronunciation of common consonant clusters. Be sure to listen to audio files we've put online for you and practice along with the pronunciations for a firm foundation for speaking Swahili like the locals.

Recognizing Familiar Words and Phrases from Pop Culture

Swahili has gained steady visibility worldwide through the influence of pop culture. Most times, when we ask new students what Swahili words they already know, there's a chorus of **Hakuna matata!** (hah-*koo*-nah mah-*tah*-tah) (*No worries!*).

Did you know that *The Lion King* has more Swahili words than **hakuna matata**? For example

>> **Simba** (*see*-mbah) (*lion*)

>> **Rafiki** (rah-*fee*-kee) (*friend*)

>> **Pumbaa** (poo-*mbah*-ah) (*chaff*) [used metaphorically to mean "*nonsense*"]

>> **Shenzi** (*sheh*-nzee) (*stupid*)

>> **Kovu** (*koh*-voo) (*a scar*)

Music is another avenue through which Swahili words and phrases have spread around the world. For example:

>> **Malaika** (mah-la-*ee*-kah) (*angel*) from the song "Malaika" by Miriam Makeba and Harry Belafonte [originally by Adam Salim]

>> **Nakupenda pia** (nah-koo-*peh*-ndah pee-ah) (*I love you, too*) from the song "Liberian Girl" by Michael Jackson

>> **Karamu** ((kah-*rah*-moo) (*party*) from the song "All Night Long" by Lionel Richie

Perhaps you've noticed some names from African–American celebrity households but had no idea they have Swahili origins. These include the following:

>> **Sanaa Lathan** ⇨ **sanaa** (sah-*nah*-ah) (*art*)

>> **Zuri Hall** ⇨ **zuri** (*zoo*-ree) (*beautiful/good*)

>> **Taraji P. Henson** ⇨ **taraji** (tah-*rah*-jee) (*hope/expectation*)

>> **Nia Long** ⇨ **nia** (*nee*-ah) (*will/resolve*)

>> **Amani Askari Toomer** ⇨ **amani** (ah-*mah*-nee) (*peace*) **askari** (ah-*skah*-ree) (*guard*)

>> **Imani Hakim** ⇨ **imani** (ee-*mah*-nee) (*faith*)

Some fictional characters also bear Swahili names. For example:

>> **Baraka** (bah-*rah*-kah) (*blessing*), a character from *Mortal Kombat Legends: Scorpion's Revenge*

>> **Zawadi** (zah-*wah*-dee) (*gift*), a Wakandan from Marvel Comics

>> **Nyota Uhura: nyota** (*nyoh*-tah) (*star*), a character from *Star Trek*

Are you planning on going on **safari**? East Africa is famous for its diverse wild-life and game parks that tourists visit in droves and loudly proclaim that they've booked a **safari**. Even Dora the Explorer uses the word **safari** for a drive around the African wilderness. To Swahili speakers, **safari** (sah-*fah*-ree) (*trip/journey*) can be a bus ride to the next town to visit a friend. (No wild animals involved.)

If you like board games and enjoy socializing with your friends and family over friendly challenges, you probably own a stack of **Jenga** blocks. Now you can tell your friends and family that **Jenga** (*jeh*-ngah) means *to build*.

Lastly, if your local cafe has chai latte or chai tea as options on the drinks menu, be aware that **chai** (*chah*-ee) just translates to *tea* in Swahili.

Discovering Swahili Words that Sound Familiar in English

Sure, there are words that have been taken over whole into the English language, but the Swahili presence in English is more complicated than that. That's because Swahili has evolved by incorporating words from languages such as Arabic, Hindi, German, Portuguese, and even English into its lexicon. You'll notice that such words also adopt vowel endings and phonetic spellings to sound like original Swahili words. If you're a keen listener, you'll be able to create connections instantly and recognize these words. Check out the examples listed below:

>> **biskuti** (bee-*skoo*-tee) (*biscuits*)

>> **bia** (*bee*-ah) (*beer*)

>> **juisi** (joo-*ee*-see) (*juice*)

>> **chokoleti** (choh-koh-*leh*-tee) (*chocolate*)

>> **keki** (*keh*-kee) (*cake*)

>> **supu** (*soo*-poo) (*soup*)

>> **aiskrimu** (ah-ee-s-*kree*-moo) (*ice-cream*)

>> **suti** (*soo*-tee) (*suit*)

>> **soksi** (*soh*-ksee) (*socks*)

>> **sketi** (*skeh*-tee) (*skirt*)

>> **blauzi** (blah-*oo*-zee) (*blouse*)

>> **glavu** (g-*lah*-voo) (*gloves*)

» **sandali** (sah-*ndah*-lee) (*sandals*)

» **tai** (*tah*-ee) (tie)

» **taulo** (tah-oo-loh) (*towel*)

» **sweta** (*sweh*-tah) (*sweater*)

» **kochi** (*koh*-chee) (*couch*)

» **kompyuta** (koh-m-p-*yoo*-tah) (*computer*)

» **sayansi** (sah-yah-*n*-see) (*science*)

» **teknolojia** (teh-knoh-loh-*jee*-ah) (*technology*)

» **maikrowevu** (mah-ee-kroh-*weh*-voo) (*microwave*)

» **mashine** (mah-*shee*-neh) (*machine*)

» **baiskeli** (bah-ee-*skeh*-lee) (*bicycle*)

» **televisheni** (teh-leh-vee-*sheh*-nee) (*television*)

» **friji** (f-*ree*-jee) (*fridge/refrigerator*)

» **video** (vee-*deh*-oh) (*video*)

» **redio** (reh-*dee*-oh) (*radio*)

» **picha** (*pee*-chah) (*picture*)

» **historia** (hee-stoh-*ree*-ah) (*history*)

» **bayolojia** (bah-yoh-loh-*jee*-ah) (*biology*)

» **fizikia** (fee-zee-*kee*-ah) (*physics*)

» **ofisi** (oh-*fee*-see) (*office*)

» **posta** (*poh*-stah) (*post office*)

» **benki** (beh-nkee) (*bank*)

» **hospitali** (hoh-spee-tah-lee) (*hospital*)

» **hoteli** (hoh-*teh*-lee) (*hotel*)

» **nesi** (*neh*-see) (*nurse*)

» **daktari** (dah-k-*tah*-ree) (*doctor*)

» **dereva** (deh-*reh*-vah) (*driver*)

» **polisi** (poh-*lee*-see) (*police*)

» **shilingi** (shee-*lee*-ngee) (*shilling*)

» **milioni** (mee-lee-*oh*-nee) (*million*)

Introducing the Swahili Alphabet

Just like English, Swahili uses the Latin alphabet and has both consonants and vowels. Unlike English, however, Swahili pronunciation is relatively easier; you read it as it is written. This section guides you through the pronunciation of Swahili vowels, consonants, and consonant clusters found in the Swahili **alfabeti** (ah-lfah-*beh*-tee) (*alphabet*).

Discovering simple Swahili sounds

Swahili has five vowels. These vowels are similar to the five English vowels. The difference is in the pronunciation. If you speak German or Italian, you already pronounce Swahili vowels as they should be. Let's have a look at Table 1-1!

TABLE 1-1   **Swahili vowels**

Letter	Pronunciation	English equivalent	Example	Translation
Aa	ah	"a" in "apple"	**mama** (*mah*-mah)	*mother*
Ee	eh	"e" in "elephant"	**pete** (*peh*-teh)	*ring*
Ii	ee	"i" in "igloo"	**giza** (*gee*-zah)	*darkness*
Oo	oh	"o" in "ostrich"	**moto** (*moh*-toh)	*fire*
Uu	oo	"oo" in "tooth"	**ukuta** (oo-*koo*-tah)	*wall*

Swahili consonants, on the other hand, are largely similar to their English counterparts in pronunciation. One major difference is that Swahili does not use the letters **q** and **x**. You'll also notice that a free-standing **c** isn't used in the Swahili alphabet; it will always be attached to the letter **h** to make **ch**. Check out the examples in Table 1-2.

TABLE 1-2   **Swahili consonants**

Letter	Pronunciation	English equivalent	Example	Translation
Bb	bah	"b" in "boy"	**baba** (*bah*-bah)	*father*
CHch	cha	"ch" in "church"	**chai** (*chah*-ee)	*tea*
Dd	dah	"d" in "dog"	**dada** (*dah*-dah)	*sister*
Ff	fah	"f" in "fun"	**farasi** (fah-*rah*-see)	*horse*

(continued)

TABLE 1-2 *(continued)*

Letter	Pronunciation	English equivalent	Example	Translation
Gg	gah	"g" in "goat"	**gari** (*gah*-ree)	*car*
Hh	hah	"h" in "hot"	**harusi** (hah-*roo*-see)	*wedding*
Jj	jah	"j" in "jug"	**joto** (*joh*-toh)	*heat*
Kk	kah	"k" in "kelp"	**kiti** (*kee*-tee)	*chair*
Ll	lah	"l" in "lily"	**lami** (*lah*-mee)	*tarmac*
Mm	mah	"m" in "man"	**maua** (mah-*oo*-ah)	*flowers*
Nn	nah	"n" in "nice"	**nanasi** (nah-*nah*-see)	*pineapple*
Pp	pah	"p" in "pot"	**paka** (*pah*-kah)	*cat*
Rr	rah	"r" in "rock"	**radi** (*rah*-dee)	*lightning*
Ss	sah	"s" in "sun"	**sakafu** (sah-*kah*-foo)	*floor*
Tt	tah	"t" in "ten"	**tembo** (*teh*-mboh)	*elephant*
Vv	vah	"v" in "vogue"	**vumbi** (*voo*-mbee)	*dust*
Ww	wah	"w" in "water"	**watu** (*wah*-too)	*people*
Yy	yah	"y" in "yeti"	**yai** (*yah*-ee)	*egg*
Zz	zah	"z" in "zest"	**zeituni** (zeh-ee-*too*-nee)	*venus*

TIP

If nasal sounds **n** and **m** appear at the beginning of a word followed by another consonant, pronounce the **n's** and **m's** as separate, single syllables. For example:

>> **nta** (*n*-tah) (*wax*)

>> **nchi** (*n*-chee) (*country*)

>> **nzi** (*n*-zee) (*fly*)

>> **mtoto** (m-*toh*-toh) (*child*)

>> **mke** (*m*-keh) (*wife*)

>> **mbwa** (*m*-bwah) (*dog*)

>> **mbao** (m-*bah*-oh) (*timber*)

>> **mlimao** (m-lee-*mah*-oh) (*lemon tree*)

Tackling Swahili consonant clusters

To truly master Swahili, you have to pay attention to the consonant and vowel arrangements in Swahili words. While pronouncing consonants separated by vowels is more straightforward, you might benefit from a little more practice with words that use consonants followed by other consonants before a vowel break. These are called consonant clusters. Consonant clusters might seem foreign at first glance, but we'll show you their English equivalents before providing Swahili examples.

dh

The **dh** consonant cluster is similar to the initial sound in English words like *that*, *there*, *this*. Listen to audio files online and repeat its pronunciation in the following words:

AUDIO
ONLINE

>> **dhamira** (dhah-*mee*-rah) (*intent*)

>> **dharura** (dhah-*roo*-rah) (*emergency*)

>> **dhaifu** (dhah-*ee*-foo) (*weak*)

>> **dhuluma** (dhoo-*loo*-mah) (*injustice*)

>> **dhalilish**a (dhah-lee-*lee*-shah) (*treat poorly*)

gh

Although this consonant cluster has no English sound equivalent, it's still possible to pronounce it correctly. Try to make a gurgling sound at the back of your throat to get it right. No cause to worry if you cannot get the gurgling sound; several Swahili speakers produce a hard /g/ sound as in *get* instead. Listen to audio files online and follow the example for the following words.

AUDIO
ONLINE

>> **ghafla** (*ghah*-flah) (*suddenly*)

>> **gharama** (ghah-*rah*-mah) (*cost*)

>> **lugha** (*loo*-ghah) (*language*)

>> **ghali** (*ghah*-lee) (*expensive*)

>> **mghahawa** (m-ghah-*hah*-wah) (*restaurant*)

ng'

Ng' is the only Swahili sound with an accent mark. To say it correctly, replicate the final sound in English words like *thing, sing, king, bring*. Listen to audio files online and repeat its pronunciation in these words.

AUDIO ONLINE

>> **ng'ombe** (*ng'oh*-mbeh) (*cow*)

>> **ng'ambo** (*ng'ah*-mboh) (*abroad*)

>> **kuong'oa** (koo-*ng'oh*-ah) (*to pluck/uproot*)

>> **kung'aa** (koo-*ng'ah*-ah) (*to shine*)

>> **kung'ang'ana** (koo-ng'ah-*ng'ah*-nah) (*to struggle*)

If a word has **ng** without the accent mark, then pronounce it as you would in words like a**ng**er, li**ng**er, hu**ng**er. For example:

>> **ngamia** (ngah-*mee*-ah) (*camel*)

>> **ngao** (*ngah*-oh) (*shield*)

>> **nguo** (*ngoo*-oh) (*clothes*)

>> **ngozi** (*ngoh*-zee) (*skin*)

>> **ngumi** (*ngoo*-mee) (*a punch*)

>> **nguzo** (*ngoo*-zoh) (*pillar*)

>> **ngano** (*ngah*-noh) (*wheat*)

Ny

Do not separate **n** from **y** when pronouncing words with the **ny** consonant cluster. To make this sound successfully, think of the underlined sounds in the words lasa**gn**a; la**ny**ard. Listen to audio online and repeat the following words.

AUDIO ONLINE

>> **nyota** (*nyoh*-tah) (*star*)

>> **nyuma** (*nyoo*-mah) (*behind*)

>> **nyufa** (*nyoo*-fah) (*cracks*)

>> **nyati** (*nyah*-tee) (*buffalo*)

>> **nyimbo** (*nyee*-mboh) (*songs*)

>> **nyanya** (*nyah*-nyah) (*tomatoes*)

>> **nyama** (*nyah*-mah) (*meat*)

>> **nyuki** (*nyoo*-kee) (*bee*)

th

The **th** sound is easy because it's also an initial sound in English words like <u>th</u>ing, <u>th</u>eatre, <u>th</u>irty. However, many foreigners make the mistake of pronouncing the **t** only. Remember that the tip of your tongue must slightly tap the space between your upper and lower front teeth to get this sound right.

AUDIO ONLINE

>> **thelathini** (theh-lah-*thee*-nee) (*thirty*)

>> **themanini** (theh-mah-*nee*-nee) (*eighty*)

>> **thibitisha** (thee-bee-*tee*-sha) (*ensure/confirm*)

>> **methali** (meh-*thah*-lee) (*proverb*)

FUN & GAMES

AUDIO ONLINE

Say the following tongue twisters as fast as possible. Listen to the recording and compare how you did.

1. **Mpishi kapika mchicha mbichi** (m-*pee*-shee kah-*pee*-kah m-*chee*-chah m-*bee*-chee) (*The chef cooked raw spinach.*)

2. **Ng'ang'a anang'ang'ana kung'oa nguzo** (*ng'ah*-ng'ah ah-nah-ng'ah-*ng'ah*-nah koo-*ng'oh*-ah *ngoo*-zoh) (*Ng'ang'a is struggling to uproot a pillar.*)

3. **Kaka kile kikuku kiko wapi kaka?** (*kah*-kah *kee*-leh kee-*koo*-koo *kee*-koh *wah*-pee *kah*-kah) (*Brother, where's that anklet, brother.*)

4. **Katibu kata wa kata ya Mkata amekataa katakata kukatakata miti katika kata ya Mkata.** (kah-*tee*-boo wah *kah*-tah yah m-*kah*-tah ah-meh-kah-*tah*-ah kah-tah-*kah*-tah koo-kah-tah-*kah*-tah *mee*-tee kah-*tee*-kah *kah*-tah yah m-*kah*-tah) (*The head of Mkata Ward has forbidden the cutting of trees in Mkata Ward.*)

5. **Wale wali walikula wali wangu** (*wah*-leh *wah*-lee wah-lee-*koo*-lah *wah*-lee *wah*-ngoo) (*Those young ladies ate my rice.*)

Chapter **2**

Getting Started with Basic Expressions

First impressions can make or break a potential relationship, be it business or personal. A sure way to create a great initial impression in Swahili culture is to greet people appropriately, an exercise that requires you to know exactly which greetings to apply in what contexts.

This chapter explains how to greet people in Swahili, respond appropriately, introduce yourself, ask and answer basic personal questions, and to excuse yourself at the end of an interaction.

Greeting People

How do you begin conversations with servers, friends, bus drivers, or passersby? Perhaps you say a quick "hi" or just dive into the conversation? In Swahili culture, every interaction begins with **salamu** (sah-*lah*-moo) (*a greeting*). It is a social faux pas to dive straight into whichever business you have with someone without first exchanging a few greetings. It is therefore important to understand which greeting to use with peers, with elders, or at different times of the day.

Saying "hello" in informal situations

You can use a range of greetings with peers in informal situations. Depending on how close you are with the person you're greeting, you can hug, bump fists, or just nod toward them while exchanging greetings. These greetings are rarely accompanied by a handshake. Table 2-1 lists some common informal greetings and their responses.

TABLE 2-1 **Informal Greetings**

salamu (a greeting).	Jibu (a response)
mambo? (*mah*-mboh) (*How are things?*).	**Poa.** (*poh*-ah) (*great*)
vipi? (*vee*-pee) (*How's it going?*)	**Safi.** (*sah*-fee) (*very well*)
Habari? (hah-*bah*-ree) (*How are you?*)	**Nzuri.** (n-*zoo*-ree) (*fine/well*)
Habari yako? (hah-*bah*-ree yah-koh) (*How are you?*)	**Salama.** (sah-*lah*-mah) (*All's well.*)
Habari gani? (hah-*bah*-ree gah-nee) (*How is it going?*)	**Njema.** (n-*jeh*-mah) (*fine/well*)
kwema? (*kweh*-mah) (*All good?*)	**Kwema.** (kweh-*mah*) (*all good*)
mzima? (m-*zee*-mah) (*Are you well?*)	**Mzima** (m-zee-*mah*) (*I am well.*)

CULTURAL WISDOM

The greeting **kwema?** and its response **kwema** are mostly used in Tanzania and the coastal regions of Kenya. You might draw a blank stare if you use it in mainland Kenya.

Jambo (*jah*-mboh) is another greeting you can use in a casual situation. In literal terms it means *an issue/matter*, so when used as a greeting, it translates to *do you/he/she/they have an issue/matter* but is understood as *how are you?* The form you choose depends on whom you are asking after because the **-jambo** greeting changes according to the personal pronoun of the individual(s) being asked after. Check out Chapter 3 for more on personal pronouns.

See Table 2-2 for different forms of the **-jambo** greeting and responses.

REMEMBER

All these greetings are posed as questions, so in speech, you'd use a rising intonation while greeting someone and a falling intonation when responding — even with the same word.

TABLE 2-2

Using -jambo Greetings

-jambo Greeting	-jambo Response
Hujambo?	**Sijambo.**
(hoo-*jah*-mboh)	(see-*jah*-mboh)
(*How are you?*)	(*I am fine.*)
Hajambo?	**Hajambo.**
(hah-*jah*-mboh)	(hah-*jah*-mboh)
(*How is he/she?*)	(*He/she is fine.*)
Hamjambo?	**Hatujambo.**
(hah-*mjah*-mboh)	(hah-too-*jah*-mboh)
(*How are you (pl.)?*)	(*We are fine.*)
Hawajambo?	**Hawajambo.**
(hah-wah-*jah*-mboh)	(hah-wah-*jah*-mboh)
(*How are they?*)	(*They are fine.*)

Talkin' the Talk

AUDIO ONLINE

Listen to the following dialogue between Malaika and Jacinta exchanging greetings using **-jambo.** Notice how the greeting is extended from asking about one person to other known members of their household.

Malaika: **Hujambo Jacinta?**
Hoo-*jah*-mboh Jacinta?
How are you, Jacinta?

Jacinta: **Mimi sijambo Malaika. Mambo?**
Mee mee See-*jah*-mboh Malaika. *Mah*-mboh
I am fine Malaika. How are things?

Malaika: **Poa sana! Baba na mama hawajambo?**
poh-ah *sah*-nah! *Bah*-bah nah *mah*-mah hah-wah-*jah*-mboh?
I am doing very well! How are your dad and mom?

Jacinta:	**Wao hawajambo kabisa! Na wewe wazazi wako hawajambo?**
	wah-oh hah-wah-*jah*-mboh kah-*bee*-sah! Nah *weh*-weh wah-*zah*-zee *wah*-koh hah-wah-*jah*-mboh?
	They are doing very well! And you, how are your parents?
Malaika:	**Wao hawajambo pia! Mtoto wako hajambo?**
	wah-oh hah-wah-*jah*-mboh *pee*-ah! M-*toh*-toh *wah*-koh hah-*jah*-mboh?
	They are doing very well as well! How is your child doing?
Jacinta:	**Yeye hajambo pia! Ninyi wote hamjambo?**
	Yeh-yeh hah-*jah*-mboh *pee*-ah! *Nee*-nyee *woh*-teh hah-m-*jah*-mboh?
	She is fine also! Are you all fine?
Malaika:	**Sisi wote hatujambo.**
	See-see *woh*-teh hah-too-*jah*-mboh.
	We are all fine.

WORDS TO KNOW

baba	*bah*-bah	father
mama	*mah*-mah	mother
wazazi	wah-*zah*-zee	parents
mtoto	m-*toh*-toh	child
mimi	*mee*-mee	I
wewe	*weh*-weh	you
yeye	*yeh*-yeh	he/she
sisi	*see*-see	we
ninyi	*nee*-nyeeh	you (pl.)
wao	*wah*-oh	they
pia	*pee*-ah	also/too
kabisa	kah-*bee*-sah	totally/absolutely

TIP

Using just **jambo!** as a greeting without specifying the recipient (you, he/she, or they) is a clear marker of being a foreigner or new to East Africa. Some locals will greet you with **jambo!** just to test the waters. How about pulling an UNO-reverse card during such instances and responding with the proper form of the greeting?

Saying "hello" in formal situations

When greeting someone who is older than you in Swahili, it is customary to say **shikamoo.** (shee-*kah*-moh) (*I touch your feet.*) The response to this is **marahaba.** (mah-rah-*hah*-bah) (*I accept your respect.*) This greeting is normally accompanied by a firm handshake, kneeling/ quick curtsy (especially children greeting adults) or a bowing of one's head.

The -**jambo** greeting is also used in formal settings, especially in Kenya. So, if you are in a formal setting and whomever you encounter is obviously younger than you, do not hesitate to use the -**jambo** greeting.

CULTURAL WISDOM

Always greet the older person first using **shikamoo**. It is considered rude for them to greet you first. If they do, salvage the situation quickly by responding appropriately to whichever greeting they use and then use the **shikamoo** greeting.

Asking about peoples' day using "habari"

You may have noticed that Swahili greetings can get lengthy, simply because greetings do not just ask after people currently involved in the conversation but also people known to be part of their households. In the same fashion, greetings also include topics relevant to the people having the conversation, such as work, school, or the day in general. Use **habari** (hah-*bah*-ree), which literally translates to *news* to achieve this; so the greetings ask for news of work, school, family, or the day.

>> **Habari za kazi?** (hah-*bah*-ree zah *kah*-zee) (*How's work?*)

>> **Habari za familia?** (hah-*bah*-ree zah fah-mee-*lee*-ah) (*How is your family?*)

>> **Habari za shule?** (hah-*bah*-ree zah *shoo*-leh) (*How is school?*)

>> **Habari za masomo?** (hah-*bah*-ree zah mah-*soh*-moh) (*How are your studies (going)?*)

>> **Habari za asubuhi?** (hah-*bah*-ree zah ah-soo-*boo*-hee) (*Good morning*)

>> **Habari za mchana?** (hah-*bah*-ree zah m-*chah*-nah) (*Good afternoon*)

>> **Habari za jioni?** (hah-*bah*-ree zah jee-*oh*-nee) (*Good evening?*)

>> **Habari za wikendi?** (hah-*bah*-ree zah wee-*keh*-ndee) (*How is/was the weekend?*)

Respond to **habari** greetings with **nzuri** (n-*zoo*-ree) or **njema** (n-*jeh*-mah) or **salama** (sah-*lah*-mah). Any one of those responses works at any given time since they all mean *well/fine*.

What if you meet at **usiku** (oo-*see*-koo) (*night*)? While it makes sense to continue with the same format of **habari za . . .** , Swahili reasons that by nighttime you will have survived the day, so it's only logical to ask how you fared during the day by saying:

» **Greeting:**

Umeshindaje? (oo-meh-shee-*ndah*-jeh) (*How did you spend your day?/How have you been?*)

» **Response:**

Vyema/salama/vizuri. (*vyeh*-mah/sah-*lah*-mah/vee-*zoo*-ree) (*Fine/well*)

Saying goodbye

Just before you part ways, say **kwaheri** (kwah-*heh*-ree) (*goodbye*). It is both a formal and informal manner of saying farewell and is frequently used to show gratitude for a nice time shared. When speaking to more than one person, you use **kwaherini** (kwah-heh-*ree*-nee) (*Goodbye to you all*) rather than **kwaheri,** which is used when bidding farewell to one person. In formal situations, provide a firm handshake as you say **kwaheri**. In informal situations, you can wave and just head out.

TIP

If parting ways with friends after a chat, just say **baadaye!** (bah-ah-*dah*-yeh) (*Later!*).

Introducing Yourself

One of the first things people do when they meet new people is to a) ask for their name and b) introduce themselves as well. Do not be surprised if your taxi driver or fruit vendor asks for your name in East Africa; they are just showing genuine interest in you. But you don't always have to wait for others to steer such interactions. This section explains how to take charge of an initial encounter by introducing yourself and asking others for their name.

Stating your name

The word **jina** (*jee*-nah) stands for *name*. You can use two phrases when stating your name:

>> **Jina langu ni . . .** (*jee*-nah *lah*-ngoo nee) (*My name is . . .*)

>> **Ninaitwa . . .** (nee-nah-*ee*-twah) (*I am called . . .*)

REMEMBER

The first option here uses a possessive *langu* (*lah*-ngoo) (*my*). Check out Chapter 3 for more information on possessives.

Asking "What is your name?"

Just like there are two ways to state your name, you also have two ways to ask someone for their name:

>> **Jina lako ni nani?** (*jee*-nah *lah*-koh nee *nah*-nee) (*What is your name?*)

>> **Unaitwa nani?** (oo-nah-*ee*-twah *nah*-nee) (*What are you called?*)

Getting Personal

You have exchanged greetings, introduced yourself, and asked the other person what their name is. Now what? Since you already have their attention, you might as well hold it by getting a bit more personal. No, do not reveal your bank account details, just background information that might help you create friendships or verify your identity to an immigration officer.

This section explains how to talk about where you come from, your place of residency, your nationality, the languages you speak, your education, and your job.

Stating where you come from/live

To ask where someone is from, say **Unatoka wapi?** (oo-nah-*toh*-kah *wah*-pee) (*Where are you from?*)

Someone may specify that they require you to state your country of residence (**nchi**; *n*–chee) by saying

>> **Unatoka nchi gani?** (oo-nah-*toh*-kah *n*-chee *gah*-nee) (*Which country are you from?*)

In answering this question, use the phrase **ninatoka** (nee–nah–*toh*–kah) (*I come from*). For example:

>> **Ninatoka Marekani.** (nee-nah-*toh*-kah Marekani) (*I come from the USA.*)

Marekani is the Swahili name for the United States. There are other countries with Swahili names, too, such as

>> **Uganda** (oo-*gah*-ndah) (*Uganda*)

>> **Uhabeshi** (oo-hah-*beh*-shee) (*Ethiopia*)

>> **Uhispania** (oo-hee-spah-*nee*-ah) (*Spain*)

>> **Ugiriki** (oo-gee-*ree*-kee) (*Greece*)

>> **Uholanzi** (oo-hoh-*lah*-nzee) (*Holland*)

>> **Uswizi** (oo-*swee*-zee) (*Switzerland*)

>> **Uswidi** (oo-*swee*-dee) (*Sweden*)

>> **Ujerumani** (oo-jeh-roo-*mah*-nee) (*Germany*)

>> **Ubelgiji** (oo-bel-*gee*-jee) (*Belgium*)

>> **Uingereza** (oo-ee-ngeh-*reh*-zah) (*The United Kingdom*)

>> **Urusi** (oo-*roo*-see) (*Russia*)

>> **Ushelisheli** (oo-sheh-lee-*sheh*-lee) (*Seychelles*)

>> **Ujapani** (oo-jah-*pah*-nee) (*Japan*)

>> **Misri** (*mee*-sree) (*Egypt*)

>> **Kolombia** (ko-loh-*mbee*-ah) (*Colombia*)

>> **Uchina** (oo-*chee*-nah) (*China*)

REMEMBER

Although many country names in Swahili are often denoted by the prefix **U–**, there are always exceptions. Also note the phonetic spelling of countries like *Colombia* (**Kolombia**; koh-loh-*mbee*-ah), *Mexico* (**Meksiko**; mehk-*see*-koh), and *Canada* (**Kanada**; kah-*nah*-dah), which are quite different from the English versions.

Two words mean *live* in Swahili. These are **kaa** (*ka*-ah) and **ishi** (*ee*-shee). This means you can use two different phrases to ask where someone lives:

>> **Unakaa wapi?** (oo-nah-*ka*-ah *wah*-pee) (*Where do you live?*)

>> **Unaishi wapi?** (oo-nah-*ee*-shee *wah*-pee) (*Where do you live?*)

To respond to questions of where you live, borrow the same wording used in the question posed; that is, if the question has the word **kaa** in it, use **kaa** in your response, and if the question has **ishi** in it, use **ishi** in your response.

>> **Ninakaa Nairobi.** (nee-nah-*ka*-ah Nairobi) (*I live in Nairobi.*)

>> **Ninaishi Nairobi.** (nee-nah-*ee*-shee Nairobi) (*I live in Nairobi.*)

Talking about nationalities

Have you ever been to a different country where everyone can tell you're not a local? What's the first thing they ask if they approach you? That's right, your nationality! This piece of information can quickly become your identity in places where others have a hard time pronouncing your name.

Nationalities are typically formed by adding a prefix **M** (singular) and **Wa** (plural) to the beginning of a country's name. For example, a Kenyan is **Mkenya** (M-*keh*-nyah), therefore Kenyans are **Wakenya** (wah-*keh*-nyah) and someone from France is **Mfaransa** (M-fah-*rah*-nsah), while people from France are **Wafaransa** (wah-fah-*rah*-nsah). A Tanzanian is **Mtanzania** (M-tah-nzah-*nee*-ah) so people from Tanzania would say **Sisi ni Watanzania** (*see*-see nee wah-tah-nzah-*nee*-ah) (*We are Tanzanian*).

When a country's initial letters begin with the vowel **u-**, form nationalities by dropping the **u-** and replacing it with **u-** in the singular and **wa-** in the plural. For example: **Uturuki** (oo-too-*roo*-kee) — **Mturiki/Waturuki** (m-too-*roo*-kee/wah-too-*roo*-kee) (*Turkey — Turkish person/Turkish people*); **Ujerumani** (oo-jeh-roo-*mah*-nee) — **Mjerumani/Wajerumani** (m-jeh-roo-*mah*-nee/(wah-jeh-roo-*mah*-nee)) (*Germany — German/Germans*).

If followed by a vowel, **m-** becomes **mw-**. For example: **Uingereza** (oo-ee-ngeh-*reh*-zah; *United Kingdom*) — **Mwingereza/Waingereza** (m-wee-ngeh-*reh*-zah/wah-ee-ngeh-*reh*-zah) (*British/English person/British/English people*; **Omani** (oh-*mah*-nee) (*Oman*) — **Mwomani/Waomani** (M-woh-*mah*-nee/ wah-oh-*mah*-nee) (*Omani person/Omani people*):

>> **Mganda** (m-*gah*-ndah) (*Ugandan*)

- » **Mhabeshi** (m-hah-*beh*-shee) *(Ethiopian)*

- » **Mhispania** (m-hee-spah-*nee*-ah) *(Spaniard)*

- » **Mgiriki** (m-gee-*ree*-kee) *(Greek)*

- » **Mholanzi** (m-hoh-*lah*-nzee) *(Dutch)*

- » **Mswizi** (m-*swee*-zee) *(Swiss)*

- » **Mswidi** (m-*swee*-dee) *(Swedish)*

- » **Mjerumani** (m-jeh-roo-*mah*-nee) *(German)*

- » **Mbelgiji** (m-bel-*gee*-jee) *(Belgian)*

- » **Mrusi** (m-*roo*-see) *(Russian)*

- » **Mshelisheli** (m-sheh-lee-*sheh*-lee) *(Seychellois)*

- » **Mjapani** (m-jah-*pah*-nee) *(Japanese)*

- » **Mmisri** (m-*mee*-sree) *(Egyptian)*

- » **Mkolombia** (m-ko-loh-*mbee*-ah) *(Colombian)*

- » **Mchina** (m-*chee*-nah) *(Chinese)*

Listing the languages you speak

If asked, you'd probably tell someone that the language focus of this book is *Swahili*; Swahili speakers, however, would say it is **Kiswahili**. Why the difference? The **Ki** denotes a language spoken by a people; in this case, the Swahili people. Therefore, to state the languages you speak in Swahili, add the prefix **Ki-** to the beginning of a region's name. For example, if you speak Chinese, the language you speak is **Kichina** (ki-*chee*-nah) *(Chinese)*; if you speak French, it is **Kifaransa** (ki-fah-*rah*-nsah) *(French)*; if you speak Japanese, it is **Kijapani** (kee-jah-*pah*-nee) *(Japanese)*. See more examples in the list below:

- » **Kihispania** (kee-hee-spah-*nee*-ah) *(Spanish)*

- » **Kigiriki** (ki-gee-*ree*-kee) *(Greek)*

- » **Kidachi** (kee-*dah*-chee) *(Dutch)*

- » **Kijerumani** (kee-jeh-roo-*mah*-nee) *(German)*

- » **Kiitaliano** (kee-ee-tah-lee-*ah*-noh) *(Italian)*

- » **Kiingereza** (kee-ee-ngeh-*reh*-zah) *(English)*

- » **Kirusi** (kee-*roo*-see) *(Russian)*

>> **Kiarabu** (kee-ah-*rah*-boo) (*Arabic*)

>> **Kireno** (kee-*reh*-noh) (*Portuguese*)

>> **Kihausa** (kee-hah-*oo*-sah) (*Hausa*)

Asking what do you study/where do you study?

We don't know what your reasons for exploring East Africa are, but perhaps you're on a study abroad program or on placement by your college. In that case, there's a good chance that you'll meet other students. **Wanafunzi** (wah-nah-*foo*-nzee) (*students*) (**mwanafunzi**; m-wah-nah-*foo*-nzee in the singular) usually ask each other about their studies within the first few minutes of meeting. To ask someone what they study, use the following phrase:

>> **Unasoma nini.** (oo-nah-*soh*-mah *nee*-nee) (*What do you study?*)

If asked, respond to this question with the phrase

>> **Ninasoma . . .** (nee-nah-*soh*-mah) (*I study . . .*)

Complete the phrase with your course or subject. Here are some options to choose from:

>> **ualimu** (oo-ah-*lee*-moo) (*education*)

>> **udaktari** (oo-dak-*tah*-ree) (*medicine*)

>> **biashara** (bee-ah-*shah*-rah) (*business*)

>> **anthropolojia** (an-throh-poh-loh-*jee*-ah) (*anthropology*)

>> **sosholojia** (soh-shoh-loh-*jee*-ah) (*sociology*)

>> **saikolojia** (sah-ee-koh-loh-*jee*-ah) (*psychology*)

>> **siasa** (see-*ah*-sah) (*politics*)

>> **masomo ya maendeleo** (mah-*soh*-moh yah mah-eh-ndeh-*leh*-oh) (*development studies*)

>> **masomo ya kiafrika** (mah-*soh*-moh yah Kee-ah-*free*-kah) (*African studies*)

>> **bayolojia** (bah-yoh-loh-*jee*-ah) (*biology*)

>> **sanaa** (sah-*nah*-ah) (*art*)

You may be interested in finding out where someone studies. The word *wapi?* (*wah*-pee) is the interrogative word for *where*. Therefore, use the phrase **unasoma wapi** (oo-nah-*soh*-mah *wah*-pee) to ask *Where do you study?*

The phrase **ninasoma katika** (nee-nah-*soh*-mah kah-*tee*-kah) (*I study at...*) precedes the name of your academic institution. For example:

>> **Ninasoma katika Chuo kikuu cha Nairobi.** (nee-nah-*soh*-mah kah-*tee*-kah *choo*-oh *kee*-koo chah Nairobi) (*I study at the University of Nairobi.*)

Chuo Kikuu stands for *university* and **chuo cha kiufundi** (*choo*-oh chah kee-oo-*foo*-ndee) stands for *technical college* However, if you have children and are asked where they might be studying, you'd want to choose from one of the following options:

>> **Shule ya upili** (*shoo*-leh yah oo-*pee*-lee) (*secondary/high school*)

>> **Shule ya msingi** (*shoo*-leh yah m-*see*-ngee) (*primary school*)

>> **Shule ya chekechea** (*shoo*-leh yah cheh-keh-*cheh*-ah) (*nursery school*)

Talkin' the Talk

Owen is studying abroad at the University of Dar Es Salaam. He meets Lydia on campus and she strikes up a conversation.

Lydia:	**Mambo vipi?** *Mah*-mboh *vee*-pee? *How is it going?*
Owen:	**Poa sana! Kwema?** *Poh*-ah *sah*-nah. *Kweh*-mah? *Really great! All good?*
Lydia:	**Kwema. Jina langu ni Lydia. Wewe unaitwa nani?** *Kweh*-mah. *Jee*-nah *lah*-ngoo nee Lydia. *Weh*-weh oo-nah-*ee*-twah *nah*-nee *All good. My name is Lydia. What are you called?*
Owen:	**Ninaitwa Owen. Nimefurahi kukufahamu. Unatoka wapi, Lydia?** Nee-nah-*ee*-twah Owen. Nee-meh-foo-*rah*-hee koo-koo-fah-*hah*-moo. Oo-nah-*toh*-kah *wah*-pee Lydia *I am called Owen. Nice to meet you. Where are you from, Lydia?*

Lydia:	**Ninatoka hapa Tanzania. Mimi ni Mtanzania. Wewe unatoka wapi?**
	Nee-nah-*toh*-kah *hah*-pah Tanzania. *Mee*-mee nee m-tah-nzah-*nee*-ah. *Weh*-weh oo-nah-*toh*-kah *wah*-pee
	I'm from here in Tanzania. I am Tanzanian. And you, where are you from?
Owen:	**Ninatoka Marekani lakini kwa sasa ninaishi hapa Tanzania. Unasoma wapi?**
	Nee-nah-*toh*-kah Marekani lah-*kee*-nee *sah*-sah nee-nah-*ee*-shee *hah*-pah Tanzania. Oo-a-nah-*soh*-mah *wah*-pee?
	I'm from the USA but live here in Tanzania for now. Where do you study?
Lydia:	**Ninasoma Historia hapa Chuo Kikuu cha Dar Es Salaam. Na wewe?**
	Nee-nah-*soh*-mah *Hee*-stoh-*ree*-ah *hah*-pah *choo*-oh *kee*-koo chah Dar Es Salaam. Nah *weh*-weh?
	I study history here at the University of Dar Es Salaam. And you?
Owen:	**Ninasoma Sosolojia katika Chuo Kikuu cha Indiana.**
	Nee-nah-*soh*-mah soh-shoh-loh-*jee*-ah kah-*tee*-kah *choo*-oh *kee*-koo chah Indiana
	I study sociology at Indiana University.
Lydia:	**Unasema lugha gani?**
	oo-nah-*seh*-mah *loo*-ghah *gah*-nee
	What languages do you speak?
Owen:	**Ninasema Kiingereza, Kiarabu na Kiswahili kidogo.**
	Nee-nah-*seh*-mah kee-ee-ngeh-*reh*-zah, kee-ah-*rah*-boo nah kee-swah-*hee*-lee kee-*doh*-goh
	I speak English, Arabic, and a little Swahili.
Lydia:	**Safi sana! Karibu Tanzania. Baadaye!**
	Sah-fee sah nah! Kah-*ree*-boo Tanzania. Ba-ah-*dah*-yeh
	Great! Welcome to Tanzania. Later!
Owen:	**Baadaye!**
	Ba-ah-*dah*-yeh
	Later!

• •

Asking about occupations

You'll probably be interested in the jobs **kazi** (*kah*-zee) of the people you meet. To ask about someone's job, say the following:

>> **Unafanya kazi gani?** (oo-nah-*fah*-nyah *kah*-zee *gah*-nee) (*What's your job?*)

If this question is posed to you, respond with the phrase **Mimi ni . . .** (*mee*-mee nee) (*I am . . .*) followed by the job title. Check out a few jobs in Swahili, as listed here:

>> **mwalimu** (m-wah-*lee*-moo) (*teacher*)

>> **mwanabiashara** (m-*wah*-nah-bee-ah-*shah*-rah) (*businessman/woman*)

>> **mkulima** (m-koo-*lee*-mah) (*farmer*)

>> **daktari** (dahk-*tah*-ree) (*doctor*)

>> **muuguzi/nesi** (moo-oo-*goo*-zee/*neh*-see) (*nurse*)

>> **dereva** (de-*reh*-vah) (*driver*)

>> **mpishi** (m-*pee*-shee) (*chef*)

>> **mwanamitindo** (m-*wah*-nah-mee-*tee*-ndoh) (*model*)

>> **msusi** (m-*soo*-see) (*hairdresser*)

>> **fundi bomba** (*foo*-ndee *boh*-mbah) (*plumber*)

>> **fundi umeme** (*foo*-ndee oo-*meh*-meh) (*electrician*)

>> **mhandisi** (m-hah-*ndee*-see) (*engineer*)

>> **mtafiti** (m-tah-*fee*-tee) (*researcher*)

TIP

Most phrases for describing a trade require adding the term **fundi** (*foo*-ndee) (*handyman/woman*), which means someone who fixes, makes, or builds things by hand. To specify what exactly they specialize in, add the second part of what they deal with, like **bomba** (*boh*-mbah) (*faucets*), **umeme** (oo-*meh*-meh) (*electricity*), **nguo** (*ngoo*-oh) (*clothes*), and **viatu** (vee-*ah*-too) (*shoes*).

FUN & GAMES

1. Match the greetings in column A to their appropriate responses in column B.

A	B
Habari za safari?	Marahaba.
Hujambo	Kwema.
Mambo vipi?	Salama.
Shikamoo	Poa.
Kwema?	Sijambo.

2. Complete the following words with the correct missing letter.

   A. HA__ __RI

   B. S__ L __M__

   C. S__ J __ M__ __

IN THIS CHAPTER

» Identifying personal pronouns

» Using personal pronouns in sentences

» Identifying nouns in different classes

» Constructing grammatically correct sentences using different nouns

Chapter 3

Navigating Nouns and Pronouns in Swahili

Do you ever wonder what the secret is to getting comfortable with a new language? For some languages, it's mastering the verb tenses; for others, it's gender forms; and for Swahili, it's noun classes. Whichever noun you can think of in Swahili belongs to a specific noun class that affects the structure of the sentence it appears in. In this chapter, we walk you through the basics of Swahili noun classes, starting with pronouns.

Introducing Personal Pronouns

A personal pronoun is the word you use instead of a name of a person or thing — saying "he" for Dick, "she" for Jane, and "it" for the house they live in, for example. You need to know personal pronouns and their markers well before you can comfortably make your own sentences. This section discusses personal pronouns in the singular and plural forms and how to use them in sentences.

Personal pronouns in the singular form

There are three personal pronouns in Swahili:

>> **mimi** (*mee*-mee) (*I/me*)

>> **wewe** (*weh*-weh) (*you*)

>> **yeye** (*yeh*-yeh) (*he/him/she/her*).

REMEMBER

Swahili has no gendered pronouns, so the word **yeye** could refer to anyone.

Personal pronouns in the plural form

The three personal pronouns have their plural forms. These are

>> **sisi** (*see*-see) (*we/us*)

>> **nyinyi/ninyi** (*nyee*-nyee/*nee*-nyee) (*you* pl.)

>> **wao** (*wah*-oh) (*they/them*)

Personal pronouns in sentences

Each personal pronoun, whether singular or plural, has its own marker, as shown in Table 3-1.

TABLE 3-1   **Pronoun Markers**

Singular pronoun	Pronoun marker	Plural pronoun	Pronoun marker
Mimi	ni-	sisi	tu-
Wewe	u-	nyinyi/ninyi	m-
Yeye	a-	wao	wa-

In a sentence, these personal pronoun markers are attached to the verb. Notice how the verbs **kuna** (*koo*-nah) (*grate*), **kamua** (kah-*moo*-ah) (*milk*) and **lipa** (*lee*-pah) (*pay*) change depending on the pronoun used in the following sentence examples:

» **Mimi ninakuna nazi.** (*mee*-mee nee-nah-*koo*-nah *nah*-zee) (*I'm grating coconut.*)

» **Sisi tunakuna nazi.** (*see*-see too-nah-*koo*-nah *nah*-zee) (*We're grating coconuts.*)

» **Wewe unakuna nazi.** (*weh*-weh oo-nah-*koo*-nah *nah*-zee) (*You're grating coconuts.*)

» **Nyinyi mnakuna nazi.** (*nyee*-nyee m-nah-*koo*-nah *nah*-zee) (*You're [pl.] grating coconuts.*)

» **Yeye anakuna nazi.** (*yeh*-yeh ah-nah-*koo*-nah *nah*-zee) (*He/she is grating coconuts.*)

» **Wao wanakuna nazi.** (*wah*-oh wah-nah-*koo*-nah *nah*-zee) (*They're grating coconuts.*)

» **Mimi nimekamua ng'ombe.** (*mee*-mee nee-meh-kah-*moo*-ah *ng'oh*-mbeh) (*I have milked a cow.*)

» **Sisi tumekamua ng'ombe.** (*see*-see too-meh-kah-*moo*-ah *ng'oh*-mbeh) (*We have milked the cows.*)

» **Wewe umekamua ng'ombe.** (*weh*-weh oo-meh-kah-*moo*-ah *ng'oh*-mbeh) (*You have milked a cow.*)

» **Nyinyi mmekamua ng'ombe.** (*nyee*-nyee m-meh-kah-*moo*-ah *ng'oh*-mbeh) (*You [pl.] have milked the cows.*)

» **Yeye amekamua ng'ombe.** (*yeh*-yeh ah-meh-kah-*moo*-ah *ng'oh*-mbeh) (*He/she has milked a cow.*)

» **Wao wamekamua ng'ombe.** (*wah*-oh wah-meh-kah-*moo*-ah *ng'oh*-mbeh) (*They have milked the cows.*)

» **Mimi nitalipa mahari kesho.** (*mee*-mee nee-tah-*lee*-pah mah-*hah*-ree *keh*-shoh) (*I will pay a dowry tomorrow.*)

» **Sisi tutalipa mahari kesho.** (*see*-see too-tah-*lee*-pah mah-*hah*-ree *keh*-shoh) (*We will pay a dowry tomorrow.*)

» **Wewe utalipa mahari kesho.** (*weh*-weh oo-tah-*lee*-pah mah-*hah*-ree *keh*-shoh) (*You will pay a dowry tomorrow.*)

» **Nyinyi mtalipa mahari kesho.** (*nyee*-nyee m-tah-*lee*-pah mah-*hah*-ree *keh*-shoh) (*You [pl.] will pay a dowry tomorrow.*)

» **Yeye atalipa mahari kesho.** (*yeh*-yeh ah-tah-*lee*-pah mah-*hah*-ree *keh*-shoh) (*He will pay a dowry tomorrow.*)

» **Wao watalipa mahari kesho.** (*wah*-oh wah-tah-*lee*-pah mah-*hah*-ree *keh*-shoh) (*They will pay a dowry tomorrow.*)

The pronoun markers are followed by tense markers in the sentence examples given: **na-** for present tense, **me-** for the perfect tense, and **ta-** for the future tense. To learn more about using verbs in sentences, check out Chapter 4 of this book.

Introducing Swahili Noun Classes

A noun is the name of a person, animal, object or an idea. For example, *girl*, *cat*, *hill*, and *love* are all nouns. In Swahili, **nomino** (noh–*mee*–noh) (*nouns*) fall into different classes depending on how they form their plurals and/or what they represent. Sometimes you can tell which class a noun belongs to by looking at its singular and plural marker.

Okay, but why are noun classes so important? The hard truth is, noun classes affect how we construct possessives, demonstratives, verbs, adjectives, and much more in Swahili. In short, for your sentence to be grammatically correct, you need to pay attention to the noun class of the main subject in that sentence, since almost every other part of the sentence relies on which class you're dealing with. We'll discuss eight noun classes in this section.

M/Wa noun class

This noun class consists of all living creatures such as human beings, animals, birds, insects, and so on. Most nouns in this class dealing with people take the prefix **m-** in the singular and **wa-** in the plural form; that's why it's called the **M/Wa** noun class. See the examples that follow:

>> **mtoto/watoto** (m-*toh*-toh/wah-*toh*-toh) (*child/children*)

>> **mkulima/wakulima** (m-koo-*lee*-mah/wah-koo-*lee*-mah) (*farmer/farmers*)

>> **mwalimu/walimu** (mwah-*lee*-moo/wah-*lee*-moo) (*teacher/teachers*)

>> **mwandishi/waandishi** (mwah-*ndee*-shee/wah-ah-*ndee*-shee) (*author/authors*)

>> **msanii/wasanii** (mh-sah-*nee*-ee/wah-sah-*nee*-ee) (*artist/artists*)

>> **mwananchi/wananchi** (m-wah-nah-*n*-chee/wah-nah-*n*-chee) (*citizen/citizens*)

>> **mkenya/wakenya** (m-*keh*-nyah/wah-*keh*-nyah) (*Kenyan/Kenyans*)

>> **mwajiri/waajiri** (mwah-*jee*-ree/wah-ah-*jee*-ree) (*employer/employers*)

>> **mtu/watu** (m-*too*/wah-too) (*person/people*)

>> **mzee/wazee** (mh-*zeh*-eh/wah-*zeh*-eh) (*older person/older people*)

>> **mzazi/wazazi** (mh-*zah*-zee/wah-*zah*-zee) (*parent/parents*)

>> **mke/wake** (*mh*-keh/*wah*-keh) (*wife/wives*)

>> **mume/waume** (*moo*-meh/wah-oo-meh) (*husband/husbands*)

>> **mchumba/wachumba** (mh-*choo*-mbah/wah-*choo*-mbah) (*fiance/fiances*)

>> **mjomba/wajomba** (m-*joh*-mbah/wah-*joh*-mbah) (*uncle/uncles*)

>> **mpwa/wapwa** (*m*-pwah/*wah*-pwah) (*niece/nieces*)

>> **mfanyabiashara/wafanyabiashara** (m-fah-nyah bee-ah-*shah*-rah/ wah-fah-nyah bee-ah-*shah*-rah) (*businessperson/businesspeople*)

>> **mwizi/wezi** (m-*wee*-zee/*weh*-zee) (*thief/thieves*)

>> **mkutubi/wakutubi** (m-koo-*too*-bee/wah-koo-*too*-bee) (*librarian/librarians*)

As in all things, there are exceptions to the **M/Wa** rules. Most significantly, several nouns in this class don't actually start with an **m-** in the singular and **wa-** in the plural. These nouns include names describing family relationships, human occupations/categorizations, animals, and insects. For example,

>> **baba/baba** (*bah*-bah) (*father/fathers*)

>> **mama/mama** (*mah*-mah/*mah*-mah) (*mother/mothers*)

>> **kaka/kaka** (*kah*-kah/*kah*-kah) (*brother/brothers*)

>> **dada/dada** (*dah*-dah/*dah*-dah) (*sister/sisters*)

>> **bibi/bibi** (*bee*-bee/*bee*-bee) (*grandmother/grandmothers*)

>> **babu/babu** (*bah*-boo/*bah*-boo) (*grandfather/grandfathers*)

>> **binamu/binamu** (bee-*nah*-moo/bee-*nah*-moo) (*cousin/cousins*)

>> **shangazi/shangazi** (shah-*ngah*-zee/shah-*ngah*-zee) (*aunt/aunts*)

Human occupations/categorizations:

>> **rais/marais** (rah-*ee*-s/mah-rah-*ee*-s) (*president/presidents*)

>> **daktari/madaktari** (dah-*ktah*-ree/mah-dah-*ktah*-ree) (*doctor/doctors*)

>> **kipofu/vipofu** (kee-*poh*-foo/vee-*poh*-foo) (*blind person/blind people*)

>> **kiziwi/viziwi** (kee-*zee*-wee/vee-*zee*-wee) (*deaf person/deaf people*)

Animal and insects:

>> **paka/paka** (*pah*-kah/*pah*-kah) (*cat/cats*)

>> **simba/simba** (*see*-mbah/*see*-mbah) (*lion/lions*)

>> **fisi/fisi** (*fee*-see/*fee*-see) (*hyena/hyenas*)

>> **chui/chui** (*choo*-ee/*choo*-ee) (*leopard/leopards*)

>> **farasi/farasi** (fah-*rah*-see/fah-*rah*-see) (*horse/horses*)

>> **ndege/ndege** (*ndeh*-geh/*ndeh*-geh) (*bird/birds*)

>> **njiwa/njiwa** (*njee*-wah/*njee*-wah) (*dove/doves*)

>> **bata/bata** (*bah*-tah/ *bah*-tah) (*duck/ducks*)

>> **kuku/kuku** (*koo*-koo/*koo*-koo) (*chicken/chicken*)

>> **samaki/samaki** (sah-*mah*-kee/(sah-*mah*-kee) (*fish/fish*)

>> **mbwa/mbwa** (*mh*-mbwah/*mh*-mbwah) (*dog/dogs*)

>> **nyoka/nyoka** (*nyoh*-kah/*nyoh*-kah) (*snake/snakes*)

>> **mbu/mbu** (*m*-mboo/*m*-mboo) (*mosquito/mosquitoes*)

>> **nzi/nzi** (*n*-zee/*n*-zee) (*fly/flies*)

>> **nyuki/nyuki** (*nyoo*-kee/*nyoo*-kee) (*bee/bees*)

>> **nge/nge** (*n*-nge/*n*-nge) (*scorpion/scorpions*)

>> **buibui/buibui** (boo-ee-*boo*-ee/boo-ee-*boo*-ee) (*spider/spiders*)

For these nouns, you will just have to memorize them and remember that they do not change in their plural form.

So how does this noun class play out in a sentence? Adjectives describing words in the M/Wa noun class also take the same **m–** and **wa–** prefixes in the singular and plural, respectively. When dealing with this noun class, you also need to affix either the prefix **a–** (for a single subject) or **wa–** (for a plural subject) to the verbs linked to that subject or subjects.

Let's use three different adjectives: **–zuri** (*zoo*–ree) (*good*), **–baya** (*bah*–yah) (*bad*), and **–dogo** (*doh*–goh) (*small*) to demonstrate.

>> **Mtoto mdogo anacheza.** (m-*toh*-toh m-*doh*-goh a-nah-*cheh*-zah) (*A small child is playing.*)

>> **Watoto wadogo wanacheza.** (wa-*toh*-toh wah-*doh*-goh wa-nah-*cheh*-zah) (*Small children are playing.*)

>> **Mtu mbaya alikuja nyumbani.** (*m*-too m-*bah*-yah ah-lee-*koo*-jah nyoo-*mbah*-nee) (*A bad person came home.*)

>> **Watu wabaya walikuja nyumbani.** (*wah*-too wah-*bah*-yah wah-lee-*koo*-jah nyoo-*mbah*-nee) (*Bad people came home.*)

>> **Mwalimu mzuri atanifundisha kusoma.** (m-wah-*lee*-moo m-*zoo*-ree ah-tah-nee-foo-*ndee*-shah koo-*soh*-mah) (*A good teacher will teach me to read.*)

>> **Walimu wazuri watanifundisha kusoma.** (wah-*lee*-moo wah-*zoo*-ree wah-tah-nee-foo-*ndee*-shah koo-*soh*-mah) (*Good teachers will teach me to read.*)

REMEMBER

All nouns in the **M/Wa** class adhere to the rule of affixing **m-** or **wa-** to the adjective and **a-** or **wa-** to the verbs depending on whether they're singular or plural. This also applies to nouns in this class that don't begin with **m-** in the singular or **wa-** in the plural. For example,

>> **Rais mbaya alichukua hongo.** (rah-*ee*-s m-*bah*-yah ah-lee-choo-*koo*-ah *hoh*-ngoh) (*The bad president took a bribe.*)

>> **Marais wabaya walichukua hongo.** (rah-*ee*-s wah-*bah*-yah wah-lee-choo-*koo*-ah *hoh*-ngoh) (*The bad presidents took bribes.*)

>> **Farasi mzuri amekula nyasi.** (fah-*rah*-see m-*zoo*-ree ah-meh-*koo*-lah *nyah*-see) (*The good horse has eaten grass.*)

>> **Farasi wazuri wamekula nyasi.** (fah-*rah*-see wah-*zoo*-ree wah-meh-*koo*-lah *nyah*-see) (*The good horses have eaten grass.*)

>> **Kaka mdogo alikataa kuosha vyombo.** (*kah*-kah m-*doh*-goh ah-lee-kah-*tah*-ah koo-*oh*-shah *vyoh*-mboh) (*The younger brother refused to wash the dishes.*)

>> **Kaka wadogo walikataa kuosha vyomboh.** (*kah*-kah wah-*doh*-goh wah-lee-kah-*tah*-ah koo-*oh*-shah *vyoh*-mboh) (*The younger brothers refused to wash the dishes.*)

Ji/Ma noun class

Nouns in this class take the prefix **ji-** in the singular and **ma-** in the plural, hence the name **Ji/Ma** noun class. However, only a small number of nouns conform to this rule. For example,

>> **jina/majina** (*jee*-nah/mah-*jee*-nah) (*name/names*)

>> **jicho/macho** (*jee*-choh/*mah*-choh) (*eye/eyes*)

» **jipu/majipu** (*jee*-poo/mah-*jee*-poo) (*boil/boils*)

» **jani/majani** (*jah*-nee/mah-*jah*-nee) (*leaf/leaves*)

» **jino/meno** (*jee*-noh/*meh*-noh) (*tooth/teeth*)

» **jiko/meko** (*jee*-koh/*meh*-koh) (stove/stoves; kitchen/kitchens)

Most nouns in this class have no singular prefix but take the plural **ma–** prefix. A lot of produce (fruits and veggies) belong in this class. For example,

» **tunda/matunda** (*too*-ndah/mah-*too*-ndah) (*fruit/fruits*)

» **chungwa/machungwa** (*choo*-ngwah/mah-*choo*-ngwah) (*orange/oranges*)

» **embe/maembe** (*eh*-mbeh/mah-*eh*-mbeh) (*mango/mangoes*)

» **pera/mapera** (*peh*-rah/mah-*peh*-rah) (*guava/guavas*)

» **papai/mapapai** (pah-*pah*-ee/mah-pah-*pah*-ee) (*pawpaw/pawpaws*)

» **nanasi/mananasi** (nah-*nah*-see/mah-nah-*nah*-see) (*pineapple/pineapples*)

» **parachichi/maparachichi** (pah-rah-*chee*-chee/mah-pah-rah-*chee*-chee) (*avocado/avocados*)

» **tofaa/matofaa** (toh-*fa*-ah/mah-toh-*fah*-ah) (*apple/apples*)

» **limau/malimau** (lee-*mah*-oo/mah-lee-*mah*-oo) (*lemon/lemons*)

» **tikiti maji/matikiti maji** (tee-*kee*-tee *mah*-jee/mah-tee-*kee*-tee *mah*-jee) (*watermelon/watermelons*)

» **tango/matango** (*tah*-ngoh/mah-*tah*-ngoh) (*cucumber/cucumbers*)

» **boga/maboga** (*boh*-gah/mah-*boh*-gah) (*pumpkin/pumpkins*)

» **ua/maua** (*oo*-ah/mah-*oo*-ah) (*flower/flowers*)

Nouns that exist in the plural form only — liquids, for example — also fall in the Ji/Ma noun class. for example

» **maji** (*mah*-jee) (*water*)

» **mafuta** (mah-*foo*-tah) (*oil*)

» **maziwa** (mah-*zee*-wah) (*milk*)

Other nouns in the **Ji/Ma** class include words such as

>> **soko/masoko** (*soh*-koh/mah-*soh*-koh) (*market/markets*)

>> **dirisha/madirisha** (dee-*ree*-shah/mah-dee-*ree*-shah) (*window/windows*)

>> **jengo/majeng**o (*jeh*-ngoh/mah-*jeh*-ngoh) (*building/buildings*)

>> **daraja/madaraja** (dah-*rah*-jah/mah-dah-*rah*-jah) (*bridge/bridges*)

>> **gari/magari** (*gah*-ree/mah-*gah*-ree) (*car/cars*)

>> **shamba/mashamba** (*shah*-mbah/mah-*shah*-mbah) (*farm/farms*)

>> **yai/mayai** (*yah*-ee/mah-*yah*-ee) (*egg/eggs*)

REMEMBER

It's always going to be easier to identify noun membership of words in this noun class by their plural forms rather than their singular forms. As a rule of thumb, nouns in this class can begin with any letter in their singular form but must take the **ma–** prefix in their plural form.

Sentence construction with nouns in the Ji/Ma class follows these rules:

>> Adjectives take no prefix in the singular but do add the prefix **ma-** in the plural.

>> Affix the prefix **li-** to the verb for singular subjects and **ya-** to the verb for plural subjects.

For example,

>> **Embe tamu litaliwa.** (*eh*-mbeh *tah*-moo lee-tah-*lee*-wah) (*The sweet mango will be eaten.*)

>> **Maembe matamu yataliwa.** (mah-*eh*-mbeh mah-*tah*-moo yah-tah-*lee*-wah) (*The sweet mangoes will be eaten.*)

>> **Jengo kubwa limeporomoka.** (*jeh*-ngoh *koo*-bwah lee-lee-poh-roh-*moh*-kah) (*The big building collapsed.*)

>> **Majengo makubwa yameporomoka.** (mah-*jeh*-ngoh mah-*koo*-bwah yah-lee-poh-roh-*moh*-kah) (*The big buildings collapsed.*)

>> **Ua zuri lilinunuliwa.** (oo-ah *zoo*-ree lee-lee-noo-noo-*lee*-wah) (*The beautiful flower was bought.*)

>> **Maua mazuri yalinunuliwa.** (mah-oo-ah mah-*zoo*-ree yah-lee-noo-noo-*lee*-wah) (*The beautiful flowers were bought.*)

M/Mi noun class

In this noun class, words take the prefix **m-** in the singular and **mi-** in the plural. A lot of plant names and body parts belong in this noun class. For example,

>> **mti/miti** (*m*-tee/*mee*-tee) *(tree/trees)*

>> **mlimao/milimao** (m-lee-*mah*-oh/mee-lee-*mah*-oh) *(lemon tree/lemon trees)*

>> **mchungwa/michungwa** (m-*choo*-ngwah/mee-*choo*-ngwah) *(orange tree/ orange trees)*

>> **mpera/mipera** (m-*peh*-rah/mee-*peh*-reh) *(guava tree/guava trees)*

>> **mtofaa/mitofaa** (m-toh-*fah*-ah/mee-toh-*fah*-ah) *(apple tree/apple trees)*

>> **mparachichi/miparachichi** (m-pah-rah-*chee*-chee/mee-pah-rah-*chee*-chee) *(avocado tree/avocado trees)*

>> **mzambarau/mizambarau** (m-zah-mbah-*rah*-oo/mee-zah-mbah-*rah*-oo) *(java plum tree/java plum trees)*

>> **mzeituni/mizeituni** (m-*zeh*-ee-too-nee/mee-*zee*-ee-too-nee) *(olive tree/olive trees)*

>> **mgomba/migomba** (m-*goh*-mbah/mee-*goh*-mbah) *(banana tree/banana trees)*

>> **mkia/mikia** (m-*kee*-ah/mee-*kee*-ah) *(tail/tails)*

>> **mgongo/migongo** (m-*goh*-ngoh/mee-*goh*-ngoh) *(back/backs)*

>> **mkono/mikono** (m-*koh*-noh/mee-*koh*-noh) *(hand/hands)*

>> **mdomo/midomo** (m-*doh*-moh/mee-*doh*-moh) *(lip/lips)*

>> **mguu/miguu** (*m*-goo/*mee*-goo) *(leg/legs)*

>> **moyo/mioyo** (*moh*-yoh/mee-*oh*-yoh) *(heart/hearts)*

>> **mfupa/mifupa** (m-*foo*-pah/mee-*foo*-pah) *(bone/bones)*

Other words in the **M/Mi** noun class include

>> **mkufu/mikufu** (m-*koo*-foo/mee-*koo*-foo) *(necklace/necklaces)*

>> **mkate/mikate** (m-*kah*-teh/mee-*kah*-teh) *(bread/breads)*

>> **mlima/milima** (m-*lee*-mah/mee-*lee*-mah) *(mountain/mountains)*

>> **mji/miji** (*m*-jee/*mee*-jee) *(town/towns)*

>> **mto/mito** (*m*-toh/*mee*-toh) *(river/rivers; pillow/pillows)*

>> **mkoba/mikoba** (m-*koh*-bah/mee-*koh*-bah) *(handbag/handbags)*

>> **mshale/mishale** (m-*shah*-leh/mee-*shah*-lee) *(arrow/arrows)*

There are a few exceptions in the **M/Mi** noun class. Such exceptions begin with the **mw-** prefix in their singular form but still take the **mi-** prefix in their plural form. Examples include

>> **mwili/miili** (m-*wee*-lee/mee-*ee*-lee) (*body/bodies*)

>> **mwamba/miamba** (m-*wah*-mbah/mee-*ah*-mbah) (*rock/rocks*)

>> **mwezi/miezi** (m-*weh*-zee/mee-*eh*-zee) (*month/months*)

>> **mwaka/miaka** (m-*wah*-kah/mee-*ah*-kah) (*year/years*)

>> **mwale/miale** (m-*wah*-leh/mee-*ah*-leh) (*ray/rays*)

>> **mwavuli/miavuli** (m-wah-*voo*-lee/mee-ah-*voo*-lee) (*umbrella/umbrellas*)

>> **mwembe/miembe** (*mweh*-mbeh/mee-*eh*-mbeh) (*mango tree/mango trees*)

>> **mwaliko/mialiko** (m-wah-*lee*-koh/mee-ah-*lee*-koh) (*invitation/invitations*)

Follow these rules to construct correct sentences that contain nouns in the M/Mi class:

>> Adjectives take the prefix **m-** in the singular and the prefix **mi-** in the plural.

>> Affix the prefixes **u-** to the verb for singular subjects and **i-** to the verb for plural subjects.

For example,

>> **Mti mrefu umekatwa.** (*m*-tee m-*reh*-foo oo-meh-*kah*-twah) (*The tall tree has been cut down.*)

>> **Miti mirefu imekatwa.** (*mee*-tee mee-*reh*-foo ee-meh-*kah*-twah) (*The tall trees have been cut down*)

>> **Mkoba mzuri umepotea.** (m-*koh*-bah m-*zoo*-ree oo-meh-poh-*teh*-ah) (*The nice handbag is lost.*)

>> **Mikoba mizuri imepotea.** (mee-*koh*-bah mee-*zoo*-ree ee-meh-poh-*teh*-ah) (*The nice handbags are lost.*)

>> **Mwavuli mkubwa umevunjika.** (m-wah-*voo*-lee m-*koo*-bwah oo-meh-voo-*njee*-kah) (*The big umbrella is broken.*)

>> **Miavuli mikubwa imevunjika.** (mee-ah-*voo*-lee mee-*koo*-bwah ee-meh-voo-*njee*-kah) (*The big umbrellas are broken.*)

N/N noun class

This is the largest noun class. Nouns beginning with an **N-** in the singular keep the same prefix in their plural form. For example,

>> **nyumba/nyumba** (*nyoo*-mbah/*nyoo*-mbah) (*house/houses*)

>> **njia/njia** (*njee*-ah/*njee*-ah) (*way/ways*)

>> **nchi/nchi** (*n*-chee/*n*-chee) (*country/countries*)

>> **nguo/nguo** (*ngoo*-oh/*ngoo*-oh) (*cloth/clothes*)

>> **ndoto/ndoto** (*ndoh*-toh/*ndoh*-toh) (*dream/dreams*)

>> **ndizi/ndizi** (*ndee*-zee/*ndee*-zee) (*banana/bananas*)

>> **nyama/nyama** (*nyah*-mah/*nyah*-mah) (*meat/meats*)

>> **nazi/nazi** (*nah*-zee/*nah*-zee) (*coconut/coconuts*)

As was to be expected, there are exceptions to this rule as well, because some words do not take the **n-** prefix in their singular or plural forms but still fall in this class. Most of these words are of foreign origin, such as the following:

>> **simu/simu** (*see*-moo/*see*-moo) (*phone/phones*)

>> **kompyuta/kompyuta** (koh-m-pee-*yoo*-tah/koh-m-pee-*yoo*-tah) (*computer/ computers*)

>> **mashine/mashine** (mah-*shee*-neh/mah-*shee*-neh) (*machine/machines*)

>> **shule/shule** (*shoo*-leh/*shoo*-leh) (*school/schools*)

>> **soda/soda** (*soh*-dah/*soh*-dah) (*soda/sodas*)

>> **biskuti/biskuti** (bee-*skoo*-tee/bee-*skoo*-tee) (*biscuit/biscuits*)

>> **meza/meza** (*meh*-zah/*meh*-zah) (*table/tables*)

>> **sketi/sketi** (*skeh*-tee/*skeh*-tee) (*skirt/skirts*)

>> **soksi/soksi** (*soh*-ksee/*soh*-ksee) (*socks/socks*)

>> **hoteli/hoteli** (hoh-*teh*-lee/hoh-*teh*-lee) (*hotel/hotels*)

Other words in the N/N noun class include the following:

>> **taa/taa** (*tah*-ah/*tah*-ah) (*lamp/lamps*)

>> **bahari/bahari** (bah-*hah*-ree/bah-*hah*-ree) (*ocean/oceans*)

>> **suruali/suruali** (soo-roo-*ah*-lee/soo-roo-*ah*-lee) (*pant/pants*)

- **karatasi/karatasi** (kah-rah-*tah*-see/kah-rah-*tah*-see) (*paper/papers*)

- **dawa/dawa** (*dah*-wah/*dah*-wah) (*pill/pills*)

- **chupa/chupa** (*choo*-pah/*choo*-pah) (*bottle/bottles*)

- **hewa/hewa** (*heh*-wah/*heh*-wah) (*air/air*)

- **kahawa/kahawa** (kah-*hah*-wah/ kah-*hah*-wah) (*coffee/coffees*)

- **chai/chai** (*chah*-ee/*chah*-ee) (*tea/teas*)

- **sabuni/sabuni** (sah-*boo*-nee/sah-*boo*-nee) (*soap/soaps*)

- **barua/barua** (bah-*roo*-ah/bah-*roo*-ah) (*letter/letters*)

- **sahani/sahani** (sah-*hah*-nee/sah-*hah*-nee) (*plate/plates*)

- **sukari/sukari** (soo-*kah*-ree/soo-*kah*-ree) (*sugar/sugars*)

- **chumvi/chumvi** (choo-*m*-vee/choo-*m*-vee) (*salt/salts*)

- **pilipili/pilipili** (pee-lee-*pee*-lee/pee-lee-*pee*-lee) (*pepper/peppers*)

How can Swahili speakers tell when someone is talking about multiple houses instead of one if there is no plural marker in the noun? They listen for plural markers in rest of the sentence! Do the following to construct sentences in which the main subject falls in the **N/N** class:

- Affix the prefix **i-** to the verb for singular subjects and **zi-** to the verb for plural subjects.

For example,

- **Nchi bora ina usalama.** (n-chee *boh*-rah *ee*-nah oo-sah-*lah*-mah) (*A good country has peace.*)

- **Nchi bora zina usalama.** (n-chee *boh*-rah *zee*-nah oo-sah-*lah*-mah) (*Good countries have peace.*)

- **Hoteli kubwa imefungwa.** (hoh-*teh*-lee *koo*-bwah ee-meh-*foo*-ngwah) (*The big hotel is closed.*)

- **Hoteli kubwa zimefungwa.** (hoh-*teh*-lee *koo*-bwah zee-meh-*foo*-ngwah) (*The big hotels are closed.*)

- **Dawa kali imetupwa.** (*dah*-wah *kah*-lee ee-meh-*too*-pwah) (*The bitter pill/ medicine has been thrown out.*)

- **Dawa kali zimetupwa.** (*dah*-wah *kah*-lee zee-meh-*too*-pwah) (*The bitter pills/ medicines have been thrown out.*)

Ki/Vi noun class

Nouns in this class take the prefix **ki–** in the singular and **vi–** in their plural forms. For example,

>> **kiatu/viatu** (kee-*ah*-too/vee-*ah*-too) *(shoe/shoes)*

>> **kitabu/vitabu** (kee-*tah*-boo/vee-*tah*-boo) *(book/books)*

>> **kioo/vioo** (kee-*oh*-oh/vee-*oh*-oh) *(mirror/mirrors)*

>> **kiti/viti** (*kee*-tee/*vee*-tee) *(chair/chairs)*

>> **kilima/vilima** (kee-*lee*-mah/vee-*lee*-mah) *(hill/hills)*

>> **kisima/visima** (kee-*see*-mah/vee-*see*-mah) *(well/wells)*

>> **kilio/vilio** (kee-*lee*-oh/vee-*lee*-oh) *(cry/cries)*

>> **kina/vina** (*kee*-nah/*vee*-nah) *(depth/depths)*

>> **kiazi/viazi** (kee-*ah*-zee/vee-*ah*-zee) *(potato/potatoes)*

>> **kidole/vidole** (kee-*doh*-leh/vee-*doh*-leh) *(finger/fingers)*

>> **kichwa/vichwa** (kee-chwah/*vee*-chwah) *(head/heads)*

>> **kiuno/viuno** (kee-*oo*-noh/vee-*oo*-noh) *(waist/waists)*

>> **kifua/vifua** (kee-*foo*-ah/vee-*foo*-ah) *(chest/chests)*

>> **kisiwa/visiwa** (kee-*see*-wah/vee-*see*-wah) *(island/islands)*

>> **kisu/visu** (*kee*-soo/*vee*-soo) *(knife/knives)*

>> **kitanda/vitanda** (kee-*tah*-ndah/vee-*tah*-ndah) *(bed/beds)*

>> ***kiungo/viungo** (kee-*oo*-ngoh/vee-*oo*-ngoh) *(spice/spices)*

Other nouns in this class begin with **ch–** in the singular and change into **vy–** in the plural. These include

>> **chakula/vyakula** (chah-*koo*-lah/vyah-*koo*-lah) *(food/foods)*

>> **chama/vyama** (*chah*-mah/*vyah*-mah) *(party/parties)*

>> **cheti/vyeti** (*cheh*-tee/*vyeh*-tee) *(certificate/certificates)*

>> **chuo/vyuo** (*choo*-oh/*vyoo*-oh) *(university/universities)*

>> **choo/vyoo** (*choh*-oh/*vyoh*-oh) *(toilet/toilets)*

>> **chombo/vyombo** (*choh*-mboh/*vyoh*-mboh) *(utensil/utensils)*

>> **chumba/vyumba** (*choo*-mbah/*vyoo*-mbah) *(room/rooms)*

>> **chuma/vyuma** (*choo*-mah/*vyoo*-mah) *(metal/metals)*

We consider **Ki/Vi** the easiest noun class to master because all you need to do when constructing sentences is to attach the prefix **ki-** for singular entities and **vi-** for plural entities to adjectives as well as verbs. For example:

>> **Kiatu kidogo kinafinya.** (kee-*ah*-too kee-*doh*-goh kee-nah-*fee*-nyah) (*The small shoe pinches.*)

>> **Viatu vidogo vinafinya.** (vee-*ah*-too vee-*doh*-goh vee-nah-*fee*-nyah) (*The small shoes pinch.*)

>> **Kisiwa kizuri kinapiganiwa.** (kee-*see*-wah kee-*zoo*-ree kee-nah-pee-gah-*nee*-wah) (*The beautiful island is being fought over.*)

>> **Visiwa vizuri vinapiganiwa.** (vee-*see*-wah vee-*zoo*-ree vee-nah-pee-gah-*nee*-wah) (*The beautiful islands are being fought over.*)

>> **Chakula kitamu kilimalizwa.** (chah-*koo*-lah kee-*tah*-moo kee-lee-mah-*lee*-zwah) (*The delicious food was finished.*)

>> **Vyakula vitamu vilimalizwa.** (vyah-*koo*-lah vee-*tah*-moo vee-lee-mah-*lee*-zwah) (*The delicious foods were finished.*)

U/N noun class

Nouns within this category use the prefix **u-** for singular and **n-** for plural. However, only a limited subset of nouns adhere to this pattern, as shown in the examples listed here:

>> **ufa/nyufa** (*oo*-fah/*nyoo*-fah) (*crack/cracks*)

>> **uwanja/nyanja** (oo-*wah*-njah/*nyah*-njah) (*field/fields*)

>> **uso/nyuso** (*oo*-soh/*nyoo*-soh) (*face/faces*)

>> **ulimi/ndimi** (oo-*lee*-mee/*ndee*-mee) (*tongue/tongues*)

>> **uma/nyuma** (*oo*-ah/*nyoo*-mah) (*fork/forks*)

Some nouns in this class begin with the prefix **u-** in their singular, as you'd expect, but then veer off and begin with **mb-** in their plural form. These include

>> **ubao/mbao** (oo-*bah*-oh/*mbah*-oh) (*board/boards*)

>> **ubavu/mbavu** (oo-*bah*-voo/m-*bah*-voo) (*rib/ribs*)

Within the **U/N** class you'll also find nouns that take the **u–** prefix in their singular, as expected, but take no prefix in their plural form. The following nouns are good examples:

>> **ukoo/koo** (oo-*koh*-oh/*koo*-oh) (*clan/clans*)

>> **ukucha/kucha** (oo-*koo*-chah/*koo*-chah) (*fingernail/fingernails*)

>> **ufagio/fagio** (oo-fah-*gee*-oh/fah-*gee*-oh) (*broom/brooms*)

>> **ufunguo/funguo** (oo-foo-*ngoo*-oh/foo-*ngoo*-oh) (*key/keys*)

>> **ukurasa/kurasa** (oo-koo-*rah*-sah/koo-*rah*-sah) (*page/pages*)

There's also a small group of nouns still within the **U/N** class that begin with the prefix **w–** in their singular form and change to begin with the prefix **ny–** in their plural form. For example,

>> **wimbo/nyimbo** (*wee*-mboh/*nyee*-mboh) (*song/songs*)

>> **wembe/nyembe** (*weh*-mbeh/*nyeh*-mbeh) (*razor blade/razor blades*)

>> **waya/nyaya** (*wah*-yah/*nyah*-yah) (*cable/cables*)

>> **wavu/nyavu** (*wah*-voo/*nyah*-voo) (*net/nets*)

>> **wakati/nyakati** (wah-*kah*-tee/nyah-*kah*-tee (*time/times*)

To form sentences with nouns in the **U/N** class, remember the following:

>> Adjectives take the prefix **m–** in the singular and the prefix **n–** in the plural.

>> Affix the prefix **u–** to the verb for singular subjects and **zi–** to the verb for plural subjects.

See these examples:

>> **Uso mzuri unapendeza.** (*oo*-soh m-*zoo*-ree oo-nah-peh-*ndeh*-zah) (*A beautiful face is attractive.*)

>> **Nyuso nzuri zinapendeza.** (*nyoo*-soh n-*zoo*-ree zee-nah-peh-*ndeh*-zah) (*Beautiful faces are attractive.*)

>> **Ukucha mrefu itakatwa.** (oo-*koo*-chah m-*reh*-foo ee-tah-*kah*-twah) (*A long fingernail will be cut/trimmed.*)

>> **Kucha ndefu zitakatwa.** (*koo*-chah *ndeh*-foo zee-tah-*kah*-twah) (*Long fingernails will be cut/trimmed.*)

» **Wavu mzito umenasa samaki.** (*wah*-voo m-*zee*-toh oo-meh-*nah*-sah sah-*mah*-kee) (*A heavy net has caught a fish.*)

» **Nyavu nzito zimenansa samaki.** (*nah*-voo n-*zee*-toh zee-meh-*nah*-sah sah-*mah*-kee) (*Heavy nets have caught fish.*)

U/U noun class

In this class, nouns take the **u-** marker in the singular and retain the same in the plural. These nouns refer to abstract notions such as the following:

» **uzuri/uzuri** (oo-*zoo*-ree/ oo-*zoo*-ree) (*beauty/worthiness*)

» **upendo/upendo** (oo-*peh*-ndoh/oo-*peh*-ndoh) (*love*)

» **upole/upole** (oo-*poh*-leh/oo-*poh*-leh) (*gentleness*)

» **ukweli/ukweli** (oo-*kweh*-lee/oo-*kweh*-lee) (*truth*)

» **ukarimu/ukarimu** (oo-kah-*ree*-moo/oo-kah-*ree*-moo) (*hospitality*)

» **utulivu/utulivu** (oo-to-*lee*-vee/oo-too-*lee*-voo) (*calmness*)

» **ukali/ukali** (oo-*kah*-lee/oo-*kah*-lee) (*severity*)

» **uvumilivu/uvumilivu** (oo-voo-mee-*lee*-voo/oo-voo-mee-*lee*-voo) (*patience*)

» **usawa/usawa** (oo-*sah*-wah/oo-*sah*-wah) (*equality*)

» **uhuru/uhuru** (oo-*hoo*-roo/oo-*hoo*-roo) (*freedom*)

» **ukatili/ukatili** (oo-kah-*tee*-lee/ oo-kah-*tee*-lee) (*cruelty/cruelty*)

» **ubaguzi/ubaguzi** (oo-bah-*goo*-zee/ oo-bah-*goo*-zee) (*discrimination*)

» **ulimwengu** (oo-lee-*mweh*-ngoo) (*the world*)

In sentences with nouns from the **U/U** class, add the prefix **u-** to verbs and **m-** to adjectives if the word can take an adjective.

» **Uvumilivu wa Asha unastaajabisha.** (oo-voo-mee-*lee*-voo wah Asha oo-nah-stah-ah-jah-*bee*-shah) (*Asha's patience is shocking.*)

» **Utilivu wa mtoto mdogo unapendeza.** (oo-too-*lee*-voo wah m-*toh*-toh m-*doh*-goh oo-nah-peh-*ndeh*-zah) (*The young child's calmness is admirable.*)

» **Ugali mkubwa umeiva.** (oo-*gah*-lee m-*koo*-bwah oo-meh-*ee*-vah) (*The big ugali is ready.*)

» **Ulimwengu unabadilika.** (oo-lee-*mweh*-ngoo oo-nah-bah-dee-*lee*-kah) (*The world is changing.*)

PA/KU/MU noun class

This class is unique because it contains only one noun: **pahali** (pah–*hah*–lee) (*place*) also known as **mahali** (mah–*hah*–lee).

In sentences, use the prefixes **pa-**, **ku-**, **m-** as subject prefixes attached to verbs and to create agreement with adjectives. For example,

>> **Pahali pazuri pamesafishwa.** (pah–*hah*–lee pah–*zoo*–ree pah–meh–sah–*fee*–shwah) (*The good place has been cleaned.*)

>> **Pahali kubaya kumefungwa.** (pah–*hah*–lee koo–*bah*–yah koo–meh–*foo*–ngwah) (*A bad place has been closed.*)

>> **Mahali mzuri ni humu.** (mah–*hah*–lee m–*zoo*–ree nee *hoo*–moo) (*A good place is inside here.*)

TIP

Use **pa-** for a definite location.

Use **ku-** for general area or indefinite location.

Use **mu-** for inside/within a location.

Although this noun class has just one original member, other words can also gain membership using the prepositional suffix **-ni**. For example

   shule (*shoo*-leh) (*school*) ⇨ **shuleni** (shoo-*leh*-nee) (*at/in school*)

   soko (*soh*-koh) (*market*) ⇨ **sokoni** (soh-*koh*-nee) (*at/in the market*)

   msitu (m-*see*-too) (*forest*) ⇨ **msituni** (m-see-*too*-nee) (*at/in the forest*)

   duka (*doo*-kah) (*shop*) ⇨ **dukani** (doo-*kah*-nee) (*at/in the shop*)

   kitanda (kee-*tah*-ndah) (*bed*) ⇨ **kitandani** (kee-tah-*ndah*-nee) (*on/in bed*)

   nyumba (*nyoo*-mbah) (*house*) ⇨ **nyumbani** (nyoo-*mbah*-nee) (*at home*)

To form sentences with these words as part of the **Pa/Ku/Mu-** noun class, adjectives take the prefixes **pa-**, **ku-**, and **m-**, respectively. For example,

>> **Msituni kunatisha.** (m-see-*too*-nee koo-nah-*tee*-shah) (*In the forest, it is scary.*)

>> **Nyumbani mnasafishwa kila siku.** (nyoo-*mbah*-nee m-nah-sah-*fee*-shwah *kee*-lah *see*-koo) (*Inside the home is cleaned every day.*)

>> **Shuleni pamejaa Watoto.** (doo-*kah*-nee pah-meh-*jah*-ah wah-*toh*-toh) (*In the school there are many children.*)

Talkin' the Talk

Salama is at the market buying fruits and vegetables from a seller's stall. Notice the different nouns they use and how they affect the sentence structures.

Salama: **Habari gani?**
Hah-*bah*-ree *gah*-nee?
How are you doing?

Maua: **Nzuri. Ungependa nini?**
N-*zoo*-ree. Oo-ngeh-*peh*-ndah *nee*-nee?
I am doing well. What would you like?

Salama: **Ninahitaji maparachichi, ndizi, machungwa, karoti, na pilipili.**
Nee-nah-hee-*tah*-jee mah-pah-rah-*chee*-chee, *ndee*-zee, mah-*choo*-ngwah, kah-*roh*-tee nah pee-lee-*pee*-lee.
I need avocados, bananas, oranges, carrots, and pepper.

Maua: **Sawa, Unataka mafungu mangapi kwa kila moja?**
Sah-wah, oo-nah-*tah*-kah mah-*foo*-ngoo mah-*ngah*-pee kwah *kee*-lah *moh*-jah?
Okay, how many piles do you want for each?

Salama: **Ninataka mafungu mawili kwa kila kitu. Je, una brokoli?**
Nee-nah-*tah*-kah mah-*foo*-ngoo mah-*wee*-lee kwah *kee*-lah *kee*-too, Jeh, oo-nah broh-*koh*-lee?
I want two piles for everything. Do you have broccoli?

Maua: **Ndiyo nina brokoli. Unataka ngapi?**
Ndee-yoh nee-nah broh-*koh*-lee. Oo-nah-*tah*-kah *ngah*-pee?
Yes, I have broccoli. How many do you want?

Salama: **Ninataka brokoli mbili. Ninaomba viazi, malimao, na mihogo.**
Nee-nah-*tah*-kah broh-koh-lee mbee-lee. Nee-nah-*oh*-mbah vee-*ah*-zee, mah-lee-*mah*-oh nah mee-*hoh*-goh.
I want two broccoli. I need potatoes, lemons, and cassavas.

Maua: **Sawa. Unataka kitu kingine?**
Sah-wah. Oo-nah-*tah*-kah *kee*-too kee-*ngee*-nee?
Okay. Do you need anything else?

Salama:	**Ninataka mdalasini viungo na majani ya chai pia.**
	Nee-nah-*tah*-kah m-dah-lah-*see*-nee vee-*oon*-go nah mah-*jah*-nee yah *chah*-ee *pee*-ah.
	I want cinnamon and tea leaves, too.

Maua:	**Sawa. Vitu vyako hivi hapa.**
	Sah-wah. *Vee*-too *vyah*-koh *hee*-vee *hah*-pah.
	Okay. Here are your things.

Salama:	**Asante sana rafiki.**
	Ah-sah-*n*-teh *sah*-nah rah-*fee*-kee.
	Thank you very much, friend.

Maua:	**Karibu tena.**
	Kah-*ree*-boo *teh*-nah.
	Please come again.

Salama:	**Asante, kwaheri.**
	Ah-sah-*n*-teh, kwah-*heh*-ree
	Thanks, goodbye.

Maua:	**Kwaheri.**
	Kwah-*heh*-ree
	Goodbye.

● ●

WORDS TO KNOW

maparachichi	mah-pah-rah-*chee*-chee	avocados
ndizi	*ndee*-zee	bananas
machungwa	mah-*choo*-ngwah	oranges
malimao	mah-lee-*mah*-oh	lemons
karoti	kah-*roh*-tee	carrots
pilipili	pee-lee-*pee*-lee	pepper
viungo	vee-*oo*-ngoh	spices
brokoli	broh-*koh*-lee	broccoli

viazi	vee-*ah*-zee	potatoes
mihogo	mee-*hoh*-goh	cassavas
mafungu	mah-*foo*-ngoo	piles
sawa	*sah*-wah	okay
taka	*tah*-kah	want
ngapi	*ngah*-pee	how many

FUN & GAMES

Sort the following nouns into the correct noun class.

mwalimu	kiatu	chuoni	parachichi	vikombe
watoto	wimbo	nyumba	upendo	Jimbo
simu	kioo	chakula	mama	Karoti
kompyuta	shati	simba	kitabu	Kiti
uso	uzuri	meza	miti	Daktari
nyumbani	chama	sahani	milimao	hospitalini

M/WA _____

M/MI _____

JI/MA _____

KI/VI _____

N/N _____

U/N _____

U/U _____

PA/KU/MU _____

Chapter **4**

Adding Action to Your Words: Verbs

What's on your to-do list? Tending to your garden? Trying out a new recipe? Running a marathon? Dancing the night away? When it comes to how you spend your day, you have an infinite variety of activities to choose from, but all such activities have one thing in common: You express them using verbs.

It should come as no surprise, then, that like in many languages, verbs are a crucial component of the Swahili sentence structure that speakers use to express action, states of being, and events. The basic form of verbs in Swahili is modified using various prefixes to communicate different grammatical functions such as subject agreement and tense.

This chapter explores some of the key features of Swahili verbs that should help you to

>> Recognize the infinitive verb form

>> Express actions in a variety of tenses

>> Use various tenses in the correct negative form

Recognizing the Infinitive Verb Form

An infinitive is the basic form of a verb before conjugation. For example, when you say "I will eat," you have conjugated the infinitive verb "to eat" before making that sentence. The infinitive is the *to* form of a verb such as to swim, to dance, to cook. Before looking at Swahili infinitives, take a look at the Swahili verb root, which is the same as infinitives but lacks the "to" marker of infinitives.

All Swahili verbs with a Bantu origin end with **-a**. For example

>> **tembea** (teh-*mbeh*-ah) (*walk*)

>> **lipa** (*lee*-pah) (*pay*)

Other verbs end with **-e**, **-i**, or **-u** and have their origins in Arabic. For example:

>> **samehe** (sah-*meh*-heh) (*forgive*)

>> **fikiri** (fee-*kee*-ree) (*think*)

>> **tabasamu** (tah-bah-*sah*-moo) (*smile*)

The infinitive form of all Swahili verbs is marked by the prefix **ku-** (koo) before the verb root. This corresponds to the use of *to* in English verbs such as *to write* (**kuandika**; koo-ah-*ndee*-kah). The prefix **ku-** is, therefore, attached to the root of the verb showing that it's in its infinitive form.

>> **ku + lala = kulala** (koo-*lah*-lah) (*to sleep*)

>> **ku + soma = kusoma** (koo-*soh*-mah) (*to read/to study*)

>> **ku + zuru = kuzuru** (koo-*zoo*-roo) (*to tour*)

>> **ku + tabasamu = kutabasamu** (koo-*tah*-bah-*sah*-moo) (*to smile*)

>> **ku + fikiri = kufikiri** (koo-*fee*-kee-ree) (*to think*)

>> **ku + jali = kujali** (koo-*jah*-lee) (*to care* (*about*))

Notice that the words used in the examples have either two or three syllables in them. A second group of monosyllabic verbs do not make much sense without the prefix **ku-**. These short verbs are always attached to the **ku-** infinitive marker even when conjugated through its various forms.

>> **ku + la = kula** (*koo*-lah) to eat

>> **ku + nywa = kunywa** (*koo*-nywah) to drink

>> **ku + fa = kufa** (*koo*-fah) to die

Using Verbs in Sentences

Identifying infinitives is a fine first step, but the trick is to get comfortable using verbs correctly when constructing actual sentences. It helps that the basic structure of a Swahili sentence is subject-verb-object. Easy enough. However, this order might be hard to recognize when the verb does not stand on its own. For example

>> **Nitalala.** (nee-tah-*lah*-lah) (*I will sleep.*)

What happened to the infinitive marker **ku-**? Well, there's a chance you'll recognize the first-person pronoun marker **ni-**. (If not, check out Chapter 3, where you can get the full story on first-, second-, and third-person markers.) This means that the actual first-person pronoun **mimi** (*mee*-mee; *I*) has been omitted in this sentence, and only its marker is used. (You can choose to include or omit the pronoun: Either way, the pronoun marker is mandatory for your sentence to make sense grammatically.) The next marker attached (**-ta-**) denotes tense — the future tense in this case. Lastly, the verb is added without its infinitive marker if it is not monosyllabic. Look at the following sentences to see how verbs get used.

>> **kusoma:** Mimi nina**soma** kitabu. (*mee*-mee nee-nah-*soh*-mah kee-*tah*-boo) (*I am reading a book.*)

>> **kuzuru:** Yeye ata**zuru** Uganda. (*yeh*-yeh ah-tah-*zoo*-roo Uganda) (*He/She will tour Uganda.*)

>> **kujali:** Sisi tuna**jali** Wanyama. (*see*-see too-nah-*jah*-lee wah-*nyah*-mah) (*We value/care about animals.*)

With monosyllabic verbs, you don't drop the **ku-**infinitive marker; everything else, however, gets treated the same. The next sentences show you what we mean.

>> **kula:** Mimi nina**kula** ukoko. (*mee*-mee nee-nah-*koo*-lah oo-*koh*-koh) (*I am eating a ukoko.*)

>> **kunywa:** Yeye ata**kunywa** uji. (*yeh*-yeh ah-tah-*koo*-nywah oo-jee) (*He/She will drink a porridge.*)

East African porridge is more like a smoothie, so it's drinkable.

>> **kufa:** Bibi yetu ali**kufa**. (*bee*-bee *yeh*-too ah-lee-*koo*-fah) (*Our grandma died.*)

CULTURAL WISDOM

Using Verbs in the Correct Tense

Verbs can be expressed in several different tenses, but every Swahili user must master five basic tenses to begin speaking confidently. The next few sections walk you through how to use each tense correctly.

The present tense

This tense describes activities or states that are currently ongoing. It is marked by inserting **-na-** before the verb root. For example:

>> **Ninatembea.** (nee-nah-teh-*mbeh*-ah) (*I am walking.*)

Breaking down **ninatembea** into its constituent parts, we have **ni-** as the pronoun marker for *I*, **na-** as the present tense marker, and **-tembea** as the conjugated verb.

REMEMBER

The present tense in Swahili corresponds with what are known as the simple present tense and present continuous tenses in English. That's right. In Swahili, one verb form corresponds to two English forms. For example:

>> Ni**na**soma. (nee-nah-*soh*-mah) (*I am studying/I study.*)

>> Ni**na**pika. (nee-nah-*pee*-kah) (*I am cooking/I cook.*)

The position of the tense marker stays the same even when using different personal pronoun markers in the singular as well as plural forms, as Table 4-1 makes clear. (Again, if you're not sure about your pronoun markers, check out Chapter 3.)

REMEMBER

Monosyllabic verbs retain **ku-** even when conjugated. Words with a foreign origin behave the same as the Bantu origin words throughout.

The past tense

This tense describes activities or states that took place in the past and have been completed. It is equivalent to the simple past tense in English. This tense is marked by inserting **-li** between the personal pronoun marker and the verb. Check out Table 4-2 to see how the past tense shows up through different pronouns.

TABLE 4-1   **Using the Present Tense with Other Pronouns**

Pronoun	Pronoun marker	Sentence Example	Translation
Sisi	tu-	Sisi tu**na**pika. (See-see too-nah-*pee*-kah)	*We are cooking/cook.*
Wewe	u-	Wewe u**na**kula. (weh-weh oo-nah-*koo*-lah)	*You are eating/eat.*
Nyinyi	m-	Nyinyi m**na**kula. (*nyee*-nyee m-nah-*koo*-lah)	*You (pl.) are eating/eat.*
Yeye	a-	Yeye a**na**tabasamu. (*yeh*-yeh ah-nah- *tah*-bah-*sah*-moo)	*He/she is smiling/smiles.*
Wao	wa-	Wao wanatabasamu. (*wah*-oh wah-nah- *tah*-bah-*sah*-moo)	*They are smiling/smile.*

TABLE 4-2   **Using the Past Tense**

Pronoun	Pronoun prefix	Sentence Example	Translation
Mimi	ni-	Mimi ni**li**suka nywele jana. (*mee*-mee nee-lee-*soo*-kah *nyweh*-leh *jah*-nah)	*I plaited my hair yesterday.*
Sisi	tu-	Sisi tu**li**suka nywele jana. (*See*-see too-lee-*soo*-kah *nyweh*-leh *jah*-nah)	*We plaited our hair yesterday.*
Wewe	u-	Wewe u**li**oleka mapema. (*weh*-weh oh-lee-oh-*leh*-kah mah-*peh*-mah)	*You got married early.*
Nyinyi	m-	Nyinyi m**li**oleka mapema. (*nyee*-nyee m-lee-oh-*leh*-kah mah-*peh*-mah)	*You (pl.) got married early.*
Yeye	a-	Yeye a**li**zuru Afrika Mashariki. (*yeh*-yeh ah- lee-*zoo*-roo Afrika mah-shah-*ree*-kee)	*He/she toured East Afrika.*
Wao	wa-	Wao wa**li**zuru Afrika Mashariki. (*wah*-oh wah-lee-*zoo*-roo Afrika mah-shah-*ree*-kee)	*They toured East Africa.*

WORDS TO KNOW

jana	*jah*-nah	yesterday
juzi	*joo*-zee	day before yesterday
wiki iliyopita	*wee*-kee ee-lee-yoh-*pee*-tah	last week
wike tatu	zilizopita *wee*-kee *tah*-too zee-lee-zoh-*pee*-tah	three weeks ago
wiki kumi zilizopita	*wee*-kee *koo*-mee zee-lee-zoh-*pee*-tah	ten weeks ago
mwezi uliopita	m-*weh*-zee oo-lee-oh-*pee*-tah	last month
mwaka jana	m-*wah*-kah *jah*-nah	last year
mwaka uliopita	m-*wah*-kah oo-lee-oh-*pee*-tah	last year

The future tense

This tense describes plans and activities that have not yet happened but will occur at a future time. This tense is marked by inserting **-ta** between the personal pronoun marker and the verb. Table 4-3 illustrates how the future tense shows up through different pronouns.

TABLE 4-3 **Using the Future Tense**

Pronoun	Pronoun prefix	Sentence Example	Translation
Mimi	ni-	Mimi ni**ta**ogelea kesho. (*mee*-mee nee-tah-ogeh-*leh*-ah *keh*-shoh)	*I will swim tomorrow.*
Sisi	tu-	Sisi tu**ta**ogelea kesho. (*see*-see too- tah-ogeh-*leh*-ah *keh*-shoh)	*We will swim tomorrow.*
Wewe	u-	Wewe u**ta**zuru pwani. (*weh*-weh oo-tah-*zoo*-roo *pwah*-nee)	*You will tour the coast.*
Nyinyi	m-	Nyinyi m**ta**zuru pwani. (*nyee*-nyee m-tah-*zoo*-roo *pwah*-nee)	*You (pl.) will tour the coast.*

Pronoun	Pronoun prefix	Sentence Example	Translation
Yeye	**a-**	Yeye **a**takunywa mvinyo jioni. (*yeh*-yeh ah- tah- *koo*-nywah m-*vee*-nyoh jee-*oh*-nee)	*He/she will drink wine in the evening.*
Wao	**wa-**	Wao watakunywa mvinyo jioni. (*wah*-oh wah- tah- *koo*-nywah m-*vee*-nyoh jee-*oh*-nee)	*They will drink wine in the evening.*

WORDS TO KNOW

kesho	*keh*-shoh	tomorrow
kesho kutwa	*keh*-shoh *koo*-twah	day after tomorrow
wiki ijayo	*wee*-kee ee-*jah*-yoh	next week
wiki tatu zijazo	*wee*-kee *tah*-too zee-*jah*-zoh	three weeks from now
wiki kumi zijazo	*wee*-kee *koo*-mee zee-*jah*-zoh	ten weeks from now
mwezi ujao	m-*weh*-zee oo-*jah*-oh	next month
mwaka ujao	m-*wah*-kah oo-*jah*-oh	next year

The perfect tense

This tense describes actions or activities that were completed in the past but whose effects are still felt/observed in the present. It is similar to the English present perfect and past perfect tenses. This tense is marked by inserting **-me** between the personal pronoun prefix and the verb.

Check out Table 4-4 to see how the perfect tense is used through different pronouns.

The habitual tense

This tense describes activities that one repeatedly engages in. Think of your routine; if you were to explain what your morning routine is usually like in Swahili, you would use the habitual tense. This tense is marked by inserting **hu-** before the verb.

TABLE 4-4   **Using the Perfect Tense**

Pronoun	Pronoun prefix	Sentence Example	Translation
Mimi	**ni-**	Mimi ni**me**vuna mahindi. (*mee*-mee nee-meh-*voo*-nah mah-*hee*-ndee)	*I have harvested maize.*
Sisi	**tu-**	Sisi tu**me** vuna mahindi. (*see*-see too-meh-*voo*-nah mah-*hee*-ndee)	*We have harvested maize.*
Wewe	**u-**	Wewe u**me**jaribu kuogelea baharini? (*weh*-weh oo-meh-jah-*ree*-boo koo-oh-geh-*leh*-ah bah-hah-*ree*-nee)	*Have you tried to swim in the ocean?*
Nyinyi	**m-**	Nyinyi m**me**jaribu kuogelea baharini? (*nyee*-nyee m-meh-jah-*ree*-boo koo-oh-geh-*leh*-ah bah-hah-*ree*-nee)	*Have you (pl.) tried to swim in the ocean?*
Yeye	**a-**	Yeye a**me**kunywa madafu. (*yeh*-yeh ah-meh-*koo*-nywah mah-*dah*-foo)	*He/she has drunk coconut water.*
Wao	**wa-**	Wao wa**me**kunywa madafu. (*wah*-oh wah-meh-*koo*-nywah mah-*dah*-foo)	*They have drunk coconut water.*

The habitual tense behaves slightly differently from the other four tenses in two ways.

> » It is never attached to a pronoun prefix.

> » Short verbs in the habitual tense drop the **ku-**.

Table 4-5 shows you how the habitual tense is used through different pronouns.

CULTURAL WISDOM

Swahili dialects differ in the use of habitual tense. In some parts of Tanzania like Arusha, you are likely to notice the addition of **-ga** at the end of verb stems to mark the habitual tense. For example:

> » Ninaamka**ga**. (nee-nah-am-*kah*-gah) (I usually wake up.)

> » Ninakula**ga**. (nee-nah-koo-*lah*-gah) (I usually eat.)

TABLE 4-5   **Using the Habitual Tense**

Pronoun	Pronoun prefix	Sentence Example	Translation
Mimi	**ni-**	Mimi **hu**amka mapema. (*mee*-mee hoo-*ah*-mkah mah-*peh*-mah)	*I wake up early.*
Sisi	**tu-**	Sisi **hu**amka mapema. (*see*-see hoo-*ah*-mkah mah-*peh*-mah)	*We wake up early.*
Wewe	**u-**	Wewe **hu**fikiri sana. (*weh*-weh hoo-*fee*-kee-ree *sah*-nah)	*You think a lot.*
Nyinyi	**m-**	Nyinyi **hu**fikiri sana. (*nyee*-nyee hoo-*fee*-kee-ree *sah*-nah)	*You (pl.) think a lot.*
Yeye	**a-**	Yeye **hu**la ugali kila siku. (*yeh*-yeh *hoo*-lah oo-*gah*-lee *kee*-lah *see*-koo)	*He/she eats ugali every day.*
Wao	**wa-**	Wao hula ugali kila siku. (*wah*-oh hoo-lah oo-*gah*-lee *kee*-lah *see*-koo)	*They eat ugali every day.*

WORDS TO KNOW

kila	*kee*-lah	every
kila siku	*kee*-lah *see*-koo	every day
kila asubuhi	*kee*-lah ah-soo-*boo*-hee	every morning
kila usiku	*kee*-lah oo-*see*-koo	every night
mara kwa mara	*mah*-rah kwah *mah*-rah	occasionally/from time to time
kila mara	*kee*-lah *mah*-rah	always

Talkin' the Talk

Lulu and Aisha are friends. Lulu wants to spend some time with Aisha but is not sure when she is free. She calls Aisha to ask about her plans. Notice the use of different tenses.

Lulu: **Aisha vipi? Unafanya nini sasa?**
Aisha *vee*-pee? Oo-nah-*fah*-nyah *nee*-nee *sah*-sah?
Hello, Aisha! What are you doing now?

Aisha: **Poa sana. Ninafua nguo zangu.**
Poh-ah *sah*-nah. Nee-nah-*foo*-ah *ngoo*-oh *zah*-ngoo.
Great. I'm washing my clothes.

Lulu: Unataka kwenda kula kitimoto mkahawani?
Oo-nah-*tah*-kah *kweh*-ndah *koo*-lah *kee*-tee *moh*-toh
m-kah-hah-*wah*-nee?
Do you want to go eat fried pork at the restaurant?

Aisha: **Duh, nimekula chakula muda sio mrefu. Bado nimeshiba. Pia nilikula kitimoto jana.**
Doo, nee-meh-*koo*-lah chah-*koo*-lah *moo*-dah *see*-oh
m-*reh*-foo. *Bah*-doh nee-meh-*shee*-bah. *Pee*-ah nee-lee-*koo*-lah *kee*-tee *moh*-toh *jah*-nah.
Oh, I have had food not long ago. I am still full. Also, I ate fried pork yesterday.

Lulu: **Haya, utamaliza kufua nguo saa ngapi?**
Hah-yah, oo-tah-mah-*lee*-zah koo-*foo*-ah saah *ngah*-pee?
Alright, when will you finish washing clothes?

Aisha: **Nitamaliza kufua nguo saa tano.**
Nee-tah-mah-*lee*-zah koo-*foo*-ah *ngoo*-oh saah *tah*-noh.
I will finish washing clothes at 11 o'clock.

Lulu: **Sawa, nitakuja saa sita mchana ili tuamue cha kufanya pamoja.**
Sah-wah, nee-tah-*koo*-jah saah *see*-tah m-*chah*-nah *ee*-lee too-ah-*moo*-eh chah koo-*fah*-nyah pah-*moh*-jah.
Ok, I will come at 12 pm so that we decide what to do together.

Aisha: **Sawa, baadaye!**
Sah-wah, bah-ah-*dah*-yeh!
Ok, later!

Negating Actions Described by Verbs

Sometimes it is necessary to express verbs in the negative. Think about the need to state ideas such as "I did not sleep," "She will not travel," "I am not a student," and so on. To make a non-affirmative sentence in Swahili, you first need to negate the pronoun prefix before the tense markers of the verb. Table 4-6 shows you what we mean.

TABLE 4-6 ## Negating Pronoun Prefix

Pronoun	Affirmative Pronoun prefix	Negative Pronoun Prefix
Mimi	ni-	si-
Sisi	tu-	hatu-
Wewe	u-	hu-
Nyinyi	m-	ham-
Yeye	a-	ha-
Wao	wa-	hawa-

For example:

» **Mimi sichemshi maji ya kuoga.** (*mee*-mee see-*cheh*-mshee *mah*-jee yah koo-*oh*-gah) (*I am not/do not boiling/boil water for showering.*)

» **Sisi hatuchanji chale.** (*see*-see hah-too-*chah*-njee *chah*-leh) (*We do not draw tattoos.*)

» **Wewe huogopi jinni.** (*Weh*-weh hoo-oh-*goh*-pee *jee*-nee) (*You are not scared of djins/genies.*)

» **Nyinyi hamli pweza.** (*Nyee*-nyee *hah*-mlee *pweh*-zah) (*You (pl.) are not eating/do not eat octopus meat.*)

» **Yeye hapendi paka.** (*Yeh*-yeh hah-*peh*-ndee *pah*-kah) (*He/she does not like cats.*)

Master these negative forms of pronoun markers to use in all the tenses.

TIP

A quick way to recall all the negative prefixes is to think of the **-jambo** greeting. (For more on greetings, see Chapter 2.) Remember that the **-jambo** greeting is always expressed in the negative. (Instead of saying "I am fine," a Swahili speaker would get the same idea across by saying "I don't have an issue.") Look at the bolded parts of the greeting directed at different persons; these are the same negative pronoun prefixes you use when negating in all other instances.

>> (Mimi) **Si**(na)jambo. (see-*jah*-mboh) (*I don't have an issue/I am fine.*)

>> (Wewe) **Hu**(na)jambo. (hoo-*jah*-mboh) (*You don't have an issue/You're fine.*)

>> (Yeye) **Ha**(na)jambo. (hah-*jah*-mboh) (*He/She doesn't have an issue/He/She is fine.*)

>> (Sisi) **Atu**(na)jambo. (hah-too-*jah*-mboh) (*We don't have an issue/We are fine.*)

>> (Nyinyi) **Ham**(na)jambo. (ham-*jah*-mboh) (*You (pl.) don't have an issue/You (pl.) are fine.*)

>> (Wao) **Hawa**(na)jambo (hah-wah-*jah*-mboh) (*They don't have an issue/They are fine.*)

The following sections examine how to negate actions expressed in the five basic Swahili tenses.

The present tense

There are five things you need to do when negating in the present tense:

>> Change the subject marker to its negative form. (Refer to Table 4-6 for guidance.)

>> Drop the present tense marker **-na**.

>> If necessary, change the final vowel **-a** to **-i**.

Only verbs of Bantu origin have the **-a** ending.

REMEMBER

>> Never change the final vowel of the verb if it ends with **-e**, **-i,** or **-u.**

>> Drop the infinitive marker **ku-** if the verb is monosyllabic.

The sentences below show statements in the affirmative as well as their negated forms.

>> **Ninasoma.** (nee-nah-*soh*-mah) (*I am studying/ I study.*)

>> **Sisomi.** (see-*soh*-mee) (*I am not studying/I do not study.*)

>> **Unasoma.** (oo-nah-*soh*-mah) (*You are studying/You study.*)

>> **Husomi.** (hoo-*soh*-mee) (*You are not studying/You do not study.*)

» **Anasoma.** (ah-nah-*soh*-mah) (*He/she is studying/studies.*)

» **Hasomi.** (hah-*soh*-mee) (*He/she does is not studying/does not study.*)

» **Tunasoma.** (tu-nah-*soh*-mah) (*We are studying/we study*)

» **Hatusomi.** (hah-too-*soh*-mee) (*We are not studying/ We do not study.*)

» **Mnasoma.** (m-nah-*soh*-mah) (*You (pl.) are studying/do not study.*)

» **Hamsomi.** (ham-*soh*-mee) (*You (pl.) are not studying/do not study.*)

» **Wanasoma.** (wah-nah-*soh*-mah) (*They are studying/they study.*)

» **Hawasomi.** (hah-wah-*soh*-mee) (*They are not studying/they do not study.*)

» **Anatabasamu.** (ah-nah-*tah*-bah-sah-moo) (*He/she is smiling.*)

» **Hatabasamu.** (hah-*tah*-bah-sah-moo) (*He/she is not smiling.*)

» **Ninakula.** (nee-nah-*koo*-lah) (*I am eating. I eat.*)

» **Sili.** (*see*-lee) (*I am not eating/I do not eat.*)

REMEMBER

» **Sili** is an example in which a monosyllabic verb (**ku-** + **la**) not only drops the **ku-** but also changes the final **-a** to an **-i**.

» **Ninafagia baraza.** (nee-nah-*fah*-gee-ah bah-*rah*-zah) (*I am sweeping the verandah.*)

» **Sifagii baraza.** (see-*fah*-gee bah-*rah*-zah) (*I am sweeping the verandah.*)

» **Tunateka maji ya mvua.** (tu-nah-*teh*-kah *mah*-jee yah m-*voo*-ah) (*We are collecting/we collect rainwater.*)

» **Hatuteki maji ya mvua.** (hah-too- *teh*-kee *mah*-jee yah m-*voo*-ah) (*We are not collecting/we do not collect rainwater.*)

» **Unauza matunda.** (oo-nah-*oo-zah* mah-*too*-ndah) (*You are selling fruits/You sell fruits.*)

» **Huuzi matunda.** (hoo-*oo*-zee mah-*too*-ndah) (*You are not selling fruits/You do not sell fruits.*)

The past tense

There are three things to remember when negating in the past tense:

>> Change the subject marker to its negative form. (Refer to Table 4-6 for guidance.)

>> Replace the past tense marker **li-** with the past tense negative marker **ku-**.

>> Keep only one **ku-** if the verb is short.

The sentences below show past tense statements in the affirmative as well as their negated forms.

>> **Nilioga.** (nee-lee-*oh*-gah) (*I showered.*)

>> **Sikuoga.** (see-koo-*oh*-gah) (*I did not shower.*)

>> **Ulioga.** (oo-lee-*oh*-gah) (*You showered.*)

>> **Hukuoga.** (hoo- koo-*oh*-gah) (*You did not shower.*)

>> **Alioga.** (ah-lee-*oh*-gah) (*He/she showered.*)

>> **Hakuoga.** (hah- koo-*oh*-gah) (*He/she did not shower.*)

>> **Tulioga.** (too-lee-*oh*-gah) (*We showered.*)

>> **Hatukuoga.** (hah-too- koo-*oh*-gah) (*We did not shower.*)

>> **Mlioga.** (m-lee-*oh*-gah) (*You (pl.) showered.*)

>> **Hamkuoga.** (ham-koo-*oh*-gah) (*You (pl.) did not shower.*)

>> **Walioga.** (wah-lee-*oh*-gah) (*They showered.*)

>> **Hawakuoga.** (hah-wah-koo-*oh*-gah) (*They did not shower.*)

>> **Alidhani nilimsaliti.** (ah-lee- *dhah*-nee nee-lee-m-sah-*lee*-tee) (*He/she thought I betrayed him/her.*)

>> **Hakudhani** nilimsaliti (hah-koo-*dhah*-nee nee-lee-m-sah-*lee*-tee) (*He/she did not think I betrayed him/her.*)

>> **Ulikunywa.** (oo-lee-*koo*-nywah) (*You drank.*)

>> **Hukunywa.** (hoo-*koo*-nywah) (*You did not drink.*)

>> **Tuliota jua asubuhi.** (too-lee-*oh*-tah *joo*-ah ah-soo-*boo*-hee) (*We basked in the sun in the morning.*)

>> **Hatukuota jua asubuhi.** (hah-too- koo-*oh*-tah *joo*-ah ah-soo-*boo*-hee) (*We did not bask in the sun in the morning.*)

>> **Mlikamua ng'ombe.** (m-lee-kah-*moo*-ah *ng'o*-mbeh) (*You (pl.) milked the cows.*)

>> **Hamkukamua ng'ombe.** (ham-koo-kah-*moo*-ah *ng'o*-mbeh) (*You (pl.) did not milk the cows.*)

The future tense

As was the case with the present and past tenses, you'll need to keep three separate things in mind when negating in the future tense:

>> Change the subject marker to its negative form. (Refer to Table 4-6 for guidance.)

>> Retain the future tense marker **ta-**.

>> Retain the infinitive marker **ku-** if the verb is short.

For example:

>> **Nitapika.** (nee-tah-*pee*-kah) (*I will cook.*)

>> **Sitapika.** (see-tah-*pee*-kah) (*I will not cook.*)

>> **Utapika.** (oo-tah-*pee*-kah) (*You will cook.*)

>> **Hutapika.** (hoo-tah-*pee*-kah) (*You will not cook.*)

>> **Atapika.** (ah-tah-*pee*-kah) (*He/she will cook.*)

>> **Hatapika.** (hah-tah-*pee*-kah) (*He/she will not cook.*)

>> **Tutapika.** (too-tah-*pee*-kah) (*We will cook.*)

>> **Hatutapika.** (hah-too-tah-*pee*-kah) (*We will not cook.*)

>> **Mtapika.** (m-tah-*pee*-kah) (*You (pl.) will cook.*)

>> **Hamtapika.** (ham- tah-*pee*-kah) (*You (pl.) will not cook.*)

>> **Watapika.** (wah-tah-*pee*-kah) (*They will cook.*)

>> **Hawatapika.** (hah-wah- tah-*pee*-kah) (*They will not cook.*)

>> **Atahesabu.** (ah- tah-*heh*-sah-boo) (*He/she will count.*)

>> **Hatahesabu.** (hah- tah-*heh*-sah-boo) (*He/she will not count.*)

>> **Watakufa.** (wah-tah-*koo*-fah) (*They will die.*)

>> **Hawatakufa.** (hah-wah-tah-*koo*-fah) (*They will not die.*)

» **Nitasahau.** (nee-tah-*sah*-hah-oo) (*I will forget.*)

» **Sitasahau.** (see- tah-*sah*-hah-oo) (*I will not forget.*)

» **Tutaoa.** (too-tah-*oh*-ah) (*We will marry.*)

» **Hatutaoa.** (hah-too-tah-*oh*-ah) (*We will not marry.*)

» **Watapona.** (wah-tah-*poh*-nah) (*They will recover/get well.*)

» **Hawatapona.** (hah-wah-tah-*poh*-nah) (*They will not recover/get well.*)

The perfect tense

By now you know the drill: To negate in the perfect tense you need to do three things:

» Change the subject marker to its negative form. (Refer to Table 4-6 for guidance.)

» Replace the perfect tense marker **-me** with the negative perfect tense marker **-ja.**

» Drop the infinitive marker **ku-** if the verb is short.

For example:

» **Nimenunua nguo.** (nee-meh-noo-*noo*-ah *ngoo*-oh) (*I have bought clothes.*)

» **Sijanunua.** (see- jah-noo-*noo*-ah *ngoo*-oh) (*I have not bought clothes.*)

» **Umenunua mshikaki.** (oo- meh-noo-*noo*-ah m-shee-*kah*-kee) (*You have bought meat skewers.*)

» **Hujanunua mshikaki.** (hoo- jah-noo-*noo*-ah m-shee-*kah*-kee) (*You have not bought meat skewers.*)

» **Amenunua kitenge.** (ah- meh-noo-*noo*-ah kee-*teh*-ngeh) (*He/she has bought kitenge.*)

» **Hajanunua kitenge.** (hah- jah-noo-*noo*-ah kee-*teh*-ngeh) (*He/she has not bought kitenge.*)

CULTURAL WISDOM

» *Kitenge* is a Swahili patterned fabric used for clothing.

» **Tumenunua mbuzi.** (too-meh-noo-*noo*-ah) (*We have bought a goat.*)

» **Hatujanunua mbuzi.** (hah-too- jah-noo-*noo*-ah m-*boo*-zee) (*We have not bought a goat.*)

- **Mmenunua maji.** (m- meh-noo-*noo*-ah *mah*-jee) (*You (pl.) have bought water.*)

- **Hamjanunua maji.** (ham- jah-noo-*noo*-ah *mah*-jee) (*You (pl.) have not bought water.*)

- **Wamenunua vikapu.** (wah- meh-noo-*noo*-ah vee-*kah*-poo) (*They have bought baskets.*)

- **Hawajanunua vikapu.** (hah-wah- jah-noo-*noo*-ah vee-*kah*-poo) (*They have not bought baskets.*)

- **Wamerudi.** (wah- meh-*roo*-dee) (*They have come back.*)

- **Hawajarudi.** (hah- wah- jah-*roo*-dee) (*They have not come back.*)

- **Umekula.** (oo-meh-*koo*-lah) (*You have eaten.*)

- **Hujala.** (hoo-*jah*-lah) (*You have not eaten.*)

- **Nimeona mbweha.** (oo-meh-*oh*-nah m-*bweh*-hah) (*I have seen a hyena.*)

- **Sijaona mbweha.** (hoo-jah-*oh*-nah m-*bweh*-hah) (*I have not seen a hyena.*)

- **Umekuna nazi.** (oo-meh-*koo*-nah *nah*-zee) (*You have grated a coconut.*)

- **Hujakuna nazi.** (hoo-*jah*-koo-nah *nah*-zee) (*You have not grated a coconut.*)

- **Amesusa chakula.** (ah-meh-*soo*-sah chah-*koo*-lah) (*He/she has refused the food.*)

- **Hajasusa chakula.** (hoo-jah- *soo*-sah chah-*koo*-lah) (*He/she has not refused the food.*)

The habitual tense

For a change of pace, it turns out you can negate the habitual tense in two differ-ent ways.

For Method 1, do the following:

- Change the subject marker to its negative form. (Refer to Table 4-6 for guidance.)

- Remove the habitual tense marker **hu-**.

- Change the final vowel **-a** to **-i** (only if the verb is of Bantu origin and thus ends with the vowel **-a**)

- Do NOT change the final vowel of the verb if it ends with **-e**, **-i**, or **-u**.

- Drop the **ku-** infinitive marker if the verb is short.

The sentences below show you how to negate statements in the habitual tense using Method 1:

>> **Mimi huvaa bangili.** (*mee*-mee *hoo*-vaah bah-*ngee*-lee) (*I (usually) wear bracelets.*)

>> **Mimi sivai bangili.** (*mee*-mee see-*vah*-ee bah-*ngee*-lee) (*I do not (usually) wear bracelets.*)

>> **Wewe huvaa kofia.** (*weh*-weh *hoo*-vaah koh-*fee*-ah) (*You (usually) wear a cap.*)

>> **Wewe huvai kofia.** (*weh*-weh hoo-*vah*-ee koh-*fee*-ah) (*You do not (usually) wear a cap.*)

>> **Yeye huvaa buibui.** (*yeh*-yeh *hoo*-vaah boo-ee-*boo*-ee) (*She (usually) wears buibui.*)

>> **Yeye havai buibui.** (*yeh*-yeh hah-*vah*-ee boo-ee-*boo*-ee) (*She does not (usually) wear buibui.*)

>> The *buibui* is a long piece of black cloth worn as a dress by Muslim women, especially on the East African coast.

CULTURAL WISDOM

>> **Sisi huvaa pete.** (*see*-see *hoo*-vaah *peh*-teh) (*We (usually) wear rings.*)

>> **Sisi hatuvai pete.** (*see*-see hah-too-*vah*-ee *peh*-teh) (*We do not (usually) wear rings.*)

>> **Nyinyi huvaa kaptula.** (*nyee*-nyee *hoo*-vaah kap-*too*-lah) (*You (pl.) (usually) wear shorts.*)

>> **Nyinyi hamvai kaptula.** (*nyee*-nyee *ham*-vah-ee kap-*too*-lah) (*You (pl.) do not (usually) wear shorts.*)

>> **Wao huvaa vitambaa.** (*wah*-oh *hoo*-vaah vee-*tah*-mbaah) (*They (usually) wear headscarves.*)

>> **Wao hawavai vitambaa.** (*wah*-oh hah-wah-*vah*-ee vee-*tah*-mbaah) (*They do not (usually) wear headscarves.*)

>> **Yeye husamehe haraka.** (*Yeh*-yeh hoo-*sah*-meh-heh hah-*rah*-kah) (*He/She (usually) forgives quickly.*)

>> **Sisi hunywa kongoro.** (*see*-see *hoo*-nywah koh-*ngoh*-roh) (*We (usually) drink ox foot soup.*)

>> **Sisi hatunywi kongoro.** (*see*-see hah-*too*-nywee koh-*ngoh*-roh) (*We (usually) do not drink ox foot soup.*)

CULTURAL
WISDOM

>> Perhaps you have heard of oxtail soup, made with white beans, carrots, potatoes, and, yes, oxtails. For generations, many people in England have considered it to be the perfect comfort food. In Tanzania, many consider ox foot soup to be equally comforting and a great cure for hangovers.

>> **Wao hulima shamba.** (*wah*-oh hoo-*lee*-mah *shah*-mbah) (*They (usually) plough the farm.*)

>> **Wao hawalimi shamba.** (*wah*-oh hah-wah-*lee*-mee *shah*-mbah) (*They (usually) do not plough the farm.*)

>> **Yeye hufuga kuku na sungura.** (*yeh*-yeh hoo-*foo*-gah *koo*-koo nah soo-*ngoo*-rah) (*They (usually) keep chickens and rabbits.*)

>> **Yeye hafugi kuku na sungura.** (*yeh*-yeh hah-*foo*-gee *koo*-koo nah soo-*ngoo*-rah) (*They (usually) do not keep chickens and rabbits.*)

TIP

You may notice that negating in the habitual tense using Method 1 looks very similar to what you would get with present tense negation. Do not worry about a mix up in meaning as it is understood in context.

With Method 1 out of the way, let's turn to Method 2. Here's what has to happen:

>> Change the subject marker to its negative form. (Refer to Table 4-6 for guidance.)

>> Add **-wa** to the habitual tense marker **hu-** to make **huwa-.**

>> Everything else mirrors Method 1.

The sentences below show you how to negate statements in the habitual tense using Method 2:

>> **Mimi huvaa miwani.** (*mee*-mee *hoo*-vaah mee-*wah*-nee) (*I (usually) wear glasses.*)

>> **Mimi huwa sivai miwani.** (*mee*-mee *hoo*-wah see-*vah*-ee) (*I do not usually wear glasses.*)

>> **Wewe huvaa kanzu.** (*weh*-weh *hoo*-vaah *kah*-nzoo) (*You (usually) wear a kanzu.*)

>> **Wewe huwa huvai kanzu.** (*weh*-weh *hoo*-wah hoo-*vah*-ee *kah*-nzoo) (*You do not usually wear a kanzu.*)

CULTURAL
WISDOM

>> The kanzu is a long white or cream-colored tunic worn in East Africa mostly by Muslim men. It is often a Ugandan man's go-to attire for wedding celebrations.

>> **Yeye huvaa hereni.** (*yeh*-yeh *hoo*-vaah heh-*reh*-nee) (*He/She (usually) wears earrings.*)

» **Yeye huwa havai hereni.** (*yeh*-yeh *hoo*-wah hah-*vah*-ee heh-*reh*-nee) (*He/She does not usually wear earrings.*)

» **Sisi huvaa vipuli.** (*see*-see *hoo*-vaah vee-*poo*-lee) (*We (usually) wear nose rings.*)

» **Sisi huwa hatuvai vipuli.** (*see*-see *hoo*-wah hah-too-*vah*-ee vee-*poo*-lee) (*We do not usually wear nose rings.*)

» **Nyinyi huvaa sketi.** (*nyee*-nyee *hoo*-vaah *skeh*-tee) (*You (pl.) (usually) wear skirts.*)

» **Nyinyi huwa hamvai sketi.** (*nyee*-nyee *hoo*-wah ham-*vah*-ee *skeh*-tee) (*You (pl.) do not usually) wear skirts.*)

» **Wao huvaa sare.** (wah-oh *hoo*-vaah *sah*-reh) (*They (usually) wear a uniform.*)

» **Wao huwa hawavai sare.** (wah-oh *hoo*-wah hah-wah-*vah*-ee *sah*-reh) (*They do not usually wear a uniform.*)

» **Yeye hustarehe jioni.** (Yeh-yeh hoo-*stah*-reh-heh jee-*oh*-nee) (*He/She (usually) relaxes in the evening.*)

» **Yeye huwa hastarehe jioni.** (*yeh*-yeh *hoo*-wah hah-*stah*-reh-heh jee-*oh*-nee) (*He/She usually does not relax in the evening.*)

» **Wao huokota kuni wikendi.** (*wah*-oh hoo-oh-*koh*-tah *koo*-nee wee-*keh*-ndee) (*They (usually) collect firewood over the weekends.*)

» **Wao huwa hawaokoti kuni wikendi.** (*wah*-oh *hoo*-wah hah-wah-oh-*koh*-tee *koo*-nee wee-*keh*-ndee)) (*They do not usually collect firewood over the weekends.*)

» **Wewe huimba bafuni.** (*weh*-weh hoo-*ee*-mbah bah-*foo*-nee) (*You (usually) sing in the shower.*)

» **Wewe huwa huimbi bafuni.** (*weh*-weh *hoo*-wah hoo-*ee*-mbee bah-*foo*-nee) (*You do not usually sing in the shower.*)

» **Sisi hukaanga dagaa.** (*see*-see *hoo*-kah-*ah*-ngah *dah*-gaah) (*We (usually) fry dagaa.*)

» **Sisi huwa hatukaangi dagaa.** (*see*-see *hoo*-wah hah-too-kah-*ah*-ngee *dah*-gaah) (*We do not usually fry dagaa.*)

CULTURAL WISDOM

Dagaa, also known as Lake Victoria sardines, are an important fish in the diet of people in eastern and southern Africa. On moonless nights, fishermen paddle out onto the lakes and then use kerosene lamps to attract zooplankton, the dagaa's main food. Hoping for a meal, the dagaa rush in, only to get caught in the fishermen's nets and soon become a meal for someone else.

Talkin' the Talk

Lulu arrives at Aisha's place. They start talking about what they want to do together. Notice the use of negatives through different tenses.

Lulu:	**Aisha, unapenda kwenda klabu?** Aisha, oo-nah-*peh*-ndah *kweh*-ndah *klah*-boo? *Aisha, do you like going to the club?*
Aisha:	**Hapana, mimi sipendi kwenda klabu.** Hah-*pah*-nah, *mee*-mee see-*peh*-ndee *kweh*-ndah *klah*-boo. *No, I do not like going to the club.*
Lulu:	**Au twende kutembea bustani leo jioni?** Ah-oo *tweh*-ndeh koo-teh-*mbeh*-ah boo-*stah*-nee *leh*-oh jee-*oh*-nee? *Or let's go walk in the park this evening.*
Aisha:	**Twende kama sio mbali.** *Tweh*-ndeh *kah*-mah *see*-oh *mbah*-lee. *Let's go if it isn't far.*
Lulu:	**Kwani umechoka baada ya kufua nguo?** *Kwah*-nee oo-meh-*choh*-kah bah-*ah*-dah yah koo-*foo*-ah *ngoo*-oh? *Are you tired after washing clothes?*
Aisha:	**Hapana, sijachoka sana. Nina uvivu tu leo. Utarudi nyumbani mapema leo?** Hah-*pah*-nah, see-jah-*choh*-kah *sah*-nah. *Nee*-nah oo-*vee*-voo too *leh*-oh. Oo-tah-*roo*-dee nyoo-*mbah*-nee mah-*peh*-mah *leh*-oh? *No, I am not very tired. I'm just a bit lazy today. Will you go back home early today?*
Lulu:	**Hapana, sitarudi nyumbani mapema. Kwa nini?** Hah-*pah*-nah, see-tah-*roo*-dee nyoo-*mbah*-nee mah-*peh*-mah. Kwah *nee*-nee? *No, I will not go back home early today. Why?*
Aisha:	**Basi tutazame filamu.** *Bah*-see too-tah-*zah*-meh fee-*lah*-moo. *Then let's watch a movie.*
Lulu:	**Sawa, una filamu gani?** *Sah*-wah, oo-nah fee-*lah*-moo *gah*-nee? *Ok, what movie do you have?*

Aisha:	**Nina filamu ya Selina. . .**
	Nee-nah fee-*lah*-moo yah Selina. . .
	I have the Selina movie. . .
Lulu:	**Ah, tulitazama filamu ya Selina wiki iliyopita!**
	Ah, too-lee-tah-*zah*-mah fee-*lah*-moo yah Selina *wee*-kee ee-lee-yoh-*pee*-tah!
	Ah, we watched the Selina movie last week!
Aisha:	**Ndiyo lakini hatukumaliza. Kumbuka ni ndefu sana.**
	Ndee-yoh lah-*kee*-nee hah-to-koo-mah-*lee*-zah. Koo-*mboo*-kah nee *ndeh*-foo *sah*-nah.
	Yes, but we did not complete it. Remember it's very long.
Lulu:	**Ah, samahani, nilikuwa nimesahau.**
	Ah, sah-mah-*hah*-nee, nee-lee-*koo*-wah nee-meh-sah-*hah*-oo
	Ah; my apologies, I had forgotten.

••

FUN & GAMES

The figure below shows a number of different activities. Put a check mark in the box next to the verbs describing each activity.

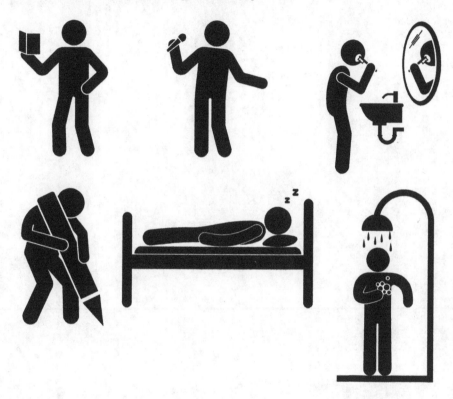

- ❑ kuvua samaki
- ❑ kulala
- ❑ kuchora
- ❑ kucheza karata

- ❑ kuoga
- ❑ kupiga deki
- ❑ kupiga mswaki
- ❑ kusoma

- ❑ kutembea
- ❑ kuimba
- ❑ kuota jua
- ❑ kupika

Chapter 5

Getting Your Numbers and Dates Right

S wahili numbers are an important part of the language and are essential for basic communication, so understanding them is crucial. You may have heard that Swahili speakers visualize time differently from the rest of the world. As a foreigner, you risk missing important appointments if you do not understand Swahili time. The secret to avoiding such a mess starts with familiarizing yourself with numbers. In fact, mastering numbers in Swahili makes a lot of things easier, including

» Talking about your family

» Understanding your bus booking or hotel check-in times

» Figuring out prices

This chapter offers a straightforward introduction to Swahili numbers. It explains how to do the following:

» Ask for someone's phone number in Swahili (and give out your own number as well)

» State your address in Swahili

» Ask others about their age and state your own

» Ask after the price of something

» Tell the time like a local

Using Cardinal Numbers

When you go to the store with your shopping list, the idea is to get 5 apples, 4 lamb chops, 1 head of lettuce, and 2 bottles of wine. To make that list, you use the counting numbers (1, 2, 3, 4 . . .) also known as *cardinal* numbers. Now, if you want to make a Swahili shopping list, you have to master Swahili numbers. The next few sections help you with that task.

Counting 0–10

Counting in Swahili is simple, but only after you master the numbers 0 through 10. Every other number greater than 10 builds upon this knowledge. Table 5-1 shows the Swahili word and pronunciation for numbers 0 through 10.

TABLE 5-1   Counting 0–10

Number	Swahili	Pronunciation
0	sufuri/sifuri	soo-*foo*-ree/see-*foo*-ree
1	moja	*moh*-jah
2	mbili	m-*bee*-lee
3	tatu	*tah*-too
4	nne	*n*-neh
5	tano	*tah*-no
6	sita	*see*-tah
7	saba	*sah*-bah
8	nane	*nah*-neh
9	tisa	*tee*-sah
10	kumi	*koo*-mee

You might notice that some of these numbers are similar to numbers in Arabic. Yes, the numbers *sita*, *saba* and *tisa* have Arabic origins.

Counting 11–100

When it comes to counting from 11 to 19, Swahili combines words for ten and the numbers from one to nine. For example, eleven is **kumi na moja** (*koo*-mee nah *moh*-jah), which literally translates to "ten and one". Twelve is therefore **kumi na mbili** (*koo*-mee nah m-*bee*-lee), which is "ten and two" and so on. (Check out Table 5-2 for whole numbers in the 11-to-19 range.) When you can apply this rule, mastering higher numbers is easy.

TABLE 5-2

Counting from 11 to 19

Number	Swahili	Pronunciation
11	**kumi na moja**	*koo*-mee nah *moh*-jah
12	**kumi na mbili**	*koo*-mee nah m-*bee*-lee
13	**kumi na tatu**	*koo*-mee nah *tah*-too
14	**kumi na nne**	*koo*-mee nah *n*-neh
15	**kumi na tano**	*koo*-mee nah *tah*-noh
16	**kumi na sita**	*koo*-mee nah *see*-tah
17	**kumi na saba**	*koo*-mee nah *sah*-bah
18	**kumi na nane**	*koo*-mee nah *nah*-neh
19	**kumi na tisa**	*koo*-mee nah *tee*-sah

The tens come with different names, as shown in Table 5-3. However, the same rule we use to form the numbers 11 to 19 applies here as well. That means 24 is "*twenty and four*"/**ishirini na nne** (ee-shee-*ree*-nee nah *n*-neh), 46 is "*forty and six*"/**arobaini na sita** (ah-roh-bah-*ee*-nee nah *see*-tah) and so on.

Counting 101–1,000,000

Counting 1 through 10 is for kindergartners. Counting up to 100 is for 1st graders. Now it's time for some higher math — counting up to 1,000,000! It's pretty easy — all you do is combine the 1 through 9 numbers with **mia** (*mee*-ah), the Swahili word for hundred. Table 5-4 shows how it is done.

TABLE 5-3

Counting the Tens

Number	Swahili	Pronunciation
20	**ishirini**	ee-shee-*ree*-nee
30	**thelathini**	thee-lah-*thee*-nee
40	**arobaini**	ah-roh-bah-*ee*-nee
50	**hamsini**	hah-m-*see*-nee
60	**sitini**	see-*tee*-nee
70	**sabini**	sah-*bee*-nee
80	**themanini**	thee-mah-*nee*-nee
90	**tisini**	tee-*see*-nee
100	**mia moja**	*mee*-ah *moh*-jah

TABLE 5-4

Counting the Hundreds

Number	Swahili	Pronunciation
200	**mia mbili**	*mee*-ah m-*bee*-lee
300	**mia tatu**	*mee*-ah *tah*-too
400	**mia nne**	*mee*-ah *n*-neh
500	**mia tano**	*mee*-ah *tah*-noh
900	**mia tisa**	*mee*-ah *tee*-sah

Knowing how to count to 10, to 100, and to 1,000,000 means you can come up with almost any number you would want — even some huge ones. Table 5-5 has some examples of some (relatively) big numbers.

For the really big numbers, however, you are going to need some new vocabulary. Use the word **elfu** (*ehl*-foo) for thousands and **milioni** (mee-lee-*oh*-nee) for millions. You can also use the word **laki** (*lah*-kee) to describe numbers in the hundreds of thousands. Table 5-6 goes for broke with some really big numbers.

TABLE 5-5

Combining Numbers in the Hundreds

Number	Swahili	Pronunciation
132	**mia moja thelathini na mbili**	*mee*-ah *moh*-jah thee-lah-*thee*-nee nah *mbee*-lee
245	**mia mbili arobaini na tano**	*mee*-ah *mbee*-lee ah-roh-bah-*ee*-nee nah *tah*-no
356	**mia tatu hamsini na sita**	*mee*-ah *tah*-too hah-m-*see*-nee nah *see*-tah
427	**mia nne ishirini na saba**	*mee*-ah *n*-neh ee-shee-*ree*-nee nah *sah*-bah
999	**mia tisa tisini na tisa**	*mee*-ah *tee*-sah tee-*see*-nee nah *tee*-sah

TABLE 5-6

Counting Thousands

Number	Swahili	Pronunciation
1000	**elfu moja**	*ehl*-foo *moh*-jah
8000	**elfu nane**	*ehl*-foo *nah*-neh
20,000	**elfu ishirini**	*ehl*-foo ee-shee-*ree*-nee
50,000	**elfu hamsini**	*ehl*-foo hah-m-see-nee
100,000	**elfu mia moja/laki moja**	*ehl*-foo *mee*-ah *moh*-jah/*lah*-kee *moh*-jah
500,000	**elfu mia tano/laki tano**	*ehl*-foo *mee*-ah *tah*-no/*lah*-kee *tah*-no
1,000,000	**milioni moja**	mee-lee-*oh*-nee *moh*-jah

Using Ordinal Numbers

The counting numbers (1, 2, 3, 4, and so on) are referred to as *cardinal* numbers. The ranking numbers (1st, 2nd 3rd, and so on) are known as *ordinal* numbers. It turns out that if you can count 1 to 10 using cardinal numbers, you are pretty much set when it comes to using ordinal numbers. Yes, there are a few slight differences with some of the numbers, but as Table 5-7 clarifies, many are exactly the same.

TABLE 5-7   # Counting Ordinal Numbers

Ordinal Number	Swahili	Pronunciation
1st	**kwanza**	*kwah*-nzah
2nd	**pili**	*pee*-lee
3rd	**tatu**	*tah*-too
4th	**nne**	*n*-neh
5th	**tano**	*tah*-no
6th	**sita**	*see*-tah
7th	**saba**	*sah*-bah
8th	**nane**	*nah*-neh
9th	**tisa**	*tee*-sah
10th	**kumi**	*koo*-mee

Notice that 1st and 2nd are different from the cardinal numbers while the rest stay the same. So how would you know whether someone was talking about 10 or 10th? Pay attention to the words said before the number. Swahili speakers add an associative **-a** (of) before the ordinal number. For example:

> » **Nina nyumba kumi.** (*nee*-nah *nyoo*-mbah *koo*-mee) (*I have ten houses.*)

> » **Nina nyumba ya kumi.** (*nee*-nah *nyoo*-mbah yah *koo*-mee) (*I have a tenth house.*)

In the second example, **ya** shows the relationship between **nyumba** and **kumi**.

Talkin' the Talk

AUDIO ONLINE

While touring Kajiado, a town in Kenya's southwest, Melissa becomes friends with Lana, a local woman who invites her home to meet her family. Read the dialogue below and pay attention to which children are present and which ones are absent.

Lana: **Dada, Melissa, karibu nyumbani kwangu!**
          dah-dah Melissa, kah-*ree*-boo nyoo-*mbah*-nee
          kwah-ngoo
          Sister Melissa, welcome to my home!

Melissa: **Ahsante sana.**
          ah-*sah*-nteh *sah*-nah
          Thank you very much.

Lana: **Karibu kiti. Utakunywa chai?**
          kah-*ree*-boo *kee*-tee. Uh-tah-*koo*-nywah *chah*-ee
          Have a seat. Would you like some tea?

Melissa: **Ndiyo, ndiyo. Nashukuru.**
          Ndee-yoh, *ndee*-yoh. Nah-shoo-*koo*-roo.
          Yes, yes. Thank you.
          (Lana's children walk in)

Lana: **Melissa, hawa ni watoto wangu. Huyu ni mtoto
          wangu wa pili anaitwa Paulo. Yeye ni mwanafunzi
          wa darasa la saba. Huyu ni wa tatu. Anaitwa Maua.
          Yeye ni mwanafunzi wa darasa la tano. Na huyu
          mdogo ni wa nne. Yeye ni mwanafunzi wa darasa
          la tatu.**
          Melissa, hah-wah nee wah-*toh*-toh *wah*-ngoo. *Hoo*-yoo
          nee m-*toh*-toh *wah*-ngoo wah *pee*-lee ah-nah-*ee*-twah
          Paulo. *Yeh*-yeh nee m-wah-nah-*foo*-nzee wah dah-*rah*-
          sah lah *sah*-bah. *Hoo*-yoo nee wah *tah*-too. Ah-nah-*ee*-
          twah Mah-*oo*-ah. *Yeh*-yeh nee m-wah-nah-*foo*-nzee wah
          dah-*rah*-sah lah *tah*-noh. Nah *hoo*-yoo m-*doh*-goh nee
          wah *n*-neh. *Yeh*-yeh nee m-wah-nah-*foo*-nzee wah dah-
          rah-sah lah *tah*-too.
          *Melissa, these are my children. This one is my second child.
          His name is Paulo. He is a sixth-grade student. This one is
          the third (child). Her name is Maua. She is a fifth-grade
          student. And this younger one is the fourth one. He is in
          third grade.*
          (Turns to her children)

Lana:	**Msalimieni mgeni.**
	m-sah-lee-mee-*eh*-nee m-*geh*-nee
	Greet the visitor.

The children:	**Shikamoo!**
	she-*kah*-moh
	Our respects!

Melissa:	**Marahaba! Habari zenu?**
	mah-rah-*hah*-bah! Hah-*bah*-ree *zeh*-noo
	How are you?

The children:	**Nzuri**
	n-*zoo*-ree
	Good!

Melissa:	**Mtoto wako wa kwanza yuko wapi?**
	m-*toh*-toh *wah*-koh wah *kwah*-nzah *yoo*-koh *wah*-pee?
	Where is your first child?

Lana:	**Mtoto wangu wa kwanza bado hajarudi kutoka shuleni. Yeye ni mwanafunzi wa darasa la nane kwa hivyo anasoma sana.**
	m-*toh*-toh *wah*-ngoo wah *kwah*-nzah *bah*-doh hah-jah-*roo*-dee koo-*toh*-kah shoo-*leh*-nee. *Yeh*-yeh nee m-wah-nah-*foo*-nzee wah dah-*rah*-sah lah *nah*-neh kwah hee-*vee*-oh ah-nah-*soh*-mah *sah*-nah.
	My first child is yet to come back from school. He is in 8th grade, so he studies a lot.

Melissa:	**Ah, sawa! Nimefurahi kuwajua watoto wako. Ahsante sana!**
	ah *sah*-wah! Nee-meh-foo-*rah*-hee koo-wah-*joo*-ah wah-*toh*-toh *wah*-koh. Ah-*sah*-nteh *sah*-nah.
	Oh, okay! It's a pleasure getting to know your children. Thank you very much!

● ●

CULTURAL WISDOM

Most Swahili speakers will offer tea to a guest. Accept the offer graciously; if you decline, your hosts might think you are being rude.

Asking For (and Giving Out) Phone Numbers

Knowing how to count is a great first step, but we can't think of any conversations in which two people just recite numbers to each other. The idea is to actually use the numbers in everyday situations. One such situation is asking somebody for their phone number.

In Swahili-speaking countries, requesting **nambari ya simu** (nah-*mbah*-ree yah *see*-moo) (*phone number*) is a popular way to show interest in getting to know someone better. It might be the same in your own culture, or it could be different. (For example, in the United States, when a man asks a woman for her phone number, it usually means he's interested in starting a romantic relationship.)

To ask for someone's phone number, you can say one of the following:

» **Nambari yako ya simu ni gani?** (nam-*bah*-ree *yah*-koh yah *see*-moo nee *gah*-nee?) (*What is your phone number?*)

» **Naomba nambari yako ya simu tafadhali.** (nah-*oh*-mbah nam-*bah*-ree *yah*-koh yah *see*-moo tah-fah-*dhah*-lee.) (*I'd like your phone number, please.*)

Most people state their phone numbers as single digits. A few people start with the first two single digits and then relay the rest as double digits. When someone asks for your phone number, you can reply with something along the following lines. (Of course, you'd have to substitute your own phone number.)

» **Nambari yangu ya simu ni tano tano tano sufuri moja nane saba** (Nah-*mbah*-ree *yah*-ngoo yah *see*-moo nee *tah*-noh *tah*-noh *tah*-noh soo-*foo*-ree *moh*-jah *nah*-neh *sah*-bah). (*My phone number is 555-0187.*)

Talkin' the Talk

Timothy is in Tanzania for a brief visit and sees the friendly face of a young man who just might be able to show him the local sights. Read their conversation as they make plans to meet again for a walk in the city.

Timothy: **Mambo vipi kaka?**
mah-mboh *vee*-pee *kah*-kah
How are things, brother?

Rajabu: **Poa! Unaitwa nani?**
poh-ah! Uh-nah-*ee*-twah *nah*-nee
Cool/fine! What's your name?

Timothy: **Ninaitwa Timothy. Na wewe je?**
nee-nah-*ee*-twah Timothy. Nah *weh*-weh jeh
My name is Timothy. How about you?

Rajabu: **Ninaitwa Rajabu. Karibu sana Tanzania!**
nee-nah-*ee*-twah Rah-*jah*-boo. Kah-*ree*-boo *sah*-nah
Tah-nah-zee-ah-*nee*-ah
My name is Rajabu. Welcome to Tanzania.

Timothy: **Asante sana! Ninapenda sana Tanzania. Unaweza kunionyesha sehemu mbalimbali nzuri hapa mjini?**
ah-*sah*-nteh *sah*-nah. Nee-nah-*peh*-ndah *sah*-nah Tanzania.
Oo-nah-*weh*-zah koo-nee-oh-*nyeh*-shah seh-*heh*-moo
mbah-lee-*mbah*-lee n-*zoo*-ree *hah*-pah m-*jee*-nee
Thank you very much! I like Tanzania very much. Could you show me more beautiful places within the city?

Rajabu: **Vizuri sana. Nitafurahi kukuona wikendi hii tutembee mjini. Naomba nambari yako ya simu tafadhali.**
Vee-*zoo*-ree *sah*-nah. Nee-tah-*foo*-rah-hee koo-koo-oh-nah
wee-*keh*-ndee hee. nah-*oh*-mbah *nah*-mbah-ree *yah*-koh
yah *see*-moo tah-fah-*dah*-lee
Thank you. I'll be happy to see you this weekend for a walk in the city. I'd like to have your phone number, please.

Timothy: **Bila shaka! Nambari yangu ya simu ni moja, mbili, mbili, tano, nne, saba, tatu, tisa, sita, nne, mbili. Nambari yako ya simu ni gani?**
Bee-lah *Shah*-kah! Nah-*mbah*-ree *yah*-ngoo yah *see*-moo
nee; *moh*-jah, m-*bee*-lee, m-*bee*-lee, tah-no, n-neh, *sah*-bah,
tah-too, *tee*-sah, *see*-tah, n-neh, m-*bee*-lee. nah-*mbah*-ree
yah-koh yah *see*-moo nee *gah*-nee?
Sure! My phone number is 12254739642. What is your phone number?

Rajabu:	**Nambari yangu ya simu ni sifuri, moja, mbili, mbili, moja, tano, nne, tatu, tatu, saba.**
	Nah-*mbah*-ree *yah*-ngoo yah *see*-moo nee: see-*foo*-ree, *moh*-jah, m-*bee*-lee, m-*bee*-lee, *moh*-jah, *tah*-noh, *n*-neh, *tah*-too, *sah*-bah
	My phone number is 0122154337.

• •

WARNING

Although exchanging phone numbers is a popular way to stay in touch with friends and family, be wary of scammers, hackers, or just bothersome people before giving someone your phone number. If asked to give out your phone number in a social setting, be sure that it is to someone you actually want to stay in touch with.

Requesting and Giving Addresses

Have you ever imagined visiting someone without an exact address to plug into Google Maps? Well, in case you find yourself in a Swahili-speaking country, this is one of the cultural shocks you're sure to encounter. But don't be disheartened; we can show you ways to navigate the challenge using local landmarks.

To request someone's home address, ask them **unakaa wapi** (oo-nah-*kah*-ah *wah*-pee) (*Where do you live?*) or **unaishi wapi** (oo-nah-*ee*-shee *wah*-pee) (*Where do you live?*). Respond with something along the lines of **ninakaa nyumba nambari sita tano nne mbili Kenyatta Avenue** (nee-nah-*kah*-ah *nyoo*-mbah nah-*mbah*-ree *see*-tah *tah*-noh *n*-neh m-*bee*-lee Kenyatta Avenue) (*I live at house number 6542 Kenyatta Avenue*) or **ninaishi nyumba nambari sita tano nne mbili Kenyatta** (nee-nah-ee-shee *nyoo*-mbah nah-*mbah*-ree *see*-tah *tah*-noh *n*-neh m-*bee*-lee Kenyatta Avenue) (*I live at 6542 Kenyatta Avenue*)

Another way to request addresses is to say **anuani yako ni gani** (ah-noo-*ah*-nee *yah*-koh nee *gah*-nee) (*What is your address?*). Respond with **anuani yangu ni sita mbili tano Mtaa wa Biashara** (ah-noo-*ah*-nee *yah*-ngoo nee) (*My address is 625 Biashara Street.*). You are more likely to encounter this phrase in official settings such as immigration offices, but it can also be used informally to communicate the idea that you need to provide an exact address and not just the general neighborhood.

Talkin' the Talk

Carley is new to Arusha, a gateway to many safari destinations in Tanzania, and has already made a new friend, Jamila. She wants to visit Jamila at her home during the weekend. Here is the conversation between them exchanging addresses.

Carley: **Mambo vipi Jamila?**
           Mam-boh *vee*-pee Jamila?
           Hello, Jamila!

Jamila: **Poa! Unaenda wapi leo?**
           Poh-ah! Oo-nah-*eh*-ndah *wah*-pee *leh*-oh?
           Hello! Where are you going today?

Carley: **Ninaenda sokoni. Na wewe?**
           Nee-nah-*eh*-ndah soh-*koh*-nee. Nah *weh*-weh?
           I'm going to the market. And you?

Jamila: **Ninarudi nyumbani.**
           Nee-nah-*roo*-dee nyoo-*mbah*-nee.
           I'm going back home.

Carley: **Unakaa wapi hapa Arusha?**
           Oo-nah-*kah*-ah *wah*-pee *hah*-pah Arusha?
           Whereabouts in Arusha do you live?

Jamila: **Ninakaa Leganga. Ninakaa na rafiki zangu na wewe?**
           Nee-nah-*kah*-ah Leh-*gah*-ngah. Nee-nah-*kah*-ah nah rah-*fee*-kee *zah*-ngoo nah *weh*-weh?
           I live in Leganga. I live with my friends, and you?

Carley: **Ninakaa Njiro katika fleti na mpenzi wangu.**
           Nee-nah-*kah*-ah Njiro kah-*tee*-kah *fleh*-tee nah m-*peh*-nzee *wah*-ngoo.
           I live in Njiro in a flat/apartment with my boyfriend.

Jamila: **Ooh sawa! Anuani yako ni gani? Ningependa kuja nyumbani kwako wikendi kama ni sawa.**
           Ooh *sah*-wah! Ah-noo-*ah*-nee *yah*-koh nee *gah*-nee? Nee-ngeh-*peh*-ndah *koo*-jah *kwah*-koh wee-*keh*-ndee *kah*-mah nee *sah*-wah.
           Oh, okay! What's your address? I'd like to come over to your place over the weekend if that is fine.

Carley:	**Hamna shida karibu sana. Anuani yangu ni nyumba nambari kumi na tano, mtaa wa Uzunguni. Kuna kanisa na mti mkubwa karibu na nyumba yangu. Anuani yako ni gani?**

Ham-nah *shee*-dah kah-*ree*-boo *sah*-nah. Ah-noo-*ah*-nee *yah*-ngoo nee *nyoo*-mbah nah-*mbah*-ree *koo*-mee nah *tah*-noh, m-*tah*-ah wah Uzunguni. *Koo*-nah kah-*nee*-sah nah *m*-tee m-*koo*-bwah kah-*ree*-boo nah *nyoo*-mbah *yah*-ngoo. Ah-noo-*ah*-nee *yah*-koh nee *gah*-nee?

No problem. You are very welcome. My address is house number 15, in Uzunguzi neighborhood. There's a church and a big tree near my house. What's your address?

Jamila:	**Anuani yangu ni nyumba nambari saba, mtaa wa Leganga. Nyumba iko karibu na shule ya msingi ya Leganga na duka la dawa.**

Ah-noo-*ah*-nee *yah*-ngoo nee *nyoo*-mbah nah-*mbah*-ree *sah*-bah m-*tah*-ah wah Leganga. *Nyoo*-mbah *ee*-koh kah-*ree*-boo nah *shoo*-leh yah m-*see*-ngee yah Lenganga nah *doo*-kah lah *dah*-wah.

My address is house number 7, in Leganga neigborhood. The house is close to a Leganga primary school and a pharmacy.

Carley:	**Ahsante sana. Tutaonana hivi karibuni.**

Ah-*sah*-nteh *sah*-nah. Too-tah-oh-*nah*-na *hee*-vee kah-ree-*boo*-nee.

Thank you. See you soon.

● ●

WORDS TO KNOW

maeneo	mah-eh-*neh*-oh	general area
anuani	ah-noo-*ah*-nee	address
mtaa	*m*-taah	street/neighborhood
nyumba	*nyoo*-mbah	house
fleti	*fleh*-tee	flat/apartment
karibu na	kah-*ree*-boo nah	near
soko	*soh*-koh	market
shule	*shoo*-leh	school
kanisa	kah-*nee*-sah	church
duka la dawa	*doo*-kah lah *dah*-wah	pharmacy

CULTURAL WISDOM

Finding your way around can be difficult in most Swahili-speaking countries. When walking down the street in cities and towns, you're not going to find any house numbers or family names on the houses you see, and the street signs may not be visible. When you venture outside of the cities and head into the country, you're not going to find any street signs at all.

TIP

If you're wondering how to find your way, then you'll be glad to know that you can use local landmarks such as

>> Shops

>> Churches

>> Mosques

>> Bars

>> Banks

>> Trees (usually very big or unique trees)

In the conversation above, Jamila uses a school and a pharmacy as landmarks to give her address. Chapter 7 of this book guides you on how to rely on word of mouth or local knowledge to find a location.

Asking "How Old Are You?" and Stating Your Age

You might have grown up in a culture where it was impolite to ask how old someone was — especially if that someone was a woman! Swahili speakers, however, think it's quite normal to ask someone's age when meeting them for the first time. For them, it is a perfect topic for small talk.

So, if you are looking for a way keep a conversation going, ask someone their age by saying **Una miaka mingapi?** (*oo*-nah mee-*ah*-kah mee-*ngah*-pee) (*how old are you?*). If someone asks about your age, respond with the phrase **Nina miaka** . . . (*nee*-nah mee-*ah*-kah) [*I am* . . . *years (old).*] Literally [I have . . . years.]

Talkin' the Talk

While on a trip to Mombasa, a city in Kenya's southeast, Marie meets Bahati. They greet each other, and naturally the topic of their ages comes up.

Marie: **Hujambo rafiki?**
hoo-*jah*-mboh rah-*fee*-kee
How are you, my friend?

Bahati: **Sijambo! Jina lako ni nani?**
see-*jah*-mboh! *Jee*-nah *lah*-koh nee *nah*-nee?
I'm doing well! What's your name?

Marie: **Jina langu ni Marie na wewe je?**
Jee-nah *lah*-ngoo nee Marie nah *weh*-weh jeh
My name is Marie, and how about you?

Bahati: **Jina langu ni Bahati. Karibu sana Kenya.**
Jee-nah *lah*-ngoo nee Bahati. Kah-*ree*-boo *sah*-nah Kenya.
My name is Bahati. Welcome to Kenya.

Marie: **Asante sana Bahati. Ninapenda Kenya sana.**
Ah-*sah*-nteh *sah*-nah Bahati. Nee-nah-*peh*-ndah Kenya *sah*-nah;
Thank you very much, Bahati. I like Kenya a lot.

Bahati: **Safi sana! Ninafurahi kusikia hivyo. Una miaka mingapi?**
Sah-fee *sah*-nah! Nee-nah-foo-*rah*-hee ku-see-*kee*-ah *hee*-vyoh. *Oo*-nah mee-*ah*-kah mee-*ngah*-pee?
That's great! I'm glad to hear that. How old are you?

Marie: **Mimi nina miaka thelathini na nane. Bahati, samahani, nina haraka kidogo. Tunaweza kuzungumza wakati mwingine?**
Mee-mee *nee*-nah mee-*ah*-kah theh-lah-*thee*-nee nah *nah*-neh. Bahati, sah-mah-*hah*-nee *nee*-nah hah-*rah*-kah kee-*doh*-goh. too-nah-*weh*-zah koo-zoo-*ngoo*-mzah wah-*kah*-tee m-wee-*ngee*-neh?
I am thirty-five years old. I apologize, but I must go now. Can we talk another time?

Bahati: **Hamna shida, Marie. Nimefurahi kukutana na wewe!**
Hah-mnah *Shee*-dah, Marie. Nee-meh-foo-*rah*-hee koo-koo-*tah*-nah nah *weh*-weh
No worries, Marie. I am glad to meet you!

Marie: **Nimefurahi kukutana na wewe pia! Baadaye!**
Nee-meh-foo-*rah*-hee koo-koo-*tah*-nah nah *weh*-weh *pee*-ah. Bah-ah-*dah*-yeh!
Glad to meet you, too. Later!

Identifying Years in Swahili

Most English speakers would refer to the year "1964," as "nineteen sixty-four" and not "one thousand nine hundreds sixty and four." If you've been following along in this chapter so far, you know that Swahili takes the second approach. So, if you want to mention a specific year in your conversation, simply state the year just as you do with regular numbers. The only difference is that you must mark the number you are using as a year by inserting the phrase **mwaka wa** (m-*wah*-kah wah) (*year of*) before the actual number. Table 5-8 shows a few examples.

TABLE 5-8

Stating Years

Year	Swahili	Pronunciation
1998	**mwaka wa elfu moja mia tisa tisini na nane**	m-*wah*-kah wah *ehl*-foo *moh*-jah *mee*-ah *tee*-sah tee-*see*-nee nah *nah*-neh
2001	**mwaka wa elfu mbili na moja**	m-*wah*-kah wah *ehl*-foo m-*bee*-lee nah *moh*-jah
2023	**mwaka wa elfu mbili ishirini na tatu**	m-*wah*-kah wah *ehl*-foo m-*bee*-lee ee-shee-*ree*-nee nah *tah*-too

TIP

Always use the full number with years. For example, 2023 cannot be **ishirini na tatu** (ee-shee-*ree*-nee nah *tah*-too) ('23). No one will understand that there is an implied *2000*. Unfortunately, that would mean one would have to change the title of Bryan Adams' hit song from "The Summer of '69" to "The Summer of 1969" if translated into Swahili. Somehow the new version doesn't have the same ring.

Getting Familiar with the Calendar

Birthdays, anniversaries, graduation days, going away parties, holidays — all of these events tend to take place on the same day each year. So, if you're wondering how to update your online calendar to Swahili while staying in East Africa, this section is for you.

Naming the days of the week

Calendars in the United States start the week with Sunday. Calendars designed for the European market choose Monday as the starting point. Technically speaking,

Swahili calendars should start the week with Saturday, since **Jumamosi** (joo-mah-*moh*-see) combines the word **Juma** (*week*) and **mosi** (*the number 1*) to get across the idea of the first day of the week. (In practice, the work week is similar to the Western calendar, that's to say running from Monday to Friday, with the weekend being Saturday and Sunday.)

REMEMBER

You might be thinking "What happened to **moja**, which is the word for the number 1 I learned at the beginning of this chapter?" **Mosi** is a variant of **moja**, but you only use it when talking about dates. **Moja** gets used for everything else.

CULTURAL WISDOM

The names of the week are a cultural crossover from earlier contact with the Arab world, where Friday is a day of prayer and rest. The Muslim faithful in East Africa still follow this custom, while those of other religions (or non-believers) treat Friday as a normal workday.

Now that we have that settled, check out Table 5-9 for a list for all the days of the week.

TABLE 5-9 **Days of the Week**

Day	Swahili	Pronunciation
Saturday	**Jumamosi**	joo-mah-*moh*-see
Sunday	**Jumapili**	joo-mah-*pee*-lee
Monday	**Jumatatu**	joo-mah-*tah*-too
Tuesday	**Jumanne**	joo-mah-*n*-neh
Wednesday	**Jumatano**	joo-mah-*tah*-noh
Thursday	**Alhamisi**	al-hah-*mee*-see
Friday	**Ijumaa**	ee-joo-*mah*-ah

Identifying months by name and numbers

Do you remember ordinal numbers from earlier in this chapter? You need them again for the calendar. You can choose whether to use ordinal numbers to name months in Swahili or their Swahili-ized names, which are just their English equivalent but with Swahili spelling and pronunciation. Table 5-10 shows months by their Swahili-ized names.

TABLE 5-10

Months by Name

Month	Swahili	Pronunciation
January	**Januari**	jah-noo-*ah*-ree
February	**Februari**	feb-roo-*ah*-ree
March	**Machi**	*mah*-chee
April	**Aprili**	ahp-*ree*-lee
May	**Mei**	*meh*-ee
June	**Juni**	*joo*-nee
July	**Julai**	joo-*lah*-ee
August	**Agosti**	ah-*goh*-stee
September	**Septemba**	sep-*teh*-mbah
October	**Oktoba**	ok-*toh*-bah
November	**Novemba**	noh-*veh*- mbah
December	**Disemba**	dee-*seh* -mbah

If you feel like using ordinal numbers, then you'd use **Mwezi** (m–*weh*–zee) for *month* and combine that with the Swahili words for *first*, *second*, *third* and so on. (By the way, **mwezi** means *month* but in other contexts it can also mean *the moon*.) To refer to months by their order, use the phrase **mwezi wa . . .** (m–*weh*–zee wah) (*month of . . .*). Table 5-11 shows the months from first to last.

TABLE 5-11

Using Ordinal Numbers for Months

Month	Swahili	Pronunciation
January	**mwezi wa kwanza**	m-*weh*-zee wah *kwah*-nzah
February	**mwezi wa pili**	m- *weh* -zee wah *pee*-lee
March	**mwezi wa tatu**	m- *weh* -zee wah *tah*-too
April	**mwezi wa nne**	m- *weh* -zee wah *n*-neh
May	**mwezi wa tano**	m- *weh* -zee wah *tah*-noh
June	**mwezi wa sita**	m- *weh* -zee wah *see*-ta
July	**mwezi wa saba**	m- *weh* -zee wah *sah*-bah

Month	Swahili	Pronunciation
August	**mwezi wa nane**	m- *weh* -zee wah *nah*-neh
September	**mwezi wa tisa**	m- *weh* -zee wah *tee*-sah
October	**mwezi wa kumi**	m- *weh* -zee wah *koo*-mee
November	**mwezi wa kumi na moja**	m- *weh* zee wah *koo*-mee nah *moh*-jah
December	**mwezi wa kumi na mbili**	m- *weh* -zee wah *koo*-mee nah m-*bee*-lee

Reading and writing dates in Swahili

If you plan on getting married, you first have to set a date and then tell all your friends and family which date you came up with. If you plan on getting married in East Africa, then you have to learn how to express dates in Swahili. To state the date [**tarehe** (tah-*reh*-heh)(*the date*)] in Swahili, begin with the day, then the month, and finally the year. For example, 31st May, 2022 in Swahili would be **tarehe thelathini na moja, mwezi wa tano, mwaka wa elfu mbili na ishirini na mbili** (tah-*reh*-heh theh-lah-*thee*-nee nah *moh*-jah, *mweh*-zee wah *tah*-noh, *mwah*-kah wah *ehl*-foo m-*bee*-lee nah ee-shee-*ree*-nee nah m-*bee*-lee). (Yes, it is a mouthful, but all dates are a mouthful in all languages when you have to use lots of numbers.) Notice the explicit stating of what each number is before the number is mentioned using **tarehe . . . , mwezi wa . . . , mwaka wa . . .**

REMEMBER

The correct arrangement of the date in Swahili-speaking countries is DD/MM/YYY. This is important to remember when filling out forms or other official communication to avoid confusion.

When you are describing different events that happened to you or to someone else in the past, are happening now, or will happen in the future, you are going to need words like "today," "tomorrow," or "next week." We have those for you in the Words to Know list below.

WORDS TO KNOW

leo	*leh*-oh	*today*
kesho	*keh*-shoh	*tomorrow*
kesho kutwa	*keh*-shoh koo-*tuh*-wah	*day after tomorrow*
jana	*jah*-nah	*yesterday*

juzi	joo-zee	day before yesterday
juzi juzi	joo-zee joo-zee	not long ago
wiki ijayo	wee-kee ee-jah-yoh	next week
mwisho wa wiki	m-wee-shoh wah wee-kee	end of the week
mwezi ujao	m-weh-zee oo-jah-oh	next month
mwisho wa mwezi	m-wee-shoh wah m-weh-zee	end of the month
mwisho wa mwaka	m-wee-shoh wah m-wah-kah	end of the year
mwaka ujao	m-wah-kah oo-jah-oh	next year
mwezi uliopita	m-wah-kah oo-lee-oh-pee-tah	last month
mwaka uliopita	m-weh-zee oo-lee-oh-pee-tah	last year

Talking about birthdays

No doubt your date of birth, **siku ya kuzaliwa** (see-koo yah koo-zah- lee-wah), is an important piece of information everywhere you go. You should expect to be asked about your birthday in both formal and informal settings.

To ask "what is your date of birth?" say **ulizaliwa lini?** (oo-lee-zah-lee-wah lee-nee).

To respond, say **nilizaliwa tarehe . . . mwezi wa . . . mwaka wa** (nee-lee-zah-lee-wah tah-reh-heh . . . m-weh-zee wah . . . m-wah-kah wah . . .) (I was born on DD/MM/YYY).

To wish someone a happy birthday, say **heri ya siku yako ya kuzaliwa** (heh-ree yah see-koo yah-koh ya koo-zah-lee-wah).

Talkin' the Talk

Jumanne is celebrating his birthday today. He meets Travis who is visiting Zanzibar and invites him to the party.

Jumanne: Hujambo rafiki?
                hoo-jah- mboh rah-fee-kee?
                How are you, friend?

Travis: Sijambo habari gani?
                see-jah-mboh! Hah-bah-ree gah-nee?
                I am fine! How are you doing?

Jumanne: Nzuri sana. Karibu Zanzibar. Unaitwa nani?
                n-zoo-ree sah-nah. Kah-ree-boo Zanzibar. Oo-nah-ee-twah
                nah-nee?
                I am very well. Welcome to Zanzibar. What's your name?

Travis: Ninatwa Travis. Na wewe?
                nee-nah-ee-twah Travis. Nah weh-weh?
                My name is Travis. And you?

Jumanne: Ninaitwa Jumanne. Karibu sana leo jioni ninasherehekea
                siku yangu ya kuzaliwa.
                nee-nah-ee-twah Jumanne. Kah-ree-boo sah-nah leh-oh
                Jee-oh-nee Nee-nah-sheh-reh-heh-keh-ah See-koo yah-ngoo
                yah koo-zah-lee-wah.
                My name is Jumanne. I will be celebrating my birthday tonight.
                You are invited.

Travis: Safi sana! Una miaka mingapi?
                sah-fee sah-nah! oo-nah mee-ah-kah mee-ngah-pee?
                That's nice! how old are you?

Jumanne: Nina miaka ishirini na tano.
                nee-nah mee-ah-kah ee-shee-ree-nee nah tah-no.
                I'm twenty-five years old.

Travis: Heri ya siku ya kuzaliwa kwako! Ulizaliwa lini?
                Heh-ree yah see-koo yah koo-zah-lee-wah kwah-koh!
                Oo-lee-zah-lee-wah lee-ni?
                Happy birthday to you! What is your date of birth?

Jumanne: Nilizaliwa tarehe kumi na mbili, mwezi wa saba mwaka wa
                elfu moja mia tisa tisini na nane.
                Nee-lee-zah-lee-wah tah-reh-heh koo-mee nah m-bee-lee
                m-weh-zee wah sah-bah m-wah-kah wah ehl-foo moh-jah
                mee-ah tee-sah tee-see-nee nah nah-neh.
                I was born on the 12th of July, 1998.

CULTURAL WISDOM

Many people in Swahili-speaking countries, especially those of the older generation, do not celebrate their birthdays for a variety of reasons, including cultural and religious beliefs. In some cultures, birthdays are not seen as an important event and, thus, are not celebrated.

Understanding Swahili Time

The Swahili concept of time, *saa (sah-ah)*, depends on whether the sun is up or down. This is because the Equator cuts across East African countries and almost divides Kenya into two equal halves. The result is all East African countries experience 12 hours of sunlight and 12 hours of darkness every single day throughout the year. Imagine having no daylight savings time!

Distinguishing between day and night in the 12-hour clock system

Swahili speakers count hours with reference to sunrise (6:00am) and sunset (6:00pm). 7:00am is, therefore, 1 hour after sunrise, 8:00am is 2 hours after sunrise and so on.

For example:

>> **First hour after sunrise** (saa moja) (*sah*-ah *moh*-jah)   7:00am

>> **Third hour after sunrise** (saa tatu) (*sah*-ah *tah*-too)   9:00am

>> **Fifth hour after sunset** (saa tano) (*sah*-ah *tah*-noh)   11:00pm

>> **Sixth hour after sunset** (saa sita) (*sah*-ah *see*-tah)   12:00am

At this point you might be wondering how to differentiate the morning from the afternoon to avoid confusion, since the Swahili phrases don't contain the words for *sunrise* and *sunset*. It's simple; include the general period of day with the exact hour! Table 5-12 shows the general periods of the day in Swahili.

TABLE 5-12 **Periods of the Day**

Alfajiri	ahl-fah-*jee*-ree	*dawn*
Asubuhi	ah-soo-*boo*-hee	*morning*
Mchana	m-*chah*-nah	*afternoon*
Jioni	jee-*oh*-nee	*evening*
Usiku	oo-*see*-koo	*night*

The periods of a 24-hour day listed above break down as follows:

>> **alfajiri**: 4:00am–6:59am

>> **asubuhi**: 7:00am–11:59am

>> **mchana**: 12:00pm–3:59pm

>> **jioni**: 4:00pm–6:59pm

>> **usiku**: 7:00pm–3:59am

With all that under your belt, you'll soon be telling time in Swahili like a pro. Putting all the pieces together, you'll be coming up with something like the following:

>> **saa tatu asubuhi**: (*sah*-ah *tah*-too ah-soo-*boo*-hee)   9:00am

>> **saa tano usiku**: (*sah*-ah *tah*-noh oo-*see*-koo)   11:00pm

>> **saa kumi jioni**: (*sah*-ah *koo*-mi jee-*oh*-nee)   4:00pm

Of course, if both speakers see the sun shining outside and are talking about something happening right now, there's no need to mention the period of day.

CULTURAL WISDOM

Before wrist watches and cellphones became common, most Swahili speakers could tell the time just by looking at the position of the sun in the sky and the length of their shadow. Seline definitely knew it was lunch time (1:00pm) when the sun was right above her head and her shadow was at its shortest! Most of the older generation in the villages can still pinpoint the exact hour of the day even without looking at a clock. (Seline has tried this trick in the United States and the United Kingdom, and it does not work; she must have been too far from the equator!)

Working with hours and minutes

The clock faces used in Swahili-speaking countries are the same as those used in countries following the European Standard Time. The only difference is how we express it in Swahili.

Recall that Swahili speakers count hours with reference to sunrise (6:00am) and sunset (6:00pm). Look at Figure 5-1 to understand how a Swahili speaker interprets the clock.

FIGURE 5-1:
Reading the hour: Saa tatu.

The time in Figure 5-1 reads 9:00 o'clock in European Standard Time. In Swahili, that is *saa tatu*, 3 o'clock. How does nine become three? Pay attention to the numbers outside the clockface. They represent the hours after sunrise or sunset (at 6 on the clock face). 9 o'clock is, therefore, 3 hours after sunrise/sunset.

TIP

A quick way to identify the correct hour is to read the number directly opposite the short hand (hour hand) of the clock. So, if the short hand is on 8 (and it's dark outside), you draw an imaginary line straight across the clockface ending up at 2. Now you know it is 2 hours past sunset — **saa mbili usiku**, in other words.

Calculate the minutes, **dakika** (dah-*kee*-kah) just as you would with European Standard Time. Figure 5-2 tells us that the current time is **saa tatu na dakika kumi** (*sah*-ah *tah*-too nah dah-*kee*-kah *koo*-mee). We'll let you work out the individual pieces — the hours part and the minutes part — on your own.

FIGURE 5-2:
Reading the time:
*saa tatu na
dakika kumi.*

REMEMBER

You must indicate that you're going to state the hour by mentioning **saa** first and then indicate that you're going to mention the minutes by saying **dakika**. When telling time you must always use the **saa** and **dakika** markers; if you don't let people know exactly what kind of number you are using — an hours number or a minutes number — no one will understand you.

Using the correct time phrases

Like most languages, Swahili has phrases that make it easier to express the number of minutes past the hour or to the hour. The list below highlights the more common ones.

WORDS TO KNOW		
kamili	kah-*mee*-lee	on the dot/on the hour
nusu	*noo*-soo	half
robo	*roh*-boh	quarter
kasoro dakika	kah-*soh*-roh dah-*kee*-kah	minutes to
kasorobo	kah-soh-*roh*-boh	quarter to

For example:

>> **Saa tatu kamili asubuhi** (*sah*-ah *tah*-too *kah*-mee-lee ah-soo-*boo*-hee) (*9: 00am [on the dot/hour]*)

>> **Saa tano na nusu asubuhi** (*sah*-ah *tah*-noh nah *noo*-soo ah-soo-*boo*-hee) (*11: 30am*)

>> **Saa sita na robo mchana** (*sah*-ah *see*-tah nah *roh*-boh m-*chah*-nah) (*quatre past midday [12:15pm]*)

>> **Saa nne kasoro dakika kumi asubuhi** (*sah*-ah *n*-neh kah-*soh*-roh dah-*kee*-kah *koo*-mee ah-soo-*boo*-hee) (*ten minutes to 10:00am [9:50am]*)

>> **Saa mbili usiku kasorobo** (*sah*-ah m-*bee*-lee oo-*see*-koo kah-soh-*roh*-boh) (*quatre to 8:00pm [7:45pm]*)

Stating the time

When asking for the time, use the phrase **Ni saa ngapi?** (nee *sah*-ah *ngah*-pee) meaning "What is the time?". Respond with the phrase **Ni saa . . .** (nee *sah*-ah. . .), "*It is . . .*"when giving the time. For example:

Luke :   **Hujambo kaka? Ni saa ngapi?**
           (hoo-*jah*-mboh *kah*-kah? Nee *sah*-ah *ngah*-pee)
           How are you, brother? What is the time?

Juma: **Sijambo. Ni saa sita na dakika ishirini na tano.**
           (see-*jah*-mboh. Nee *sah*-ah *see*-tah nah dah-*kee*-kah
           ee-shee-*ree*-nee nah *tah*-noh)
           I am well. It is 12:25pm.

Luke: **Ahsante.**
           (ah-*sah*-nteh)
           Thank you.

Good job mastering Swahili numbers! Now you can update your calendar with confidence and not worry about mixing up Swahili time with European Standard Time.

Talkin' the Talk

Listen to the dialogue below between Shauna and Paulo. Try to figure out what time it is and when their biology class starts.

Shauna: **Paulo, mambo?**
Paulo, *mah*- mboh?
How are things, Paulo?

Paulo: **Poa sana, Shauna. Kwema?**
Poh-ah *sah*-nah, Shauna. *kweh*-mah?
Great, Shauna. All good?

Shauna: **Kwema. Simu yangu imezima na sina saa. Sasa ni saa ngapi?**
Kweh-mah. *See*-moo *yah*-ngoo ee-meh-*zee*-mah nah *see*-nah *sah*-ah. *Sah*-sah nee *sah*-ah *ngah*-pee?
All good. My phone's dead, and I don't have a watch. What is the time now?

Paulo: **Oh, pole. Sasa ni saa sita na dakika thelathini na nne**.
Oh, *poh*-leh. *Sah*-sah nee *sah*-ah *see*-tah nah dah-*kee*-kah the-lah-*thee*-nee nah *n*-neh
Oh, sorry. It is 12:34pm.

Shauna: **Na darasa la Bayolojia ni saa ngapi?**
Nah dah-*rah*-sah lah Bah-yoh-lo-*jee*-ah nee *sah*-ah *ngah*-pee?
And what time is the biology class?

Paulo: **Darasa la Bayolojia ni kutoka saa saba na dakika kumi hadi saa tisa.**
dah-*rah*-sah lah Bah-yoh-lo-*jee*-ah nee koo-*toh*-kah sah *sah*-bah nah dah-*kee*-kah *koo*-mee *hah*-dee sah *tee*-sah.
The biology class is from 1:10pm to 3:00pm.

Shauna: **Lo! Acha nikimbie chumbani nichukue vitabu vyangu halafu niende darasani. Ahsante Paulo!**
Loh! *Ah*-chah nee-kee-*mbee*-eh choo-*mbah*-nee nee-choo-*koo*-eh vee-*tah*-boo *vyah*-ngoo hah-*lah*-foo nee-*eh*-ndeh dah-rah-*sah*-nee; Ah-*sah*-nteh Paulo!
Oh, my! Let me run to my room and get my books then go to class. Thanks, Paulo!

Paulo: **Haya, kwaheri!**
Hah-yah, kwah-*heh*-ree!
Ok then, bye!

FUN & GAMES

1. Write a check to Ms. Zahara Moshi for $1357. Write the dollar amount in words.

JOHN DOE OR JANE DOE
123 MAIN STREET
ANYTOWN, TN 01234
PHONE 555-1212

2670
87-823/641

DATE: _____

Pay to the
Order of _____ $ [   ]

_____ Dollars 🔒 Security details on back.

6–73

🏛 **Bank Of Yourtown**
YOURTOWN, TN

FOR _____ _____ MP

⑆012345678⑆   ⑈987654321⑈

2. Write the following numbers in Swahili numerals.

9 _____

18 _____

177 _____

1888 _____

16,000 _____

150,000 _____

3,330,000 _____

3. Match the times shown to their correct Swahili descriptions.

A. 8:00   B. 11:10   C. 3:15

D. 9:30   E. 4:40   F. 7:45

saa tatu na nusu   _____

saa kumi na moja kasoro dakika ishirini   _____

saa tano na dakika kumi   _____

saa moja na dakika arobaini na tano   _____

saa mbili kamili   _____

saa mbili kasorobo   _____

saa kumi na dakika arobaini   _____

saa tisa na robo   _____

2

Swahili in Action

Chapter **6**

Making Small Talk

Have you ever been nervous meeting new people because you don't know what to talk about with them beyond the initial introductions? Are you looking for ways to avoid the dreaded "awkward silence"? Make small talk! Each culture has topics they consider acceptable or not acceptable for small talk. This section explores some topics that the Swahili culture considers small-talk safe.

Revealing Your Marital Status

Here's a little secret to prepare you for interaction with Swahili speakers; we're nosy. We'll ask about your personal business, but we mean no harm. It's perfectly acceptable to ask someone you've met and struck up a conversation with whether they're married or not.

REMEMBER

You'll, of course, have to phrase your question or response to reflect gender. Read on to find out how.

As a man

If you're a man, a speaker will ask you **Umeoa?** (oo-meh-*oh*-ah) (*Have you married?/Are you married?*)

To respond in the affirmative, say **Ndiyo, nimeoa.** (*ndee*-yoh nee-meh-*oh*-ah) (*Yes, I have married/Yes, I am married.*)

Kuoa (koo-*oh*-ah) (*to marry*) is the verb. Speakers conjugate this verb to include a subject marker **u-** for *you* and a perfect tense marker **-me-**. Take a look at Chapter 4 for pointers on verb conjugation.

To respond in the negative, say **Hapana, bado sijaoa.** (hah-*pah*-nah, *bah*-doh see-jah-*oh*-ah) (*No, I haven't married yet/No, I am not married.*)

The pronoun marker and tense marker in **nimeoa** change into their negated forms to create **sijaoa.** If this is an unfamiliar concept, hop over yet again to Chapter 4 to see how one negates verbs in Swahili.

As a woman

If you're a woman, a speaker will ask you **Umeolewa?** (oo-meh-oh-*leh*-wah) (*Have you been married?/Are you married?*)

To respond in the affirmative, say **Ndiyo, nimeolewa.** (*ndee*-yoh nee-meh-oh-*leh*-wah) (*Yes, I have been married/Yes, I am married*)

To respond in the negative, say **Hapana, bado sijaolewa.** (hah-*pah*-nah, *bah*-doh see-jah-oh-*leh*-wah) (*No, I have not been married yet./No, I am not yet married.*)

CULTURAL WISDOM

In Swahili culture, the terms "**oa** (*oh*-ah) (*marry*)" and "**olewa** (oh-*leh*-wah) (*be married*)" are used to describe the process of getting married, and they carry cultural significance that reflects the belief that it is the woman who "gets married" in a more explicit way than the man.

In this case, the verb **kuoa** (koo-*oh*-ah) (*to marry*) changes to its passive form **kuolewa** (koo-oh-*leh*-wah) (*to be married*). **Wa-** is therefore a passive marker.

In East African communities, the man pays a dowry to his bride's parents (sometimes even to the bride herself depending on the community) as a gesture of his ability to take care of her in the marriage. Also, the bride usually leaves her parents' home to join the man wherever he lives — he brings the bride to his home (active), the bride is brought to the man's home (passive).

You've no doubt noticed the use of **bado** (*bah*-doh) (*not yet*) while giving negative responses here. It indicates that you expect or at least hope that you'll marry/get married someday. **Bado** is also a complete response on its own to questions with verbs in the perfect tense, understood to mean *not yet*. For example:

Q. **Chakula kimeiva?** (chah-*koo*-lah kee-meh-*ee*-vah) *Is the food ready?*

A. **Bado.** (*bah*-doh) (*Not yet.*)

Q. **Umesafisha chumba chako?** (oo-meh-sah-*fee*-shah *choo*-mbah *chah*-koh)
(*Have you cleaned your room?*)

A. **Bado.** (*bah*-doh) (*Not yet.*)

Talking about Your Family

The family is another safe topic for small talk with Swahili speakers. It's not unusual to be bombarded with questions of your immediate family ties when you strike up a conversation with a local. Although you don't have to reveal your mother's maiden name, you might find it useful to know how to state who you have in your family in Swahili and what they do for work. This section covers the basics of family relationships, including how to ask others about their families.

Introducing immediate family relationships

When visiting a Swahili family, it is important to remember that family is of utmost importance in their culture. Immediate family members are highly respected and are expected to be treated with the utmost respect. Family members include:

>> **baba** (*bah*-bah) (*dad*)

>> **mama** (*mah*-mah) (*mother*)

>> **kaka** (*kah*-kah) (*brother*)

>> **dada** (*dah*-dah) (*sister*)

>> **mke** (*m*-keh) (*wife*, coastal region of Kenya) / (**bibi**) (*bee*-bee) (*wife*, everywhere else in Kenya)

>> **mume** (*moo*-meh) (*husband*)

>> **mtoto** (m-*toh*-toh) (*child*) / **watoto** (wah-*toh*-toh) (*children*)

>> **mama wa kambo** (*mah*-mah wah *kah*-mboh) *stepmother*

>> **baba wa kambo** (*bah*-bah wah *kah*-mboh) *stepfather*

Introducing extended family relationships

Extended family members play an important role among Swahili speakers because they are responsible for looking out for one another and aiding each other when needed. When it comes to asking about extended family members, ask about the following members:

>> **bibi** (*bee*-bee) (*grandmother,* coastal regions of Kenya) **nyanya** (*nyah*-nyah) (*grandmother,* everywhere else in Kenya)

>> **babu** (*bah*-boo) (*grandfather*)

>> **babu mzaa baba** (*bah*-boo m-*zah*-ah *bah*-bah) (*paternal grandfather*)

>> **bibi mzaa baba** (*bee*-bee m-*zah*-ah *bah*-bah) (*paternal grandmother*)

>> **babu mzaa mama** (*bah*-boo m-*zah*-ah *mah*-mah) (*maternal grandfather*)

>> **bibi mzaa mama** (*bee*-bee m-*zah*-ah *mah*-mah) (*maternal grandmother*)

>> **baba mkubwa** (*bah*-bah m-*koo*-bwah) (uncle, *dad's older brother*)

>> **baba mdogo** (*bah*-bah m-*doh*-goh) (uncle, *dad's younger brother*)

>> **mama mkubwa** (*mah*-mah m-*koo*-bwah) (aunt, *mom's older sister*)

>> **mama mdogo** (*mah*-mah m-*doh*-goh) (aunt, *mom's younger sister*)

>> **shangazi** (shah-*ngah*-zee) (aunt, *dad's older or younger sister*)

>> **binamu** (bee-*nah*-moo) (*cousin*)

>> **mpwa** (*m*-pwah) (*niece/nephew*))

>> **mjukuu** (m-joo-*koo*-oh) (*grandchild*)

>> **shemeji** (sheh-*meh*-jee) (*brother-in-law*)

>> **wifi** (*wee*-fee) (*sister-in-law*)

>> **mama mkwe/mavyaa** (*mah*-mah m-kweh/mah-*vyah*-ah) (*mother-in-law*)

>> **baba mkwe/bavyaa** (*bah*-bah m-kweh/bah-*vyah*-ah) (*father-in-law*)

>> **mwali** (*mwah*-lee) (*daughter-in-law*)

>> **mkwe** (*m*-kweh) (*son-in-law*)

CULTURAL WISDOM

Swahili speakers value extended family relationships very highly. This is evident in the way they refer to each other as **kaka** (*kah*-kah) (*brother*) and **dada** (*dah*-dah) (*sister*) or **ndugu** (*ndoo*-goo) (*sister/brother*) even if they are not related by blood. This is because they understand that family is not just limited to those related by blood, but also to those who are related by marriage or by friendship.

Asking probing questions about family using "do you have. . .?"

If you're curious about someone's family life or just want to fit in with the locals, feel free to shoot probing questions. For example, you can use **una . . .** (*oo*–na) (*do you have . . .?*) to ask about specific family relations:

» **Una kaka?** (*Oo*-nah *kah*-kah) (*Do you have a brother?*)

» **Una dada?** (*Oo*-nah *dah*-dah) (*Do you have a sister?*)

» **Una kaka wangapi?** (*Oo*-nah *kah*-kah wah-*ngah*-pee) (*How many brothers do you have?*)

» **Una binamu wangapi?** (*Oo*-nah bee-*nah*-moo wah-*ngah*-pee) (*How many cousins do you have?*)

» **Una shangazi?** (*Oo*-nah shah-*ngah*-zee) (*Do you have an aunt?*)

If someone asks you a **una** question, here's how you would respond:

Q. Una kaka? (*oo*-nah *kah*-kah) (*Do you have a brother?*)

A. Ndio nina kaka. (*ndee*-yoh *nee*-nah *kah*-kah) (*Yes, I have a brother.*)

Q. Una dada? (*oo*-nah *dah*-dah) (*Do you have a sister?*)

A. Ndio nina dada. (*ndee*-yoh *nee*-nah *dah*-dah) (*Yes, I have a sister.*)

Q. Una shangazi? (*oo*-nah shah-*ngah*-zee) (*Do you have an aunt?*)

A. Ndio nina shangazi. (*ndee*-yoh *nee*-nah shah-*ngah*-zee) (*Yes, I have an aunt.*)

Talking about Pets

Although not as widespread as in other societies, pets are present in some Swahili households. Cats, dogs, birds, and even rabbits are kept as companions, but dogs mostly provide protection to the household. It's not unusual to see gates marked **Mbwa mkali!** (*m*–bwah m–*kah*–lee) (*fierce dog!*) as a warning for trespassers. Here are the Swahili names for some of the more popular pets:

» **mbwa** (*mh*-mbwah) (*dog*)

» **paka** (*pah*-kah) (*cat*)

» **sungura** (soo-*ngoo*-rah) (*rabbit*)

» **ndege** (*ndeh*-geh) (*bird*)

CULTURAL WISDOM

East Africans keep a lot of farm animals for food and business, not as pets. In the villages, families rear animals such as **mbuzi** (m-*boo*-zee) (*goats*), **ng'ombe** (*ng'oh*-mbeh) (*cows*), **kuku** (*koo*-koo) (*chickens*), and **kondoo** (koh-*ndo*-oh) (*sheep*). While the idea of pets is easily understood, some pets are bound to raise eyebrows from the typical East African. Say you have **nyoka** (*nyoh*-kah) (*a snake*) or **mjusi** (m-*joo*-see) (*a lizard*) for a pet; you'll likely be branded **mchawi** (m-*chah*-wee) (*witch/wizard*).

Using Numbers as Adjectives

Questions about one's family usually include the number of people in it. Use the word **ngapi** (*ngah*-pee) (*how many*) to pose such questions. For example:

» **Una dada wangapi?** (*Oo*-nah *dah*-dah wah-*ngah*-pee) (*How many sisters do you have?*)

» **Una watoto wangapi?** (*Oo*-nah wah-*toh*-toh wah-*ngah*-pee) (*How many children do you have?*)

Notice that the question word **ngapi**, adopts a **wa-** prefix when used in these sentences. This is because the question word must agree with the noun class of the word it describes. In this case, the **wa-** prefix is used because the noun used here is in the **M/WA** noun class. (For more on how noun classes work in Swahili, check out Chapter 3.)

In a similar fashion, you also need to affix the noun class marker to numbers used as adjectives. For example:

» **Nina dada mmoja.** (*nee*-nah *dah*-dah m-*moh*-jah) (*I have one sister.*)

» **Nina watoto watatu.** (*nee*-nah wah-*toh*-toh wah-*tah*-too) (*I have three children.*)

In the first sentence, the noun marker is **m-**, so that marker gets added to **moja** (one), resulting in **mmoja**. In the second sentence, the noun marker is **wa-**, so that gets added to **tatu** (three), which means you end up with **watatu**.

Look at Table 6-1 for a summary of how to use numbers as adjectives with living things such as people.

TABLE 6-1 ## Using numbers as adjectives for people

People	Number	English
baba (*bah*-bah) (*father*)	**mmoja** (mh-*moh*-jah)	one father
mama (*mah*-mah) (*mother*)	**wawili** (wah-*wee*-lee)	two mothers
kaka (*kah*-kah) (*brother*)	**watatu** (wah-*tah*-too)	three brothers
dada (*dah*-dah) (*sister*)	**wanne** (wah-*n*-neh)	four sisters
wajomba (m-*joh*-mbah) (*uncle*)	**watano** (wah-*tah*-noh)	five uncles
rafiki (rah-*fee*-kee) (*friend*)	**sita** ** (*see*-tah)	six friends
jirani (jee-*rah*-nee) (neighbor)	**saba**** (*sah*-bah)	seven neighbors
wajukuu (wah-*joo*-koo) (*grandchildren*)	**wanane** (wah-*nah*-neh)	eight grandchildren
shemeji (sheh-*meh*-jee) (*brother-in-law*)	**tisa** ** (*tee*-sah)	nine brothers-in-law
binamu (bee-*nah*-moo) (*cousin*)	**kumi**** (*koo*-mee)	ten cousins

** *Notice that the numbers* **sita, saba, tisa,** *and* **kumi** *do not adopt the plural* **wa-** *prefix. This is because they're not of Bantu origin. You would, therefore, be making a grammatical error by saying, for example,* **watoto wasita** (*wah-toh-toh wah-see-tah*) (*wa six children*). *Instead, say* **watoto sita** (*wah-toh-toh see-tah*) (*six children*).

Talkin' the Talk

AUDIO ONLINE

Jessica is in Dodoma, the capital city of Tanzania. She is meeting her host family for the first time.

Jessica: **Shikamoo baba na mama!**
Shee-kah-*moh*-oh *bah*-bah nah *mah*-mah!
I give you my respect, Dad and Mom!

Baba & Mama: **Marahaba Jessica! Karibu sana Dodoma!**
Mah-rah-*hah*-bah Jessica! Kah-*ree*-boo *sah*-nah Doh-doh-*mah*!
We accept your respect, Jessica! Welcome to Dodoma!

Jessica: **Asante sana! Habari za familia yenu?**
Ah-sah-*nh*-teh *sah*-nah! Hah-*bah*-ree zah fah-mee-*lee*-ah *yeh*-noo?
Thanks! How is your family doing?

Baba & Mama:	**Nzuri. Watoto wako shuleni. Wanasoma shule ya bweni.** N-*zoo*-ree. Wah-*toh*-toh *wah*-koh shoo-*leh*-nee. Wah-nah-*soh*-mah *shoo*-leh yah *bweh*-nee. *Our family is doing well. Our children are in boarding school.*
Jessica:	**Mna watoto wangapi?** M-nah wah-*toh*-toh wah-*nga*-pee? *How many children do you all have?*
Baba & Mama:	**Tuna watoto wanne. Una ndugu?** *Too*-nah wah-*toh*-toh wah-*n*-neh. *Oo*-nah *ndoo*-goo? *We have four children. Do you have siblings?*
Jessica:	**Nina ndugu wawili. Mimi ni kifungua mimba. Wao ni mapacha.** *Nee*-nah *ndoo*-goo wah-*wee*-lee. *Mee*-mee nee kee-foo-*ngoo*-ah *mee*-mbah. *Wah*-oh nee mah-*pah*-chah. *I have two siblings. I am the first born. My siblings are twins.*
Baba & Mama:	**Safi. Je, una binamu?** *Sah*-fee. Jeh, *oo*-nah bee-*nah*-moo? *Great. Do you have cousins?*
Jessica:	**Nina binamu saba. Mna mbwa au paka?** *Nee*-nah bee-*nah*-moo *sah*-bah. M-nah *m*-mbwah ah-oo *pah*-ka? *I have seven cousins. Do you all have a dog or cat?*
Baba & Mama:	**Ndiyo, tuna mbwa mmoja na paka mmoja.** *Ndee*-yoh. *Too*-nah *m*-mbwah m-*moh*-jah na *pah*-ka m-*moh*-jah. *Yes. We have one dog and one cat.*
Jessica:	**Wao wanaitwa nani?** *Wah*-oh wah-nah-*ee*-twah *nah*-nee? *What are their names?*
Baba & mama:	**Hawana majina. Wewe una mbwa au paka?** Hah-*wah*-nah mah-*jee*-nah. *Weh*-weh oo-nah *m*-mbwah ah-oo *pah*-ka? *They don't have names. Do you have a dog or a cat?*
Jessica:	**Nina paka wawili. Majina yao ni Pru na Bob.** *Nee*-nah *pah*-kah wah-*wee*-lee. Mah-*jee*-nah *yah*-oh nee Pru nah Bob. *I have two cats. Their names are Pru and Bob.*

· ·

WORDS TO KNOW

ndugu	*ndoo*-goo	*siblings*
mapacha	mah-*pah*-chah	twins
bweni	*bweh*-nee	*dormitory*
kifungua mimba	kee-foo-*ngoo*-ah *mee*-mbah	*firstborn*

Identifying Professions

Initial meetings at a lot of social settings usually include revealing **facts about your professional life.** You should also expect follow-up questions about the **kazi** (*kah*-zee) (*job*) of your family members when you mention them. This section highlights how to ask and respond to **the question** "What *exactly* do you do?"

Responding to "what do you do?"

Whether on a date, at the bar chatting to a stranger, or in a taxi heading to the market, you might hear **Unafanya kazi gani?** (oo-nah-*fah*-nyah *kah*-zee *gah*-nee) (*What's your job?*) as part of the small talk.

Respond with **Mimi ni** (*mee*-mee nee) (*I am . . .*) followed by your job title. Here's a short list to choose from, but there's lots more in Chapter 2.

>> **mwalimu** (m-wah-*lee*-moo) (*teacher*)

>> **mkulima** (m-koo-*lee*-mah) (*farmer*)

>> **daktari** (dahk-*tah*-ree) (*doctor*)

>> **dereva** (de-*reh*-vah) (*driver*)

>> **mpishi** (m-*pee*-shee) (*chef*)

>> **mwanamitindo** (m-*wah*-nah-mee-*tee*-ndoh) (*model*)

>> **msusi** (m-*soo*-see) (*hairdresser*)

>> **mhandisi** (m-hah-*ndee*-see) (*engineer*)

>> **mtafiti** (m-tah-*fee*-tee) (*researcher*)

Revealing your family members' professions

It's natural for people to ask about what your family members do — at least Swahili speakers think so. Questions such as **Una dada?** (*Oo*-nah *dah*-dah) (*Do you have a sister?*) are usually followed with **Dada yako anafanya kazi gani?** (*dah*-dah *yah*-koh ah-nah-*fah*-nyah *kah*-zee *gah*-nee) (*What job does your sister do?*)

Other similar questions include

>> **Kaka yako anafanya kazi gani?** (*kah*-kah *yah*-koh ah-nah-*fah*-nyah *kah*-zee *gah*-nee) (*What job does your brother do?*)

>> **Mke wako anafaya kazi gani?** (*m*-keh *wah*-koh ah-nah-*fah*-nyah *kah*-zee *gah*-nee) (*What job does your wife do?*)

>> **Mume wako anafanya kazi gani?** (*moo*-meh *wah*-koh ah-nah-*fah*-nyah *kah*-zee *gah*-nee) (*What job does your husband do?*)

Swahili sentences follow the same basic Subject–Verb–Object structure as English sentences. However, other modifying elements like possessives and adjectives, follow the subject rather than precede it as in English. The verb carries several elements like the subject marker, tense marker, and sometimes even an object marker. Also, **wh-** question words are usually placed in the sentence final position. Let's look at the different parts of the sentence **Mke wako anfanya kazi gani?**

Mke	wako	a	na	fanya	kazi	gani?
subject	possessive	subject marker	tense marker (present tense)	Verb (infinitive; **kufanya**)	object	**wh-** question word
wife	*your*	*does*			*job*	*what?*

To respond, say **Dada yangu ni . . .** (*dah*-dah *yah*-ngoo nee . . .) (*My sister is . . .*). For example,

>> **Dada yangu ni makanika.** (*dah*-dah *yah*-ngoo nee mah-kah-*nee*-kah) (*My sister is a mechanic.*)

>> **Kaka yangu ni seremala.** (*Kah*-kah *yah*-ngoo nee seh-reh-*mah*-lah) (*My brother is a carpenter.*)

>> **Mke wangu ni hakimu.** (*m*-keh *wah*-ngoo nee hah-*kee*-moo) (*My wife is a judge.*)

In Swahili, the possessive prefixes change depending on the noun class. When you are talking about family members, in most cases, you will use **yangu** (*yah*-ngoo) (*my*) for singular and **zangu** (*zah*-ngoo) (*my*) for plural. If the nouns fall into the **M-** class in the singular and **Wa-** class in the plural, then you will use **wangu** (*wah*-ngoo) (*my*) for both singular and plural. This means that you would use a different possessive prefix depending on the person you're addressing. Please visit Chapter 3 for in-depth information on noun classes.

Again, check out Chapter 2 for more options of professions in Swahili.

Having Fun

One way to establish common ground with people you meet is to ask them about their hobbies or how they spend their evenings or weekends. In this section, we highlight words and phrases describing uraibu (oo-*rah*-ee-boo) (hobbies), which might come in handy when you're trying to make friends in East Africa.

Describing your hobbies

To know someone's hobbies, ask **Una uraibu gani?** (oo-nah oo-rah-*ee*-boo *gah*-nee) (*What's your hobby?*) or **Unapenda kufanya nini?** (oo-nah-*peh*-ndah koo-*fah*-nyah *nee*-nee) (*What do you like to do?*)

If asked, respond with **Nina uraibu wa . . .** (*nee*-nah oo-rah-*ee*-boo wah . . .) (*My hobbies are . . .*) or **Ninapenda ku . . .** (nee-nah-*peh*-ndah koo . . .) (*I like to . . .*) followed by your hobby.

Some of the most popular hobbies include the following:

>> **kusoma** (koo-*soh*-mah) (*to read*)

>> **kucheza mpira wa miguu/soka** (koo-*cheh*-zah m-*pee*-rah wah *mee*-goo/*soh*-kah) (*to play soccer*)

>> **michezo ya video** (mee-*cheh*-zoh yah vee-*deh*-oh) (*to play video games*)

>> **kupika** (koo-*pee*-kah) (*to cook*)

>> **kutazama filamu** (koo-tah-*zah*-mah fee-*lah*-moo) (*to watch movies*)

>> **kusikiliza muziki** (koo-see-kee-*lee*-zah moo-*zee*-kee) (*to listen to music*)

>> **kuvua samaki** (koo-*voo*-ah sah-*mah*-kee) (*to fish*)

- >> **kufuma** (koo-*foo*-mah) *(to crochet)*
- >> **kupiga picha** (koo-*pee*-gah *pee*-chah) *(to take photos)*
- >> **kuchora** (koo-*choh*-rah) *(to draw/paint)*
- >> **kucheza dansi** (koo-*cheh*-zah dah-*n*-see) *(to dance)*
- >> **kukwea milima** (koo-*kweh*-ah-ah mee-lee-*mah*-nee) *(to hike)*
- >> **kushona** (koo-*shoh*-nah) *(to sew)*
- >> **kuigiza** (koo-ee-*gee*-zah) *(to act)*
- >> **kuimba** (koo-*ee*-mbah) *(to sing)*
- >> **kukimbia** (koo-kee-*mbee*-ah) *(to run)*
- >> **kufanya mazoezi** (koo-*fah*-nyah mah-zoh-*eh*-zee) *(to exercise)*
- >> **kupiga gitaa** (koo-*pee*-gah gee-*tah*-ah) *(to play the guitar)*
- >> **Kupiga kinanda** (koo-*pee*-gah kee-*nah*-ndah) *(to play the piano)*
- >> **kufuga nyuki** (koo-*foo*-gah *nyoo*-kee) *(to keep bees)*
- >> **mpira wa kikapu** (m-*pee*-rah wah kee-*kah*-poo) *(basketball)*
- >> **kuwinda** (koo-*wee*-ndah) *(to hunt)*
- >> **kuruka kamba** (koo-*roo*-kah k*ah*-mbah) *(to skip rope)*
- >> **Kucheza karata** (koo-*cheh*-zah kah-*rah*-tah) *(to play cards)*

Talking about errands, chores, and daily activities

Taking care of errands and chores is essential for maintaining a household. The following are Swahili words and phrases that describe **shughuli za kila siku** (shoo-*ghoo*-lee zah *kee*-lah *see*-koo) *(daily activities)* that you may carry out on a regular basis:

- >> **kupika** (koo-*pee*-kah) *(to cook)*
- >> **kufua nguo** (koo-*foo*-ah *ngoo*-oh) *(to do laundry/to wash clothes)*
- >> **kusafisha nyumba** (koo-sah-*fee*-shah *nyoo*-mbah) *(to clean the house)*
- >> **kukata nyasi** (koo-*kah*-tah *nyah*-see) *(to cut the grass)*
- >> **kutupa takataka** (koo-*too*-pah tah-kah-*tah*-kah) *(to take out the trash)*
- >> **kupiga pasi** (koo-*pee*-gah *pah*-see) *(to iron clothes)*

- » **kupiga deki** (koo-*pee*-gah *deh*-kee) (*to mop*)

- » **kufagia** (koo-*fah*-gee-ah) (*to sweep*)

- » **kuosha gari** (koo-*oh*-shah *gah*-ree) (*to clean the car*)

- » **kubadilisha matandiko** (koo-bah-dee-*lee*-shah mah-tah-*ndee*-koh) (*to change bed linen*)

- » **kutandika kitanda** (koo-tah-*ndee*-kah kee-*tah*-ndah) (*to make the bed*)

- » **kutembeza mbwa** (koo-teh-*mbeh*-zah m-mbwah) (*to walk the dog*)

- » **kuosha vyombo** (koo-*oh*-shah *vyoh*-mboh) (*to wash dishes*)

- » **kukunja nguo** (koo-*koo*-njah *ngoo*-oh) (*to fold laundry*)

- » **kusafisha choo na bafu** (koo-sah-*fee*-shah *choh*-oh nah *bah*-foo) (*to clean the toilet and bathroom*)

- » **kununua mahitaji** (koo-*noo*-noo-ah mah-hee-*tah*-jee) (*to shop*)

- » **kutuma barua pepe** (koo-*too*-mah bah-*roo*-ah *peh*-peh) (*to send emails*)

- » **kuweka miadi** (koo-*weh*-kah mee-*ah*-dee) (*to book appointments*)

- » **kupiga simu** (koo-*pee*-gah *see*-moo) (*to make phone calls*)

Describing Your Routine

How did you spend your time last weekend? Chances are that you did more than one activity, so when you talk about what you did, you use specific words and phrases to link those activities. These words and phrases are called *sequence adverbs* (also known as *sequencers*). They are used to describe the order in which two or more actions happen; they can also help us understand the time relationship between sentences and ideas. For example,

> Mark went to the store/ Mark went fishing. Mark watched a basketball game on TV.

These three ideas are disjointed, and there's no sense of what Mark did when. We could link the same ideas together using sequence adverbs such as *first*, *then*, and *later*; for example, "First, Mark went fishing; then he went to the store. Later, he watched a basketball game on TV."

In this section, we discuss how you can use sequence adverbs to create smooth-flowing ideas in your sentences.

Using sequence adverbs in sentences: from . . . to, before, after, and more

Some common sequence adverbs include the following:

>> **kwanza** (*kwah*-nzah) (*first*)

>> **baadaye** (bah-ah-*dah*-yeh) (*later*)

>> **kisha** (*kee*-shah) (*then*)

>> **kabla ya** (*kah*-blah yah) (*before*)

>> **baada ya** (bah-*ah*-dah yah) (*after*)

>> **mara kwa mara** (*mah*-rah kwah *mah*-rah) (*occasionally*)

>> **kawaida** (kah-wah-*ee*-dah) (*usually*)

>> **mwishowe** (m-wee-*shoh*-weh) (*lastly*)

Here are some sentence examples:

>> **Kesho nitapiga deki baada ya kufua nguo zangu.** (*keh*-shoh nee-tah-*pee*-gah *deh*-kee bah-*ah*-dah yah koo-*foo*-ah *ngoo*-oh *zah*-ngoo) (*Tomorrow I will mop the floor after washing my clothes.*)

>> **Mama yangu alipiga pasi kabla ya kuoga.** (*mah*-mah *yah*-ngoo ah-lee-*pee*-gah *pah*-see *kah*-blah yah koo-*oh*-gah) (*My mother ironed clothes before showering.*)

>> **Kawaida, Ali hukimbia jioni kisha yeye hurudi nyumbani kupika chakula.** (kah-wah-*ee*-dah Ali hoo-kee-*mbee*-ah jee-*oh*-nee *kee*-shah *yeh*-yeh hoo-*roo*-dee nyoo-*mbah*-nee koo-*pee*-kah chah-*koo*-lah) (*Usually, Ali runs in the evenings and then he goes back home to cook food.*)

>> **Kawaida, mimi husoma vitabu vya hadithi kabla ya kulala lakini mara kwa mara mimi hutazama filamu za Netflix.** (kah-wah-*ee*-dah *mee*-mee hoo-*soh*-mah vee-*tah*-boo vyah hah-*dee*-thee *kah*-blah yah koo-*lah*-lah lah-*kee*-nee *mah*-rah kwah *mah*-rah *mee*-mee hoo-tah-*zah*-mah fee-*lah*-moo zah Netflix) (*Usually, I read novels before falling asleep, but occasionally I watch Netflix films.*)

>> **Wikendi hii tunapanga kufanya mambo mengi; kwanza, tutacheza mpira wa miguu, kisha tutaogelea ziwani na mwishowe tutachoma nyama.** (wee-*keh*-ndee hee too-nah-*pah*-ngah koo-*fah*-nyah *mah*-mboh *meh*-ngee: *kwah*-nzah too-tah-*cheh*-zah m-*pee*-rah wah *mee*-goo *kee*-shah too-tah-oh-geh-*leh*-ah zee-*wah*-nee nah m-wee-*shoh*-weh too-tah-*choh*-mah *nyah*-mah) (*We're planning to do a lot this weekend: first, we'll play soccer; then we'll swim in the lake; and lastly we'll have a barbecue.*)

Making Plans

It's Wednesday and you want to make weekend plans with your friends. How do you broach the subject? Most people ask what the others have planned for the weekend first. Say **Unapanga kufanya nini wikendi hii?** (oo-nah-*pah*-ngah koo-*fah*-nyah *nee*-nee wee-*keh*-ndee hee) (*What are you planning to do this weekend?*) This is a question frequently asked by friends or anyone who wants to know your **mipango** (mee-pah-*ngoh*-oh) (*plans*).

If asked, respond with **Ninapanga . . .** (nee-nah-*pah*-ngah) (*I plan . . .*) followed by the planned activity(ies). For example,

> » **Ninapanga kusafiri** (nee-nah-*pah*-ngah koo-sah-*fee*-ree) (*I plan to travel.*)
>
> or
>
> » **Nitasafiri** (nee-tah-sah-*fee*-ree) (*I will travel.*)

If you don't have any plans, say **Sina mipango.** (*see*-nah mee-*pah*-ngoh) (*I don't have plans.*)

CULTURAL WISDOM

Swahili people generally have a laid-back and accepting approach to life. Most people tend to take things as they come, rather than making detailed future plans. This attitude is reflected in their hospitality and generosity, as they often welcome visitors into their homes without prior notice.

Talkin' the Talk

AUDIO ONLINE

Simone talks about her daily activities.

Rehema: Habari gani Simone?
Hah-*bah*-ree *gah*-nee See-*moh*-nee?
How are you doing, Simone?

Simone: Nzuri sana Rehema. Unafanya nini?
N-*zoo*-ree *sah*-nah Reh-*heh*-mah. Oo-nah-*fah*-nyah *nee*-nee?
I am doing well, Rehema. What are you doing?

Rehema: Ninasafisha nyumba.
Nee-nah-sah-*fee*-shah *nyoo*-mbah
I am cleaning the house.

Simone:	Safi. Unataka msaada?
	Sah-fee. Oo-nah-*tah*-kah m-sah-*ah*-dah?
	Nice. Do you need help?

Rehema:	Ndiyo. Nisaidie kufua nguo tafadhali.
	Ndee-yoh. Nee-sah-ee-*dee*-eh koo-*foo*-ah *ngoo*-oh
	tah-fah-*dhah*-lee.
	Yes. Help me with laundry, please?

Simone:	Sawa. Unasafisha nyumba kila siku?
	Sah-wah. Oo-nah-sah-*fee*-shah *nyoo*-mbah *kee*-lah *see*-koo?
	Okay. Do you clean the house every day?

Rehema:	Hapana. Ninasafisha wikiendi tu. Na wewe je?
	Hah-*pah*-nah. Nee-nah-sah-*fee*-shah wee-kee-*eh*-ndee too.
	Nah *weh*-weh?
	No. I only clean it during the weekend. And you?

Simone:	Wikendi mimi ninapika, ninafua nguo, na ninasafisha
	nyumba.
	Wee-kee-*eh*-ndee *mee*-mee nee-nah-*pee*-kah, nee-nah-
	foo-ah *ngoo*-oh nah nee-nah-sah-*fee*-shah *nyoo*-mbah.
	On the weekend, I cook, do laundry, and I clean the house.

Rehema:	Baada ya kufanya usafi, unafanya nini?
	Bah-*ah*-dah yah koo-*fah*-nyah oo-*sah*-fee oo-nah-*fah*-nyah
	nee-nee?
	What do you do after cleaning?

Simone:	Ninakata majani na kuchoma nyama.
	Nee-nah-*kah*-tah mah-*jah*-nee nah koo-*choh*-mah *nyah*-mah.
	I cut grasses and grill.

Rehema:	Unapenda kufanya nini kujiburudisha?
	Oo-nah-*peh*-ndah koo-*fah*-nyah *nee*-nee koo-jee-boo-
	roo-*dee*-shah?
	What are your hobbies?

Simone:	Nina uraibu wa kutazama filamu na kucheza mpira wa
	kikapu. Na wewe je?
	Nee-nah oo-rah-*ee*-boo wah koo-tah-*zah*-mah fee-*lah*-
	moo nah koo-*cheh*-zah m-*pee*-rah wah kee-*kah*-poo. Nah
	weh-weh jeh?
	My hobbies are watching film and playing basketball. And you?

Rehema:	Ninapenda kusikiliza muziki na kufuma.
	Nee-nah-*peh*-ndah koo-see-kee-*lee*-zah moo-*zee*-kee nah
	koo-*foo*-mah.
	I like listening to music and crochet.

• •

WORDS TO KNOW

kufuma	koo-*foo*-mah	to crotchet
mpira wa kikapu	m-*pee*-rah wah kee-*kah*-poo	basketball
kuchoma nyama	koo-*choh*-mah *nyah*-mah	to grill
kufua nguo	koo-*foo*-ah ngoo-*oh*	to do laundry

FUN & GAMES

Complete the sentences with the correct relationships as illustrated in the family tree.

bibi   **baba**   **mama**

mume   **mke**

annasunny / Adobe Systems Incorporated

a. Jamila ni . . . . wa Nalah na Amana.

b. Djimon ni . . . . wa Jokia na Zuri

c. Kenyatta ni . . . . wa Catherine

d. Hasnaa ni . . . . wa Djimon

e. Dara ni . . . . wa Ayanna na Kondo

Chapter 7

Finding Your Way

Imagine being in an unfamiliar Nairobi city, and you need to walk to a specific building for a meeting. You haven't managed to get a local SIM card yet, so you cannot get online for Google Maps. What's a person to do? That's right; ask a local for directions! As much as you prepare for any eventualities by downloading or printing maps, you can never rule out the need to ask for directions whenever you travel.

This chapter outlines some basic phrases to use when seeking help with directions as well as how to follow the directions given.

Getting from Place to Place

If you ever plan to travel to a country in East Africa, finding your way around can be a bit of a challenge if you don't know the street names or landmarks. Fortunately, the people there are very friendly and helpful. They can guide you to the right places, tell you about the best attractions, and even suggest restaurants or activities. Some of those suggestions will explicitly mention that an event is taking place *at* a specific location. To get the idea of *at* across, Swahili speakers add the suffix -ni to the noun for that particular place. For example:

>> **Hoteli** (hoh-*teh*-lee) (*hotel*) becomes **hotelini** (hoh-teh-*lee*-nee) (*at the hotel*)

» **Kanisa** (kah-*nee*-sah) (*church*) becomes **kanisani** (kah-nee-*sah*-nee) (*at the church*)

» **Nyumba** (*nyoo*-mbah) (*house*) becomes **nyumbani** (nyoo-*mbah*-nee) (*at home*)

» **Chuo** (*choo*-oh) (*university*) becomes *chuoni* (choo-*oh*-nee) (*at the university*)

» **Hospitali** (hoh-spee-*tah*-lee) becomes **hospitalini** (hoh-spee-tah-*lee*-nee) (*at the hospital*)

» **Mkahawa** (m-kah-*hah*-wah) (*restaurant*) becomes **mkahawani** (m-kah-hah-*wah*-nee) (*at the restaurant*)

Identifying places and landmarks

Since street signs are not omnipresent, Swahili speakers tend to reference land-marks (buildings, objects, social spaces, and so on) when giving directions. That means the first step to understanding directions is recognizing those places used as landmarks in the instructions.

Here are some places, spaces, and objects you may see in an East African town/city.

» **kibanda** (kee-*bah*-ndah) (*kiosk*)

» **duka** (*doo*-kah) (*shop*)

» **soko** (*soh*-koh) (*market*)

» **kanisa** (kah-*nee*-sah) (*church*)

» **msikiti** (m-see-*kee*-tee) (*mosque*)

» **kaburini** (kaa-boo-*ree*-nee) (*graveyard*)

» **benki** (beh-*n*-kee) (*bank*)

» **daraja** (da-*rah*-jah) (*bridge*)

» **posta** (*poh*-stah) (*post office*)

» **bustani** (boo-*stah*-nee) (*park/garden*)

» **hospitali** (hoh-spee-*tah*-lee) (*hospital*)

» **zahanati** (zah-hah-*nah*-tee) (*clinic/dispensary*)

» **hoteli** (ho-*teh*-lee) (*hotel*)

» **mkahawa** (mh-kah-*hah*-wah) (*restaurant*)

» **kituo cha polisi** (kee-*too*-oh chah poh-*lee*-see) (*police station*)

>> **kituo cha basi** (kee-*too*-oh chah *bah*-see) *(bus station)*

>> **taa za barabarani** (*tah*-ah zah bah-rah-bah-*rah*-nee) *(traffic lights)*

Asking where questions

You're sightseeing in Nairobi and have an urgent need for the toilet. (Hey, it happens to everyone!) You approach a mall security guard for directions, and all you can manage to say is **choo** (*choh*-oh) *(toilet)*. Will the security guard understand that you need directions? Not unless you do a little dance showing your discomfort and urgent need for the facilities! You must learn how to ask for directions properly to avoid such scenarios.

Use the question word **wapi** (*wah*-pee) *(where)* to seek answers on the position of places, things, or people. For example:

Choo kiko wapi? (*choh*-oh *kee*-koh *wah*-pee) *Where is the toilet?*

REMEMBER

English uses the indefinite articles *a*, *an*, and the definite article *the* before mentioning nouns. Swahili, on the other hand, does not use definite articles. For example, *a pen* in Swahili is just **kalamu** (kah-*lah*-moo) — notice the lack of an article before the noun.

Notice that the name of the place/thing you seek comes first, followed by a locative **-ko** and finally the question word — **wapi.** The locative will change prefixes depending on the class of the noun it modifies. In the preceding example, the word **choo** is in the Ki-Vi noun class, so its locative uses the singular **ki-** noun class marker. (For more on the locative, see Chapter 3; for more on the different noun classes, see Chapter 3 as well.)

Other examples of places you might need help looking for may include:

>> **Maegesho ya magari yako wapi?** (mah-eh-*geh*-shoh yah mah-*gah*-ree yah-koh *wah*-pee) *(Where is the parking lot?)*

>> **Ubalozi wa Marekani uko wapi?** (oo-bah-*loh*-zee wah mah-reh-*kah*-nee oo-koo *wah*-pee) *(Where is the American embassy?)*

>> **Duka la vitabu liko wapi?** (*doo*-kah lah vee-*tah*-boo *lee*-koh *wah*-pee) *(Where is the bookshop?)*

>> **Benki iko wapi?** (*beh*-nkee *ee*-koh *wah*-pee) *(Where is the bank?)*

>> **Baa iko wapi?** (*bah*-ah *ee*-koh *wah*-pee) *(Where is the bar?)*

» **Klabu iko wapi?** (*klah*-boo *ee*-koh *wah*-pee) (*Where is the club?*)

» **Kituo cha basi kiko wapi?** (kee-*too*-oh chah *bah*-see *kee*-koh *wah*-pee) (*Where is the bus terminal?*)

Getting answers to your location questions

Before responding to your request for directions, the person helping you considers two things: your proximity to the intended destination and the position of your intended destination in relation to other buildings or places.

If considering proximity, the person will probably point (with a finger or lips) or nod in a given direction and say one of the following:

» **hapa** (*hah*-pah) (*here*: You're probably standing at the location you're looking for.)

» **pale** (*pah*-leh) (*there*: The location is close by and can be seen from where you are standing.)

» **huko** (*hoo*-koh) (*there*: The location is far and cannot be seen from where you're standing.)

For example:

» **Duka hili hapa** (*doo*-kah *hee*-lee *hah*-pah) (*Here is the shop.*)

» **Choo kiko pale.** (*Choh*-oh *kee*-koh *pah*-leh) (*There is the toilet.*)

» **Kituo cha polisi kiko huko.** (Kee-*too*-oh chah poh-*lee*-see *kee*-koh *huh*-koh) (*The police station is over there.*)

REMEMBER

If considering the position of the place in relation to other places, a Swahili speaker will provide a general location using prepositions. Check out the "Using prepositions to give directions" section, later in this chapter, to understand this technique.

Giving Directions

So, Google Maps tells you "In three hundred feet, turn north . . ." and You panic slightly as you try to remember where north is so you don't miss your exit. If you're ever confused when Google Maps or people give directions using compass directions, you'll be glad to know that East Africans give directions in a more simplified manner. That doesn't mean Swahili has no use for compass directions, as the following list makes clear:

» **kaskazini** (Kah-ska-*zee*-nee) (*North*)

» **kusini** (Koo-*see*-nee) (*South*)

» **mashariki** (Mah-sha-*ree*-kee) (*East*)

» **magharibi** (Mah-gha-*ree*-bee) (West)

» **kaskazini mashariki** (Kah-ska-*zee*-nee Mah-sha-*ree*-kee) (*Northeast*)

» **kaskazini magharibi** (Kah-ska-*zee*-nee Mah-gha-*ree*-bee) (*Northwest*)

» **kusini mashariki** (Koo-*see*-nee Mah-sha-*ree*-kee) (*Southeast*)

» **kusini magharibi** (Koo-*see*-nee Mah-gha-*ree*-bee) (*Southwest*)

Swahili speakers use compass directions to pinpoint the direction of large land masses from other equally large land masses such as city to city, region to region, country to country. For example:

» **Nchi ya Uganda iko magharibi mwa nchi ya Kenya.** (*N*-chee yah Oo-*gah*-ndah *ee*-koh mah-gha-*ree*-bee mwah *n*-chee yah *Keh*-nyah)(*Uganda is west of Kenya.*)

» **Nchi ya Tanzania iko kusini magharibi mwa nchi ya Kenya.** (*N*-chee yah Tah-n-*zah*-nee-ah *ee*-koh koo-*see*-nee mah-gha-*ree*-bee mwah *n*-chee yah *Keh*-nyah) (*Tanzania is southwest of Kenya.*)

» **Nchi ya Uhabeshi iko kaskazini mwa nchi ya Kenya.** (*N*-chee yah Oo-hah-*beh*-shee *ee*-koh kah-ska-*zee*-nee mwah *n*-chee yah *Keh*-nyah) (*Ethiopia is north of Kenya.*)

So how do Swahili speakers simplify the process of giving directions? We use prepositions and/or commands. Read on to get the details.

Using prepositions to give directions

When Swahili speakers give someone more detailed directions, they assume that these someones have a good working knowledge of the area already and are familiar with a neighborhood's landmarks. Assuming such knowledge makes it easy to say that something is *next to*, *behind*, or *in front of* something else. The Swahili counterparts for such English prepositions are listed below:

» **karibu na** (kah-*ree*-boo nah) (*close to/ next to*)

» **mbele ya** (*mbeh*-leh yah) (*in front of*)

» **nyuma ya** (*nyuh*-mah yah) (*behind*)

» **kando ya** (*kah*-ndoh yah) (*beside*)

» **juu ya** (*joo*-oo yah) (*on top of*)

» **chini ya** (*chee*-nee yah) (*below/under*)

» **katikati ya** (*kah*-tee-*kah*-tee yah) (between/in the middle/at the center)

» **ndani ya** (*ndah*-nee yah) (*inside*)

Here are some sentences showing prepositions in action:

» **Kitabu kiko karibu na kikombe** (kee-*tah*-boo *kee*-koh kah-*ree*-boo nah kee-*koh*-mbeh) (*The book is next to the cup.*)

» **Gari liko mbele ya nyumba** (*gah*-ree *lee*-koh *mbeh*-leh yah *nyoo*-mbah) (*The car is in front of the house.*)

» **Viatu viko chini ya kitanda** (vee-*ah*-too *vee*-koh *chee*-nee yah kee-*tah*-ndah) (*The shoes are under the table.*)

» **Soko liko katikati ya mji** (*soh*-koh *lee*-koh kah-tee-*kah*-tee yah *m*-jee) (*The market is in the middle of the city.*)

Using imperatives to give directions

Let's say you want to go to a phone repair shop, and you've been told it's located next to the gym. Do you know how to get to the gym? As much as location answers provide the general position of a place you're looking for, you still need to be familiar with the area to understand where to go. You probably need clear directions to get to the place.

This is where imperatives come in. Imperatives are command words: They instruct you on the steps to take in order to achieve something. Swahili imperatives are formed by using the stem of the verbs which (in most cases) end with **-a**. When commanding one person to do something, you use the verb as is, but if you are addressing a group of people you have to add **-eni** at the end of the verb to indicate that you are commanding more than one person. For example:

» **Tembea** ⇨ **tembeeni**

» **Geuka** ⇨ **geukeni**

» **Vuka** ⇨ **vukeni**

Imagine asking someone for directions to the gym. Their answer would be in the form of commands. The greatest assumption here is that you know your right hand from your left! Here are some imperatives to use when giving directions.

» **Pinda/geuka kushoto.** (*pee*-ndah/ geh-*oo*-kah koo-*shoh*-toh) (*Turn left.*)

» **Pinda/geuka kulia.** (*pee*-ndah/ geh-*oo*-kah koo-*lee*-ah) (*Turn right*)

» **Nenda moja kwa moja.** (*neh*-ndah *moh*-jah kwah *moh*-jah) (*Go straight.*)

» **Tembea.** (teh-*mbeh*-ah) (*Walk.*)

» **Vuka.** (*voo*-kah) (*Cross.*)

Figure 7-1 is a part of a map of Nairobi city center from Google Maps. Study the map and the dialogue that follows giving directions from the National Archives to Kilimanjaro restaurant.

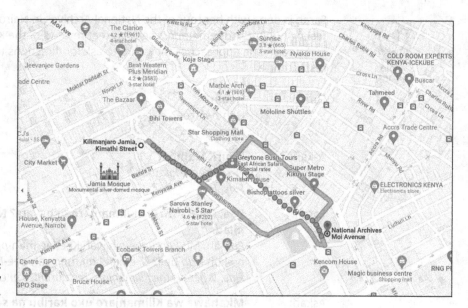

FIGURE 7-1: Nairobi's city center.

The imperative is used for more than just giving directions. Here are some examples of using the imperative in everyday situations:

>> **Pika sambusa.** (*pee*-kah sah-*mboo*-sah) (*Cook samosas.*)

>> **Soma kitabu.** (*soh*-mah kee-*tah*-boo) (*Read the book.*)

>> **Safisha nyumba.** (sah-*fee*-shah *nyoo*-mbah) (*Clean the house.*)

>> **Tembea haraka.** (teh-*mbeh*-ah hah-*rah*-kah) (*Walk faster.*)

>> **Endesha polepole.** (eh-*ndeh*-shah poh-leh-*poh*-leh) (*Drive slowly.*)

>> **Piga picha.** (*pee*-gah *pee*-chah) (*Take photos.*)

.... Talkin' the Talk ....

AUDIO
ONLINE

Sarah is done with her tour of the National Archives in Nairobi. She's feeling hungry and remembers seeing great reviews of the Kilimanjaro restaurant. She approaches the guard to ask for directions to the restaurant.

Sarah: **Habari?**
Hah-*bah*-ree?
How are you?

Askari: **Nzuri. Mambo?**
N-*zoo*-ree. *Mah*-mbo?
Fine. Hi

Sarah: **Poa. Mkahawa wa Kilimanjaro uko wapi? Nina hamu ya pilau.**
Poh-ah. Mh-kah-*hah*-wah wah Kee-lee.mah-*njah*-roh oo-koh *wah*-pee? *Nee*-nah *hah*-moo yah pee-*lah*-oo.
Fine. Where is the Kilimanjaro restaurant? I'm craving pilau.

Askari: **Mkahawa wa Kilimanjaro uko karibu na soko la City Market.**
Mh-kah-*hah*-wah wah Kee-lee.mah-*njah*-roh oo-koh kah-*ree*-boo nah *soh*-koh lah City Market.
The Kilimanjaro restaurant is located near the city market.

Sarah:	**Ninataka kwenda Mkahawa wa Kilimanjaro. Unaweza kunielekeza njia?**
	Nee-nah-tah-kah kweh-ndah mh-kah-hah-wah wah Kee-lee. mah-njah-roh. Oo-nah-weh-zah Koo-nee-eh-leh-keh-zah njee-ah?
	I want to go to the Kilimanjaro restaurant. Can you direct me how to get there?
Askari:	**Ndio. Kutoka hapa National Archives, tembea Barabara ya Moi Avenue moja kwa moja. Geuka kushoto katika mtaa wa Kenyatta Avenue. Tembea moja kwa moja hadi ufike njia panda. Geuka kulia katika mtaa wa Kimathi. Pita duka la keki la Black Forest, na mtaa wa Banda. Tembea kwa mita chache na utaona mkahawa wa Kilimanjaro kwa upande wako wa kushoto.**
	Ndee-oh. Koo-toh-kah hah-pah National Archives, teh-mbeh-ah bah-rah-bah-rah yah Moi Avenue moh-jah kwah moh-jah. Geh-oo-kah koo-shoh-toh kah-tee-kah mh-tah-ah wah Kenyatta Avenue. Teh-mbeh-ah moh-ja kwah moh-ja. hah-dee oo-fee-keh njee-ah pah-ndah. Geh-oo-kah koo-lee-ah kah-tee-kah mh-tah-ah wah Kimathi. Pee-tah doo-kah lah keh-kee lah Black Forest, nah mh-tah-ah wah Bah-ndah. Teh-mbeh-ah kwah mee-tah chah-cheh nah oo-tah-oh-nah mh-kah-hah-wah wah Kee-lee.mah-njah-roh kwah oo-pah-ndeh wah-koh wah koo-shoh-toh.
	Yes. Starting from the National Archives, head straight down Moi Avenue. Turn left onto Kenyatta Avenue and continue straight until you reach an intersection. Turn right onto Kimathi Street and pass by the Black Forest cake shop and Banda Street. After a few meters, you will see the Kilimanjaro restaurant on your left.
Sarah:	**Ahsante sana! Kwaheri!**
	Ah-sah-nteh sah-nah! Kwah-heh-ree!
	Thank you very much! Goodbye!

Talkin' the Talk

Greg is a visiting ophthalmologist posted at the International Eye Hospital in Dar es Salaam. (See Figure 7-2.) He has an appointment at the U.S. Embassy after his shift. His colleague, Asia, gives him directions.

Greg: **Vipi dada? Unaweza kunielekeza njia ya kwenda ubalozi wa Marekani?**

Vee-pee dah-dah? Oo-nah-weh-zah koo-nee-eh-leh-keh-zah njee-ah yah kweh-ndah oo-bah-loh-zee wah Mah-reh-kah-nee?

Hi, sister? Could you give me directions to go to the American embassy?

Asia: **Freshi. Ndio. Kutoka hapa hospitali ya macho, pinda kulia katika barabara ya Bagamoyo. Tembea moja kwa moja hadi mwisho. usivuke barabara. Pinda kushoto katika barabara ya Mwai Kibaki halafu nenda moja kwa moja hadi Barabara ya Old Bagamoyo.Pinda kulia hapo kisha tembea kwa mita chache utaona lango la ubalozi wa Marekani kwa upande wako wa kushoto.**

Freh-shee. Ndee-oh. Koo-toh-kah hah-pah hos-pee-tah-lee yah mah-choh, pee-ndah koo-lee-ah kah-tee-kah bah-rah-bah-rah yah Bah-gah-moh-yoh. Tem-beh-ah moh-jah-kwah moh-jah hah-dee m-wee-shoh. Oo-see-voo-keh bah-rah-bah-rah. Pee-ndah koo-shoh-toh kah-tee-kah bah-rah-bah-rah yah M-wah-ee Kee-bah-kee hah-lah-foo neh-ndah moh-jah kwah moh-jah hah-dee bah-rah-bah-rah yah Old Bah-gah-moh-yoh. Pee-ndah koo-lee-ah hah-poh kee-shah tehm-beh-ah kwah mee-tah chah-cheh oo-tah-oh-nah lah-ngoh lah oo-bah-loh-zee wah Mah-reh-kah-nee kwah oo-pah-ndeh wah-koh wah koo-shoh-toh.

Hey! Yes. From the eye hospital here, turn right at Bagamoyo Road. Walk straight to the end. Don't cross the road. Turn left at Mwai Kibaki Road; then go straight until Old Bagamoyo Road. Turn right there; then walk for a few meters. You'll see the American embassy gate to your left.

Greg: **Safi sana. Ahsante!**

Sah-fee sah-nah. Ah-sah-nteh!

Very well. Thank you!

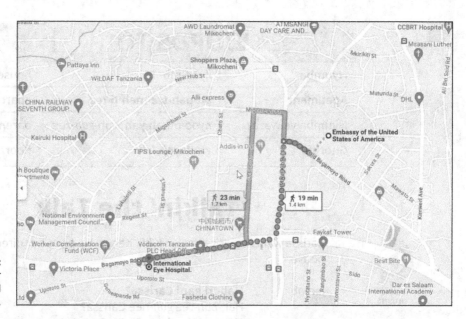

FIGURE 7-2:
Finding your way around Dar es Salaam.

TIP

You may have noticed that sometimes we use the **pinda** (*pee*-ndah) and other times **geuka** (geh-*oo*-kah) to mean *turn*. Choose the word to use depending on whether you're in Kenya or Tanzania. Tanzanian Swahili favors **pinda** while Kenyan Swahili uses **geuka**. Learn both and communicate seamlessly between the two dialects.

CULTURAL
WISDOM

Some streets do not have official names in East African cities. Smaller towns and villages rarely have street names and home addresses, but house numbers do not exist. Directions in such places use local landmarks such as shops, big/unique trees, schools, big anthills, farms, and so on.

Some of the phrases you would use in planning to visit a friend follow:

» **Karibu nyumbani kwangu.** (Kah-*ree*-boo *nyoo*-mbah-nee *kwah*-ngoo) (*Welcome to my place.*)

» **Unaishi katika nyumba au apatimenti?** (Oo-nah-ee-*shee* kah-tee-kah *nyoo*-mbah *ah*-oo ah-pah-*tee*-meh-n-*tee*?) (*Do you live in a house or an apartment?*)

» **Ninaishi katika nyumba ya wazazi wangu.** (Nee-nah-*ee*-shee kah-tee-kah *nyoo*-mbah yah wah-*zah*-zee *wah*-ngoo.) (*I live at my parent's house.*)

» **Nyumba yenu iko wapi?** (*Nyoo*-mbah *yeh*-noo ee-koh *wah*-pee?) (*Where is your house located?*)

» **Nyumba yetu iko mtaa wa Kilifi ghorofa la nne.** (*Nyoo*-mbah *yeh*-too ee-koh m-*tah*-ah wah Kee-*lee*-fee ghoh-*roh*-fah lah n-neh.) (*Our house is located at Kilifi Street fourth floor.*)

WORDS TO **KNOW**

Nyumba	*nyoo*-mbah	house
Apatiment	ah-pah-*tee*-meh-n-*tee*	apartment
Nyumba ya wazazi	*nyoo*-mbah yah wah-*zah*-zee	parent's house
Ghorofa	ghoh-*roh*-fah	floor/story house

Talkin' the Talk

**AUDIO
ONLINE**

Carissa wants to visit Jamal in Kilifi, Kenya. He gives her directions to his house.

Jamal: **Habari gani Carissa?**
Hah-*bah*-ree *gah*-nee Carissa?
How are you doing Carissa?

Carissa: **Nzuri sana Jamal.**
N-*zoo*-ree *sah*-nah Jamal.
I am doing well, Jamal.

Carissa: **Utafanya nini wikiendi hii?**
Oo-tah-*fah*-nyah *nee*-ne wee-kee-*eh*-ndee hee?
What will you be doing this weekend?

Jamal: **Mimi na rafiki zangu tutafanya sherehe.Karibu sana.**
Mee-mee nah rah-*fee*-kee *zah*-ngoo too-tah-*fah*-nyah sheh-*reh*-heh kah-*ree*-boo *sah*-nah.
Me and my friends will be having a party. You are welcome to join us.

Carissa: **Asante sana nitakuja. Unaweza kunielekeza kwako?**
Ah-*sah*-nteh *sah*-nah Nee-tah-*koo*-jah. Oo-nah-*weh*-zah koo-nee-eh-leh-*keh*-zah *kwah*-koh?
Thank you very much; I will come. Can you give me directions to your house?

Jamal:

Ndiyo. Endesha gari kutoka Mtwapa moja kwa moja kwa kilomita sitini na nane. Pinda kulia barabara ya Kilifi, endesha kwa dakika tano, utaona duka la dawa na hospitali kushoto kwako. Endelea kwa kilomita moja na utaona mti mkubwa na hospitali nyingine. Baada ya hospitali, utaona geti jekundu mbele yako na hapo ni nyumbani kwangu.

Ndee-yoh. Eh-*ndeh*-shah *gah*-ree koo-*toh*-kah Mtwapa *moh*-jah kwah *moh*-jah kwah kee-loh-*mee*-tah see-*tee*-nee nah *nah*-neh. *Pee*-ndah koo-*lee*-ah bah-rah-*bah*-rah yah Kee-*lee*-fee, eh-*ndeh*-shah kwah dah-*kee*-kah *tah*-noh, oo-tah-*oh*-nah *doo*-kah lah *dah*-wah nah hoh-spi-*tah*-lee koo-*shoh*-toh *kwah*-koh. Eh-ndeh-*leh*-ah kwah kee-loh-*mee*-tah *moh*-jah nah oo-tah-*oh*-nah *m*-tee m-*koo*-bwah nah hoh-spi-*tah*-lee nyee-*ngee*-neh . Bah-*ah*-dah yah hoh-spi-*tah*-lee, oo-tah-*oh*-nah *geh*-tee jeh-*koo*-ndoo *mbeh*-leh *yah*-koh nah *hah*-poh nee nyoo-*mbah*-nee *kwah*-ngoo.

Yes. Take Mtapwa Road and drive for 68 km. Turn left onto Kilifi Road, and after 5 minutes you will spot a pharmacy and a hospital on your left. Keep going for another kilometer and you will see a large tree and another hospital. After the hospital, you will see a red gate ahead, and that's where my house is located.

Carissa:

Vizuri. Tutaonana wikendi!
Vee-*zoo*-ree. *Too*-tah-oh-*nah*-nah wee-kee-*eh*-ndee!
Good. See you over the weekend.

• •

FUN & GAMES

1. Guide the ball out of the maze using imperatives.

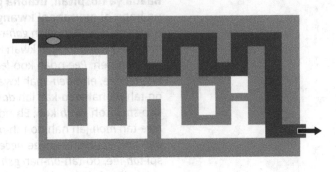

_____

_____

_____

_____

2. Which of the following would Swahili speakers use as local landmarks?

    a. Kibanda

    b. jua

    c. Shule ya msingi

    d. Nyumbani kwa Bwana Omari

    e. mto

Chapter **8**

Eating in and Dining Out

Just think about all the travel blogs/vlogs, vacation pictures from your friends, or destination brochures: What do they all have in common? Food! That's right. Sharing all these display pictures or videos of food from various parts of the world is all the rage. But in addition to imagining how fantastic all these dishes will taste, you can also learn a lot about a culture by exploring its food. In this chapter, you can start identifying Swahili food, gain the language skills to express your preferences, and finally learn how to place your order at a restaurant.

Choosing Food Options for All Times of the Day

Different mealtimes call for different **vyakula** (vyah-*koo*-lah) (*food* pl.). The list below gives you the Swahili for the three basic mealtimes:

> » **kiamsha kinywa/chakula cha asubuhi/staftahi** (kee-ah-*m*-shah *kee*-nywah/chah-*koo*-lah chah ah-soo-*boo*-hee/stah-fuh-*tah*-hee) (*breakfast;* literally *food of the morning*)

> » **chakula cha mchana/chamcha** (chah-*koo*-lah chah m-*chah*-nah/chah-m-chah) (*lunch;* literally *food of the afternoon*)

>> **chakula cha usiku/chakula cha jioni/chajio** (chah-*koo*-lah chah oo-*see*-koo/ chah-*koo*-lah chah jee-*oh*- nee) (*supper; literally food of the evening*)

Read through the following sections for vocabulary to use when talking about food options at different times throughout the day.

Having breakfast

Do you consider yourself a breakfast person, or do you prefer a quick **chai** (*chah*–ee) (*tea*) or **kahawa** (kah–*hah*–wah) (*coffee*) on the go? Whichever the case, knowing the names of breakfast food items comes in handy when you need your order made just right. Here are some of the items you'll typically find in a Swahili breakfast setup:

>> **chai ya maziwa** (*chah*-ee yah mah-*zee*-wah) (*tea with milk*)

>> **chai ya rangi** (*chah*-ee yah *rah*-ngee) (*black tea*)

>> **mkate** (m-*kah*-teh) (*bread*)

>> **andazi** (ah-*ndah*-zee) (*doughnut* — but tastier)

>> **chapati maji/pankeki**(chah-*pah*-tee *mah*-jee/pah-nee-keh-kee) (*crepes*)

>> **siagi** (see-*ah*-gee) (*butter*)

>> **mayai** (mah-*yah*-ee) (*eggs*)

>> **uji** (oo-jee) (*porridge*)

>> **sukari** (soo-*kah*-ree) (*sugar*)

>> **viazi vitamu** (vee-*ah*-zee vee-*tah*-moo) (*sweet potatoes*)

>> **mihogo** (mee-*hoh*-goh) (*cassava*)

>> **jibini** (jee-*bee*-nee) (*cheese*)

>> **chumvi** (*choo*-mvee) (*salt*)

>> **asali** (ah-*sah*-lee) (*honey*)

>> **magimbi** (mah-*gee*-mbee) (*arrow root*)

>> **soseji** (soh-*seh*-jee) (*sausage*)

>> **vitumbua** (vee-too-*mboo*-ah) (*fried coconut rice cakes*)

Eating lunch

After a morning filled with work and activities, you'll probably say **ninahisi njaa** (nee-nah-*hee*-see n-*jah*-ah) (*I feel hungry*) or **nina njaa** (*nee*-nah n-*jah*-ah) (*I am hungry*). That means it's time for lunch! Check out this list of food options for a typical Swahili lunch:

» **wali** (*wah*-lee) (*steamed rice*)

» **pilau** (pee-*lah*-oo) (*spice-filled fried rice with beef or chicken in it*)

» **biryani** (bee-ree-*ah*-nee) (*aromatic spice-filled fried rice cooked with veggies or other types of meat*)

» **nyama** (*nyah*-mah) (*meat*)

» **chapati** (chah-*pah*-tee) (*fried flat bread*)

» **samaki** (sah-*mah*-kee) (*fish*)

» **githeri/makande/pure** (gee-*dhe*-ree/mah-*kah*-ndeh/*poo*-ree) (*mix of maize and beans*)

» **mbaazi** (m-bah-*ah*-zee) (*pigeon peas*)

» **matoke** (mah-*toh*-keh) (*green bananas cooked in stew*)

» **vibanzi/chipsi** (vee-*bah*-nzee/*chee*-psi) (*French fries*)

Having supper

Many East Africans have their last meal of the day between 7:00pm and 9:00pm. While breakfast and lunch do not have to be family affairs, as people are involved in different activities and probably rushing out or not at home, supper is a communal event where members of a household meet at the end of the day to share a meal and talk about the day. Here are some common items for supper:

» **ugali** (oo-*gah*-lee) (*maize meal mush*)

» **nyama** (*nyah*-mah) (*meat*)

» **mboga za majani** (m-*boh*-gah zah mah-*jah*-nee) (*leafy vegetables*)

» **tambi** (*tah*-mbee) (*spaghetti*)

» **dagaa/omena** (dah-*gah*-ah/ oh-*meh*-nah) (*sardines*)

» **maharage wa nazi** (mah-hah-*rah*-ge yah *nah*-zee) (*beans fried in coconut milk*)

» **utumbo** (oo-*too*-mboh) (*tripe*)

There's no clear division between Swahili food options for lunch and dinner, so choose whatever you fancy based on whether you prefer a light lunch and heavy dinner or vice versa. Tread carefully, though, because **ugali** (*maize meal mush*) for lunch renders many people useless for afternoon activities as they feel too full and sleepy.

REMEMBER

Be specific when asking for **nyama** (*meat*). State whether you need **nyama ya kuku** (*nyah*-mah yah *koo*-koo) (*chicken meat*), **nyama ya mbuzi** (*nyah*-mah yah m-*boo*-zee) (*goat meat*), **nyama ng'ombe** (*nyah*-mah yah *ng'o*-mbeh) (*beef*), **nyama ya kondoo** (*nyah*-mah yah koh-*ndo*-oh) (*lamb meat*), or **nyama ya nguruwe** (*nyah*-mah yah ngoo-*roo*-weh) (*pork*). You may also want to clarify the method of preparation such as **kuchoma** (koo-*choh*-mah) (*grilled*), **kukaanga** (koo-kah-*ah*-ngah) (*fried*), and **mchuzi** (m-*choo*-zee) (*curry*). For example:

>> **Naomba mchuzi wa nyama ya ng'ombe.** (*Nah*-oh-mbah m-*choo*-zee wah *nyah*-mah yah *ng'oh*-mbeh) (*I'd like beef curry.*)

>> **Naomba nyama ya kuku wa kuchoma.** (Nah-*oh*-mbah *nyah*-mah yah *koo*-koo wah koo-*choh*-mah) (*I'd like barbecued chicken.*)

>> **Naomba nyama ya mbuzi wa kukaanga.** (Nah-*oh*-mbah *nyah*-mah yah m-*boo*-zee wah koo-kah-*ah*-ngah) (*I'd like fried goat meat.*)

CULTURAL WISDOM

The Muslim faithful do not eat **nyama ya nguruwe**; this is important to remember so that you don't make the mistake of ordering pork at a Muslim-run establishment or worse, offer your Muslim guest food with pork in it. Other religious groups that do not eat pork include Seventh Day Adventists, who are also found across East Africa.

Beverages

There's no better way to wash down a good meal or stay hydrated than with freshly made **maji ya matunda** (*mah*-jee yah mah-*too*-ndah) (*juice*) — also known as **juisi** (joo-*ee*-see) (*juice*) — from the wide variety of tasty homegrown tropical fruits in East Africa. First, learn to express your thirst by saying **ninahisi kiu** (nee-nah-*hee*-see *kee*-oo) (*I feel thirsty*) or **nina kiu** (nee-nah *kee*-oo) (*I am thirsty*) and then choose the drink you fancy from the following list:

>> **maji** (*mah*-jee) (*water*)

>> **maji ya machungwa** (*mah*-jee yah mah-*choo*-ngwah) (*orange juice*)

>> **maji ya maembe** (*mah*-jee yah mah-*eh*-mbe) (*mango juice*)

>> **maji ya mananasi** (*mah*-jee yah mah-nah-*nah*-see) (*pineapple juice*)

» **maji ya ukwaju** (*mah*-jee yah oo-*kwah*-joo) (*tamarind juice*)

» **soda** (*soh*-dah) (*soda*)

» **mvinyo** (m-*vee*-nyoh) (*wine*)

» **bia** (*bee*-ah) (*beer*)

» **pombe** (*poh*-mbeh) (*hard liquor*)

You can make (and ask for) endless juice combinations if you know fruit names. Check out Chapter 10 for the Swahili names for a variety of fruits.

REMEMBER

State your preference of chilled or room temperature water/soda by saying **Naomba maji/soda baridi** (na-*oh*-mbah *mah*-jee/*soh*-dah bah-*ree*-dee) (*I'd like cold/chilled water/soda*) or **naomba maji/soda moto** (na-*oh*-mbah *mah*-jee/*soh*-dah *moh*-toh) (*I'd like hot water/soda*). Although moto means hot, you will receive room temperature water/soda. You can also clarify the type and size of soda you want by saying **Naomba soda ya Sparletta kubwa/ndogo** (na-*oh*-mbah *soh*-dah yah Sparletta *koo*-bwah/n-*doh*-goh) (*I'd like a big/small Sparletta soda*). Adding ice to your drink is usually not an option.

CULTURAL WISDOM

Sparletta is a soft drink manufactured by The Coca-Cola Company for distribution in East African and Southern African countries. It comes in a range of great flavors and is particularly popular in Tanzania.

Snacking

Vitafunio (vee-tah-foo-*nee*-oh) (*snacks*) come in handy when you need a quick bite to keep you going until your next full meal. And don't worry about sitting down; it is socially acceptable to eat while walking in East Africa. Now, what looks tempting from the list below?

» **njugu karanga** (n-*joo*-goo kah-*rah*-ngah) (*roasted groundnuts*)

» **korosho** (koh-*roh*-shoh) (*cashew nuts*)

» **kitumbua** (kee-too-*mboo*-ah) (*fried coconut rice cakes*)

» **bagia** (bah-*gee*-ah) (*fritters*)

» **mahindi ya kuchoma** (mah-*hee*-ndee yah koo-*choh*-mah) (*roasted green maize on the cob*)

» **mahindi ya kuchemsha** (mah-*hee*-ndee yah koo-*cheh*-mshah) (*steamed green maize on the cob*)

» **viazi karai** (vee-*ah*-zee kah-*rah*-ee) (*spicy fried potatoes*)

» **chipsi mayai** (*chee*-psee mah-*yah*-ee) (*French fried omelette*)

» **kaimati** (kah-ee-*mah*-tee) (*fried sweet dumplings*)

Sharing a Meal with Others

Did you know that East Africans must offer food and/or a drink to a guest in their home? That's right, culture dictates that we do not let a guest leave without offering some form of refreshment or food. If they were about to serve food for the household anyway, the host will invite you to eat by saying **karibu tule** (kah-*ree*-boo *too*-leh) (*Welcome, let's eat.*). If your visit does not coincide with a mealtime, the host will provide snacks and a drink (usually tea) and say **karibu chai** (kah-*ree*-boo *chah*-ee) (*Have some tea*).In both cases, respond with **Ahsante sana** (Ah-*sah*-nteh) (*Thank you very much*) before digging in.

Since you're likely to find yourself sharing a meal with locals at their homes, check out the following sections for ways of stating food preferences and talking about food allergies (if you have any).

Stating food preferences

If you're ever invited for a meal and you suspect that the options might not cater to your dietary restrictions, feel free to speak up. The last thing you want to do is to embarrass your host by not eating the food they offer and not telling them why. Check out the following phrases that could be useful in such instances:

» **Mimi ni mla mboga.** (*mee*-mee nee *m*-lah m-*boh*-gah) (*I am vegetarian.*)

» **Mimi ni mla samaki tu.** (*mee*-mee nee *m*-lah sah-*mah*-kee too) (*I do eat fish/ am pescatarian.*)

» **Sili mayai.** (*see*-lee mah-*yah*-ee) (*I don't eat eggs.*)

» **Sili nyama yoyote wala mazao ya wanyama.** (*see*-lee *nyah*-mah *wah*-lah mah-*zah*-oh yah wah-*nyah*-mah) (*I don't eat any meat or animal products/I am vegan.*)

Making food allergies known

Here's a safety rule for you: If you have allergies, never make assumptions about the ingredients of a dish. Of course, no host wants to be grilled about every single ingredient they might have used, but you must be proactive in protecting your health. Inform your host of your food allergy — **mzio** (m-*zee*-oh) — before digging into a curry you're not sure about by saying.

>> **nina mzio wa maziwa.** (*nee*-na m-*zee*-oh wah mah-*zee*-wah) (*I have a dairy allergy.*)

>> **nina mzio wa pilipili hoho.** (*nee*-na m-*zee*-oh wah pee-lee-*pee*-lee *hoh*-hoh) (*I have a bell pepper allergy.*)

CULTURAL WISDOM

Traditionally, Swahili cuisine was enjoyed using fingers. However, most people today use cutlery and prefer to use bare hands only when the dish includes ugali or has bones. That said, always wash your hands (**nawa mikono**) (*nah*-wah mee-*koh*-noh) with soap and water before sitting down to eat even if you'll be using cutlery. If you're hosting, let your guests know where they can wash their hands immediately before you bring out the food. If you're a guest, don't be shy to ask **Ninaweza kunawa mikono wapi?** (nee-nah-*weh*-zah koo-*nah*-wah mee-*koh*-noh *wah*-pee) (*Where can I wash my hands?*).

Eating at a Restaurant

It's nice to receive an invitation to share a meal at someone's home, but those instances can be few and far between. How about continuing your cultural experience by visiting different **mikahawa** (mee-kah-*hah*-wah) (*restaurants*)? Afterall, they offer a more flexible way to sample local cuisine because you can order whatever you want, however you like it. Read on to find out how to order from a menu and pay your bill.

Ordering from a menu

Most restaurants in East Africa don't require prior booking, so you can always walk in and find a table. Smaller ones display the **menyu** (*meh*-nyoo) (*menu*) or **orodha ya vyakula** (oh-*roh*-dhah yah vyah-*koo*-lah) (*menu; literally list of food*) on a **ubao** (oo-*bah*-oh) (*board*). The norm, however, is that a **mhudumu** (m-hoo-*doo*-moo) (*waitstaff*) will politely greet you and hand you a **menyu** at your table. Take your time to decide what you'd like, and the waitstaff will come back with questions such as:

>> **Ungependa kinywaji gani?** (oo-ngeh-*peh*-ndah kee-*nywah*-jee *gah*-nee) (*What drink would you like?*)

» **Utakula nini leo?** (oo-tah-*koo*-lah *nee*-nee *leh*-oh) (*What will you have to eat today?*)

» **Ungependa kitu kingine tena?** (oo-ngeh-*peh*-ndah *kee*-too kee-*ngee*-neh *teh*-nah) (*Would you like something else?*)

Order your food and drinks using the phrase **naomba** (nah-*oh*-mbah) (*I would like*) or **nipe** (*nee*-peh) (*give me*). For example

» **Naomba juisi/sharubati ya ukwaju.** (nah-*oh*-mbah joo-*ee*-see/shah-roh-*bah*-tee yah oo-*kwah*-joo) (*I'd like tamarind juice.*)

» **Nipe wali, nyama ya mbuzi wa kukaanga na kabeji.** (nee-peh *wah*-lee, *nyah*-mah yah m-*boo*-zee wah koo-ka-*ah*-ngah nah kah-*beh*-jee (*Give me steamed rice, fried goat meat, and cabbage.*)

REMEMBER

Be sure to say **ahsante** (ah-*sah*-nteh) (*Thank you*) to the wait staff when you receive your order.

A few times during your meal, your waitstaff might come around to check if everything is alright with the meal by asking **Kila kitu kiko sawa?** (*kee*-lah *kee*-too *kee*-koh *sah*-wah) (*Is everything alright?*). Here are a few responses that you might find handy during such a situation:

» **Ndiyo, ahsante.** (n-*dee*-yoh ah-*sah*-nteh) (*Yes, thank you.*)

» **Naomba chumvi.** (nah-*oh*-mbah *choo*-mvee) (*I'd like some salt.*)

» **Naomba maji ya kunywa.** (nah-*oh*-mbah *mah*-jee yah *koo*-nywah) (*I'd like some water to drink.*)

» **Niongeze juisi.** (nee-oh-*ngeh*-zeh joo-*ee*-see) (*Please bring me some juice.*)

Paying your bill

Exactly when you should pay your **bili** (*bee*-lee) (*bill*) depends on the restaurant: Some will ask for payment after your meal while others will want payment up front. To request your bill, say

» **Naomba bili yangu.** (nah-*oh*-mbah *bee*-lee *yah*-ngoo) (*I'd like my bill.*)

» **Naomba kulipa.** (nah-*oh*-mbah koo-*lee*-pah) (*I'd like to pay.*)

While every establishment accepts **pesa taslimu** (*peh*-sah tah-*slee*-moo) (*cash payments*), a lot of the smaller restaurants will not accept **kadi** (*kah*-dee) (*credit/debit cards*). If you're not sure, just ask **Munakubali kadi?** (moo-nah-koo-*bah*-lee kah-dee) (*Do you accept cards?*)

CULTURAL WISDOM

Tipping is not a common practice in East Africa. However, it is fast becoming more acceptable and expected in some areas, especially in more upscale tourist locations.

Talkin' the Talk

AUDIO ONLINE

Carlos is visiting Forodhani, Zanzibar, Tanzania (one of the best places to sample Zanzibari food in the evenings). He orders different food from Jamila, the **Mhudumu** (mhoo-*doo*-moo) (*waitress*).

Carlos:	**Habari gani? Una kuku choma?**
	Hah-*bah*-ree *gah*-nee? Oo-nah *koo*-koo *choh*-mah?
	How are you doing? Do you have grilled chicken?

Jamila:	**Nzuri. Karibu sana! Kuku zipo. Unahitaji kiasi gani?**
	N-*zoo*-ree. Kah-*ree*-boo *sah*-nah! *Koo*-koo *zee*-poh. Oo-nah-hee-*tah*-jee kee-*ah*-see *gah*-nee?
	I am doing well. Welcome. I have chicken. How much do you want?

Carlos:	**Ninahitaji nusu.**
	Nee-nah-hee-*tah*-jee *noo*-soo.
	I need a half (chicken).

Jamila:	**Sawa. Ungependa kinywaji au kitu kingine?**
	Sah-wah. Oo-ngeh-*peh*-ndah kee-*nywah*-jee *ah*-oo *kee*-too kee-*ngee*-nee?
	Would you like a drink or anything else?

Carlos:	**Ndiyo. Ninaomba menyu kama unayo.**
	N-*dee*-yoh. Nee-nah-*oh*-mbah *meh*-nyoo *kah*-mah oo-*nah*-yoh.
	Yes, Can I have a menu if you have it, please?

Jamila:	**Menyu ya vyakula na vinywaji hii hapa.**
	Meh-nyoo yah vyah-*koo*-lah nah vee-*nywah*-jee hee *hah*-pah.
	Here is the menu for food and drinks.

Carlos:	**Asante sana. Ninaomba pilau, kuku choma nusu, mrenda, na soda ya Fanta.**
	Ah-*sah*-nteh *sah*-nah. Nee-nah-*oh*-mbah pee-*lah*-oo koo-koo *choh*-mah *noo*-soo, m-*reh*-ndah nah *soh*-dah yah fantah.
	Thank you very much. I would like spice-filled fried rice, half a grilled chicken, the leafy vegetable of the day, and a Fanta soda.
Jamila:	**Utakula hapa au unabeba?**
	oo-tah-*koo*-lah *hah*-pah *ah*-oo oo-tah-*beh*-bah
	Will you eat here or take it away?
Carlos:	**Nitakula hapa.**
	Nee-tah-*koo*-lah *hah*-pah
	I'll eat here.
Jamila:	**Vyakula na kinywaji hivi hapa**
	Vyah-*koo*-lah nah vee-*nywah*-jee *hee*-vee *hah*-pah.
	Here's your food and drink.
Carlos:	**Asante sana. Ninaomba bili tafadhali**
	Ah-*sah*-nteh *sah*-nah. Nee-nah-*oh*-mbah *bee*-lee tah-fah-*dhah*-lee
	Thank you very much. Can I have my bill please?
Jamila:	**Bili yako hii hapa. Jumla ni shilingi elfu nane.**
	Bee-lee *yah*-koh hee *hah*-pah. *Joo*-mlah nee shee-*lee*-ngee *ehl*-foo *nah*-neh
	Here is your bill. The total is eight thousand shillings.
Carlos:	**Asante sana. Kwaheri.**
	Ah-*sah*-nteh *sah*-nah. Kwah-*heh*-ree.
	Thank you very much. Goodbye.
Jamila:	**Asante. Karibu tena siku nyingine.**
	Ah-*sah*-nteh. Kah-*ree*-boo *teh*-nah *see*-koo nyee-*ngee*-neh.
	Thanks. Welcome again another day.

• •

WORDS TO KNOW

kiasi	kee-*ah*-see	quantity
nusu	*noo*-soo	half
robo	*roh*-boh	quatre
mzima	m-*zee*-mah	whole
jumla	*joo*-mlah	total
chakula cha kubeba	chah-*koo*-lah chah koo-*beh*-bah	take away food

FUN & GAMES

Match the names of different food and drinks to their pictures.

Sukari

Mayai

Samaki

Nyama

Asali

Chapter **9**

Using Technology to Keep in Touch

W e're lucky to live at a time in which we can still maintain constant communication with those we hold dear even when we travel very far from them. But is technology only good for maintaining communication with those back home? Absolutely not! You can have a richer East African experience by using technology to make and maintain social and business relationships, too. Read on to find out basic telephone and electronic communication etiquette for a smooth transition to building lasting, respectful relationships with Swahili speakers.

Talking and Texting with Cellphones

If you look at people walking by on any busy street, you'll see them on their phones, either texting, calling, reacting in some way to social media, or perhaps emailing. **Simu za mkono** (*see*-moo zah m-*koh*-noh) (*cellphones*) [literally, "phones of the hand"] enable us to stay in touch easily with our friends and family and even do business while on the go. It's no different in East Africa; everyone uses **simu za mkono** on a daily basis. But what are the rules of communication here? Seline recalls calling a new American friend and hearing a voice dripping with concern on the other end of the line. Since Seline was only calling to make plans for the weekend, she couldn't figure out why her friend sounded as if the sky was falling. It turned out that her friend was convinced that phone calls were meant only for emergencies and that one would — of course! — use text messages for everything else. Seline and I are still not convinced about this unwritten communication rule, but to ensure you don't run into the same dilemma, we'll explain general cellphone and electronic communication etiquette in this chapter.

Asking someone to call you

When it comes to asking someone **kukupigia simu** (koo-oo-pee-*gee*-ah *see*-moo) (*to call you*) you can leave them a voicemail, or you can send them a **ujumbe** (oo-joo-mbeh) (*text*). You can use the following phrases to do so.

>> **Tafadhali nipigie.** (tah-fah-*dhah*-lee nee-pee-*gee*-eh) (*Please call me.*)

>> **Nipigie baadaye tafadhali.** (nee-pee-*gee*-eh bah-ah-*dah*-yeh tah-fah-*dhah*-lee) (*Please call me later.*)

>> **Nipigie haraka iwezekanavyo.** (nee-pee-*gee*-eh hah-*rah*-kah ee-weh-zeh-kah-*nah*-vyoh) (*Call me as soon as possible.*)

>> **Usisahau kunipigia ni muhimu.** (oo-see-sah-*hah*-oo koo-nee-pee-*gee*-ah) (*Don't forget to call me; it is urgent.*)

>> **Nipigie ukiwa hewani.** (nee-pee-*gee*-eh oo-*kee*-wah heh-*wah*-nee) (*Call me when you are online.*)

>> **Natarajia kuona simu yako.** (nah-tah-tah-rah-*jee*-ah koo-*oh*-nah *see*-moo yah-koh) (*I will be expecting to see your call.*)

>> **Tuzungumze baada ya kazi.** (too-zoo-ngoo-*m*-zeh bah-*ah*-dah yah *kah*-zee) (*Let's talk after work.*)

>> **Tunahitaji kuzungumza.** (too-nah-hee-*tah*-jee koo-zoo-ngoo-*m*-zah) (*We need to talk.*)

Talkin' the Talk

AUDIO ONLINE

Emily is studying abroad in Mombasa. One day she calls her best friend Maua who is in the United States to share her experience.

Emily: **Ninazungumza na Maua?**
Nee-nah-zoo-ngoo-*m*-zah nah mah-*oo*-ah?
Am I speaking with Maua?

Maua: **Ndiyo, ni mimi! Habari za Mombasa?**
N-*zoo*-ree *sah*-nah. *Ndee*-yoh, nee *mee*-mee. Hah-*bah*-ree zah Moh-*mbah*-sah?
Yes, this is Maua. How is Mombasa?

Emily: **Safi sana! Ninafurahia muda wangu hapa.**
Sah-fee *sah*-nah! Nee-nah-foo-rah-*hee*-ah *moo*-dah *wah*-ngoo *hah*-pah.
It's cool! I am enjoying my time here.

Maua: **Ni vizuri kusikia hivyo. Nimejaribu kukupigia simu mara kadhaa lakini sikukupata.**
Nee vee-*zoo*-ree koo-see-*kee*-ah *hee*-vyoh. Nee-meh-jah-*ree*-boo koo-koo-pee-*gee*-ah *see*-moo *mah*-rah kah-*dha*-ah lah-*kee*-nee see-koo-koo-*pah*-tah.
I am glad to hear that. I have tried to call you several times, but I couldn't reach you.

Emily: **Ni kweli niliona simu kadhaa na jumbe lakini hakukuwa na mtandao.**
Nee *kweh*-lee nee-lee-*oh*-nah *see*-moo kah-*dhah*-ah nah *joo*-mbeh lah-*kee*-nee hah-koo-*koo*-wah nah m-tah-*ndah*-oh.
It's true I saw several calls and messages, but there was no Internet.

Maua: **Pole sana. Naelewa. Niliamua kukutumia barua pepe.**
Poh-leh *sah*-nah. Nah-eh-*leh*-wa. Nee-lee-ah-*moo*-ah koo-koo-too-*mee*-ah bah-*roo*-ah *peh*-peh.
I am very sorry. I understand. I decided to send you an email.

Emily: **Nilisahau kukupa nambari yangu mpya ya simu ya hapa Kenya.**
Nee-lee-sah-*hah*-oo koo-*koo*-pah nah-*mbah*-ree *yah*-ngoo m-pyah yah *see*-moo yah *hah*-pah *Keh*-nyah.
I forgot to give you my new Kenyan number.

Maua: **Sikujua ulibadilisha namba ya simu.**
See-koo-*joo*-ah oo-le-bah-dee-*lee*-shah *nah*-mbah yah *see*-moo
I didn't know you changed your phone number.

Emily: **Ilibidi nibadilishe kwa sababu nilihitaji kuwasiliana na wenyeji.**
Eee-lee-*bee*-dee nee-bah-dee-*lee*-sheh kwah sah-*bah*-boo nee-lee-hee-*tah*-jee koo-wah-see-lee-*ah*-nah nah weh-*nyeh*-jee.
I had to change it because I needed to communicate with the locals.

Maua:	**Unaweza kununua kifurushi cha intaneti cha mwezi mmoja?**
	Oo-nah-*weh*-zah koo-noo-*noo*-ah kee-foo-*roo*-shee chah ee-n-tah-*neh*-tee cha *mweh*-zee m-*moh*-jah?
	Can you buy a one-month Internet bundle?
Emily:	**Ndiyo. Ninaweza kununua kifurushi cha siku moja, wiki moja au mwezi mmoja.**
	Ndee-yoh. Nee-nah-*weh*-zah koo-noo-*noo*-ah kee-foo-*roo*-shee chah *see*-koo *moh*-jah, *wee*-kee *moh*-jah ah-oo *mweh*-zee m-*moh*-jah.
	Yes. I can buy an Internet bundle for a day, one week, or one month.
Maua:	**Sawa. Nimefurahi kukusikia. Nitakupigia baadaye nikiwa na muda.**
	Sah-wah. Nee-meh-foo-*rah*-hee koo-koo-see-*kee*-ah nee-tah-koo-pee-*gee*-ah bah-ah-*dah*-yeh nee-*kee*-wah nah *moo*-dah.
	Okay. I am happy to hear you. I will call you later when I have time.
Emily:	**Asante sana. Siku njema!**
	Ah-sah-*n*-teh *sah*-nah. *See*-koo *njeh*-mah.
	Thank you very much. Have a good day.

WORDS TO KNOW

kifurushi cha intaneti	kee-foo-*roo*-shee chah ee-n-tah-*neh*-tee	Internet bundle
wenyeji	weh-*nyeh*-jee	locals
barua pepe	bah-*roo*-ah *peh*-peh	email
ujumbe	oo-*joo*-mbeh	message/text
mtandao	m-tah-*ndah*-oh	Internet
piga namba	*pee*-gah *nah*-mbah	dial the number
mpokeaji	m-poh-keh-*ah*-jee	receiver

Asking to speak with someone

If you call an office or home phone and you're not sure that whoever picks up is the person you're looking for, you can ask **Ninazungumza na Juma?** (nee-nah zoo-*ngoo*-mzah nah Juma) (*Am I speaking with Juma?*) If you're out of luck, and they respond **hapana** (hah-*pah*-nah) (*No.*), ask them to put whomever you're looking for on the phone using any of the following phrases:

>> **Juma yupo?** (Juma *yoo*-poh?) (*Is Juma there?*)

>> **Ninaweza kuzungumza na Juma?** (*nee*-nah-weh-zah *koo*-zoo-ngoo-m-*zah* nah Juma) (*May I speak with Juma?*)

>> **Mpatie Juma simu tafadhali.** (m-pah-*tee*-eh *Joo*-ma *see*-moo tah-*fah*-dhah-lee) (*Put Juma on, please.*)

Leaving a message

People aren't always available to speak with you when you call them, so you leave an **ujumbe** (oo-*joo*-mbeh) (*a message*). If you're calling from a new number or calling a landline, greet the recipient, state your **jina** (*jee*-nah) (*name*), **ujumbe** (oo-*joo*-mbeh) (*a message*), and **nambari ya simu** (nah-*mbah*-ree yah *see*-moo) (*phone number*). For example:

>> **Ni Almasi.** (*nee* Almasi) (*It's Almasi.*) [very informal, for people you know well]

>> **Jina langu ni Almasi.** (*jee*-nah *lah*-ngoo nee Almasi) (*My name is Almasi.*)

>> **Tafadhali nipigie simu kwa nambari yangu ya simu . . .** (tah-fah-*dhah*-lee nee-pee-*gee*-eh *see*-moo kwah nah-*mbah*-ree *yah*-ngoo yah *see*-moo . . .) (*Please call me on my phone number . . .*)

Sometimes a second person like a spouse, sibling, child, or co-worker picks up the phone instead of the person you were calling. You'd still leave a message with them, but you'd want to preface it with phrases like the following:

>> **Nilikuwa namtafuta Juma.** (nee-lee-*koo*-wah nah-m-tah-*foo*-tah Juma) (*I was looking for Juma.*)

>> **Mwambie Juma anipigie simu.** (mwah-*mbee*-eh Juma ah-nee-pee-*gee*-eh *see*-moo) (*Tell Juma to call me.*)

>> **Mwambie Juma nilimpigia.** (mwah-*mbee*-eh *Joo*-mah nee-lee-m-pee-*gee*-ah (*Tell Juma I called.*)

CULTURAL WISDOM

Kenyans and Tanzanians rarely leave voicemails, and none of our friends back home have their voicemail box set up. If we don't pick up when our friends call, they'd rather disconnect and send a quick text message than leave a voicemail after the beep. This is perfectly understandable considering that airtime is billed per minute and leaving a voicemail doesn't provide the instant connection they were after.

Texting to check in

You might just brighten someone's day by texting to check on them because it assures them that you care. If you haven't heard from a friend for a while, it's normal to send them a quick message for the purpose of **kumjulia hali** (koo-m-joo-*lee*-ah *hah*-lee) (*finding out how they're doing*). Send any of the following messages to prompt a response.

>> **Habari za kazi?** (hah-*bah*-ree zah *kah*-zee) (*How's work?*)

>> **Habari za siku?** (hah-*bah*-ree zah *see*-koo) (*How are your days?*)

>> **Uko salama?** (oo-koh sah-*lah*-mah) (*Are you okay?*)

>> **Unaendeleaje?** (oo-nah-eh-ndeh-leh-*ah*-jeh) (*How are you fairing?*)

>> **Umepotea! Kwema?** (oo-meh-poh-*teh*-ah! *Kweh*-mah) (*You're so lost! All good?*) *["Lost" here is used for someone you haven't seen or interacted with in a while.]*

>> **Umenyamaza! Kwema?** (oo-meh-nyah-*mah*-zah! *Kweh*-mah) (*You're so quiet! All good?*)

If they're fine and respond as such, let them know you were just checking up on them by texting **nilikuwa nakujulia tu hali.** (nee-lee-*koo*-wah nah-koo-joo-*lee*-ah too *hah*-lee) (*I was just checking in on you.*) Then proceed to make plans to talk or meet later.

Making Arrangements over the Phone

Whether you're planning to meet a friend or a business partner, you're likely to make arrangements over the phone to check the best time and place to meet up. Here are some important phrases to know.

>> **jioni** (jee-*oh*-nee) (*evening*)

>> **wikendi** (wee-*keh*-ndee) (*weekend*)

» **kutana** (koo-*tah*-nah) (*to meet*)

» **mkahawa** (m-kah-*hah*-wah) (*cafe/restaurant*)

» **sinema** (see-*neh*-mah) (*cinema*)

» **klabu** (k-*lah*-boo) (*club*)

» **mpango/mipango** (m-*pah*-ngoh; mee-*pah*-ngoh) (*plan; plans*)

Talkin' the Talk

Travis is planning to visit Kikuletwa Hot Springs in Moshi, Tanzania, this weekend. He texts Sara to check if she can join him. Here is their conversation via texts:

Travis: **Vipi Sara! Uko poa?**
            Vee-pee Sah-rah oo-koh poh-ah?
            Hi, Sara! Are you good?

Sara: **Niko poa kabisa. Habari za siku?**
            Nee-koh poh-ah kah-bee-sah. Hah-bah-ree zah see-koo?
            I am doing very well. How has it been?

Travis: **Nzuri tu. Umepotea! Una mpango gani wikendi hii?**
            N-zoo-ree too. Oo-meh-poh-teh-ah! Oo-nah m-pah-ngoh gah-nee wee-keh-ndee hee-ee?
            I am okay! Long time, no see! What are you planning to do this weekend?

Sara: **Mimi niko. Ni shughuli nyingi tu za maisha. Wikendi hii sina mpango.**
            Mee-mee nee-koh. Nee shoo-ghoo-lee nyee-ngee too zah mah-ee-shah. Wee-keh-ndee hee-ee see-nah m-pah-ngoh.
            I am around. Just busy with life. I don't have plans for this weekend.

Travis: **Ninataka kwenda Kikuletwa kuogelea. Unataka kwenda na mimi?**
            Nee-nah-tah-kah kweh-ndah Kee-koo-leh-twah koo-oh-geh-leh-ah. Oo-nah-tah-kah kweh-ndah nah mee-mee?
            I want to go to Kikuletwa Hot Springs to swim. Do you want to go with me?

Sara: **Ndiyo, ningependa kwenda pia!**
            Ndee-yoh, nee-ngeh-peh-ndah kweh-ndah pee-ah!
            Yes, I would love to go, too!

Travis:	**Safi! Tukutane nje ya hoteli ya Kibo Palace saa mbili kasorobo. Tutaondoka Arusha mjini saa mbili asubuhi.**

Travis: **Safi! Tukutane nje ya hoteli ya Kibo Palace saa mbili kasorobo. Tutaondoka Arusha mjini saa mbili asubuhi.**
Sah-fee! Too-koo-*tah*-neh *n*-jeh yah hoh-*teh*-lee yah *Kee*-boh Palace *sah*-ah m-*bee*-lee kah-soh-*roh*-boh. Too-tah-oh-*ndoh*-kah Ah-*roo*-shah m-*jee*-nee *sah*-ah *mbee*-lee ah-soo-*boo*-hee.
Great! Let's meet outside Kibo Palace hotel at quarter to eight. We'll depart Arusha town at 8am.

Sara: **Ni sawa. Nitakuwa tayari. Ninahitaji kubeba nini?**
Nee *sah*-wah. Nee-tah-*koo*-wah tah-*yah*-ree. Nee-nah-hee-*tah*-jee koo-*beh*-bah *nee*-nee?
That's fine. I will be ready. What should I bring?

Travis: **Beba nguo ya kuogelea na miwani ya jua.**
Beh-bah *ngoo*-oh yah koo-oh-geh-*leh*-ah nah mee-*wah*-nee yah *joo*-ah.
Bring a swimming suit and sunglasses.

Sara: **Sawa. Nitafanya hivyo.**
Sah-wah. Nee-tah-*fah*-nyah *hee*-vyoh.
Okay. I'll do that.

Travis: **Haya. Nitakupigia simu kabla ya kuondoka.**
Hah-yah. Nee-tah-koo-pee-*gee*-ah *see*-moo kah-*b*-lah yah koo-oh-*ndoh*-kah.
Alright. I will call you before I leave.

Sara: **Asante sana. Tutaonana.**
Ah-sah-*n*-teh *sah*-nah. Too-tah-oh-*nah*-nah
Thanks. See you.

Travis: **Sawa. Kwaheri.**
Sah-wah. Kwah-*heh*-ree.
Okay. Goodbye.

• •

WORDS TO KNOW

nguo ya kuogelea	*ngoo*-oh yah koo-oh-geh-*leh*-ah	swimming suit
miwani ya jua	mee-*wah*-nee yah *joo*-ah	sunglasses
mpango	m-*pah*-ngoh	a plan
kuogelea	koo-oh-geh-*leh*-ah	to swim

You'd use more formal language with business or official appointments. Here are some important phrases to remember.

» **mkutano** (m-koo-*tah*-noh) (*meeting*)

» **miadi** (mee-*ah*-dee) (*appointment*)

» **ratiba** (rah-*tee*-bah) (*schedule*)

» **Una nafasi siku gani?** (*oo*-nah nah-*fah*-see *see*-koo *gah*-nee) (*On what day do you have time?*)

» **Ningependa tukutane** (nee-ngeh-*peh*-ndah too-koo-*tah*-neh) (*I'd like us to meet.*)

» **Naomba fursa ya kukutana nawe** (nah-*oh*-mbah *foo*-rsah yah koo-koo-*tah*-nah *nah*-weh) (*I'd like a time slot to meet with you*)

Talkin' the Talk

AUDIO ONLINE

Tamara is calling Wema Trust, an NGO based in Kajiajo North to make an appointment.

Tamara: **Habari za asubuhi? Ninazungumza na mtu kutoka Wema Trust?**
Hah-*bah*-ree zah ah-soo-*boo*-hee? Nee-nah-zoo-ngoo-m-zah nah *m*-too koo-*toh*-kah Wema Trust?
Good morning! Am I speaking with someone from Wema Trust?

Juliana: **Nzuri sana. Ndiyo, Ninaitwa Juliana. Niko mapokezi. Nikusaidiaje?**
N-*zoo*-ree *sah*-nah. *Ndee*-yoh, nee-nah-*ee*-twah Joo-lee-*ah*-nah. *Nee*-koh mah-poh-*keh*-zee. Nee-koo-sah-ee-dee-*eh*-jeh?
I am doing well. Yes, my name is Juliana. I am at the reception. How can I help you?

Tamara: **Ninaiwa Tamara. Ninatoka Marekani. Ningependa kujitolea.**
Nee-nah-*ee*-twah Tah-*mah*-rah. Nee-nah-*toh*-kah Mah-reh-*kah*-nee. Nee-ngeh-*peh*-ndah koo-jee-toh-*leh*-ah.
My name is Tamara. I am from the United States. I would like to volunteer.

CHAPTER 9 **Using Technology to Keep in Touch**   165

Juliana:	**Nimefurahi kukufahamu Tamara. Karibu sana Wema Trust.**
	Nee-meh-foo-*rah*-hee koo-koo-fah-*hah*-moo Tah-*mah*-rah. Kah-*ree*-boo sah-nah Weh-mah Trust.
	I am happy to meet you, Tamara. Welcome to Wema Trust.
Tamara:	**Asante sana. Ninaweza kuzungumza na mkurugenzi?**
	Ah-sah-*n*-teh *sah*-nah. Nee-nah-*weh*-zah koo-zoo-ngoo-*m*-zah nah m-koo-roo-*geh*-nzee?
	Thank you very much. May I speak with the director?
Juliana:	**Mkurugenzi hayupo. Amesafiri lakini atarudi wiki ijayo.**
	M-koo-roo-*geh*-nzee hah-*yoo*-poh. Ah-meh-sah-*fee*-ree lah-*kee*-nee ah-tah-*roo*-dee *wee*-kee ee-*jah*-yoh.
	The director is not around. She is travelling but will be back next week.
Tamara:	**Ninaweza kumwachia ujumbe?**
	Nee-nah-*weh*-zah koo-mwah-*chee*-ah oo-*joo*-mbeh?
	Can I leave a message for her?
Juliana:	**Ndiyo. Au kama unataka kuonana naye ninaweza kukuwekea miadi.**
	Ndee-yoh. *Ah*-oo *kah*-mah oo-nah-*tah*-kah koo-oh-*nah*-nah *nah*-yeh nee-nah-*weh*-zah koo-koo-weh-*keh*-ah mee-*ah*-dee.
	Yes. Or if you want to meet with her, I can book an appointment for you.
Tamara:	**Wazo zuri sana. Ningependa tukutane Jumatatu. Kuna nafasi saa ngapi?**
	Wah-zoh *zoo*-ree *sah*-nah. Nee-ngeh-*peh*-ndah too-koo-*tah*-neh Joo-mah-*tah*-too. *Koo*-nah nah-*fah*-see *sah*-ah *ngah*-pee?
	That's a good idea. I'd like us to meet on Monday. What time is available?
Juliana:	**Sawa. Unaweza kukutana naye Jumatatu saa mbili asubuhi. Nitamjulisha.**
	Sah-wah. Oo-nah-*weh*-zah koo-koo-*tah*-nah *nah*-yeh Joo-mah-*tah*-too *sah*-ah *mbee*-lee ah-soo-*boo*-hee. Nee-tah-m-joo-*lee*-shah.
	Okay. You can meet with her on Monday at 8am. I will let her know.
Tamara:	**Asante sana.**
	Ah-*sah*-nteh *sah*-nah.
	Thank you very much.

WORDS TO KNOW		
wazo	*wah*-zoh	idea
miadi	mee-*ah*-dee	appointment
kujiitolea	koo-jee-toh-*leh*-ah	to volunteer
ujumbe	oo-*joo*-mbeh	message
kujulisha	koo-joo-*lee*-shah	to let (sb) know

Staying Informed through the Internet

How do you keep up with world news? If you are one of those people who rely on the Internet to stay informed and stay up to date, then the **intaneti** (ee-ntah-neh-tee) (*Internet*) is your best friend. Depending on your preference, you can scroll to watch breaking news or socialize with your friends and family from all over the world. Read through this section to get started with basic technology terms, email vocabulary, and social media terminology.

Familiarizing yourself with basic technology terms

The first step to navigating communication through the Internet is learning important terminology. Here are some basic technology terms to get you started.

>> **mtandao** (m-tah-*ndah*-oh) (*network*)

>> **intaneti** (ee-ntah-*neh*-tee) (*Internet*)

>> **barua pepe** (bah-*roo*-ah *peh*-peh) (*email*)

>> **tovuti** (toh-*voo*-tee) (*website*)

>> **kiungo** (kee-*oo*-ngoh) (*link*)

>> **nywila/neno la siri** (*nywee*-lah/*neh*-noh lah *see*-ree) (*password*)

>> **mtandao wa kijamii** (m-tah-*ndah*-oh wah kee-*jah*-mee) (*social media*)

>> **kompyuta/tarakilishi** (koh-*mpyoo*-tah/tah-rah-kee-*lee*-shee) (*computer*)

>> **kalenda** (kah-*leh*-ndah) (*calendar*)

>> **mubashara** (moo-bah-*shah*-rah) (*live*)

» **mlio** (m-*lee*-oh) (*ringtone*)

» **simu janja** (*see*-moo *jah*-njah) (*smartphone*)

» **hati miliki** (*hah*-tee mee-*lee*-kee) (*copyright*)

» **digitali** (dee-gee-*tah*-lee) (*digital*)

» **kikashani** (kee-kah-*shah*-nee) (*inbox*)

» **pakua** (pah-*koo*-ah) (*download*)

» **pakia**(pah-*kee*-ah) (*upload*)

» **teknolojia ya habari** (teh-k-noh-loh-*jee*-ah yah hah-*bah*-ree) (*information technology*)

» **habari za hivi punde** (hah-*bah*-ree zah *hee*-vee *poo*-ndeh) (*breaking news*)

Engaging over email

When it comes to doing business, you can't escape sending and receiving emails as snail mail is too slow, and phone calls aren't always convenient. Besides, emails are a great way to keep a record of your communication! All of our retired friends prefer communicating over email, too, so sending informal emails is also an important skill to learn.

If you're sending a business email, address the recipient as

» **Bwana. . ./Bw. . .** (*bwah*-nah) (*Mister . . ./Mr. . .*)

» **Bibi . . ./Bi. . .** (*bee*-bee/bee) (*Miss/Ms./Mrs.*)

If it's an email to a friend or family member, use terms of endearment such as

» **Mpendwa Mama/Baba** (m-*peh*-ndwah *mah*-mah/*bah*-bah) (*Dearest mother/father*)

» **Mpenzi wangu Lulu** (m-*peh*-nzee *wah*-ngoo Lulu) (*My love, Lulu*) [to a boyfriend/girlfriend/wife/husband]

» **Mpendwa . . .** (m-*peh*-ndwah . . .) (*Dearest [name]*)

» **Rafiki mpendwa** (rah-*fee*-kee m-*peh*-ndwah) (*Dearest friend*)

Choose an appropriate greeting to use depending on whether you're writing a formal or informal email. Check out Chapter 2 for formal and informal greetings to use.

To close your business email, choose one of these phrases:

>> **Wako** (*wah*-koh) (*Yours*)

>> **Wako mwaminifu** (*wah*-koh m-wah-mee-*nee*-foo) (*Yours sincerely*)

>> **Natanguliza shukrani** (nah-tah-ngoo-*lee*-zah shoo-*kra*-nee) (*thanks in advance*)

Close your informal email in a more friendly tone using one of the following:

>> **Mwanako akupendaye** (m-wah-*nah*-koh ah-koo-peh-*ndah*-yeh) (*Your loving child*)

>> **Mpenzi wako daima** (m-*peh*-nzee *wah*-koh dah-ee-mah) (*Your forever love*)

>> **Rafiki yako** (rah-*fee*-kee *yah*-koh) (*Your friend*)

>> **Ni mimi,** (nee *mee*-mee) (*It's me,*)

>> **Kila la kheri** (*kee*-lah lah *kheh*-ree) (*best wishes*)

>> **Shukrani nyingi** (shoo-*krah*-nee *nyee*-ngee) (*many thanks*)

Socializing on social media

Have you ever stopped to imagine what would happen if all social media platforms were shut down for a few days? If you're a 90s baby or younger, you'd probably think that it would be hard for some people to cope — and you'd probably be right! In this era of science and technology, people use **mitandao ya kijamii** (mee-tah-ndah-oh yah kee-*jah*-mee) (*social media*) to communicate with their friends, families, and fans. To communicate this way in a Swahili context, you'll need to know the following words and phrases:

>> **urafiki** (oo-rah-*fee*-kee) (*friendship*)

>> **mwaliko** (mwah-*lee*-koh) (*invitation*)

>> **ujumbe wa moja kwa moja** (oo-*joo*-mbeh wah *moh*-jah kwah *moh*-jah) (*direct message*)

>> **ombi la urafiki** (*oh*-mbee lah oo-rah-*fee*-kee) (*friend request*)

>> **maoni** (mah-*oh*-nee) (*comments*)

>> **bofya** (*boh*-fyah) (*click*)

>> **acha maoni** (*ah*-chah mah-*oh*-nee) (*leave a comment*)

» **programu tumishi** (pro-g-*rah*-moo too-*mee*-shee) (*application/program*)

» **haipatikani** (hah-ee-pah-tee-*kah*-nee) (*is not available/reachable*)

» **alika** (ah-*lee*-kah) (*invite*)

» **haipo hewani** (hah-*ee*-poh heh-*wah*-nee) (*is not online*)

» **kamera** (kah-*meh*-rah) (*camera*)

» **spika** (*spee*-kah) (*speaker*)

» **video** (vee-*deh*-oh) (*video*)

FUN & GAMES

Sort the following phrases into the correct email inbox: B or C.

i. Mambo!

ii. Shikamoo!

iii. Mpenzi wangu,

iv. Wako mwaminifu,

v. Bw. Otieno,

vi. Mpenzi wako daima

B: <u>Your spouse</u>	C: <u>Your new business partner</u>

Chapter **10**
Shopping Made Easy

D id you know that farming is the leading economic activity in East Africa? Most families depend on fresh produce from their land for food, and whatever they don't consume goes to the **soko** (soh-koh) (*market*). You're, therefore, sure to find a dizzying spread of organic produce in every market you visit. This chapter introduces you to the language used in markets as well as to the delicate art of buying and bargaining with sellers at flea markets.

Shopping at Flea Markets

One of the best ways to experience Swahili culture is by shopping at flea markets. These are open-air markets that operate on a schedule such as weekends only, evenings only, or twice a week. It's a one-of-a-kind opportunity to window-shop and purchase a range of merchandise at relatively reasonable costs. Goods sold at flea markets include **matunda** (mah-*too*-ndah) (*fruits*), **mboga** (m-*boh*-gah) (*vegetables*), **nyama** (*nyah*-mah) (*meat*), **viungo** (vee-*un*-goh) (*spices*), **nguo** (*ngoo*-oh) (*clothes*), and so on. (The range of goods offered differentiates them from the many so-called "farmer's markets" found in the United States.) Make sure you buy fruits, vegetables, spices, or souvenirs to enrich your experience. Read on to find out how to navigate flea markets in East Africa.

Buying fruits

When you get an opportunity to visit any Swahili-speaking country make sure you go to the local **soko** (*soh*-koh) (*market*) and buy some fresh fruits. (Your tastebuds will thank you!) First, you'll need to know the names of the **matunda** (mah-*too*-ndah) (*fruits*) being offered. Here's a helpful list:

>> **parachichi** (pah-rah-*chee*-chee) (*avocado*)

>> **embe** (*eh*-mbeh) (*mango*)

>> **tikiti maji** (tee-*kee*-tee *mah*-jee) (*watermelon*)

>> **chungwa** (*choo*-ngwah) (*orange*)

>> **nanasi** (nah-*nah*-see) (*pineapple*)

>> **ndizi** (*ndee*-zee) (*banana*)

>> **fenesi** (feh-*neh*-see) (*jackfruit*)

>> **papai** (pah-*pah*-ee) (*papaya*)

>> **chenza** (cheh-*n*-zah) (*tangerine*)

>> **peasi** (peh-*ah*-see) (*pear*)

>> **zabibu** (zah-*bee*-boo) (*grapes*)

>> **tofaa/tufaha** (toh-*fah*-ah/too-*fah*-ha) (*apple*)

>> **stroberi** (stroh-*beh*-ree) (*strawberry*)

>> **pasheni** (pah-*sheh*-nee) (*passion fruit*)

>> **pera** (*peh*-rah) (*guava*)

>> **tunda damu** (*too*-ndah *dah*-moo) (*tamarillo/tree tomato*)

>> **ndimu** (*ndee*-moo) (*lime*)

>> **limao** (lee-*mah*-oh) (*lemon*)

>> **fenesi** (feh-*neh*-see) (*jackfruit*)

If a particular fruit catches your eye, approach the seller and say one of the following:

>> **Unauzaje fenesi?** (oo-*nah*-oo-*zah*-jeh feh-*neh*-see) (*How much is a jackfruit?* [literally: *how do you sell the jackfruit?*])

>> **Fenesi ni bei gani?** (feh-*neh*-see nee *beh*-ee *gah*-nee) (*What's the price for the jackfruit?*)

174 **PART 2** *Swahili in Action*

The seller will state a price by stating **Fenesi ni shilingi sabini** (feh-*neh*-see nee shee-*lee*-ngee sah-*bee*-nee) (*The jackfruit is seventy shillings*), for example. If that price is agreeable to you, ask for the number of fruits you'd like to buy. Say one of the following:

>> **Naomba fenesi mbili.** (nah-*oh*-mbah feh-*neh*-see *moh*-jah) (*I'd like one jackfruit.*)

>> **Nitachukua fenesi moja.** (nee-tah-choo-*koo*-ah feh-*neh*-see *moh*-jah) (*I'll take one jackfruit.*)

Getting vegetables

The following **mboga** (*mboh*-gah) (*vegetables*) are commonly found in the **soko**:

>> **karoti** (kah-*roh*-tee) (*carrot*)

>> **brokoli** (broh-*koh*-lee) (*broccoli*)

>> **kitunguu** (kee-too-*ngoo*-oo) (*onion*)

>> **pilipili hoho** (pee-lee-*pee*-lee *hoh*-hoh) (*bell pepper*)

>> **biringanya** (bee-ree-*ngah*-nyah) (*eggplant*)

>> **kabichi** (kah-*bee*-chee) (*cabbage*)

>> **sukuma wiki** (soo-*koo*-mah *wee*-kee) (*collard greens*)

>> **spinachi** (spee-*nah*-chee) (*spinach*)

>> **nyanya** (*nyah*-nyah) (*tomato*)

>> **tango** (*tah*-ngoh) (*cucumber*)

>> **dania** (*dah*-nee-ah) (*coriander*)

>> **kitunguu saumu** (kee-too-*ngoo*-oo sah-*oo*-moo) (*garlic*)

>> **bamia** (bah-*mee*-ah) (*okra*)

>> **figili** (fee-*gee*-lee) (*celery*)

>> **kiazi sukari** (kee-*ah*-zee soo-*kah*-ree) (*beetroot*)

>> **magimbi** (mah-*gee*-mbee) (*arrow root*)

>> **muhogo** (moo-*hoh*-goh) (*cassava*)

>> **kiazi** (kee-*ah*-zee) (potato) **viazi** (vee-*ah*-zee) (*potatoes*)

>> **kiazi kitamu** (kee-*ah*-zee kee-*tah*-moo) (*sweet potato*)

>> **pilipili hoho** (pee-lee-*pee*-lee *hoh*-hoh) (*green, red, yellow pepper*)

Talkin' the Talk

AUDIO ONLINE

Jim is visiting Kariakoo (the biggest market in Dar Es Salaam, Tanzania). He decides to buy **matunda** (*fruits*) and **mboga** (*vegetables*) from a **mwuzaji** (mw-oo-*zah*-jee) (*seller*).

Mwuzaji: **Karibu sana. Unataka nini?**
Kah-*ree*-boo *sah*-nah. Oo-nah-*tah*-kah *nee*-nee?
Welcome! What would you like?

Jim: **Asante sana! Ninataka maparachichi na maembe.**
Ah-*san*-teh sah-nah! Nee-nah-*tah*-kah mah-pah-rah-*chee*-chee nah mah-*eh*-mbeh.
Thank you very much! I need avocados and mangoes.

Mwuzaji: **Sawa. Unahitaji mboga pia?**
Sah-wah. Oo-nah-hee-*tah*-jee *mboh*-gah *pee*-ah?
Okay. Do you need vegetables, too?

Jim: **Ndiyo! Ninahitaji karoti, pilipili hoho, nyanya, na vitunguu.**
Ndee-yoh! Nee-nah-hee-*tah*-jee kah-*roh*-tee, pee-lee-*pee*-lee *hoh*-hoh nah vee-*too*-ngoo.
Yes! I need carrots, green peppers, tomatoes, and onions.

Mwuzaji: **Matunda na mboga hizi hapa. Karibu tena**
Mah-*too*-ndah nah *mboh*-gah *hee*-zee *hah*-pah. Kah-*ree*-boo teh-nah.
Here are the fruits and vegetables. Come again.

Jim: **Asante. Kwaheri.**
Ah-*sah*-nteh. Kwah-*heh*-ree-nee.
Thanks. Goodbye.

Purchasing meat

If you want to buy **nyama** (*nyah*-mah) (*meat*), then you want to go to **buchani** (boo-*chah*-nee) (*butcher shop*) to get them. If you only want to purchase **samaki** (sah-*mah*-kee) (*fish*) go to **soko la samaki** (*soh*-koh lah sah-*mah*-kee) (*fish market*). Here's a list of the different meats available at a **buchani**:

» **nyama ya kuku** (*nyah*-mah yah *koo*-koo) (*chicken*)

» **nyama ya mbuzi** (*nyah*-mah yah *mboo*-zee) (*goat*)

» **nyama ya kondoo** (*nyah*-mah yah koh-*ndoh*-oh) (*lamb*)

» **nyama ya ngómbe** (*nyah*-mah yah *ngóh*-mbeh) (*beef*)

» **nyama ya nguruwe/kitimoto** (*nyah*-mah yah ng-oo-*roo*-weh/kee-tee-*moh*-toh) (*pork*)

» **nyama ya bata** (*nyah*-mah yah *bah*-tah) (*duck*)

» **nyama ya bata mzinga** (*nyah*-mah yah *bah*-tah mh-*zee*-ngah) (*turkey*)

» **nyama ya sungura** (*nyah*-mah yah soo-*ngoo*-rah) (*rabbit*)

» **utumbo** (oo-*too*-mboh) (*tripe*)

If your tastes run more to seafood, here's a list of the kinds of seafood you'd find in a **samaki**:

» **uduvi** (oo-*doo*-vee) (*shrimp*)

» **kambale** (kah-*mbah*-leh) (*catfish*)

» **chaza** (*chah*-zah) (*oyster*)

» **pweza** (*pweh*-zah) (*octopus*)

» **ngisi** (*ngee*-see) (*squid*)

» **kaa** (*kah*-ah) (*crab*)

» **samakigamba** (sah-mah-kee-*gah*-mbah) (*shellfish*)

» **sato** (*sah*-toh) (*tilapia*)

Adding spices to your list

You cannot claim to have experienced Swahili culture without indulging in its rich variety of spices. Afterall, the Spice Island, Zanzibar, ensures that the whole region forever stays immersed in aromatic spicy food. If you're adventurous, include the following **viungo** (vee-*oo*-ngoh) (*spices*) in your shopping list

» **masala ya pilau** (mah-*sah*-lah yah pee-*lah*-oo) (*pilau masala*)

» **masala ya chai** (mah-*sah*-lah yah *chah*-ee) (*chai masala*)

» **iliki** (ee-*lee*-kee) (*cardamom*)

» **mdalasini** (mh-dah-*lah*-see-nee) (*cinnamon*)

» **manjano** (mah-*njah*-noh) (*turmeric*)

» **tangawizi** (tah-ngah-*wee*-zee) *(ginger)*

» **pilipili kichaa** (pee-lee-*pee*-lee kee-*chah*-ah) *(bird's eye pepper)*

» **pilipili mbuzi** (pee-lee-*pee*-lee *mboo*-zee) *(habanero peppers)*

» **pilipili kali** (pee-lee-*pee*-lee *kah*-lee) *(chili pepper)*

» **karafuu** (kah-*rah*-foo) *(cloves)*

» **jira** (*jee*-rah) *(cumin)*

» **mchaichai** (mh-chah-ee-*chah*-ee) *(lemongrass)*

» **pilipili manga** (pee-lee-*pee*-lee *mah*-ngah) *(black pepper)*

» **chumvi** (*choo*-mvee) *(salt)*

Understanding units of measurement

A lot of the goods you'll find at flea markets do not come pre-packaged. They are, after all, fresh farm produce sold mostly sold by the farmers themselves. This means that, as a buyer, you won't have a label to look at to determine the amount you're buying. Instead, you'll have to direct the seller on how much you need, and they'll measure that amount for you. Here are some common units of **kipimo** (kee-*pee*-moh) *(measurement)* at the market setting:

» **Kilo** (kee-loh) [*kilogram* (kg) for weight.]

» **Nusu kilo** (noo-soo kee-loh) *(half a kilo)*

» **Robo kilo** (*roh*-boh *kee*-loh) *(quarter)*

» **Robo tatu** (*roh*-boh *tah*-too) *(three quarters)*

» **Lita** (*lee*-tah) [*liter* (l), for volume]

» **Mita** (*mee*-tah) [*meter* (m), for length]

Other units of measurement may include

» **Sentimita** (seh-ntee-*mee*-tah) [*centimeter)* (cm), for length]

» **Mililita** (mee-lee-*lee*-tah) [*milliliter* (ml), for volume]

» **Gramu** (g-*rah*-moo) [*gram* (g), for weight]

» **Doti** (*doh*-tee) *(pair, for fabric)*

» **Fungu** (*foo*-ngoo) (*pile*)

Vegetables such as tomatoes, sweet potatoes, and small sized fruits like oranges, lemons are usually sold in "piles" of three or four. For example, a seller would say "20 shillings "for one pile." They will be arranged in piles as well.

» **Pakiti** (pah-*kee*-tee) (*packet*)

» **Dazeni** (dah-*zeh*-nee) (*dozen*)

The idea is to combine a unit of measurement with whatever you want to buy. For example,

» **Sukari kilo moja** (soo-*kah*-ree *kee*-loh *moh*-jah) (*one kilo of sugar*)

» **Mafuta lita tano** (mah-*foo*-tah *lee*-tah *tah*-noh) (*five liters of cooking oil*)

» **Kanga doti mbili** (*kah*-ngah *doh*-tee *mbee*-lee) (*two pairs of kanga — a colorful, preprinted cloth especially popular in East Africa*)

The **kanga** is usually sold in pairs. The piece of cloth has a clear border separating it from the next one where a buyer can cut it to wear as head and shoulder cover and skirt if they wish.

» **Karoti fungu moja** (kah-*roh*-tee *foo*-ngoo *moh*-jah) (*one pile of carrots*)

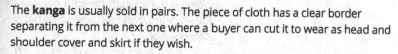

Talkin' the Talk

Tetiana is in the Nairobi Central Business District (popularly known as CBD), and she decides to stop at the City Market to purchase some spices and meat from the mwuzaji.

Tetiana: **Kuna nyama ya ngo'mbe?**
Koo-nah *nyah*-mah yah *ngóh*-mbeh?
Do you have beef?

Muuzaji: **Ndiyo. Unataka kilo ngapi?**
Ndee-yoh. Oo-nah-*tah*-kah *kee*-loh *ngah*-pee?
Yes. How many kilos do you want?

Tetiana: **Ninataka kilo tatu.**
Nee-nah-*tah*-kah *kee*-loh *tah*-too.
I need three kilos.

Muuzaji: **Kitu kingine?**
Kee-too kee-*ngee*-nee?
Anything else?

Tetiana:	**Ninataka samakigamba pia.**
	Nee-nah-*tah*-kah sah-*mah*-kee-gah-mbah *pee*-ah.
	I also need shellfish.

Muuzaji:	**kilo ngapi?**
	Sah-*mah*-kee *kee*-loh *ngah*-pee?
	How many kilos?

Tetiana:	**kilo moja**
	kee-loh *moh*-jah
	One kilo.

Muuzaji:	**Sawa. Kuna viungo pia kama unataka.**
	Sah-wah. *Koo*-nah vee-oo-ngoh *pee*-ah *kah*-mah
	oo-nah-*tah*-kah.
	Alright. We have spices, too, if you want.

Tetiana:	**Ndiyo. Ninataka pilipili manga, karafuu, tangawizi, na kitunguu saumu**
	Ndee-yoh. Nee-nah-*tah*-kah pee-lee-*pee*-lee *mah*-ngah,
	kah-*rah*-foo, tah-ngah-*wee*-zee, nah *kee*-too-ngoo
	sah-*oo*-moo.
	Yes. I need black pepper, cloves, ginger, and garlic.

Muuzaji:	**Sawasawa. Nyama, samaki na viungo hivi hapa. Karibu tena.**
	Sah-wah-*sah*-wah. *Nyah*-mah sah-*mah*-kee nah vee-*too*-
	ngoo hee-vee *hah*-pah. Kah-*ree*-boo *teh*-nah.
	Alright. Here is your meat, fish, and spices.Come again
	[literally; welcome again.]

Tetiana:	**Asante, kwaheri.**
	Ah-*sah*-nteh, kwah-*heh*-ree.
	Thanks, goodbye.

• •

Dealing with Money

As a foreigner in East Africa, it is important to be aware of the local currency and exchange rates. We recommend that you exchange money at a bank or authorized money exchange center, as this is the safest and most reliable way to obtain local currency. Be aware of any fees associated with exchanging money, as well as any restrictions on the amount of money that you can exchange at one time.

TIP

Avoid walking around with a lot of cash because it can make you a target for criminals; as a foreigner you may be perceived as an easy target for robbery.

Dealing with Kenyan and Tanzanian currencies

It is important to understand currencies in East African countries, especially Tanzania and Kenya. The Kenyan Shilling (KES) is the official currency of Kenya and comes in the following denominations:

» **shilingi tano** (shee-*lee*-ngee *tah*-no) (*five shillings*)

» **shilingi kumi** (shee-*lee*-ngee *koo*-mee) (*ten shillings*)

» **shilingi ishirini** (shee-*lee*-ngee ee-shee-*ree*-nee) (*twenty shillings*)

» **shilingi hamsini**) (shee-*lee*-ngee ha-m-*see*-nee) (*fifty shillings*)

» **shilingi mia** (shee-*lee*-ngee *mee*-ah) (*a hundred shillings*)

» **shilingi mia tano** (shee-*lee*-ngee *mee*-ah *tah*-noh) (*five hundred shillings*)

» **shilingi elfu moja** (shee-*lee*-ngee eh-*l*-foo-*moh*-jah) (*one thousand shillings*)

The Tanzanian Shilling (TZS) is the official currency of Tanzania. The currency is available in coins and banknotes. The denominations of coins are as follows:

» **shilingi hamsini** (shee-*lee*-ngee ha-m-*see*-nee) (*fifty shillings*)

» **shilingi mia** (shee-*lee*-ngee *mee*-ah) (*a hundred shillings*)

» **shilingi mia mbili** (shee-*lee*-ngee *mee*-ah *mbee*-lee) (*two hundred shillings*)

» **shilingi mia tano**) (shee-*lee*-ngee *mee*-ah *tah*-noh) (*five hundred shillings*)

The banknotes used are

» **shilingi elfu moja** (shee-*lee*-ngee eh-*l*-foo-*moh*-jah) (*one thousand shillings*)

» **shilingi elfu mbili** (shee-*lee*-ngee eh-*l*-foo-*mbee*-lee) (*two thousand shillings*)

» **shilingi elfu tano** (shee-*lee*-ngee eh-*l*-foo *tah*-noh) (*five thousand shillings*)

» **shilingi elfu kum**i (shee-*lee*-ngee eh-*l*-foo *koo*-mee) (*ten thousand shillings*)

MANAGING MOBILE MONEY TRANSACTIONS

Dealing with money in a foreign country can be a bit of a challenge, especially if you are used to paying your bills with your debit or credit card. Many shops don't accept such cards, but thanks to technology, you can often use your mobile phone to transfer money or pay your bills. If you ever find yourself in Tanzania, Kenya, Uganda, or any other African country, look into one of the many different mobile money services — such as M-Pesa, Tigo Pesa, Airtel Money, and Halopesa — you can use to handle transactions. These money services make it easier for people to pay their bills or transfer money from their bank account securely.

Asking for prices

If you're unfamiliar with how one goes about buying items at a Swahili-speaking store or market, you might find it odd that prices aren't listed. You'll need to ask a seller how much that **matunda, mboga,** or whatever else you wish to buy costs. Although it may seem frustrating at first, it is a great way to learn about cultural differences and may be quite enjoyable.

There are different ways of asking sellers for the **bei** (*beh-ee*) (*price*) of an item. Choose any of the following:

>> **Ni bei gani?** (nee *beh-ee gah-nee?*) (*What's the price*)

>> **Ni shilingi ngapi?** (nee shee-*lee*-ngee *ngah-pee?*) (*How many shillings is it?*)

>> **Ni pesa ngapi?** (nee *peh-sah ngah-pee*) (*How much is it?*)

>> **Unauzaje?** (oo-nah-oo-*zah*-jeh) (*How much are you asking for it? — Literally, "How do you sell it?"*)

Bargaining with sellers

Now that you know your **matunda** (*fruits*), **mboga** (*vegetables*), **nyama** (*meat*), and **viungo** (*spices*) in Swahili, it's time for you to practice your bargaining skills in order to get the best deal for goods and services. You, as a buyer, will have to start the conversation by making an initial offer, followed by a counteroffer from the seller, and then an exchange of offers until you both reach an agreement.

In East Africa, bargaining is an integral part of the culture and is a tradition that has been passed down through generations. It is a way of life that is based on mutual respect and trust and is used to get the best deal possible. Bargaining is seen as a way to build relationships and foster trust between buyers and sellers and is a common practice in the region.

If you perceive an item to be **ghali** (*ghah*–lee) (*expensive*) you can ask the seller to **punguza bei** (poo–*ngoo*–zah beh–ee) (*lower the price*)

Talkin' the Talk

At Kilombero market in Arusha, Tanzania, Ann is bargaining with the **mwuzaji** (*seller*) for the best prices on fruits and vegetables. She is an expert negotiator!

Mwuzaji:	**Karibu! Karibu!** Kah-*ree*-boo! Kah-*ree*-boo! *Welcome!*
Ann:	**Asante. Mapapai matano ni shilingi ngapi?** Ah-*sah*-nteh. Mah-pah-*pah*-ee mah-*tah*–noh nee shee-*lee*-nn-gee nn-*gah*-pee? *Thanks. How much are the five papayas?*
Mwuzaji:	**Ni Shilingi mia tano.** Nee shee-lee-nn-gee *mee*-ah tah-*noh* *It's five hundred shillings.*
Ann:	**Na boga ni bei gani?** Nah *boh*-gah nee *beh*-ee *gah*-nee? *And how much is the pumpkin?*
Mwuzaji:	**Shilingi mia tano.** Shee-lee-nn-gee *mee*-ah *tah*-no. *Five hundred shillings.*
Ann:	**Ni ghali sana! Punguza bei tafadhali!** Nee *gah*-lee *sah*-nah! Poo-nn-*goo*-zah *beh*-ee tah-fah-*dhah*-lee *That's very expensive! Lower the price please.*
Mwuzaji:	**Haipungui. Bei ni rahisi sana. Hakuna. Faida.** Hah-ee-poo-nn-*goo*-ee. *Beh*-ee nee rah-*hee*-see *sah*-nah. Hah-*koo*-nah. Fah-*ee*-dah. *The price can't be lowered. It's a very cheap price. No profit.*

Ann:	**Ninataka vitunguu vitano pia**
	Nee-nah-*tah*-kah *vee*-too-nn-goo vee-*tah*-noh *pee*-ah
	I also want five onions.

Mwuzaji:	**Sawa, vitunguu vitano ni shilingi mia tano lakini nitakuuzia kwa shilingi mia tatu.**
	Sah-wah, *vee*-too-nn-goo vee-*tah*-noh nee *shee*-lee-nngee *mee*-ah *tah*-no lah-*kee*-nee nee-tah-*koo*-zee-ah kwah *shee*-lee-nngee *mee*-ah *tah*-too.
	Alright. Five onions cost five hundred shillings, but I will sell it for three hundred.

Ann:	**Jumla bei gani?**
	Joo-*m*-lah nee *beh*-ee *gah*-nee?
	How much is the total?

Mwuzaji:	**Jumla ni shilingi elfu moja mia tatu.**
	Joo-*m*-lah nee *shee*-lee-ngee eh-*ll*-foo *moh*-jah *mee*-ah *tah*-too
	The total is one thousand three hundred.

Ann:	**Sawa, pesa hii hapa!**
	Sah-wah, *peh*-sah hee *hah*-pah.
	Okay. Here is the money.

Mwuzaji:	**Asante sana. Karibu tena!**
	Ah-sah-*n*-teh *sah*-nah. Kah-*ree*-boo *teh*-nah.
	Thank you very much. Come back again (literally, Welcome back again.)

• •

WORDS TO KNOW

bei	*beh*-ee	price
faida	fah-*ee*-dah	profit also maslahi (mah-slah-hee)
punguza	poo-*ngoo*-zah	lower/decrease
pesa/hela	*peh*-sah/*heh*-lah	money
jumla	joo-*m*-lah	total
-uza	*oo*-zah	sell
ghali	*ghah*-lee	expensive
bei rahisi	beh-ee rah-*hee*-see	cheap

Delving into Comparative Adjectives

Comparative adjectives compare the qualities of two or more things. In Swahili, they are formed by adding prefixes — **m-**, **ma-**, **vi-**, **ki-**, **pa-** and so on — to the adjectives. The basic form of these adjectives are as follows:

>> **zuri** (*zoo*-ree) (*nice, good*)

>> **kubwa** (*koo*-bwah) (*big*)

>> **dogo** (*doh*-goh) (*small*)

>> **eusi** (eh-*oo*-see) (*black*)

>> **eupe** (eh-*oo*-peh) (*white*)

>> **ekundu** (eh-*koo*-ndoo) (*red*)

>> **epesi** (eh-*peh*-see) (*light*)

>> **chungu** (*choo*-ngoo) (*bitter*)

>> **tamu** (*tah*-moo) (*sweet*)

>> **refu** (*reh*-foo) (*tall*)

>> **fupi** (*foo*-pee) (*short*)

>> **ghali** (*ghah*-lee) (*expensive*)

>> **rahisi** (*rah*-hee-see) (*cheap*)

Swahili uses the word **kuliko** (koo–*lee*–koh) (*than*) to compare things. For example,

>> **Yeye ni mrefu kuliko kaka yake.** (*yeh*-yeh nee m-*reh*-foo koo-*lee*-koh kah-kah *yah*-keh) (*He is taller than his brother.*)

>> **Maembe ni matamu kuliko malimao.** (mah-*eh*-mbeh nee mah-*tah*-moo koo-*lee*-koh mah-lee-*mah*-oh) (*Mangoes are sweeter than lemons.*)

>> **Viatu vyako ni vizuri kuliko vyangu.** (vee-*ah*-too *vyah*-koh nee vee-*zoo*-ree koo-*lee*-koh *vyah*-ngoo) (*His/her shoes are nicer than mine.*)

>> **mananasi ni ghali Zaidi kuliko machungwa** (mah-nah-*nah*-see nee *ghah*-lee zah-*ee*-dee koo-*lee*-koh mah-*chung*-wah) (*Pineapples are more expensive than oranges.*)

>> **ndizi ni bei rahisi kuliko tikiti maji** (*ndee*-zee nee *beh*-ee rah-*hee*-see koo-*lee*-koh tee-*kee*-tee *mah*-jee) (*Bananas are cheaper than watermelons.*)

FUN & GAMES

1. **Match the following word and phrases with their English equivalents.**

i. Punguza bei tafadhali   a. Avocado

ii. Vitunguu ni shilingi ngapi   b. Lower the price please.

iii. Mafungu   c. Green pepper

iv. Pilipili hoho   d. Piles

v. Parachichi   e. How much are the onions

2. **Find the following words in Swahili in the puzzle**

apple	grapes	guava	banana	coconut
lemon	mangoes	avocado	cabbage	spinach
okra	beans	cucumber	tomato	potato
onion	pumpkin			

```
S   W   R   Y   F   R   Y   L   I   P   R   W   U   D   P
Q   B   I   W   E   I   Z   A   N   E   G   V   Q   F   J
R   I   R   H   T   O   F   A   A   R   U   A   M   I   L
O   G   N   A   T   O   X   R   M   A   P   A   M   X   K
I   I   I   N   J   Z   A   C   A   R   B   H   A   X   A
D   Y   Z   B   D   A   G   S   E   D   D   C   H   R   B
S   V   A   B   B   B   O   D   M   D   Z   I   A   P   E
G   C   I   G   S   I   B   I   B   P   C   H   R   D   J
H   F   V   W   L   B   O   K   E   L   E   C   A   O   I
B   G   M   H   E   U   E   W   V   O   W   M   G   G   Q
U   Q   Z   F   N   D   I   L   R   S   N   O   E   S   I
N   D   I   Z   I   G   U   U   G   N   U   T   I   K   H
N   A   E   U   J   P   A   R   A   C   H   I   C   H   I
B   O   B   P   J   N   Y   A   N   Y   A   R   E   E   L
F   P   L   G   O   B   A   M   I   A   G   D   R   L   S
```

Chapter **11**

Dressing Your Best

"Clothes make the man" is a popular saying reminding us that how we dress can influence how other people initially think of us. When it comes to visiting another culture separate from your own, you have to be careful not to offend the locals with how you dress. So, what do you throw in your bag for your East African experience? This section explains things to consider before packing your bags, talks about formal and informal clothing items, and fills you in on the colors in Swahili.

Dressing for Different Occasions and Local Weather

What factors usually come into play when you're deciding what to pack for an extended trip? Or before getting dressed in general? If you're set on traveling to East Africa, it is important that you take into consideration the climate and varying temperatures. Be aware that it isn't always hot and dry in East Africa. Depending on the time of year and location, the weather can range from hot and humid to cold and wet. Did you know that during the cold season (usually July through August), temperatures in parts of Kenya and Tanzania can go as low as 44 degrees F? That's right, so packing for summer only without doing the proper research first might have you freezing and questioning your choices. Also be careful to dress appropriately for each occasion. You don't want to stand out as the clueless foreigner in flip–flops at church or shorts at a wedding.

Here are some suggestions for dressing for different occasions:

- **»** **Harusini** (hah-roo-*see*-nee) (*weddings*):
  - **suti** (*soo*-tee) (*tailored suit*)
  - **gauni** (gah-*oo*-nee) (*dress*)
  - **kanzu** (kah-*n*-zoo) (ankle-length tunic worn by Muslim men)
  - **gauni la kitenge** (gah-*oo*-nee lah kee-*tee*-ngeh) (*a dress made out of kitenge cloth*) The next section explains what kitenge cloth looks like.
  - **sketi ya kitenge** (*skeh*-tee yah kee-*tee*-ngeh) (*a skirt made out of kitenge*)
  - **blauzi ya kitenge** (blah-*oo*-zee yah kee-*tee*-ngeh) (*a blouse made out of kitenge*)

TIP

What works for a wedding in terms of wardrobe choices would work for almost any formal event in East Africa.

- **»** **Shughuli za nje au safari** (shoo-*ghoo*-lee zah *n*-njeh *ah*-oo sah-*fah*-ree) (*outdoor activities or safaris*):
  - **kofia** (koh-*fee*-ah) (*hat*)
  - **fulana** (foo-*lah*-nah) (*t-shirt*)
  - **kaptula** (kah-p-*too*-lah) (*shorts*)
  - **viatu vya kukwea mlimani** (vee-*ah*-too vyah koo-*kweh*-ah m-lee-*mah*-nee) (*hiking shoes*)
  - **suruali** (soo-roo-*ah*-lee) (*pants*)
  - **koti la mvua** (*koh*-tee lah m-*voo*-ah) (*rain coat*)

- **»** **Ufukweni au maeneo ya pwani** (oo-foo-*kweh*-nee ah-oo mah-eh-*neh*-oh yah pwah-nee) (*beach or coastal areas*):
  - **nguo nyepesi** (*ngoo*-oh nyeh-*peh*-see) (*light clothing*)
  - **nguo za kuogelea** (*ngoo*-oh zah koo-oh-geh-*leh*-ah) (*swimwear*)
  - **mafuta ya jua** (mah-*foo*-tah yah *joo*-ah) (*sunscreen*)
  - **miwani ya jua** (mee-*wah*-nee yah *joo*-ah) (*sunglasses*)

Msibani (M-see-*bah*-nee) (*at a funeral*)
  - **kanga** (*kah*-ngah) (*kah-ngah*)

- **kitenge** (kee-*teh*-ngeh) (*kitenge*)

  Keep reading to the next section for descriptions and uses of kanga and kitenge amongst East Africans.

  - **gauni** (gah-oo-nee) (*dress*)
  - **suruali na shati** (soo-roo-*ah*-lee nah *shah*-tee) (*dress pants with a shirt*)
  - **sketi na blauz**i (*skeh*-tee nah blah-oo-zee) (*skirt and a blouse*)

» **Mikutano** (mee-koo-*tah*-noh) (*business meetings and conferences*):

  - **suti** (*soo*-tee) (*suit*)
  - **suruali na shati** (soo-roo-*ah*-lee nah *shah*-tee) (*dress pants with a shirt*)
  - **tai** (*tah*-ee) (*tie*)
  - **gauni** (gah-oo-nee) (*dress*)
  - **sketi na blauzi** (*skeh*-tee nah blah-oo-zee) (*skirt and a blouse*)

Identifying Swahili Cultural Clothing and Their Uses

East Africa is home to hundreds of cultural attires owing to the numerous native tribes living there. However, a few pieces stand out as the whole region has embraced them for various functions. This section introduces you to the three most common cultural clothes of Swahili speakers.

The kanga

The most common type of clothing worn by Swahili people is the **kanga** (kah-ngah) (*kanga*). This is a brightly colored rectangular piece of cloth that is worn around the waist or shoulders, similar to the way you would wear a large scarf over your head and draped down your shoulders or a sarong. The kanga is typically made from cotton and is often decorated with proverbs, sayings, and symbols within and outside of its bold border. It is often used to express a person's feelings, identity, or beliefs. The kanga has various uses such as:

» **kubeba vitu** (koo-*beh*-bah *vee*-too) (*to carry things*)

» **kilemba** (kee-*leh*-mbah) (*a head wrap*)

- **» taulo** (tah-*oo*-loh) (*towel*)

- **» mbeleko** (mbeh-*leh*-koh) (*baby carrier*)

- **» mapazia** (mah-pah-*zee*-ah) *(curtains)*

- **» kitambaa cha meza** (kee-tah-*mbah*-ah chah *meh*-zah) *(table cloth)*

- **» gauni** (gah-*oo*-nee) (*dress*)

- **» zawadi** (zah-*wah*-dee) (*gift*)

- **» sketi** (*skeh*-tee) (*skirt*)

CULTURAL WISDOM

Kanga is traditionally worn by women but is also becoming increasingly popular among men. It is used to communicate messages, such as love, friendship, and respect. For example, a husband can give his wife a kanga that has a proverb about love. Kanga is also used to celebrate special occasions, such as weddings, births, and graduations. Messages on a kanga are not always positive; they can be cautionary or even passive aggressive. In such cases, the wearer would make sure that the person for whom the message was intended would see them. If you thought subs on social media were a new invention, think again!

The shuka

A **shuka** (*shoo*-kah) (*shuka*) is a plaid-patterned rectangular heavy cotton fabric that is traditionally worn by the Maasai community found in Kenya and Tanzania. Men and women drape a **shuka** around their body and accessorize it with elaborate traditional necklaces and belts made of beads and leather. The shuka is durable against the elements, which comes in handy since the Maasai are hunters, warriors, and semi-nomadic. It's common to see men and women wearing bright red **shuka** with faint white stripes, but they also come in bold blue stripes. Other communities have also embraced the **shuka** as an extra layer of cover during chilly days, as a picnic blanket, or as a throw blanket to brighten up their rooms.

The kitenge

Kitenge (kee-*teh*-ngeh) (*kitenge*) is a type of fabric made from cotton and decorated with bright colors and designs. The designs tend to be geometric, floral, or feature animals or other symbols. It is used to make a variety of clothing items, like dresses, skirts, and shirts and is often worn for special occasions like weddings, burial ceremonies, and religious ceremonies. In the recent past, however, more and more fashion-forward East Africans are exploring the use of kitenge in official wear by making skirt suits, pant suits, or blazers out of the material. This trend has even extended to street wear, where shorts, bomber jackets, and sweatshirts now use kitenge cloth.

Introducing Swahili Terms for Types Clothing

In addition to traditional apparel, East Africans also wear more mainstream clothing pieces, especially when there's no special event going on. Expect to see people in regular shirts, jeans, dresses, and so on while undertaking everyday activities such as going to work, to the market, or taking a stroll in the neighborhood. Check out this section for some guidance on what to wear depending on the formality of where you're going.

Dressing casually

Here's a list of some common clothes for casual wear:

>> **kaptula** (kah-*ptoo*-lah) (*shorts*)

>> **jinsi** (*jee*-nsee) (*jeans*)

>> **fulana ya mikono** (foo-*lah*-nah yah mee-*koh*-noh) (*t-shirt*)

>> **sketi** (*skeh*-tee) (*skirt*)

>> **dera** (*deh*-rah) (*free-size moo moo, like a dress for women*)

>> **kofia** (koh-*fee*-ah) (*cap, hat*)

>> **nguo za kuogelea** (*ngoo*-oh zah koo-oh-geh-*leh*-ah) (*swimming suits*)

>> **nguo za kulala** (*ngoo*-oh zah koo-*lah*-lah) (*pajamas*)

>> **ndala/champali/patipati** (*ndah*-lah/chah-*mpah*-lee/pah-tee-*pah*-tee) (*sandals*)

>> **kandambili/malapa** (kah-ndah-*mbee*-lee/mah-*lah*-pah) (*flip-flops*)

CULTURAL WISDOM

While casual wear is all about comfort, beware of your surroundings and the acceptable level of skin exposure. For example, some beaches are fine with dainty bikinis, while you risk drawing unnecessary attention with the same at other beaches. As always, if in doubt, observe the locals first and follow suit. On a lighter note, did you know that flip-flops are essentially bathroom slippers in East Africa? We often joke that foreigners wander around town in flip-flops like they expect an outdoor shower experience any minute. Don't be the target of this joke; reserve **kandambili/malapa** (kah-ndah-*mbee*-lee/mah-*lah*-pah) (*flip-flops*) for indoor use only.

Dressing formally

Don't be surprised to see churchgoers decked in their Sunday best to go to church. For Swahili speakers, the church is a formal place that calls for sharp dressing. Other such places include work (if white-collar), funerals, and weddings (usually for men). Some common clothes include

>> **tai** (*tah-ee*) (*tie*)

>> **rinda/gauni** (*ree*-ndah/gah-*oo*-nee) (*dress*)

>> **sketi** (*skeh*-tee) (*skirt*)

>> **shati** (*shah*-tee) (*shirt*)

>> **koti** (*koh*-tee) (*coat*)

>> **sweta** (*sweh*-tah) (*sweater*)

>> **suti** (*soo*-tee) (*suit*)

>> **suruali** (soo-roo-*ah*-lee) (*pants*) or (*underwear* in non-coastal parts of Kenya)

>> **blauzi** (blah-*oo*-zee) (*blouse*)

Notice how similar names for "western" clothes are to English terms? You shouldn't have much trouble explaining what you need to a clothes vendor with these.

Here are some clothing items and accessories that fit both formal and informal occasions.

>> **viatu** (vee-*ah*-too) (*shoes*)

>> **buti** (*boo*-tee) (*boots*)

>> **miwani** (mee-*wah*-nee) (*glasses*)

>> **miwani ya jua** (mee-*wah*-neeh yah *joo*-ah) (*sunglasses*)

>> **fulana** (foo-*lah*-nah) (*vest*)

>> **sidiria** (see-dee-*ree*-ah) (*bra*)

>> **chupi** (*choo*-pee) (*underwear*)

>> **soksi** (*soh*-ksee) (*socks*)

>> **glavu** (*glah*-voo) (*gloves*)

>> **skafu** (*skah*-foo) (*scarf*)

>> **mkanda/mshipi** (m-*kah*-ndah/m-*shee*-pee) (*belt*)

» **saa ya mkono**(*sa*-ah yah m-*koh*-noh) (*wristwatch*)

» **hereni** (heh-*reh*-ni) (*earrings*)

» **mkufu** (m-*koo*-foo) (*necklace*)

» **pete** (*peh*-teh) (*ring*)

» **barakoa** (bah-rah-*koh*-ah) (*mask*)

You're also likely to notice some religious clothing while in East Africa. These include

» **buibui** (*boo*-ee-*boo*-ee) (*long black gown with head cover worn by Muslim women*)

» **ushungi/mtandio** (oo-*shoo*-ngee/m-tah-*ndee*-oh) (*headscarf worn by Muslim women*)

» **kanzu** (*kah*-nzoo) (*ankle-length tunic worn by Muslim men*)

» **barakashia** (bah-rah-kah-*shee*-ah) (*circular hat worn by Muslim men*)

» **kilemba** (kee-*leh*-mbah) (*a head wrap worn by men of Sikh and other traditional religious groups*)

Describing Clothes

What's your favorite **rangi** (*rah*–ngee) (*color*)? Your wardrobe might already be full of clothes and accessories in your favorite colors, but nothing beats shopping for a sentimental piece to remind you of your travels. Read this section to pick up vocabulary related to colors in Swahili and how to describe clothes using their colors.

Here are some popular colors to get you started:

» **ekundu** (-eh-*koo*-ndoo) (*red*)

» **eusi** (-eh-*oo*-see) (*black*)

» **eupe** (-eh-*oo*-peh) (*white*)

» **rangi ya manjano** (*rah*-ngee yah mah-*njah*-noh) (*yellow*)

» **buluu/rangi ya samawati** (*boo*-loo/*rah*-ngee yah sah-mah-*wah*-tee) (*blue*)

» **rangi ya kijani** (*rah*-ngee yah kee-*jah*-nee) (*green*)

- » **rangi ya zambarau** (*rah*-ngee yah zah-mbah-*rah*-oo) (*purple*)

- » **rangi ya chungwa** (*rah*-ngee yah mah-*choo*-ngwah) (*orange*)

- » **rangi ya kahawia** (*rah*-ngee yah kah-hah-*wee*-ah) (*brown*)

- » **rangi ya kijivu** (*rah*-ngee yah kee-*jee*-voo) (*grey*)

- » **rangi ya waridi** (*rah*-ngee yah wah-*ree*-dee) (*pink*)

- » **rangi ya dhahabu** (*rah*-ngee yah dhah-*hah*-boo) (*gold*)

- » **rangi ya fedha** (*rah*-ngee yah *feh*-dhah) (*silver*)

REMEMBER

Notice that when stating colors, only three — **ekundu** (-eh-*koo*-ndoo) (*red*), **eusi** (-eh-*oo*-see) (*black*), and **eupe** (-eh-*oo*-peh) (*white*) — have no descriptors. Every other color is described as **rangi ya . . .** (*rah*-ngee yah . . .) (*the color of . . .*). For example, **rangi ya kijivu** literally translates to *the color of ash*, **rangi ya machungwa**, *the color of oranges*, **rangi ya manjano**, *the color of turmeric*, and so on. Using this second set of colors as adjectives is easy; just mention the item then add the color. For example:

- » **suti ya buluu** (*soo*-tee yah *boo*-loo) (*blue suit*)

- » **mkoba wa kijivu** (m-*koh*-bah wah kee-*jee*-voo) (*a grey handbag*)

- » **soksi za kijani** (*soh*-ksee zah kee-*jah*-nee) (*green socks*)

- » **miwani ya zambarau** (mee-*wah*-nee yah zah-mbah-*rah*-oo) (*purple glasses*)

The colors **ekundu** (-eh-*koo*-ndoo) (*red*), **eusi** (-eh-*oo*-see) (*black*), and **-eupe** (-eh-*oo*-peh) (*white*) adopt a prefix consistent with the noun class of the item they are describing. For example, **viatu** (vee-*ah*-too) (*shoes*) is plural and is in the Ki/Vi noun class. If the shoes are black, you'd say **viatu vyeusi** (vee-*ah*-too vyeh-oo-see) (*black shoes*). Table 11-1 outlines this process.

You may have noticed that these rules do not always fit as expected. For example, **kiatu** does not take **kieusi** but instead takes **cheusi**. Remember the following rules:

- » KI before a, e, or o = CH

- » VI before a, e, or o = VY

- » M before any vowel mostly = MW

- » MI before e = ME

- » JI before e = JE

TABLE 11-1   Matching prefixes with noun classes.

Noun Class	Noun Class Marker	Noun	Adjective (-ekundu, -eusi, -eupe)	Verb
JI	li-	Gauni	jekundu	limefuliwa (lee-meh-foo-*lee*-wah)
MA	ya-	Magauni	mekundu	yamefuliwa (vee-meh-foo-*lee*-wah)
				(*has been washed/have been washed*)
KI	ki-	Kiatu	Cheusi	kimepotea (kee-meh-poh-*teh*-ah)
VI	vi-	Viatu	vyeusi	vimepotea (vee-meh-poh-*teh*-ah)
CH				(*has been lost/have been lost*)
VY				
M	u-	Mkanda	mweupe	umekatika (oo-meh-kah-*tee*-kah)
MI	i-	Mikanda	meupe	imekatika (ee-meh-kah-*tee*-kah)
				(*has been torn/have been torn*)
N	i-	Soksi	nyeupe	imetoboka (ee-meh-toh-*boh*-kah)
N	zi-	Soksi	nyeupe	zimetoboka (zee-meh-toh-*boh*-kah)
				(*has a hole/has holes*)

Here are more examples:

>> **shati jekundu** (*shah*-tee jeh-*koo*-ndoo) (*red shirt*)

>> **mkanda mweupe** (m-*kah*-ndah mweh-oo-peh) (*white belt*)

>> **buti nyekundu** (*boo*-tee nyeh-*koo*-ndoo) (*red boots*)

>> **magauni meupe** (mah-gah-oo-nee meh-oo-peh) (*white dresses*)

Check out "Introducing Swahili Noun Classes" in Chapter 3 for more explanation.

Talkin' the Talk

AUDIO ONLINE

Kristen is at Gikomba market (East Africa's largest open-air market in Nairobi, Kenya) buying **nguo** (*ngoo*-oh) (*clothes*) from **muuzaji** (moo-oo-*zah*-jee) (*seller*).

Muuzaji: **Karibu sana rafiki! Unataka nini?**
Kah-*ree*-boo *sah*-nah rah-*fee*-kee. Oo-nah-*tah*-kah *nee*-nee?
Welcome friend! What would you like?

Kristen:	**Ninataka magauni marefu mawili.**
	Nee-nah-*tah*-kah mah-gah-*oo*-nee mah-*reh*-foo
	mah-*wee*-lee.
	I want two long dresses.

Muuzaji:	**Magauni yapo mengi sana leo. Unataka rangi gani?**
	Mah-gah-*oo*-nee *yah*-poh *meh*-ngee *sah*-nah *leh*-oh.
	Oo-nah-*tah*-kah *rah*-ngee *gah*-nee?
	There are so many dresses today. Which color do you want?

Kristen:	**Ninataka gauni moja jekundu na moja jeupe.**
	Nee-nah-*tah*-kah gah-*oo*-nee *moh*-jah jeh-*koo*-ndoo na
	moh-jah jeh-*oo*-peh
	I want one red dress and one white dress.

Muuzaji:	**Sawa. Jaribu haya mawili ni saizi ndogo uone kama**
	yanakutosha.
	Sah-wah. Jah-*ree*-boo *hah*-yah mah-*wee*-lee nee sah-*ee*-zee
	ndoh-goh oo-*oh*-neh *kah*-mah yah-nah-koo-*toh*-shah.
	Okay. Try these two, they are small size. See if they fit you.

Kristen:	**Haya. Yananitosha vizuri kabisa. Una masweta?**
	Hah-yah. Yah-nah-nee-*toh*-shah vee-*zoo*-ree kah-*bee*-sah.
	Oo-nah mah-*sweh*-tah?
	Okay. They fit me very well. Do you have sweaters?

Muuzaji:	**Ndiyo. Unataka mangapi?**
	Ndee-yoh. Oo-nah-*tah*-kah mah-*ngah*-pee
	Yes. How many do you want?

Kristen:	**Ninataka moja jeusi.**
	Nee-nah-*tah*-kah *moh*-jah jeh-*oo*-see
	I want one black sweater.

Muuzaji:	**Hili hapa. Jaribisha.**
	Hee-lee *hah*-pah. Jah-ree-*bee*-shah.
	Here it is. Try it on.

Kristen:	**Ninalipenda sana sweta hili!**
	Nee-nah-lee-*peh*-ndah *sah*-nah *sweh*-tah *hee*-lee!
	I like this sweater very much.

Muuzaji:	**Unataka kitu kingine?**
	Oo-nah-*tah*-kah *kee*-too kee-*ngee*-nee?
	Do you want something else?

Kristen:	**Ndiyo. Ninaomba kanga doti moja na kitenge mita moja**
	Ndee-yoh. Nee-nah-*oh*-mbah *kah*-ngah *doh*-tee *moh*-jah
	nah kee-*tee*-ngeh *mee*-tah *moh*-jah.
	Yes. Give me two kangas and one metre of kitenge.

Muuzaji: **Kanga hii hapa. Inasema "Nani kama mama". Kitenge hiki hapa.**
Kah-ngah *hee*-ee *hah*-pah. Ee-nah-*seh*-mah "*Nah*-nee *kah*-mah *mah*-mah". Kee-*tee*-ngee *hee*-kee *hah*-pah.
Here is the kanga. It says "No one is like a mother," and here is your kitenge.

Kristen: **Sawa. Asante sana!**
Sah-wah. Ah-*sah*-nteh *sah*-nah!
Okay. Thank you very much.

Muuzaji: **Karibu tena!**
Kah-*ree*-boo *teh*-nah.
come back again!

• •

WORDS TO KNOW		
saizi	sah-*ee*-zee	size
doti	*doh*-tee	pair
mita	*mee*-tah	metre
Jaribisha	jah-ree-*bee*-shah	try on

Chapter **12**

Swahili at Work

onducting business in a foreign language can be a daunting task. It's easy to piece together a few words and phrases to get by on the street, but the stakes are significantly higher when your intention is to create a good relationship with partners and reel in clients. We also believe that you're likely to find your colleagues being more helpful if you try to speak Swahili with them and observe the cultural nuances around office interactions. To help you make the best impression at work, in this chapter we discuss the basics of interacting with your colleagues as well as how to conduct yourself at meetings and business dinners.

Getting Down to Work

Unless your work is fully remote, you most likely spend time in **ofisi** (oh-*fee*-see) (*the office*) where you meet **wafanyakazi wenzi** (wah-*fah*-nyah-*kah*-zee *weh*-nzee) (*your colleagues*). In this situation, how you interact with others could be the difference between a good working environment and a nightmare situation in which everyone makes things difficult for you at work. Get ahead of it all by learning some key words and phrases related to the workplace. Some examples include the following:

> » **kazi** (*kah*-zee) (*work/job*)

> » **kampuni** (kah-*mpoo*-nee) (*company*)

- **sekta ya umma** (*seh*-ktah yah *oo*-mah) (*public sector*)

- **sekta binafsi** (*seh*-ktah bee-*nah*-fsee) (*private sector*)

- **shirika lisilo la kiserikali** (shee-*ree*-kah lee-*see*-loh lah kee-seh-ree-*kah*-lee) (*non-governmental organization/NGO*)

- **idara** (ee-*dah*-rah) (*department*)

- **mtaji** (m-*tah*-jee) (*capital*)

- **mkataba** (m-kah-*tah*-bah) (*contract*)

- **mteja; wateja** (m-*teh*-jah; wah-*teh*-jah) (*client; clients*)

- **warsha** (*wah*-rshah) (*workshop*)

- **kongamano** (koh-ngah-*mah*-noh) (*conference*)

Interacting with your colleagues

Whether you have just a couple of **wafanyakazi wenzi** or several, you'll have to know how to navigate interactions with them.

The first thing you want to get right is everyone's title. Before a male colleague's name, use the title **Bwana** (*bwah*–nah) (*Mister/Mr.*) and before a female colleague's name, use the title **Bi** (*bee*) (*Mrs/Ms.*)

The second thing you need to get right is job titles; here are some titles to get you started:

- **bosi** (*boh*-see) (*boss*)

- **mwajiri** (m-wah-*jee*-ree) (*employer*)

- **kuajiri** (koo-ah-*jee*-ree) (*to employ*)

- **bodi ya wakurugenzi** (*boh*-dee yah wah-koo-roo-*geh*-nzee) (*board of directors*)

- **mwanabodi; wanabodi** (m-wah-nah-*boh*-dee; wah-nah-*boh*-dee) (*board member; board members*)

- **mwekezaji; wawekezaji** (m-weh-keh-*zah*-jee; wah-weh-keh-*zah*-jee) (*investor; investors*)

- **mkurugenzi** (m-koo-roo-*geh*-nzee) (*director*)

- **karani** (kah-*rah*-nee) (*clerk*)

- **katibu** (kah-*tee*-boo) (*secretary*)

» **katibu mkoo** (kah-*tee*-boo m-koo) (*principal secretary*)

» **msaidizi** (m-sah-ee-*dee*-zee) (*assistant*)

» **mlinzi** (m-*lee*-nzee) (*security guard*)

CULTURAL WISDOM

In Swahili culture, it's customary to greet your colleagues as you come into work. Say a cheerful **habari za asubuhi** (hah–*bah*–ree zah ah–soo–*boo*–hee) (*good morning*) to those you meet in the morning to show respect and politeness while acknowledging their presence. Check out Chapter 2 for more greetings to use in different situations.

Following are some important phrases to help you interact professionally with your colleagues.

» **Ninaweza kukusaidia vipi?** (nee-nah-*weh*-zah koo-koo-sah-ee-*dee*-ah *vee*-pee) (*How can I help you?*)

» **Unahitaji usaidizi?** (oo-nah-hee-*tah*-jee oo-sah-ee-*dee*-zee) (*Do you need help?*)

» **Tungependa kukualika kwenye mkutano.** (too-ngeh-*peh*-ndah koo-koo-ah-*lee*-kah *kweh*-nyeh m-koo-*tah*-noh) (*We'd like to invite you to a meeting.*)

» **Tutakutana saa ngapi?** (too-tah-koo-*tah*-nah *sah*-ah *ngah*-pee) (*What time shall we meet?*)

» **Ulipata ujumbe wangu?** (oo-lee-*pah*-tah oo-*joo*-mbeh *wah*-ngoo) (*Did you get my message?*)

» **Nina swali kuhusu kazi hii.** (*nee*-nah s*wah*-lee koo-*hoo*-soo *kah*-zee *hee*-ee) (*I have a question about this task.*)

» **Ninatumai kila kitu kinaenda vizuri.** (nee-nah-too-*mah*-ee *kee*-lah *kee*-too kee-nah-*eh*-ndah vee-*zoo*-ree) (*I hope everything's going well.*)

» **Tunaweza kujadili hili zaidi kesho?** (too-nah-*weh*-zah koo-jah-*dee*-lee *hee*-lee zah-*ee*-dee *keh*-shoh?) (*Can we discuss this further tomorrow?*)

» **Ninashukuru kwa ushirikiano wako.** (nee-nah-shoo-*koo*-roo kwah oo-shee-ree-kee-*ah*-noh *wah*-ko) (*I appreciate your cooperation.*)

» **Ninafurahi kufanya kazi na wewe.** (nee-nah-foo-*rah*-hee koo-*fah*-nyah *kah*-zee nah *weh*-weh) (*I'm happy to work with you.*)

» **Ninathamini mchango wako.** (nee-nah-thah-*mee*-nee m-*chah*-ngoh *wah*-koh) (*I value your input.*)

» **Tuko pamoja katika hili.** (*too*-koh pah-m*oh*-jah kah-*tee*-kah *hee*-lee) (*We're together in this.*)

» **Ninafurahi kufanya kazi katika timu hii.** (nee-nah-foo-*rah*-hee koo-*fah*-nyah *kah*-zee kah-*tee*-kah *tee*-moo *hee*-ee) (*I'm glad to work on this team.*)

» **Ninashukuru kwa msaada wako.** (nee-nah-shoo-*koo*-roo kwah m-sah-*ah*-dah *wah*-koh) (*I'm grateful for your assistance.*)

Finding people or things at the office

Unless you're prepared to go searching for people and things for hours on end, it's wise to ask your colleagues for help using the verb **kutafuta** (koo-tah-*foo*-tah) (*to look for*) or the question word **wapi?** (*wah*-pee) (*where?*)

REMEMBER

Use **ninatafuta . . .** (nee-nah-tah-*foo*-tah) (*I'm looking for . . .*) for inanimate things, **ninamtafuta . . .** (nee-nah-mtah-*foo*-tah) (*I'm looking for . . .*) for one person, and **ninawatafuta . . .** (nee-nah-wah-tah-*foo*-tah) (*I'm looking for . . .*) for multiple people . The **-m-** is an object marker for animate things in the singular and the **-wa-** is an object marker for animate things in plural.

Here are some Swahili words and phrases you might find useful when looking for people or things in an office or work setting:

» **Ninamtafuta Bi. Sofia.** (nee-nah-mtah-*foo*-tah Bi. Sofia) (*I'm looking for Ms Sofia.*)

» **Ninawatafuta Bi. Sofia na Bw. Otieno.** (nee-nah-wah-tah-*foo*-tah Bee Sofia nah *Bwah*-nah Otieno) (*I'm looking for Ms Sofia and Mr. Otieno.*)

» **Ninatafuta kalamu.** (nee-nah-tah-*foo*-tah kah-*lah*-moo) (*I'm looking for a pen.*)

» **Ninatafuta faili la ripoti.** (nee-nah-tah-*foo*-tah fah-*ee*-lee lah ree-*poh*-tee) (*I'm looking for the report file.*)

» **Faili liko karibu na kompyuta yako.** (fah-*ee*-lee *lee*-koh kah-*ree*-boo nah koh-m-pee-*yoo*-tah *yah*-ko) (*The file is near your computer.*)

» **Simu yako iko juu ya meza.** (*see*-moo *yah*-koh *ee*-koh *joo*-oo yah *meh*-zah) (*Your phone is on the table.*)

» **Ripoti iko juu ya meza.** (ree-*poh*-tee *ee*-koh *joo*-oo yah *meh*-zah) (*The report is on the table.*)

» **Mkurugenzi amesimama mbele ya jukwaa.** (m-koo-roo-geh-*n*-zee ah-meh-see-*mah*-mah *mbeh*-leh yah joo-*kwah*-ah) (*The director is standing in front of the podium.*)

» **Unaweza kupata karatasi kwenye rafu.** (oo-nah-*weh*-zah koo-*pah*-tah kah-rah-*tah*-see *kweh*-nyeh *rah*-foo) (*You can find paper on the shelf.*)

>> **Ninaweza kupata mashine ya kuchapisha wapi?** (nee-nah-*weh*-zah koo-*pah*-tah mah-*shee*-nee yah koo-chah-*pee*-shah wah-pee?) (*Where can I find the printer?*)

Talkin' the Talk

Shirley is volunteering with the Peace Corps in Iringa Tanzania. She will be working at a Peace Corps office. She meets Maua (a receptionist at the Peace Corps office in Iringa, Tanzania).

Shirley: **Habari za leo?**
Hah-*bah*-ree zah *leh*-oh?
How are you doing today?

Maua: **Nzuri sana. Jina langu ni Maua. Nikusaidieje?**
N-*zoo*-ree *sah*-nah. *Jee*-nah *lah*-ngoo nee Mah-*oo*-ah. Nee-koo-sah-ee-dee-*ah*-jeh?
I am doing very well. My name is Maua. How can I help you?

Shirley: **Jina langu ni Shirley. Ninatoka Marekani. Ninajitolea na programu ya Peace Corps. Nitafanya kazi hapa ofisini na leo ni siku yangu ya kwanza.**
Jee-nah *lah*-ngoo nee Shirley. Nee-nah-*toh*-kah Mah-reh-*kah*-nee. Nee-nah-jee-toh-*leh*-ah nah proh-*grah*-moo yah Peace Corps. Nee-tah-*fah*-nyah *kah*-zee *hah*-pah oh-fee-*see*-nee nah *leh*-oh nee *see*-koo *yah*-ngoo yah *kwah*-nzah.
My name is Shirley. I am from the United States. I am volunteering with the Peace Corps Program. I will be working here in the office, and today is my first day of work.

Maua: **Ooh! Karibu sana Shirley. Nitakuonyesha ofisi yetu na nitakutembeza.**
Oooh! Kah-*ree*-boo *sah*-nah Shirley, Nee-tah-koo-oh-*nyeh*-shah oh-*fee*-see *yeh*-too nah ne-tah-koo-the-*mbeh*-zah.
Oooh. You are warmly welcome, Shirley. I will show you our office, and I will take you around.

Shirley: **Samahani. Ninahitaji kutumia msala. Msala uko wapi?**
Sah-mah-*hah*-nee. Nee-nah-hee-*tah*-jee koo-too-*mee*-ah m-*sah*-lah. M-*sah*-lah *oo*-koh *wah*-pee?
Excuse me, I need to use the bathroom. Where is the bathroom located?

Maua:	**Msala uko upande wako wa kushoto. Utaona neno "wanawake".**
	M-sah-lah oo-koh oo-pah-ndeh wah-koh wah koo-shoh-toh. Oo-tah-oh-nah neh-noh wah-nah-wah-keh.
	The bathroom is on your left. You will see the word "Women".
Shirley:	**Sawa. Asante sana. Je, kuna mkahawa hapa karibu na ofisi?**
	Sah-wah. Ah-sah-nteh. Jeh, koo-nah m-kah-hah-wah kah-ree-boo nah oh-fee-see?
	Okay. Thanks. Is there a restaurant near the office?
Maua:	**Ndiyo kuna mkahawa nje ya jengo hili.**
	Ndee-yoh koo-nah m-kah-hah-wah n-jeh yah jeh-ngoh hee-lee.
	Yes, there is a restaurant outside this building.
	(Maria goes to the bathroom and comes back.)
Maua:	**Haya, Nitakuoyesha kwa mratibu wa programu zetu kwanza. Ofisi yake iko chumba nambari sita.**
	Hah-yah. Nee-tah-koo-oh-nyeh-shah kwah m-rah-tee-boo wa pro-grah-moo zeh-too kwah-nzah. Oh-fee-see yah-keh ee-koh choo-mbah nah-mbah-ree see-tah.
	Okay. I will show you our programs coordinator's office. His office is in room number six.
Shirley:	**Sawa, ningependa kuzungumza na mratibu huyu baadaye kama inawezekana.**
	Sah-wah, nee-ngeh-peh-ndah koo-zoo-ngoo-m-zah nah m-rah-tee-boo hoo-yoo- bah-ah- dah-yeh kah-mah ee-nah-weh-zeh-kah-nah.
	Okay, I would like to speak with the coordinator later if possible.
Maua:	**Ndiyo, nitamjulisha. Ofisi iliyoko nyuma yako ni ya mhasibu wetu.**
	Ndee-yoh, nee-tah-m-joo-lee-shah. Oh-fee-see ee-lee-yoh-koh nyoo-mah yah-koh nee yah m-hah-see-boo weh-too.
	Yes, I will let him know. The office behind you is for our bursar.
Shirley:	**Naona. Je, mnashirikiana na mashirika mengine hapa Iringa kusaidia wananchi?**
	Nah-oh-nah. Jeh, m-nah-shee-ree-kee-ah-nah nah mah-shee-ree-kah meh-ngee-nee hah-pah Ee-ree-ngah koo-sah-ee-dee-ah wah-nah-n-chee?
	I see. Do you collaborate with other organizations here in Iringa to help citizens?

Maua: **Ndiyo, tunafanya kazi na mashirika ya kiserikali na yasiyo ya kiserikali.**

Ndee-yoh,too-nah-*fah*-nyah *kah*-zee nah mah-shee-*ree*-kah yah kee-seh-ree-*kah*-lee nah yah-*see*-yoh yah kee-seh-ree-*kah*-lee.

Yes, we work with both governmental and non-governmental organizations.

Shirley: **Vizuri sana. Asante sana Maua. Ninafurahi kufanya kazi hapa.**

Vee-*zoo*-ree *sah*-nah. Ah-sah-*n*-teh *sah*-nah Mah-*oo*-ah. *Nee*-nah-foo-*rah*-hee koo-*fah*-nyah *kah*-zee *hah*-pah.

That's very good. Thank you very much Maua. I am happy to be working here.

• •

WORDS TO KNOW

mashirika ya kiserikali	mah-shee-*ree*-kah yah kee-seh-ree-*kah*-lee	governmental organizations
mashirika yasiyo ya kiserikali	mah-shee-*ree*-kah yah-*see*-yoh yah kee-seh-ree-*kah*-lee	non-governmental organizations
kujitolea	koo-jee-toh-*leh*-ah	to volunteer
mhasibu	m-hah-*see*-boo	bursar
mratibu wa program	m-rah-*tee*-boo wah proh-g-*rah*-moo	program coordinator
mashirika	mah-shee-*ree*-kah	organizations
msala	m-*sah*-lah	bathroom/toilet

Attending meetings

Sometimes we wish we could skip most meetings and just take care of business via emails, but meetings are unavoidable — and sometimes quite necessary. You'd be wise to prepare yourself to speak up in a meeting whenever called upon. This section discusses the proper way to make introductions and speak up in a meeting held in Swahili. But before that, familiarize yourself with the following words and phrases relevant to meetings conducted in Swahili:

>> **kufungua mkutano** (koo-foo-*ngoo*-ah m-koo-*tah*-noh) (*opening the meeting*)

>> **ajenda za mkutano** (ah-*jeh*-ndah zah m-koo-*tah*-noh) (*meeting agenda*)

>> **malengo ya mkutano** (mah-*leh*-ngoh yah m-koo-*tah*-noh) (*purpose of the meeting*)

>> **kumbukumbu ya mkutano** (koo-mboo-*koo*-mboo yah m-koo-*tah*-noh) (*minutes*)

>> **katibu** (kah-*tee*-boo) (*secretary*)

>> **mwenyekiti** (mweh-nyeh-*kee*-tee) (*chairperson*)

>> **tuanze** (too-ah-*n*-zeh) (*Let's begin.*)

>> **mengineyo** (meh-ngee-*neh*-yoh) (*AOB/any other business*)

>> **maoni** (mah-*oh*-nee) (*comments*)

>> **asante kwa kujumuika nasi leo** (aha-sah-n-*teh*-nee kwah koo-joo-moo-*ee*-kah *nah*-see *leh*-oh) (*Thanks for joining us today.*)

>> **asanteni wote kwa kuja** (ah-sah-n-*tee*-nee *woh*-teh kwah *koo*-jah) (*Thanks all for coming.*)

>> **mapendekezo** (mah-peh-ndeh-*keh*-zoh) (*suggestions*)

>> **mwaliko** (mwah-*lee*-koh) (*invitation*)

>> **utambulisho** (oo-tah-mboo-*lee*-shoh) (*introductions*)

>> **kuongoza mkutano** (koo-oh-*ngoh*-zah m-koo-*tah*-noh) (*leading the meeting*)

Making introductions

When dealing with introductions in a workplace setting, particularly within Swahili society, it's important to show respect and take time for pleasantries before diving into business discussions. Make sure you take your time to build rapport and make a positive impression. Here are some essential words and phrases you can use:

>> **salamu** (sah-*lah*-moo) (*greetings*)

>> **utambulisho** (oo-tah-mboo-*lee*-shoh (*introductions*)

>> **Ninavutiwa na** (nee-nah-voo-*tee*-wah nah) (*I'm interested in . . .*)

>> **Unafanya kazi gani hapa?** (oo-nah-*fah*-nyah *kah*-zee *gah*-nee *hah*-pah) (*What do you do here?*)

>> **Ninashughulika na** (nee-nah-shoo-ghoo-*lee*-kah nah) (*I deal with. . .*)

>> **Ninafanya kazi kama** (nah-*fah*-nyah *kah*-zee *kah*-mah) (*I work as a . . .*)

>> **Ninafurahi kukutana nawe.** (*nee*-nah-foo-*rah*-hee koo-koo-*tah*-nah nah weh-weh) (*I'm glad to meet you.*)

>> **Nina hamu ya kujifunza zaidi kuhusu kazi yako.** (nee-nah *hah*-moo yah koo-jee-foo-*n*-zah zah-*ee*-dee koo-*hoo*-soo *kah*-zee yah-ko) (*I'm eager to learn more about your work.*)

>> **Ninashukuru kwa fursa ya kufanya kazi Pamoja.** (nee-nah-shoo-*koo*-roo kwah foo-*r*-sah yah koo-*fah*-nyah *kah*-zee pah-*moh*-jah) (*I'm grateful for the opportunity to work together.*)

Speaking up in a meeting

When attending a meeting, it's important to join the discussion with your colleagues, listen to other people's ideas, and share your ideas as well. You can only achieve this by observing the rules of turn-taking; otherwise, you risk coming across as obnoxious, and your colleagues won't like you. We suggest that you always be on the lookout for an opportunity to speak and then come in with phrases such as the following:

>> **Kuna mtu mwingine angependa kuchangia mada?** (*koo*-nah mwee-*ngee*-neh angeh-*peh*-ndah koo-chah-*ngee*-ah *mah*-dah) (*Would anyone else like to contribute to the topic?*)

>> **Bwana Karim, labda una la kusema?** (*bwah*-nah Karim *lah*-bdah oo-nah lah koo-*seh*-mah) (*Mr. Karim, maybe you have something to say?*)

>> **Kuna mawazo mengine?** (*koo*-nah mah-*wah*-zoh meh-*ngee*-neh) (*Are there other ideas?*)

>> **Kuna maoni tofauti?** (*koo*-nah mah-*oh*-nee toh-fah-*oo*-tee) (*Are there different ideas?*)

>> **Tunakubali?** *(*too-nah-koo-*bah*-lee) (*Do we agree?*)

Offer your opinions politely whether you agree or disagree. For example,

>> **Ninakubaliana na maoni ya Bi. Tausi . . .?** (nee-nah-koo-bah-lee-*ah*-nah nah mah-*oh*-nee yah Bee Tausi) (*I agree with Ms Tausi's ideas . . .*)

>> **Ninadhani maoni ya Bw. Rashid ni muhimu, ila nina wazo tofauti.** (nee-nah-*dhah*-nee mah-*oh*-nee yah *bwah*-nah Rashid nee moo-*hee*-moo *ee*-lah *nee*-nah wah-zoh toh-fah-*oo*-tee) (*I think Mr. Rashid's comments are important, but I have a different idea.*)

>> **Sikubaliani na wazo la kuuza hisa zetu mwaka huu.** (see-koo-bah-lee-*ah*-nee nah wah-zoh lah koo-*oo*-zah *hee*-sah *zeh*-too m-*wah*-kah hoo) (*I don't agree with the idea of selling our stock this year.*)

>> **Ningependa kutoa maoni tofauti.** (nee-ngeh-*peh*-ndah koo-*toh*-ah mah-*oh*-nee toh-fah-*oo*-tee) (*I'd like to make opposing comments.*)

Invite others into the conversation using phrases such as

>> **Mnaonaje?** (m-nah-oh-*nah*-jeh) (*What do you think?*)

>> **Nawaalika kutoa mawazo yenu kuhusu mada hili.** (nah-wah-ah-*lee*-kah koo-*toh*-ah mah-*wah*-zoh yeh-noo koo-*hoo*-soo *mah*-dah *hee*-lee) (*I invite you to share your thoughts on this topic.*)

>> **Natanguliza shukrani kwa mwitiko wowote.** (nah-tah-ngoo-*lee*-zah shoo-*krah*-nee kwah m-wee-*tee*-koo woh-*woh*-teh) (*Thanks in advance for any feedback.*)

Making the Rounds: Business Dinners

Whether formal or more social and relaxed, business dinners still call for attend-ees to maintain a professional image. In this section, we'll guide you through drinking norms in Swahili business dinners.

Drinking politely

Business dinners will most likely be accompanied by drinks, either alcoholic, non-alcoholic or both. Check out Chapter 8 for drinks options and how to request them if your business dinner is at a restaurant. Here are some drink options to expect.

>> **maji** (*mah*-jee) (*water*)

» **juisi** (joo-*ee*-see) (*juice*)

» **soda** (*soh*-dah) (*soda*)

» **kahawa** (kah-*hah*-wah) (*coffee*)

» **mvinyo** (m-*vee*-nyoh) (*wine*)

» **bia** (*bee*-ah) (*beer*)

» **pombe** (*poh*-mbeh) (*alcohol in general*)

» **pombe kali** (*poh*-mbeh *kah*-lee) (*whiskey/gin/vodka*)

You can make polite conversation about the drinks' origin. Use the associative **ya** (*yah*) (*of*) to link the drink and its place of origin. For example:

» **Hii ni bia ya wapi?** (hee nee *bee*-ah yah *wah*-pee) (*From which region is this beer?*)

» **Hii ni mvinyo ya Tanzania?** (hee nee m-*vee*-nyoh yah Tanzania) (*Is this Tanzanian wine?*)

» **Ninapenda bia ya Uganda.** (nee-nah-*peh*-ndah *bee*-ah yah Uganda) (*I like Ugandan beer.*)

» **Kahawa ya Kenya ni tamu sana.** (kah-*hah*-wah yah Kenya nee *tah*-moo *sah*-nah) (*Kenyan coffee is very delicious.*)

Join your colleagues in **pongezi/kutakia kheri** (poh-*ngeh*-zee/koo-tah-*kee*-ah *kheh*-ree) (*a toast*) by following the lead of **mtangazaji wa pongezi** (m-tah-ngah-*zah*-jee wah poh-*ngeh*-zee) (*the toastmaster*). Some phrases you might hear and repeat during a toast include the following:

» **Kwa mwaka mpya!** (kwah m-*wah*-kah *m*-pyah) (*To the new year!*)

» **Kwa faida tele!** (kwah fah-*ee*-dah *teh*-leh) (*To more profits!*)

» **Kwa biashara bora!** (kwah bee-ah-*shah*-rah *boh*-rah) (*To good business!*)

» **Kwa afya!** (kwah *ah*-fyah) (*To health!*)

Remember to thank your host at the end of the evening. Say **Ninashukuru kwa mualiko wako** (nah-shoo-*koo*-roo kwah moo-ah-*lee*-koh *wah*-koh) (*I'm grateful for your invitation.*) or **Ahsante kwa kunialika** (Ah-*sah*-nteh kwah koo-nee-ah-*lee*-kah) (*Thanks for inviting me.*)

CULTURAL WISDOM

Part of drinking politely is making sure you don't go overboard with your alcohol intake. Swahili society views drunkenness as a weakness so you risk being labelled untrustworthy or unpredictable if you become visibly drunk at a business dinner.

Declining drinks

Unlike invitations to have tea, water, or juice when in someone's home, you can decline offers to drink without offending your business partner/host.

» **Hapana, asante.** (hah-*pah*-nah, ah-sah-*n*-teh) *(no, thank you)*

» **Ahsante, lakini mimi sinywi pombe.** (ah-*sah*-nteh lah-*kee*-nee *mee*-mee *see*-nywee *poh*-mbeh) *(Thank you, but I don't drink alcohol.)*

» **Nashukuru, sina kiu.** (nee-nah-shoo-*koo*-roo, *see*-nah *kee*-oo) *(I appreciate it, I'm not thirsty.)*

» **Samahani, nimeshakunywa.** (sah-mah-*hah*-nee nee-meh-shah-*koo*-nywah) *(I'm sorry, I've already had a drink)*

» **Asante kwa mualiko, lakini sihitaji kinywaji.** (ah-sah-*n*-teh kwah moo-ah-*lee*-koh lah-*kee*-nee see-hee-*tah*-jee kee-*nywah*-jee) *(Thank you for the invitation, but I don't need a drink.)*

» **Ningependa kuendelea na maji tu.** (nee-ngeh-*peh*-ndah koo-eh-ndeh-*leh*-ah nah *mah*-jee *too*-oo) *(I'd prefer to stick with water.)*

» **Hakika, sina haja ya kinywaji kwa sasa.** (hah-*kee*-kah, *see*-nah *hah*-jah yah kee-*nywah*-jee kwah *sah*-sah) *(Certainly, I don't need a drink for now.)*

» **Ninashukuru, nimechoka sana kunywa.** (nee-nah-shoo-*koo*-roo nee-meh-*choh*-kah *sah*-nah *koo*-nywah) *(I appreciate it, I've had quite enough to drink.)*

» **Ningependa kujaribu kitu kingine wakati huu.** (nee-ngeh-*peh*-ndah koo-jah-*ree*-boo *kee*-too kee-*ngee*-neh wah-*kah*-tee *hoo*-oo) *(I'd like to try something else at the moment.)*

FUN & GAMES

Sort the following words into the correct box.

   i. kalamu

  ii. mkurugenzi

 iii. katibu

  iv. ripoti

  v. mwajiri

 vi. rafu

People at the office	Things at the office

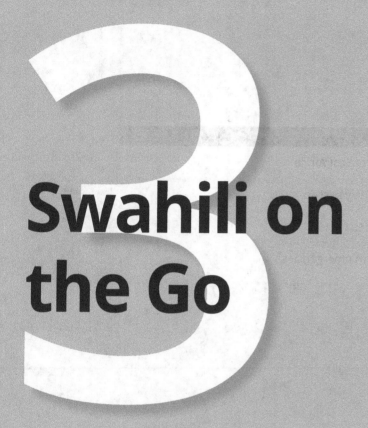

Swahili on the Go

Chapter **13**

Planning a Safari

H as watching *National Geographic* episodes made you hunger for first-hand experiences of the East African savannah? Whether your desire is to climb Mount Kilimanjaro or enjoy a sighting of a lioness hunting in the wilderness of the Amboseli National Park, you'll need to plan your itinerary well in advance. In this chapter, we'll highlight important factors to consider when choosing a destination for your **safari** (sah-*fah*-ree) (*journey*), communicating with your travel agency, and packing for your trip.

Choosing a Travel Destination

What do you look for when vacationing? Relaxation, knowledge, or adventure? For most people traveling to East Africa, their choices lead them to **mbuga za wanyama** (m-*boo*-gah zah wah-*nyah*-mah) (*animal parks*), **makumbusho** (mah-koo-*mboo*-shoh) (*museums*), and **ufukweni** (oo-foo-*kweh*-ni) (*the beaches*).

Looking at national parks

East Africa has several national parks to choose from, plus animal orphanages, reserves, and conservancies. Here are some basic words and phrases to help you navigate your visit to **mbuga za wanyama** (m-*boo*-gah zah wah-*nyah*-mah) (*animal parks*).

- » **kiingilio** (kee-ee-ngee-*lee*-oh) (*entrance fee*)

- » **Mlango wa kuingilia uko wapi?**(m-*lah*-ngoh wah koo-ee-ngee-*lee*-ah *oo*-koh *wah*-pee) *(Where is the entrance?)*

- » **wanyamapori** (wah-*nyah*-mah-*poh*-ree) (*wild animals*)

- » **kupanda milima** (koo-*pah*-ndah m-*lee*-mah) (*hiking*)

- » **kutazama ndege** (koo-tah-*zah*-mah *ndeh*-geh) (*birdwatching*)

- » **upigaji picha** (oo-pee-*gah*-jee *pee*-chah) (*photography*)

- » **uwindaji** (oo-wee-*ndah*-jee) (*hunting*)

- » **uwindaji haramu** (oo-wee-*ndah*-jee hah-*rah*-moo) (*poaching*)

- » **ramani** (rah-*mah*-nee) *(map)*

- » **njia** (*njee*-ah) *(trail)*

- » **kupiga kambi** (koo-*pee*-gah *kah*-mbee) (*camping*)

- » **mahali pa kupiga kambi** (mah-*hah*-lee pah koo-*pee*-gah *kah*-mbee) *(campground)*

- » **mlinzi wa hifadhi** (m-lee-*n*-zee wah hee-*fah*-dhee) (*park ranger*)

TIP

Learn the names of **wanyamapori** (wah–*nyah*–mah–*poh*–ree) (*wild animals*) before your safari so you can easily engage your tour guide in small talk about what you want to see. Some useful names to remember include the following:

- » **simba** (*see*-mbah) (*lion*)

- » **ndovu/tembo** (n-*doh*-voo/*teh*-mboh) (*elephant*)

- » **kifaru** (kee-*fah*-roo) (*rhino*)

- » **chui** (*choo*-ee) (*leopard*)

- » **nyati** (*nyah*-tee) (*buffalo*)

- » **twiga** (*twee*-gah) (*giraffe*)

- » **nyumbu** (*nyoo*-mboo) (*wildebeest*)

- » **fisi** (*fee*-see) (*hyena*)

- » **duma** (*doo*-mah) (cheetah)

- » **punda milia** (*poo*-ndah mee-*lee*-ah) (*zebra*)

- » **swara** (*swah*-rah) (*gazelle*)

- » **paa** (*pah*-ah) (*antelope*)

>> **kobe** (*koh*-beh) (*tortoise*)

>> **kasuku** (kah-*soo*-koo) (*parrot*)

>> **mwewe** (*mweh*-weh) (*hawk*)

>> **kunguru** (koo-*ngoo*-roo) (*crow*)

>> **njiwa** (*njee*-wah) (*dove*)

>> **mbuni** (*mboo*-nee) (*ostrich*)

Visiting heritage sites and museums

These phrases should help you communicate effectively while visiting heritage sites and museums:

>> **makumbusho** (mah-koo-*mboo*-shoh) (*museum*)

>> **maonyesho** (mah-oh-*nyeh*-sho) (*exhibition*)

>> **historia** (hee-stoh-*ree*-ah) (*history*)

>> **kipande cha historia** (kee-*pah*-ndeh chah hee-stoh-*ree*-ah) (*artifact*)

>> **utamaduni** (oo-tah-mah-*doo*-nee) (*culture*)

>> **mwongozaji wa ziara** (mwoh-ngoh-*zah*-jee wah zee-*ah*-rah) (*tour guide*)

>> **tiketi** (tee-*keh*-tee) (*ticket*)

>> **kuingia** (koo-ee-*ngee*-ah) (*entrance*)

>> **ukumbi wa maonyesho** (oo-*koo*-mbee wah mah-oh-*nyeh*-shoh) (*exhibition hall*)

>> **sanamu** (sah-*nah*-moo) (*sculpture*)

>> **picha** (*pee*-chah) (*painting*)

>> **uchunguzi wa kale** (oo-choo-*ngoo*-zee wah *kah*-leh) (*archaeology*)

>> **kale** (*kah*-leh) (*ancient*)

>> **uhifadhi** (oo-hee-*fah*-dhee) (*preservation*)

>> **elimu** (eh-*lee*-moo) (*education*)

>> **kituo cha wageni** (kee-*too*-oh chah wah-*geh*-nee) (*visitor center*)

>> **kumbukumbu** (koo-mboo-*koo*-mboo) (*souvenir*)

» **Makumbusho yanafunguliwa/fungwa saa ngapi?** (mah-koo-*mboo*-shoh yah-nah-foo-ngoo-*lee*-wah/*foo*-ngwah *sah*-ah *ngah*-pee? *(What time does the museum open/close?)*

» **Kiingilio ni shilingi ngapi?** (kee-ngee-*lee*-oh nee shee-*lee*-ngee *ngah*-pee) *(How much is the entrance fee?)*

» **Onyesho la historia ya kale liko wapi?** (oh-*nyeh*-shoh lah hee-sto-*ree*-ah yah k*ah*-leh *lee*-koh *wah*-pee) *(Where is the exhibit on ancient history?)*

» **Niambie zaidi kuhusu kipande hiki cha historia** (nee-ah-*mbee*-eh zah-ee-dee koo-*hoo*-soo kee-*pah*-ndeh *hee*-kee chah hee-stoh-*ree*-ah) *(Tell me more about this artifact.)*

Taking in the beaches

Get ready to hit the beach for a fun or relaxing time with the following words and phrases at your fingertips:

» **ufukwe** (oo-*foo*-kweh) *(beach)*

» **mchanga** (m-*chah*-ngah) *(sand)*

» **bahari** (bah-*hah*-ree) *(ocean)*

» **mawimbi** (mah-*wee*-mbee) *(waves)*

» **kuogelea** (koo-geh-*leh*-ah) *(swimming)*

» **kuogelea kwa bodi ya mawimbi** (koo-oh-geh-*leh*-ah kwa *boh*-dee yah mah-*wee*-mbee) *(surfing;* literally *swimming by using the surfing board)*

» **konokono wa baharini** (koh-noh-*koh*-noh wah bah-hah-*ree*-nee) *(seashells)*

» **matumbawe** (mah-too-*mbah*-weh) *(coral reef)*

» **kupwa na kujaa kwa bahari** (*koo*-pwah nah koo-j*ah*-ah kwah bah-*hah*-ree) *(tide;* literally *fall and rise of ocean levels)*

» **mwavuli wa ufukweni** (mwah-*voo*-lee wah oo-foo-*kweh*-nee) *(beach umbrella)*

» **mlinzi wa sehemu ya kuogelea** (m-lee-*n*-zee wah seh-*heh*-moo yah koo-oh-geh-*leh*-ah) *(lifeguard)*

» **nazi** (*nah*-zee) *(coconut)*

» **sherehe ya ufukweni** (sheh-*reh*-heh yah oo-foo-*kweh*-nee) *(beach party)*

» **machweo** (mah-*chweh*-oh) *(sunset)*

» **mawio** (mah-*wee*-oh) *(sunrise)*

Communicating with a Travel Agency

Whether you choose to plan and book your vacations by yourself or through a travel agent, you'll still want to find out if a destination is going to align with your interests. In this section, we show you how to communicate your expectations, itinerary, and weather concerns ahead of time in this section.

Articulating your expectations

Ever heard of the phrase "Stay ready so you don't have to get ready?" When it comes to traveling, especially overseas, it's important to research as much as you can so that you know what to expect. Check out these words and phrases to use with your travel agent or whomever your contact is.

>> **Ninahitaji msaada wako.** (nee-nah-hee-*tah*-jee m-sah-*ah*-dah *wah*-koh) (*I need your assistance.*)

>> **Ninaomba ushauri kuhusu vivutio vya utalii.** (nee-nah-*oh*-mbah oo-shah-*oo*-ree koo-*hoo*-soo vee-voo-*tee*-oh vyah oo-*tah*-lee) (*I request advice about tourist attractions.*)

>> **Tafadhali nieleze kuhusu vifurushi vyako vya safari.** (tah-fah-*dhah*-lee nee-eh-*leh*-zeh koo-*hoo*-soo vee-foo-*roo*-shee *vyah*-koh vyah sah-*fah*-ree) (*Please tell me about your travel package.*)

>> **Nitahitaji visa?** (nee-tah-hee-*tah*-jee *vee*-sah) (*Will I need a visa?*)

>> **Unaweza kutusaidia na visa?** (oo-nah-*weh*-zah koo-too-sah-ee-*dee*-ah *vee*-sah) (*Can you assist us with visas?*)

>> **Ninataka kuuliza kuhusu safari za ndege.** (nee-nah-*tah*-kah koo-*lee*-zah koo-*hoo*-soo sah-*fah*-ree zah *ndeh*-geh) (*I want to inquire about flights.*)

>> **Tafadhali nipe taarifa zaidi kuhusu malazi.** (tah-fah-*dhah*-lee *nee*-peh tah-ah-*ree*-fah zah-*ee*-dee koo-*hoo*-soo mah-*lah* zee) (*Please provide more details about the accommodations.*)

>> **Je, kuna punguzo lolote la bei?** (jeh, *koo*-nah poo-*ngoo*-zoh loh-*loh*-teh lah *beh*-ee) (*Is there any discount available?*)

>> **Ninaweza kulipa kwa kadi ya mkopo?** (nee-nah-*weh*-zah koo-*lee*-pah nah *kah*-dee yah m-*koh*-poh) (*Can I pay with a credit card?*)

>> **Ninashukuru kwa msaada wako.** (nee-nah-shoo-*koo*-roo kwah m-sah-*ah*-dah *wah*-koh) (*I appreciate your help.*)

Figuring out your to-do list

What do you want to do on your vacation? State your desired activities so that your travel agent can curate an attractive package for you. Use **ningependa** (nee–nge–peh–ndah) (*I'd like . . .*) to state your desires in the form of a to–do list. For example,

>> **Ningependa kupanda mlima Kilimanjaro.** (nee-nge-*peh*-ndah koo-*pah*-ndah m-*lee*-mah Kilimanjaro) (*I'd like to climb Mount Kilimajaro.*)

>> **Ningependa kuona ndovu.** (nee-nge-*peh*-ndah koo-*oh*-nahn-*doh*-voo) (*I'd like to see an elephant.*)

>> **Ningependa kulisha twiga chakula.** (nee-nge-*peh*-ndah koo-*lee*-shah *twee*-gah chah-*koo*-lah) (*I'd like to feed a giraffe.*)

>> **Ningependa kucheza densi na Wamaasai.** (nee-nge-*peh*-ndah koo-*cheh*-zah *deh*-nsee nah wah-ma-ah-*sah*-ee) (*I'd like to dance with the Maasai people.*)

>> **Ningependa kutembelea maonyesho ya Sanaa.** (nee-nge-*peh*-ndah koo-teh-mbeh-*leh*-ah mah-oh-*nyeh*-shoh yah sah-*nah*-ah) (*I'd like to visit art shows.*)

>> **Ningependa kutembelea majumba ya makumbusho.** (nee-nge-*peh*-ndah koo-teh-mbeh-*leh*-ah mah-*joo*-mbah yah mah-koo-*mboo*-shoh) (*I'd like to visit museums.*)

>> **Ningependa kuota jua.** (nee-nge-*peh*-ndah koo-*oh*-tah *joo*-ah) (*I'd like to bask in the sun.*)

Checking on the weather

Imagine packing a full suitcase of light summer clothes only to find that your destination is experiencing heavy downpours and cold temperatures! Or you miss witnessing the Great Wildebeest Migration because your truck is stuck in the mud on your way to the Maasai Mara! The major thing overlooked in these two scenarios is **hali ya hewa** (*hah*–lee yah *heh*–wah) (*weather conditions*). You cannot skip checking the weather forecast before arranging your safari. Some common weather terminology include

>> **mvua** (m-*voo*-ah) (*rain*)

>> **jua** (*joo*-ah) (*sunshine*)

>> **joto** (*joh*-toh) (*warm*)

>> **baridi** (bah-*ree*-dee) (*cold*)

>> **upepo** (oo-*peh*-poh) (*wind*)

>> **radi** (*rah*-dee) (*lightning*)

>> **ngurumo za radi** (ngoo-*roo*-moh zah *rah*-dee) (*thunderstorm*)

>> **rasharasha/manyunyu** (rah-shah-*rah*-shah/ mah-*nyoo*-nyoo) (*drizzle*)

>> **mafuriko** (mah-foo-*ree*-koh) (*floods*)

>> **dhoruba** (dhoh-*roo*-bah) (*storm*)

>> **ukame** (oo-*kah*-meh) (*drought*)

>> **matope** (mah-*toh*-eh) (*mud*)

>> **barafu** (bah-*rah*-foo) (*ice*)

>> **theluji** (theh-*loo*-jee) (*snow*)

>> **ukungu** (oo-*koo*-ngoo) (*fog*)

>> **lindi/upinde wa mvua** (*lee*-ndee/oo-*pee*-ndeh wah m-*voo*-ah) (*rainbow*)

>> **wingu;mawingu** (*wee*-ngoo;mah-*wee*-ngoo) (*clouds*)

>> **viwango vya joto** (vee-*wah*-ngoh vyah *joh*-toh) (*temperature*)

To describe what's happening with the day's weather, use the verb **kuna** (*koo*-nah) (*there is*). For example,

>> **Kuna baridi leo.** (*koo*-nah bah-*ree*-dee *leh*-oh) (*It is cold today.* [literal translation: *There is cold today.*])

>> **Kuna joto.** (*koo*-nah *joh*-toh) (*It is warm/hot; there is warmth.* [literal translation: *There is heat.*])

>> **Kuna mvua.** (*koo*-nah m-*voo*-ah) (*It is raining.* [literal translation: *There is rain.*])

If you'd like to express the weather condition in the negative, use **hakuna** (hah-*koo*-nah) (*there is no . . .*). For example,

>> **Leo hakuna mawingu.** (*leh*-oh hah-*koo*-nah mah-*wee*-ngoo) (*There are no clouds today.*)

>> **Hakuna jua.** (hah-*koo*-nah *joo*-ah) (*There is no sunshine.*)

>> **Hakuna upepo mkali.** (hah-*koo*-nah oo-*peh*-poh m-*kah*-lee) (*There are no strong winds.*)

To ask about future weather conditions, use **kutakuwa na** (koo-tah-*koo*-wah nah . . .) (*there will be . . .*). For example,

» **Kutakuwa na matope mwezi wa tatu?** (koo-tah-*koo*-wah nah mah-*toh*-peh m-*weh*-zee wah *tah*-too) (*Will it be muddy in March? [literal translation: Will there be mud in March?]*)

» **Kutakuwa na baridi kali mwezi wa sita?** (koo-tah-*koo*-wah nah bah-*ree*-dee *kah*-lee m-*weh*-zee wah *see*-tah) (*Will it be very cold in June? [literal translation: Will there be a lot of cold in June?]*)

» **Kutakuwa na joto jingi mwezi wa nane?** (koo-tah-*koo*-wah nah *joh*-toh *jee*-ngee m-*weh*-zee wah *nah*-neh) (*Will it be very hot in August? [literal translation: Will there be a lot of heat in August?]*)

REMEMBER

East Africa uses the metric system; therefore, temperature is measured in **digrii** (*dee*-gree) (*degree Celsius*). For example, you'd state a temperature reading as **Viwango vya joto leo ni kati ya digrii ishirini na tatu na digrii ishirini na nane.** (vee-*wah*-ngoh vyah *joh*-toh *leh*-oh nee *kah*-tee yah *dee*-gree ee-shee-*ree*-nee nah *tah*-too nah *dee*-gree ee-shee-*ree*-nee nah *nah*-neh) (*Today's temperatures are lows of twenty-three degrees Celsius and highs of twenty-eight degrees Celsius.*)

When talking to your travel agency, you may want to inquire about **majira/msimu** (mah-*jee*-rah/m-*see*-moo; mee-*see*-moo) (*seasons/season*). Use the following words to describe different seasons:

» **majira ya vuli/majira ya maanguko** (mah-*jee*-rah yah *voo*-lee/mah-*jee*-rah yah mah-ah-*ngoo*-koh) (*fall/autumn season*)

» **majira ya baridi/majira ya kipupwe** (mah-*jee*-rah yah bah-*ree*-dee/mah-*jee*-rah yah kee-*poo*-pweh) (*winter season*)

» **majira ya kuchipua** (mah-*jee*-rah yah mah-*see*-kah) (*spring season*)

» **majira ya joto/majira ya kiangazi** (mah-*jee*-rah yah *joh*-toh/mah-*jee*-rah yah kee-ah-*ngah*-zee) (*summer*)

Be aware that East Africa experiences seasons differently from most Northern and Southern Hemisphere countries. Our seasons are, therefore, divided into **msimu wa mvua** (m-*see*-moo wa m-*voo*-ah) (*rainy season*) and **msimu wa kiangazi** (m-*see*-moo wa kee-ah-*ngah*-zee) (*summer/sunny season*).

Packing for Your Trip

Some people travel light while others try to fit their whole life into two suitcases for vacations. No matter what group you fall in, you must have a list of items that you consider traveling essentials. This means that if you forget them at home, you might have to buy them at your destination — or not be allowed on the plane at all if you've managed to forget your passport. Read on to familiarize yourself with Swahili words for items you might need when you **fungasha mzigo** (foo-*ngah*-shah m-*zee*-goh) (*pack your luggage*).

» **pasipoti** (pah-see-*poh*-tee) (*passport*)

» **cheti cha chanjo** (*cheh*-tee chah *chah*-njoh) (*vaccination certificate*)

» **dawa** (*dah*-wah) (*medicine*)

» **dawa za maumivu** (*dah*-wah zah mah-oo-*mee*-voo) (*pain medication/ painkillers*)

» **mafuta ya kuzuia jua** (mah-*foo*-tah yah koo-zoo-*ee*-ah *joo*-ah) (*sunscreen*)

» **mafuta ya kuzuia mbu** (mah-*foo*-tah yah koo-zoo-*ee*-ah *m*-boo) (*mosquito repellent*)

» **kofia ya jua** (koh-*fee*-ah yah *joo*-ah) (*sun hat*)

» **kamera** (kah-*meh*-rah) (*camera*)

» **kitabu cha hadithi** (kee-*tah*-boo chah hah-*dee*-thee) (*novel*)

» **viatu vya kukwea mlima** (vee-*ah*-too vyah koo-*kweh*-ah m-*lee*-mah) (*climbing boots*)

» **nguo za kuogelea** (*ngoo*-oh zah koo-oh-geh-*leh*-ah) (*swimming suits*)

Check out Chapter 11 for more names of specific clothing items that you'd need to pack.

Talkin' the Talk

Olivia is planning to travel to Tanzania this summer. She calls **wakala wa safari** (wah-*kah*-lah wah sah-*fah*-ree) (*a travel agent*) to plan for her trip.

Olivia: **Habari za leo?**
             Hah-*bah*-ree zah *leh*-oh?
             How are you doing today?

Loma: **Nzuri sana. Nikusaidieje?**
             N-*zoo*-ree *sah*-nah. Nee-koo-sah-ee-dee-*eh*-jeh?
             I am doing fine. How can I help you?

Olivia:	**Ninazungumza na mtu kutoka ofisi ya kampuni ya utalii ya Zara.**
	Nee-nah-zoo-ngoo-mzah nah m-too koo-toh-kah oh-fee-see yah kah-mpoo-nee yah koo-tah-lee yah Zah-rah?
	Am I speaking with someone from Zara tours company?

Loma:	**Ndiyo. Jina langu ni Loma. Mimi ni wakala wa safari hapa.**
	Ndee-yoh. Jee-nah lah-ngoo nee Loh-mah. Mee-mee nee wah-kah-lah wah sah-fah-ree hah-pah.
	My name is Loma. I am the travel agent here.

Olivia:	**Sawa. Jina langu ni Olivia. Ninapiga simu kupanga safari yangu ya kuja Tanzania.**
	Sah-wah. Jee-nah lah-ngoo nee Oh-lee-vee-ah. Nee-nah pee-gah see-moo koo-pah-ngah sah-fah-ree yah-ngoo yah koo-jah Tah-nzah-nee-ah.
	Okay. My name is Olivia. I am calling to plan for my trip to Tanzania.

Loma:	**Karibu sana Olivia! Unapanga kusafiri tarehe ngapi?**
	Kah-ree-boo sah-nah Oh-lee-vee-ah oo-nah-pah-ngah koo-sah-fee-ree tah-reh-heh ngah-pee?
	Welcome Olivia! On which date are you planning to travel?

Olivia:	**Ninapanga kusafiri mwezi wa nane tarehe kumi hadi kumi na nne.**
	Nee-nah-pah-ngah koo-sah-fee-ree mweh-zee wah nah-neh tah-reh-heh koo-mee hah-dee koo-mee nah n-neh.
	I am planning to travel between August 10th and 14th.

Loma:	**Safi sana. Unapanga kutembelea wapi?**
	Sah-fee sah-nah. Oo-nah-pah-ngah koo-teh-mbeh-leh-ah wah-pee?
	That's great! Where do you plan to visit?

Olivia:	**Sijui. Unaweza kupendekeza sehemu nzuri za kutembelea?**
	See-joo-ee oo-nah-weh-zah koo-peh-ndeh-keh-zah seh-heh-moo n-zoo-ree zah koo-teh-mbeh-leh-ah?
	I don't know. Can you recommend nice places to visit?

Loma: **Ndiyo, kuna sehemu nyingi nzuri sana za kutembelea kama Serengeti, Ngorongoro, na ufukweni katika mji wa Dar Es Salaam au Tanga.**

Ndee-yoh, koo-nah seh-heh-moo nyee-ngee n-zoo-ree sah-nah zah koo-teh-mbeh-leh-ah kah-mah Seh-reh-ngeh-tee,Ngoh-roh-ngoh-roh nah oo-foo-kweh-nee kah-tee-kah m-jee wah Dah Eh-Sah-lah-am ah-oo Tah-ngah.

Yes, there are many nice places to visit, such as the Serengeti, Ngorongoro (Conservation Area), and the beaches near the cities of Dar Es Salaam or Tanga.

Olivia: **Kuna wanyama gani katika mbuga hizi?**

Koo-nah wah-nyah-mah gah-nee kah-tee-kah mboo-gah hee-zee?

What animals are there in these parks?

Loma: **Kuna simba, chui,tembo, vifaru, na nyati**

Koo-nah see-mbah, choo-ee, teh-mboh, vee-fah-roo, nah nyah-tee.

There are lions, leopards, elephants, rhinos, and buffalo.

Olivia: **Sawa! Ninatamani sana kuwaona wanyama wakubwa watano.**

Sah-wah! Nee-nah-tah-mah-nee sah-nah koo-wah-oh-nah wah-nyah-mah wah-koo-bwah wah-tah-noh.

Okay! I wish to see all the big five.

Loma: **Utawaona wote katika mbuga hizi.**

Oo-tah-wah-oh-nah woh-teh kah-tee-kah mboo-gah hee-zee.

You will see all of them in these parks.

Olivia: **Ningependa kujua kuhusu hali ya hewa ya mwezi wa nane.**

Nee-ngeh-peh-ndah koo-joo-ah koo-hoo-soo hah-lee yah heh-wah yah mweh-zee wah nah-neh.

I would like to know about weather in August.

Loma: **Hali ya hewa ni nzuri wakati huu. Anga linaonekana vizuri na joto ni la wastani. Watu wengi wanapenda kutembelea Tanzania wakati huu.**

Hah-lee yah heh-wah nee n-zoo-ree wah-kah-tee hoo-oo. Ah-ngah lee-nah-oh-neh-kah-nah vee-zoo-ree nah joh-toh nee lah wah-stah-nee. Wah-too weh-ngee wah-nah-peh-ndah koo-teh-mbeh-leh-ah Tah-n-zah-nee-ah wah-kah-tee hoo-oo.

The weather is nice during this time. The sky is clear with moderate temperatures. Many people like to visit Tanzania during this time.

Olivia: **Mna ofa yoyote?**
M-nah oh-fah yoh-yoh-teh?
Do you have any offers?

Loma: **Ndiyo! Una bahati sana. Tuna ofa ya safari ya siku tatu kwenda Serengeti, Ngorongoro na Zanzibar. Kuna punguzo la bei. Unapata kutembelea sehemu zote hizi kwa dola mia tano tu!**
Ndee-yoh! Oo-nah bah-hah-tee sah-nah. Too-nah oh-fah yah sah-fah-ree yah see-koo tah-too kweh-ndah Seh-reh-ngeh-tee, Ngoh-roh-ngoh-roh nah Zah-nzee-bah-r. Koo-nah poo-ngoo-zoh lah beh-ee. Oo-nah-pah-tah koo-teh-mbeh-leh-ah seh-heh-moo zoh-teh hee-zee kwah doh-lah mee-ah tah-noh too!
Yes! You are very lucky. We have a three-day safari offer to Serengeti, Ngorongoro, and Zanzibar. There is a discount. You get to visit all these places for five hundred dollars only!

Olivia: **Safi sana! Nimependa ofa hii. Je, ofa inajumuisha nini?**
Sah-fee sah-nah! Nee-meh-peh-ndah oh-fah hee-ee. Jeh, oh-fah ee-nah-joo-moo-ee-shah nee-nee?
That's great! I like this offer. What does it include?

Loma: **Ofa inajumuisha usafiri, malazi, na chakula.**
Oh-fah ee-nah-joo-moo-ee-shah oo-sah-fee-ree, mah-lah-zee nah chah-koo-lah.
The offer includes transportation, accommodations, and food.

Olivia: **Safi sana! Tafadhali niwekee nafasi. Na nitahitaji kubeba nini ninapojiandaa na safari yangu?**
Sah-fee sah-nah. Tah-fah-dhah-lee nee-wee-kee-eh nah-fah-see. Nah nee-tah-hee-tah-jee koo-beh-bah nee-nee nee-nah-poh-jee-ah-nda-ah nah sah-fah-ree yah-ngoo?
That's great! Please reserve a spot for me. And what do I need to carry when preparing for my trip?

Loma: **Nitafanya hivyo. Utahitaji kubeba mabuti kwa ajili ya safari na kutembea, jaketi la mvua, miwani ya jua, nguo za kuogelea, viza, na pesa taslimu kidogo.**
Nee-tah-fah-nyah hee-vyoh. Oo-tah-hee-tah-jee koo-beh-bah mah-boo-tee kwah ah-jee-lee yah sah-fah-ree nah koo-teh-mbeh-ah, jah-keh-tee lah m-voo-ah, mee-wah-nee yah joo-ah, ngoo-oh zah koo-eh-geh-leh-ah, vee-zah nah peh-sah tah-slee-moo kee-doh-goh.
I will do that. You will need to carry boots for walking, a raincoat, sunglasses, swimming suits, a visa, and some cash.

Olivia: **Asante sana! Tutaonana**
Ah-*sah*-nteh *sah*-nah! Too-tah-oh-*nah*-nah
Thank you very much! I'll see you (soon) !.

Loma: **Asante, kwaheri.**
Ah-*sah*-nteh, kwah-*heh*-ree.
Thanks, goodbye!

WORDS TO KNOW

punguzo la bei	poo-*ngoo*-zoh lah *beh*-ee	discount
ofa	*oh*-fah	offer
jumuisha	joo-moo-*ee*-shah	include
bahati	bah-*hah*-tee	luck
usafiri	oo-sah-*fee*-ree	transport
malazi	mah-*lah*-zee	accommodation
wakala wa safari	wah-*kah*-lah wah sah-*fah*-ree	travel agent
kampuni ya utalii	kah-*mpoo*-nee yah oo-*tah*-lee	tour company

FUN & GAMES

Name each of the Big 5 animals shown here in Swahili.

setory / Adobe Systems Incorporated

1. _____
2. _____
3. _____
4. _____
5. _____

IN THIS CHAPTER

» **Flying the friendly (Swahili) skies**

» **Hitting the road**

» **Taking to the water**

Chapter **14**

Getting Around: Planes, Trains, Taxis, Buses, and More

Mtaka cha mvunguni sharti ainame (m-*tah*-kah chah m-voo-*ngoo*-nee shah-*r*-tee ah-ee-*nah*-meh) (*Whoever needs something from under the bed must bend over*), so goes a popular Swahili proverb. In this case, whoever desires to explore the world must get comfortable traveling, unless you have mastered the enviable art of teleportation. Choose your mode of **usafiri** (oo-sah-*fee*-ree) (*transportation*) depending on your schedule, spirit of adventure, availability of transportation, distance, and, of course, your budget. This chapter outlines some key phrases and information you need for a smooth journey around Swahili towns.

Taking Flights

Usafiri wa ndege (oo-sah-*fee*-ree wah n-*deh*-geh) (*air travel/travel by plane*) is fast, reliable, and convenient for long-distance travel. You can book flights connecting various East African cities and towns online from airline websites with ease as they're all in English. However, it's best to prepare for airport lingo as you're bound to encounter a barrage of signs in Swahili. Here's a list of common terms you are sure to come across:

>> **uwanja wa ndege** (oo-*wah*-njah wah n-*deh*-geh) (*airport*)

>> **kitambulisho** (kee-tah-mboo-*lee*-shoh) (*identification*)

>> **pasipoti** (pah-see-*poh*-tee) (*passport*)

>> **chanjo** (*chah*-njoh) (*vaccine*)

>> **wenyeji** (weh-*nyeh*-jee) (*locals/residents*)

>> **wageni** (wah-*geh*-nee) (*visitors/ non-residents*)

>> **viza** (*vee*-zah) (*visa*)

>> **foleni** (foh-*leh*-nee) (*queue/line*)

>> **ushuru** (oo-*shoo*-roo) (*tax*)

>> **lango** (*lah*-ngoh) (*gate*)

>> **mizigo** (mee-*zee*-goh) (*luggage*)

>> **sanduku** (sah-*ndoo*-koo) (*suitcase*)

>> **chunga mizigo yako** (*choo*-ngah mee-*zee*-goh *yah*-koh) (*watch your luggage*).

>> **choo** (*choh*-oh) (*toilet*)

>> **usivute sigara hapa** (oo-see-*voo*-teh see-*gah*-rah *hah*-pah) (*no smoking*)

>> **afisa wa uhamiaji** (ah-*fee*-sah wah oo-hah-mee-*ah*-jee) (*immigration officer*)

>> **tiketi ya ndege** (tee-*kee*-tee yah n-*deh*-geh) (*plane ticket*)

>> **pasi ya kuabiri ndege** (*pah*-see yah koo-ah-*bee*-ree *ndeh*-geh) (*boarding pass*)

Here are some common phrases you might hear at the airport:

>> **Naomba kuona pasipoti yako.** (nah-*oh*-mbah koo-*oh*-nah pah-see-*poh*-tee *yah*-koh) (*May I see your passport.*)

>> **Hii hapa.** (*hee*-ee *hah*-pah) (*Here it is.*)

>> **Lazima upitie lango la usalama.** (lah-*zee*-mah oo-pee-*tee*-eh *lah*-ngoh lah oo-sah-*lah*-mah) (*You must go through the security gate.*)

>> **Tafadhali vua viatu vyako.** (tah-fah-*dhah*-lee *voo*-ah vee-*ah*- too *vyah*-koh) (*Please remove your shoes.*)

>> **Tutapima uzito wa mzigo wako.** (too-tah-*pee*-mah oo-*zee*-toh wah m-*zee*-goh wah- koh) (*We'll weigh your luggage.*)

>> **Mzigo wako ni mzito sana. Itabidi ulipe ada ya uzito wa ziada.** (m-*zee*-goh wah-koh nee m-*zee*-toh *sah*-nah. Ee-tah-*bee*-dee oo-*lee*-peh *ah*-dah yah oo-*zee*-toh wah zee-*ah*-dah) (*Your bag is too heavy. You'll have to pay a fee for the excess weight.*)

>> **Ndege yako inaondoka wakati kamili.** (*ndeh*-geh *yah*-koh ee-nah-oh-*ndoh*-kah wah-*kah*-tee kah-*mee*-lee) (*Your flight is on time.*)

>> **Ndege nambari . . .inayoelekea mji wa Arusha itachelewa kuondoka kwa masaa mawili.** (*ndeh*-geh nah-*mbah*-ree . . . ee-nah-yoh-eh-leh-*keh*-ah m-jee wah Arusha ee-tah-cheh-*leh*-wah kwah mah-*sah*-ah mah-*wee*-lee) (*Flight number . . . to Arusha is delayed by two hours.*)

>> **Safari ya ndege nambari . . .inayoelekea mji wa Mombasa imetamatizwa.** (sah-*fah*-ree yah *ndeh*-geh nah-*mbah*-ree . . . ee-nah-yoh-eh-leh-*keh*-ah m-jee wah Mombasa ee-meh-tah-ma-*tee*-zwah) (*flight number . . . to Mombasa is cancelled*)

>> **Itabidi ukate tiketi ya ndege tena** (ee-tah-*bee*-dee oo-*kah*-teh tee-*keh*-tee teh-nah) (*You must rebook.*) [Literally *You must buy a plane ticket again.*]

Navigating Road Transport

The most popular form of transport is **usafiri wa barabara** (oo-sah-*fee*-ree wah bah-rah-*bah*-rah) (*ground transportation*) because it is the cheapest way of getting around. You have the following options:

>> **basi** (*bah*-see) (*bus*)

>> **matatu/daladala** (mah-*tah*-too/dah-lah dah-lah) (*minibus*)

>> **teksi** (*teh*-ksee) (*taxi*)

>> **pikipiki/bodaboda** (pee-kee-*pee*-kee/ boh-dah-*boh*-dah) (*motorcycle*)

>> **bajaji/tuktuk** (bah-*jah*-jee/*tuck*-tuck) (*auto rickshaw*)

>> **treni** (*treh*-nee) (train)

Taking daladala/matatu

Matatu in Kenya, known as **daladala** in Tanzania, serve as a primary transportation option for many people. These are privately owned minibuses that are often brightly decorated and usually have music playing. They are typically used for short- to medium-distance journeys in cities and towns. They are usually operated by a **dereva** (deh-*reh*-vah) (*driver*) and a **kondakta** (koh-*ndah*-ktah) (*conductor*). The **Kondakta** collects money from the passengers and lets the driver know when to stop for a potential passenger or let a passenger off at a particular place. When taking **matatu** or **daladala** use these words and phrases:

» **nauli** (nah-*oo*-lee) (*fare*)

» **abiria** (ah-bee-*ree*-ah) (*passengers*)

» **kupanda** (koo-*pah*-ndah) (*to get on the bus*)

» **kushuka** (koo-*shoo*-kah) (*to get off/ to alight*)

» **kituo cha basi** (kee-*too*-oh chah *bah*-see/ste-jee) (*bus station*)

» **mizigo** (mee-*zee*-goh) (*luggage*)

» **chenji** (*che*-njee) (*change*)

» **utingo** (oo-*tee*-ngoh) (*bus conductor* – in Tanzania)

» **shusha!** (*shoo*-shah) (*let me off!*)

Most cities and towns don't have designated stations or stops for **matatus/daladalas** outside the downtown area, so where do you take a **matatu** if you need one? Just stand along the road and hail one down as it approaches you! A lot of times, the **kondakta** will poke his head out to ask if you need a **matatu** to a specific place. Ask the conductor **Nauli kwenda, . . . ni ngapi?** (nah-*oo*-lee *kweh*-ndah . . ., nee *ngah*-pee) (*How much is the fare to . . .?*) If the price seems right, hop in and wait for **kondakta** to ask you to pay.

TIP

Always have cash in hand when using **matatu/daladala** and ensure they're in lesser denominations, like 10, 20, 50, 100, 200 in Kenya and 500, 1000, 5000 in Tanzania. Request your balance by telling the **kondakta Nipe/Naomba salio/ chenji.** (*nee*-peh/nah-*oh*-mbah sah-*lee*-oh/*che*-njee) (*Give me the change.*)

To alight, just shout **Shusha!** (*shoo*-shah) (*let me off!*), and the **kondakta** will signal **dereva** to stop.

Nairobi is home to a robust **matatu** culture. (If you've ever watched *Pimp My Ride*, you'll have a somewhat clearer picture of what to expect from a **matatu**.) A lot of minibuses bear colorful graffiti showcasing portrait art that celebrates local and international stars. These minibuses also come fitted with TV screens and high-speed Internet for entertainment during your journey. Most of them come close to party buses rather than commuter buses because of the disco lighting and popular music they play for passengers. Be careful not to miss your stop; lots of people tend to do so because they're having too much fun aboard!

Traveling by bus

Basi (*bah*-see) (*bus*) is more suitable for cross-country distances so you can catch a glimpse of local life and a wide variety of beautiful landscapes as you make your way through different regions. **Basi** are also convenient and economical if you're a budget traveler. Unlike the **matatu/daladala**, **basi** have designated stops and stations known as **kituo cha basi** (kee-*too*-oh chah *bah*-see) (*bus stop/station*). You'll find a ticketing office at each **kituo cha basi** where you can get travel information and purchase your **tiketi** (tee-*keh*-tee) (*ticket*) using cash, mobile money transfer, or card. Some major bus companies have online booking options so you won't have to go for **tiketi** in person.

Be sure to do research beforehand so you can select the bus that best suits your needs. Make sure you are aware of the following:

>> **njia ya basi** (*njee*-ah yah *bah*-see) (*bus route*)

>> **muda wa kuondoka na muda wa kuwasili** (*moo*-dah wah koo-oh-*ndoh*-kah nah *moo*-dah wah koo-wah-*see*-lee) (*the departure and arrival times*)

>> **Nunua tiketi mapema.** (noo-*noo*-ah tee-*kee*-tee mah-*peh*-mah) (*Purchase your ticket ahead of time.*)

>> **Chunga mizigo yako.** (*choo*-ngah mee-*zee*-goh yah-koh) (*Watch your luggage.*)

>> **daraja la kwanza** (dah-*rah*-jah lah *kwah*-nzah) (*first- class*)

Only major bus companies have a few first-class seats with the rest being economy. These seats are usually towards the front of the bus with extra leg room and no seatmates.

>> **Safari inaweza kuwa ndefu kwa sababu ya foleni.** (sah-*fah*-ree ee-nah-*weh*-zah *koo*-wah *ndeh*-foo kwah sah-*bah*-boo yah foh-*leh*-nee). (*The journey might take longer than expected due to traffic.*)

Some **basi** have **kondakta** while others don't. A **kondakta** here will mostly keep the **dereva** company, make announcements of stops/lengths of breaks, and supervise luggage collection from the storage space underneath the bus.

Long-distance buses stop at intervals to allow for bathroom breaks, refreshments, and stretching. Pay keen attention to **muda wa mapumziko** (*length of breaks*). These rest stops are usually equipped with **vyoo** (vee-*yoh*-oh) (*toilets*), **maduka** (mah-*doo*-kah) (*shops*), and **migahawa** (mee-gah-*hah*-wah) (*restaurants*). Remember to carry cash to pay for toilet use.

If traveling through Tanzania, don't be surprised if your **basi** stops in the middle of nowhere and **kondakta/dereva** announces **Ni muda wa kuchimba dawa** (nee moo-dah wah koo-*chee*-mbah *dah*-wah). (*It's time to dig up medicine.*) This means it's time to relieve yourself in the bushes. (Hopefully just a bladder-emptying issue.) If this happens, watch for where the local men and women go and join your gender to answer the call of nature. Hopefully this serves as a reminder to pack your sanitizer and antibacterial wipes for such journeys.

To notify the **kondakta** that you have luggage underneath the bus, say **Nina mzigo chini ya basi** (*nee*-nah m-*zee*-goh *chee*- nee yah *bah*-see). (*I have luggage underneath the bus.*) Notify the **dereva** if your bus has no **kondakta**.

Talkin' the Talk

Jerry wants to travel from Dar Es Salaam to Nairobi by bus this weekend. He is at Ubungo bus station booking for his trip from **wakala wa basi** (wah-*kah*-lah wah *bah*-see) (*bus agent*).

Wakala wa basi:	**Habari za leo? Unasafiri kwenda wapi?** Hah-*bah*-ree zah *leh*-oh? Oo-nah-sah-*fee*-ree *kwe*-ndah *wah*-pee? *How are you doing today? Where are you traveling to?*
Jerry:	**Nzuri sana. Ninasafiri kwenda Nairobi.** N-*zoo*-ree *sah*-nah. Nee-nah-sah-*fee*-ree *kwe*-ndah Nah-ee-*roh*-bee. *I am doing very well. I am travelling to Nairobi.*
Wakala wa basi:	**Safi. Unataka kusafiri lini?** *Sah*-fee. Oo-nah-*tah*-kah koo-sah-*fee*-ree *lee*-nee? *That's great. When do you want to travel?*
Jerry:	**Ninataka kusafiri kesho asubuhi.** Nee-nah-*tah*-kah koo-sah-*fee*-ree *keh*-sho ah-soo-*boo*-hee *I want to travel tomorrow morning.*

Wakala wa basi:	**Sawa. Unataka daraja la kwanza au la kawaida?**
	Sah-wah. Oo-nah-*tah*-kah dah-*rah*-jah lah *kwah*-nza *ah*-oo *chee*-nee?
	Thats okay. Do you want first class or economy class?

Jerry:	**Ninataka daraja la kwanza. Muda wa kuondoka kituoni ni saa ngapi?**
	Nee-nah-*tah*-kah dah-*rah*-jah lah *kwah*-nza. *Moo*-dah wah koo-oh-*ndoh*-kah kee-too-*oh*-nee nee *sah*-ah *ngah*-pee?
	I want the first class. What time do we leave from the bus station?

Wakala wa basi:	**Basi linaondoka saa kumi na mbili kamili.**
	Bah-see lee-tah-oh-*ndoh*-kah *sah*-ah *koo*-mee nah *mbee*-lee kah-*mee*-lee.
	The bus will leave at 6:00am sharp.

Jerry:	**Basi litawasili Nairobi saa ngapi?**
	Bah-see lee-tah-wah-*see*-lee Nah-ee-*roh*-bee *sah*-ah *ngah*-pee?
	What time will the bus arrive in Nairobi?

Wakala wa basi:	**Basi litawasili saa tatu usiku.**
	Bah-see lee-tah-wah-*see*-lee *sah*-ah *tah*-too oo-*see*-koo
	The bus will arrive at 9pm.

Jerry:	**Asante sana. Tutaonana kesho.**
	Ah-sah-*n*-teh *sah*-nah. Too-tah-oh-*nah*-nah *keh*-shoh.
	Thank you very much. Will see you tomorrow.

Wakala wa basi:	**Asante. Kwaheri.**
	Ah-sah-*n*-teh.Kwah-*heh*-ree.
	Thanks. Goodbye.

●●●●●●●●●●●●●●●●●●●●●●●●●●●●●●●●●●●●●●

Hailing and arranging taxi pickups

Usafiri wa teksi (oo-sah-*fee*-ree wah *teh*-ksee) (*taxi rides*) can be inexpensive or expensive depending on the demand and distance. Whatever the case, there's no denying how convenient they are since they come to you and drop you off at your destination in comfort. Big cities like Nairobi, Mombasa, Kisumu, and Dar es Salaam also have popular rideshare apps like Uber and Lyft, so arranging a pickup is straightforward. You can still hail a taxi the old-fashioned way in these cities and other towns if they're marked as taxis. Remember the following important phrases while using a **teksi**:

> » **Unaenda wapi?** (oo-nah-*eh*-ndah *wah*-pee) (*Where are you going?*)

> » **Kwenda . . . ni shilingi ngapi?** (*kweh*-ndah . . .nee- shee-*lee*-ngee *ngah*-pee) (*How much does it cost to go to . . .?*)

> » **Funga mkanda.** (*foo*-ngah m-*kah*-ndah) (*Fasten the seatbelt.*)

> » **Nishushe hapa.** (nee-*shoo*-sheh *hah*-pah) (*Drop me off here.*)

Some town centers (in Dodoma, for example) will have color-coded taxis for easy identification. Most times, however, the vehicles will not be marked as taxis, but you quickly learn to identify the drivers by how alert they are to spot potential clients. A good practice by locals is to identify one good **dereva wa teksi** (deh-*reh*-vah wah *teh*-ksee) (*taxi driver*) based on your ride experience and save their phone number for any future rides.

Using smaller vehicles (tuktuk, motorcycle, bicycle)

In the mood for some adventure? How about using a **tuktuk** (called **bajaji** (bah-*jah*-jee) in Tanzania), or a **bodaboda** (boh-dah-*boh*-dah) (*motorcycle taxi*)? All of these are great options for quick errands around town and easy to find. Need to carry a lot of shopping bags, sit with a friend or two, and shelter from the sun on the go? Choose a **tuktuk**. Late for an appointment and need to beat traffic? Hop on a **bodaboda**, sitting right behind the driver. Walking through a remote area and need to give your feet a rest, hail a **bodaboda ya baisikeli** (boh-dah-*boh*-dah yah bah-ee-see-*keh*-lee) (*bicycle taxi*).

TIP

Some town centers have marked stations for **bodaboda** operators, but you can flag them down anytime you need one and notice there's no one on the **bodaboda's** passenger seat. Do the same with **tuktuks** and **bodaboda ya baisikeli**. Ask the **dereva** "**Nauli ya kwenda . . . ni shilingi ngapi?**"(nah-*oo*-lee yah *kweh*-ndah . . . nee shee-*lee*-ngee *ngah*-pee) (*How much is the fare to . . .?*) If the price is acceptable, hop on and pay in cash when you arrive at your destination.

Remember some of these useful phrases for your **bodaboda** ride:

> » **Punguza mwendo kiasi.** (poo-*ngoo*-zah m-*weh*-ndoh kee-*ah*-see) (*Slow down a bit.*)

> » **Kuwa makini.** (*koo*-wah mah-*kee*-nee) (*Be careful.*)

> » **Angalia Barabara.** (ah-ngah-*lee*-ah bah-rah-*bah*-rah) (*Eyes on the road.*)

REMEMBER

You may need to provide directions to your drivers during the journey. You're lucky if your destination is a well-known landmark, but if not, check out Chapter 7 for easy ways to give directions.

Traveling by train

Most traveling by **garimoshi/treni** (*gah*-ree *moh*-shee/*treh*-nee) (*train*) in East Africa can be an exciting and rewarding experience, especially when it is your first time in the region. Depending on the country, expect to find a variety of train services, ranging from slow cross-country trains to high-speed city commuter and cross-country trains. Before embarking on a train, familiarize yourself with the following words and phrases:

>> **muda wa kuondoka** (*moo*-dah wah koo-oh-*ndoh*-kah) (*departure time*)

>> **muda wa kuwasili** (*moo*-dah wah koo-wah-*see*-lee (*arrival time*)

>> **stesheni** (steh-*sheh*-nee) (*station*)

>> **behewa** (beh-*heh*-wah)

>> **daraja la kwanza** (dah-*rah*-jah lah *kwah*-nzah) (*first class*)

>> **daraja la kawaida** (dah-*rah*-jah lah kah-wah-*ee*-dah) (*economy class*)

Using Ships of All Kinds

Need an escape from the mainland? Try visiting the islands for a unique experience of Swahili cuisine, slow island life, and pristine beaches. Use a **kivuko** (kee-*voo*-koh) (*ferry*) if you need to access the islands off the coast of the Indian Ocean and a **meli** (*meh*-lee) (*waterbus*) or **mashua** (mah-*shoo*-ah) (*boat*) to access the islands found in Lake Victoria. This section describes some key points to pay attention to when using ships to travel in East Africa.

Taking Ferry/Boats/Water Bus Rides

All water vessels work on a strict schedule, so be sure to buy a **tiketi** (tee-*keh*-tee) (*ticket*) ahead of time at the ticketing offices and keep it with you for the whole ride in case attendants ask for proof of payment at the end of the journey. Note that the ferry rides from Likoni to Mombasa Island (coastal Kenya) are free to foot passengers and only charge a ferry toll to vehicles. If unsure of what to do, observe the locals first and follow suit.

Pay attention to these phrases when using any water vessel:

» **daraja la kwanza** (dah-*rah*-jah lah *kwah*-nzah) *(first class)*

» **kitambulisho** (kee-tah-mboo-*lee*-shoh) *(identification)*

» **pasipoti** (pah-see-*poh*-tee) *(passport)*

» **usisimame hapa** (oo-see-see-*mah*-meh *hah*-pah) *(Do not stand here.)*

» **zima injini ya gari** (*zee*-mah ee-*njee*-nee yah *gah*-ree) *(Switch off the car's engine.)*

» **usivute sigara hapa** (oo-see-*voo*-teh see-*gah*-rah *hah*-pah) *(Do not smoke here.)*

CULTURAL WISDOM

As you would expect, the terrain of the land and various out-of-pocket costs affect one's choice of transportation. Businesspeople dealing with bulky goods like farm produce routinely favor non-motorized forms of transportation over relatively short distances (0–5 miles). The most popular choice is **mkokoteni** (m-koh-koh-*teh*-nee)/**rukwama** (roo-*kwah*-mah) *(hand cart)*. Even within big cities like Nairobi you will see **mkototeni/rukwama** drivers ferrying fresh produce from central farmers markets to smaller estate markets as directed by sellers. Don't be surprised to see **mkokoteni/rukwama** drivers ferrying people across flooded roads during the rainy seasons: It's quick money for them, and the passengers get to save their footwear and clothes from ruin! A win-win for both sides.

In places like Lamu Old Town, residents use **punda** (*poo*-ndah) *(donkeys)* to transport goods. These streets are so narrow that most motorized vehicles cannot weave through them. Lamu residents are so adept at handling donkeys that they included donkey racing in their annual cultural festival. In arid and semi-arid places like northern parts of Kenya, residents sometimes ferry goods using **ngamia** (ngah-*mee*-ah) *(camels)*.

Talkin' the Talk

AUDIO ONLINE

Amanda is in Mombasa, Kenya, experiencing coastal life and culture. She decides to take the SGR (Standard Gauge Railway) **treni** (t-*reh*-nee) *(train)* to Nairobi.

Amanda:	**Habari za asubuhi? Treni ya kwanza kwenda Nairobi inaondoka saa ngapi?**
	Hah-*bah*-ree zah ah-soo-*boo*-hee? *Treh*-nee yah *kwah*-nzah *kweh*-ndah Nairobi ee-nah-oh-*ndoh*-kah sah-ah *ngah*-pee?
	Good morning! What time does the first train to Nairobi leave?

Rajabu:	**Inaondoka saa mbili kamili asubuhi.**
	Ee-nah-oh-*ndoh*-kah *sah*-ah *mbee*-lee kah-*mee*-lee ah-soo-*boo*-hee.
	It leaves at 8:00am.

Amanda:	**Inawasili Nairobi saa ngapi?**
	Ee-nah-wah-*see*-lee Nah-ee-*roh*-bee *sah*-ah *ngah*-pee?
	What time does in arrive in Nairobi?

Rajabu:	**Inawasili saa nane mchana.**
	Ee-nah-wah-*see*-lee *sah*-ah *nah*-neh m-*chah*-nah
	It arrives at 2pm.

Amanda:	**Sawa. Ninataka tiketi ya kesho asubuhi saaa mbili.**
	Sah-wah. Nee-nah-*tah*-kah tee-*kee*-tee yah *keh*-shoh ah-soo-*boo*-hee *sah*-ah *mbee*-lee
	Okay. I need a ticket for tomorrow at 8am.

Rajabu:	**Ungependa kukaa daraja la ngapi?**
	Oo-ngeh-*peh*-ndah koo-*kah*-ah dah-*rah*-jah lah *ngah*-pee?
	Which class would you like to book/sit?

Amanda:	**Ningependa kukaa daraja la kwanza. Kuna Wifi na vitafunio?**
	Nee-ngeh-*peh*-ndah koo-*kah*-ah dah-*rah*-jah lah *kwah*-nzah. *Koo*-nah WiFi nah vee-tah-foo-*nee*-oh?
	I would like to get a seat in first class. Is there Wi-Fi and snacks?

Rajabu:	**Ndiyo, kuna WiFi, vitafunio, na vyakula vinauzwa.**
	Ndee-yoh, *koo*-nah WiFi, vee-tah-*foo*-nee-oh nah vyah-*koo*-lah vee-nah-*oo*-zwah.
	Yes. There are Wi-Fi and snacks, and food is available for purchase.

Amanda:	**Vizuri sana. Nauli ni shilingi ngapi?**
	Vee-*zoo*-ree *sah*-nah. Nah-*oo*-lee nee shee-*lee*-ngee *ngah*-pee?
	That's great. How much is the fare?

Rajabu:	**Nauli ni shilingi elfu tatu.**
	Nah-*oo*-lee nee shee-*lee*-ngee *el*-foo t*ah*-too.
	The fair is three thousand.

Amanda:	**Haya. Nauli hii hapa.**
	Hah-yah. Nah-oo-lee hee-ee hah-pah
	Okay. Here is the fare.
Rajabu:	**Asante. Tiketi yako hii hapa. Tutaonana asubuhi.**
	Ah-sah-nteh. Tee-keh-tee yah-koh hee-ee hah-pah. Too-
	tah-oh-nah-nah ah-soo-boo-hee.
	Thanks. Here is your ticket. See you tomorrow morning.
Amanda:	**Asante sana. Kwaheri**
	Ah-sah-nteh sah-nah. Kwah-heh-ree.
	Thank you very much. Goodbye.

●●●

WORDS TO **KNOW**

ondoka	oh-*ndoh*-kah	leave
wasili	wah-*see*-lee	arrive
nauli	nah-*oo*-lee	fare
vitafunio	vee-tah-*foo*-nee-oh	snacks

FUN & GAMES

Identify these vehicles by their Swahili names.

1.

   _____

2.

   _____

3.

   _____

4.

   _____

Identify these vehicles by their correct names.

Chapter **15**

Arranging Accommodations

L ook around your home right now; can you name the things you see in Swahili? What is the Swahili name for your favorite room in the home? This chapter helps you to develop the language skills to start talking about everyday things in your home, booking accommodations for trips, and renting an apartment for long-term stays.

Describing Different Spaces in Your Apartment/Home

A **nyumba** (*nyoo*-mbah) (*house*) has different **vyumba** (vee-*oo*-mbah) (*rooms*). [A single room is a **chumba** (*choo*-mbah).] Your home may include the following rooms:

» **sebule** (seh-*boo*-leh) (*sitting room*)

» **chumba cha kulia** (*choo*-mbah chah koo-*lee*-ah) (*dining room*)

» **chumba cha kulala** (*choo*-mbah chah koo-*lah*-ah) (*bedroom*)

>> **jikoni** (jee-*koh*-ni) (*kitchen*)

>> **bafu** (*bah*-foo) (*bathroom*)

**CULTURAL
WISDOM**

Traditional homes in East Africa will not have **bafu** and **jikoni** as part of the rooms in the **nyumba**. These structures will be found outside and near the main house — with the bathroom/toilet (thankfully) being a bit further away than the kitchen. The toilets are outhouses modestly constructed using wood or bricks; they have a simple hole in the ground where you must squat to use rather than sit as you might be accustomed to doing. The bathrooms outside make use of *bucket showers*; that means you have to carry your bucket of water with you using a **beseni** (beh-seh-ni) (*bucket*). (Make sure you bring enough water; otherwise you might end up with shampoo still in your hair.) As for the separate **jikoni** outside, these are necessary if the family uses **kuni** (*koo*-nee)(*firewood*) for fuel to ensure no one dies of carbon monoxide poisoning or ends up with a house that smells constantly of smoke. Although having a kitchen and bathroom/toilet within the main house has mostly been a luxury for city dwellers, more and more village dwellers are gaining access to proper plumbing and using gas to cook instead of firewood. With such improvements, they have adjusted their accommodations accordingly.

Read on to discover the names of items typically found in different rooms.

The sitting room

Here are some of the items you'd expect to find in a **sebule** (seh–*boo*–leh) (*sitting room*):

>> **meza** (*meh*-zah) (*table*)

>> **sofa/kochi** (*soh*-fah/*koh*-chee) (*sofa/couch*)

>> **zulia** (zoo-*lee*-ah) (*carpet*)

>> **televisheni** (teh-leh-vee-*sheh*-nee) (*television*)

>> **taa** (*tah*-ah) (*lamp*)

>> **maua** (mah-oo-ah) (*flowers*)

>> **picha za ukutani** (*pee*-chah zah oo-koo-*tah*-nee) (*wall pictures*)

>> **rafu ya vitabu** (*rah*-foo yah vee-*tah*-boo) (*bookshelf*)

>> **mito** (*mee*-toh) *pillows*

>> **kiyoyozi** (kee-yoh-*yoh*-zee) *air conditioner*

>> **viti** (*veh*-tee) (*chairs*)

>> **saa ya ukutani** (*sah*-*ah* yah oo-koo-*tah*-nee) (*wall clock*)

REMEMBER

A lot of homes in East Africa do not have air conditioning. Some homes will use fans in the hot months, but most people just open their windows and doors to cool their rooms.

The dining room

A typical dining room would have the following items:

>> **meza** (*meh*-zah) (*table*)

>> **kitambaa cha meza** (kee-tah-*mba*-ah chah *meh*-zah) (*tablecloth*)

>> **maua** (mah-*oo*-ah) (*flowers*)

>> **taa** (*tah*-ah) (*lamp*)

>> **viti** (*vee*-tee) (*chairs*)

>> **kabati** (kah-*bah*-tee) (*cupboard/sideboard*)

The bedroom

You can expect to find the following items in a bedroom:

>> **kitanda** (kee-*tah*-ndah) (*bed*)

>> **godoro** (goh-*doh*-roh) (*mattress*)

>> **mito** (*mee*-toh) (*pillows*)

>> **blanketi** (blah-*nkeh*-tee) (*blanket*)

>> **mashuka** (mah-*shoo*-kah) (*bedsheets*)

>> **kabati ya nguo** (kah-*bah*-tee yah n-*goo*-oh) (*wardrobe*)

The kitchen

A typical **jikoni** (jee–*koh*-nee) (*kitchen*) includes the following appliances and utensils:

>> **jiko** (*jee*-koh) (*stove/cooker*)

- **jiko la umeme** (*jee*-koh lah oo-*meh*-meh) (*electric cooker/stove*)

- **jiko la gesi** (*jee*-koh lah *geh*-see) (*gas cooker/stove*)

- » **joko** (*joh*-koh) (*oven*)

- » **maikrowevu** (mah-ee-kroh-*weh*-voo) (*microwave*)

- » **jokofu/friji** (joh-*koh*-foo/ f-*reeh*-jee) (*fridge*)

- » **kabati ya vyombo** (kah-*bah*-tee yah **vyoh**-mboh) (*kitchen cabinet*)

- » **masufuria** (mah-soo-foo-*ree*-ah) (*pots*)

- » **kisu** (*kee*-soo) (*knife*)

- » **kijiko** (kee-*jee*-koh) (*spoon*)

- » **uma** (oo-mah) (*fork*)

- » **kisukumio** (kee-soo-koo-*mee*-oh) (*rolling pin*)

- » **mashine ya kuosha vyombo** (mah-*shee*-neh yah koo-*oh*-shah *vyoh*-mboh) (*dishwasher*)

- » **sinki** (*see*-nkee) (*sink*)

- » **bilauri/gilasi** (bee-lah-*oo*-ree/gee-*lah*-see) (*glass*)

- » **bakuli** (bah-*koo*-lee) (*bowl*)

- » **sahani** (sah-*hah*-nee) (*plate*)

- » **mwiko** (m-*wee*-koh) (*large wooden spoon*)

- » **jaa la taka** (*ja*-ah lah *tah*-kah) (*trash can*)

CULTURAL WISDOM

Most East Africans hand-wash their utensils as machines like dishwashers are a luxury for the very few. In most families, children from about age ten upward are assigned dishwashing as one of their daily chores. Everyone contributes in some way to keeping the home clean, and this is one example of how it works.

The bathroom

Here is a list of what you can expect to find in a bathroom:

- » **choo/msala** (*choh*-oh/m-*sah*-lah) (*toilet*)

- » **mfereji** (m-feh-*reh*-jee) (*tap/faucet*)

- » **bomba la maji** (*boh*-mbah lah *mah*-jee) (*faucet/tap*)

- » **bomba la kuogea** (*boh*-mbah lah koo-oh-*geh*-ah) (*shower head*)

- » **beseni la kuogea** (beh-*seh*-nee lah koo-oh-*geh*-ah) (*bathtub*)

- » **taulo** (tah-*oo*-loh) (*towel*)

>> **karatasi ya chooni** (kah-rah-*tah*-see yah choo-*oh*-nee) (*toilet paper*)

>> **sabuni** (sah-*boo*-nee) (*soap*)

>> **kioo** (*kee*-oh) (*mirror*)

>> **kabati** (kah-*bah*-tee) (*cabinet*)

>> **pazia la bafuni** (pah-*zee*-ah lah bah-*foo*-ni) (*shower curtain*)

>> **sinki** (*see*-nkee) (*sink*)

REMEMBER

Not all bathrooms will be as fully equipped as the list shows. Only newer, more modern houses will have them.

Finding a Place to Stay

Everybody needs a haven to get back to after a long day or night of dealing with traffic, crowds, work, loud music, trekking across town, and so on. If you're anything like us, this haven translates to suitable accommodation. Seline had one vacation ruined by a spontaneous decision to book a room in a hotel without much thought. Big mistake. A good lesson from that experience is that research and planning are essential when looking for ideal lodging for your vacation or while renting an apartment.

Asking about amenities using "kuna"

Do you mind showering with cold water or going without Wi-Fi at your hotel? If you have specific things that your room must have, use **kuna** . . . (*koo-nah; is there/are* . . .) to check whether a room comes with specific amenities before your booking. For example:

>> **Kuna wifi?** (*koo*-nah wifi) (*Is there Wi-Fi?*)

>> **Kuna kiyoyozi?** (*koo*-nah kee-yoh-*yoh*-zee) (*Is there air conditioning?*)

>> **Kuna televisheni?** (*koo*-nah teh-leh-vee-*sheh*-nee) (*Is there a television?*)

>> **Kuna kuogelea?** (*koo*-nah *bwah*-wah lah koo-oo-geh-*leh*-ah) (*Is there a swimming pool?*)

>> **Kuna maji moto bafuni?** (*koo*-nah *mah*-jee *moh*-toh bah-*foo*-nee) (*Is there hot water in the shower?*)

>> **Kuna friji/jokofu?** (*koo*-nah f-*ree*-jee/joh-*koh*-foo) (*Is there a fridge?*)

Stating your wishes using "-nge-"

If you're planning to stay at a hotel and you want to be sure that your room comes with what you need, you can also use the phrase **ningependa** . . . (nee-ngeh-*peh*-ndah) (*I would like* . . .) to express your wishes to the booking agent.

For example:

>> **Ningependa mto mkubwa.** (nee-ngeh-*peh*-ndah *m*-toh m-*koo*-bwah) (*I would like a big pillow.*)

>> **Ningependa televisheni katika chumba changu.** (nee-ngeh-*peh*-ndah teh-leh-vee-*sheh*-nee kah-*tee*-kah *chooh*-mbah *chah*-ngoo) (*I would like a TV in my room.*)

>> **Ningependa friji katika chumba changu.** (nee-ngeh-*peh*-ndah f-*ree*-jee kah-*tee*-kah *choo*-mbah *chah*-ngoo) (*I would like a refrigerator in my room.*)

>> **Ningependa pasi.** (nee-ngeh-*peh*-ndah *pah*-see) (*I would like an iron.*)

>> **Ningependa chupa za maji.** (nee-ngeh-*peh*-ndah *choo*-pah zah *mah*-jee) (*I would like bottles of water.*)

Making a reservation

Where do you stay when you travel? Hotels, motels, bed and breakfasts, backpacker hostels? In Swahili, most temporary accommodations have the same name; **hoteli** (hoh-*teh*-lee) (*hotel*). Hostels, locally known as **mabweni** (mah-*bweh*-nee) [singular form is **bweni** (*bweh*-nee) (*hostel*)] are mainly for single-gender students and are, thus, not open for booking to travelers.

A lot of hotels use online reservation forms, which ensure you don't need to speak to a person while booking your room. If you prefer to speak to a hotel clerk instead, greet them and say

>> **Ningependa kukodi chumba.** (nee-ngeh-*peh*-ndah koo-*koh*-dee *choo*-mbah) (*I would like to book a room.*)

The booking clerk will ask you a series of questions to determine whether they have a vacant room that fits your needs. This section explains the kind of questions to expect and how to respond appropriately.

Stating your length of stay

After you have stated that you would like to book a room, the first question will be about the date you plan to check in:

>> **Kutoka tarehe gani?** (koo-*toh*-kah tah-*reh*-heh *gah*-nee) (*From what date?*)

If you plan on checking in on December 20th, say

>> **Kutoka tarehe ishirini mwezi wa Disemba.** (koo-*toh*-kah tah-*reh*-heh ee-shee-*ree*-nee m-*weh*-zee wah Dee-*seh*-mbah) (*From December 20*th)

The booking clerk will then be interested in knowing how long you plan to stay at the hotel. They may ask for your check-out date by saying

>> **Hadi tarehe gani?** (*hah*-dee tah-*reh*-heh *gah*-nee) (*Until what date?*)

If you plan on checking out the day after Christmas Day (**Krismasi**) (kree-s-*mah*-see), say

>> **Hadi tarehe ishirini na sita mwezi wa Disemba.** (*hah*-dee tah-*reh*-heh ee-shee-*ree*-nee nah *see*-tah m-*weh*-zee wah Dee-*seh*-mbah) (*until December 26*)

Alternatively, the clerk may ask for the number of days you'll spend at the hotel.

>> **Kwa siku ngapi?** (Kwah *see*-koo *ngah*-pee) (*For how many days?*)

Respond by saying

>> **Kwa siku tano.** (kwah *see*-koo *tah*-noh) (*For five days*)

If you're not yet comfortable with Swahili numbers and dates, check out Chapter 5 for guidance.

TIP

Minimize the chance of any confusion by using **tarehe** (*dates*) in all your responses, as dates provide clarity on the number of days and nights you plan on spending at the hotel. The phrase **kutoka tarehe kumi na tano hadi tarehe ishirini na mbili** (koo-*toh*-kah tah-*reh*-heh *koo*-mee nah *tah*-noh *hah*-dee tah-*reh*-heh ee-shee-*ree*-nee nah *mbee*-lee) (*From January 15th to January 22nd*) comes in handy while stating your length of stay.

Comparing prices for different room offers

The amount you pay for a room depends on the type of room you book. You must, therefore, familiarize yourself with the different types of rooms available, such as

>> **chumba cha mtu mmoja** (*choo*-mbah cha *m*-too m-*moh*-jah) (*single room*) (literally; a room for one person)

>> **chumba cha watu wawili** (*choo*-mbah cha *wah*-too wah-*wee*-lee) (*double room*) (literally a room for two people)

REMEMBER

Most hotels in East Africa charge rooms per person sharing, so a single room is meant for one person and a double room is meant for two people. If you show up with company in a single room, expect a double charge on your bill.

When you have specified the type of room you want, ask about the price by saying

>> **Chumba hicho ni pesa ngapi?** (*choo*-mbah *hee*-choh nee *peh*-sah *ngah*-pee) (*How much is that room?*)

You might hear different prices for the type of room you want, depending on the number of guests sharing, floor number, view, balcony access, level of noise, amenities in the rooms, and so on. A double room with a view to the beach will cost more than a double room facing the car park. Use the word **kuliko** (koo-*lee*-koh) *(than)* to express such comparisons. For example,

>> **Chumba cha watu wawili kinachoangalia ufukweni ni ghali kuliko chumba cha watu wawili kinachoangalia maegesho ya magari.**

(*choo*-mbah chah *wah*-too wah-*wee*-lee kee-nah-choh-ah-ngah-*lee*-ah oo-foo-*kweh*-nee nee *ghah*-lee koo-*lee*-koo *choo*-mbah chah *wah*-too wah-*wee*-lee kee-nah-choh-ah-ngah-*lee*-ah mah-eh-*geh*-shoh yah mah-*gah*-ree)

A double room facing the beach is more expensive than a double room facing the parking lot.

>> **Chumba cha mtu mmmoja bila huduma ya chakula cha asubuhi ni bei rahisi kuliko chumba cha mtu mmoja na huduma ya chakula cha asubuhi.**

(*choo*-mbah chah *m*-too m-*moh*-jah *bee*-lah hoo-*doo*-mah yah chah-*koo*-lah chah ah-soo-*boo*-hee nee *beh*-ee rah-*hee*-see koo-*lee*-koh *choo*-mbah chah *m*-too m-*moh*-jah nah hoo-*doo*-mah yah chah-*koo*-lah chah ah-soo-*boo*-hee)

A single room without breakfast service is cheaper than a single room with breakfast service.

Checking into the hotel

You've survived a long flight, are perhaps feeling hot and sweaty, and just need somewhere to keep you and your luggage so you can finally relax; it's time to check into your hotel! This is a very straightforward process if you have a prior reservation. We don't know how you feel about it, but we always get very excited whenever we check into hotels. The staff will greet you and ask about your journey using **Habari za safari?** (hah-*bah*-ree zah sah-*fah*-ree) (*How was your journey?*) (Chapter 2 has some tips on the best way to respond to such greetings.)

The check-in staff will go through the process of verifying your identity by asking for your **jina** (*jee*-nah) (*name*), **nambari ya pasipoti** (nah-*mbah*-ree yah pah-see-poh-tee) (*passport number*), **barua pepe** (bah-*roo*-ah *peh*-peh) (*email*), and/or **nambari ya simu** (nah-*mbah*-ree yah *see*-moo) (*phone number*). After all is verified, they will tell you **nambari ya chumba chako** (nah-*mbah*-ree yah *choo*-mbah *chah*-koh) (*your room number*) and hand over the **funguo** (foo-*ngoo*-oh) (*key*) to your room.

Then comes the payment. Yes, most hotels in East Africa will swipe your card for payment details while you check in and not while checking out. The check-in staff will say **Naomba kadi yako ya benki** (nah-*oh*-mbah *kah*-dee *yah*-koh yah *beh*-nkee) (*I'd like your bank card.*) to which the correct response is for you to hand over your debit or credit card.

Before you leave the front desk for your room, you might want to ask a few questions for a smooth experience. For example:

>> **Chakula cha asubuhi ni saa ngapi?** (*chah*-koo-lah chah ah-soo-*boo*-hee nee *sah*-ah *ngah*-pee) (*What time is breakfast?*)

>> **Chumba cha mazoezi kiko wapi?** (*choo*-mbah chah mah-zoh-*eh*-zee *kee*-koh *wah*-pee) (*Where is the gym?*)

>> **Kuna huduma ya kukanda mwili?** (*Koo*-nah hoo-*doo*-mah yah koo-*kah*-ndah m-*wee*-lee) (*Is there a massage service?*)

>> **Kuondoka hotelini siku ya mwisho ni saa ngapi?** (koo-oh-*ndoh*-kah hoh-teh-*lee*-nee *see*-koo yah m-*wee*-shoh nee *sah*-ah *ngah*-pee) (*What time do I have to check out on the last day?*)

Talkin' the Talk

AUDIO
ONLINE

Amanda is in Zanzibar, Tanzania, for the summer. She's just arrived at the Hotel Verde and is checking in. Here is the conversation between her and Aisha, the **mhudumu wa mapokezi** (m-hoo-*doo*-moo wah mah-poh-*keh*-zee) (*receptionist*).

Aisha: **Habari za leo? Karibu sana Zanzibar!**
Hah-*bah*-ree zah *leh*-oh? Kah-*ree*-boo *sah*-nah Zan-*zee*-bar?
How are you doing today? Welcome to Zanzibar!

Amanda: **Nzuri sana! Asante sana. Nilipiga simu juzi kuweka chumba.**
N-*zoo*-ree *sah*-nah! Ah-*sah*-nteh *sah*-nah. Nee-lee-*pee*-gah *see*-moo *joo*-zee koo-*weh*-kah *choo*-mbah.
I am doing very well! Thanks. I called the day before yesterday to reserve a room.

Aisha: **Sawa. Ninaomba pasipoti chako tafadhali.**
Sah-wah. Nee-nah-*oh*-mbah pah-see-*poh*-tee *chah*-koh tah-fah-*dhah*-lee.
Okay. Can I have your passport please?

Amanda: **Pasipoti hii hapa.**
pah-see-*poh*-tee *hee*-ee *hah*-pah.
Here's my passport.

Aisha: **Asante. Utakaa chumba nambari kumi.**
Ah-*sah*-nteh. oo-tah-*kah*-ah *choo*-mbah nah-*mbah*-ree *koo*-mee.
Thanks. You'll stay in room number ten.

Amanda: **Sawa. Je, chakula cha asubuhi ni saa ngapi?**
Sah-wah. Jeh, chah-*koo*-lah chah ah-soo-*boo*-hee nee *sah*-ah *ngah*-pee?
What time is breakfast?)

Aisha: **Chakula cha asubuhi ni kutoka saa kumi na mbili na nusu hadi saa tatu.**
Chah-koo-lah chah ah-soo-*boo*-hee nee koo-*toh*-kah *sah*-ah *koo*-mee nah m-*bee*-lee nah *noo*-soo *hah*-dee *sah*-ah *tah*-too.
Breakfast is from at 6:30 to 9:00am.

Amanda:	**Sawa. Kuondoka hotelini siku ya mwisho ni saa ngapi?**
	Sah-wah. Koo-oh-ndoh-kah hoh-teh-lee-nee see-koo yah m-wee-shoh nee sah-ah ngah-pee;
	What time do I have to check out on the last day?
Aisha:	**Kuondoka hotelini siku ya mwisho ni saa nne asubuhi**
	Koo-oh-ndoh-kah hoh-teh-lee-nee see-koo yah m-wee-shoh nee sah-ah n-neh ah-soo-boo-hee
	Check-out time is at 10:00am on the last day.
Amanda:	**Asante sana!**
	Ah-sah-nteh sah-nah!
	Thank you very much.
Aisha:	**Karibu. Kama una swali piga simu mapokezi.**
	Kah-ree-boo. Kah-mah oo-nah swah-lee pee-gah see-moo mah-poh-keh-zee.
	You are welcome. If you have any questions call reception.
Amanda:	**Ahsante**.
	Ah-sah-nteh
	Thanks.

Checking out of the hotel

When the last day of your vacation comes, it's time **kuondoka hotelini** (koo-oh-ndoh-kah hoh-teh-lee-nee) (*to check out of the hotel*). (**Kuondoka hotelini** literally translates to *leave the hotel* but it's used to mean *to check out* as well.) Pack your bags and head out to the reception again. Greet the staff and say **Ninaondoka sasa.** (Nee-nah-oh-ndoh-kah *sah*-sah) (*I am leaving now.*) as you hand over the keys.

Remember the payment details you provided while checking in? They take out the payment on the day you check out after ensuring there are no other charges on top of your room charge. Your receipt will be sent to the email address you provided while checking in, but you can request a physical copy by saying **Naomba risiti ya karatasi.** (nah-*oh*-mbah ree-*see*-tee yah kah-rah-*tah*-see) (*I'd like a paper receipt.*)

You might ask for help with a few things such as taxis or airport transfers. Here's how:

>> **Nisaidie kuita teksi tafadhali.** (nee-sah-ee-*dee*-eh koo-*ee*-tah *teh*-ksee tah-fah-*dhah*-lee) (*Help me call a taxi, please.*)

>> **Je mna basi la kwenda uwanja wa ndege?** (jeh *m*-nah *bah*-see lah *kweh*-ndah oo-*wah*-njah wah n-*deh*-geh) (*Do you (pl.) have a bus going to the airport?*)

And that's it! Say **kwaheri** (kwah-*heh*-ree) (*goodbye*) to the staff and head out to your next adventure.

Renting an Apartment

Are you looking to travel and live in East Africa for a longer period, say for more than three months? Hotels are great and come in handy for short-term stays, but they aren't the most cost-effective accommodation solution for longer stays. If you're going to be somewhere for a long time, it makes sense to rent an apartment for that duration. This section explores things to consider during your search, including how to get in touch with leasing agents and potential landlords and what all those clauses in your lease actually mean.

Narrowing down your search area

Apartment hunting is like shopping; only your shopping list contains qualities you desire in a property. Some things to consider while searching for a place to rent may include the following:

>> **gharama** (ghah-*rah*-mah) (*cost*)

>> **usafiri wa umma** (oo-sah-*fee*-ree wah *oo*-mah) (*public transportation*)

>> **umbali na jiji** (oo-*mbah*-lee nah *jee*-jee) (*distance to the city*)

>> **usalama** (oo-sah-*lah*-mah) (*safety*)

>> **umbali na hospitali** (oo-*mbah*-lee nah hoh-spee-*tah*-lee) (*distance to the hospital*)

>> **umbali na kituo cha polisi** (oo-*mbah*-lee nah kee-*too*-oh chah poh-*lee*-see) (*distance to the police station*)

>> **huduma ya maji** (hoo-*doo*-mah yah *mah*-jee) (*water supply*)

>> **huduma ya umeme** (hoo-*doo*-mah yah oo-*meh*-meh) (*power supply*)

>> **umbali na ofisi yako** (oo-*mbah*-lee nah oh-*fee*-see *yah*-koh) (*distance to your office*)

>> **kelele** (keh-*leh*-leh) (*noise*)

>> **mtaa** (m-*tah*-ah) (*neighborhood*)

Communicating with leasing agents

Madalali (mah–dah–*lah*–lee) (*leasing agents*) can help to make the process of looking for an apartment/house easier. But where do you find them? Everywhere! As you walk around East African towns, you are likely to spot boards advertising various houses/apartments to let with phone numbers provided. Those phone numbers belong to **madalali**. Be sure to approach established leasing companies if you need to rent a place.

Begin by letting any leasing agent you end up working with know your **bajeti** (bah–*jeh*–tee) (*budget*). Then list your preferences so they can help you get you what you are looking for. Here are some phrases that can help with that conversation:

>> **nyumba yenye samani/fanicha** (*nyoo*-mbah *yeh*-nyeh sah-*mah*-nee/*fah*-nee-chah) (*furnished house*)

>> **nyumba isiyo na samani/fanicha** (*nyoo*-mbah ee-*see*-yoh nah sah-*mah*-nee/*fah*-nee-chah) (*unfurnished house*)

>> **huduma ya maji** (hoo-*doo*-mah yah *mah*-jee) (*water supply*)

>> **huduma ya umeme** (hoo-*doo*-mah yah oo-*meh*-meh) (*power supply*)

>> **nyumba yenye eneo maalum** (*nyoo*-mbah *yeh*-nyeh eh-*neh*-oh ma-*ah*-loom) (*house in its own compound*)

Leasing agents will do all the footwork of looking for places that fit your needs before coming back to you for confirmation and viewing options.

Communicating with landlords

Madalali hand you over to the **mwenye nyumba** (m-*weh*-nyeh *nyoo*-mbah) (*landlord*) after you have zeroed in on a possible suitable choice. At this stage, be sure to ask the following questions:

>> **Kodi ya nyumba ni shilingi ngapi?** (*koh*-dee yah *nyoo*-mbah nee shee-*lee*-ngee *ngah*-pee?) (*How much is the rent?*)

>> **Amana ni shilingi ngapi?** (ah-*mah*-nah nee shee-*lee*-ngee *ngah*-pee?) (*How much is the deposit?*)

>> **Mkataba ni wa muda gani?** (mh-kah-*tah*-bah nee wah *moo*-dah *gah*-nee?) (*How long is the lease?*)

>> **Makubaliano ya amana ni yapi?** (mah-*koo*-bah-lee-*ah*-noh yah ah-*mah*-nah nee yah–pee?) (*What are the terms for deposit?*)

>> **Mwisho wa kulipa kodi ni tarehe ngapi?** (*mwee*-shoh wah koo-*lee*-pah koh-dee nee tah-*reh*-heh *ngah*-pee?) (*When is the deadline for paying rent?*)

CULTURAL WISDOM

In Tanzania, landlords enforce a minimum six-month lease with full rent for that duration paid up front. In Kenya, most places do not have a minimum lease period, and landlords collect rent monthly.

Understanding your lease restrictions

A lease is a legal document, so pay close attention to the details before signing one. It's also not unusual for landlords to provide some rules verbally which, if broken, would allow them to terminate your lease. Check out some rules you might be told or might appear on a lease owing to cultural, religious, safety, or social ties.

>> **Usipike nguruwe hapa** (oo-see-*pee*-keh ngoo-*roo*-weh *hah*-pa) (*Do not cook pork here.*)

>> **Usitumie mishumaa** (oo-see-too-*mee*-eh mee-shoo-*mah*-ah) (*Do not use candles.*)

>> **Kelele za muziki baada ya saa tatu usiku haziruhusiwi** (keh-*leh*-leh zah moo-*zee*-kee bah-*ah*-dah yah *sah*-ah *tah*-too oo-*see*-koo hah-zee-roo-hoo-*see*-wee) (*No loud music after 9pm.*)

>> **Huruhusiwi kufanya sherehe katika nyumba** (hoo-roo-hoo-*see*-wee koo-*fah*-nyah sheh-*reh*-heh kah-*tee*-kah *nyoo*-mbah) (*No house parties allowed.*)

>> **Usivute sigara ndani ya nyumba** (oo-see-*voo*-teh see-*gah*-rah *ndah*-nee yah *nyoo*-mbah) (*Do not smoke on the property.*)

>> **Wanyama hawaruhusiwi humu** (wah-*nyah*-mah hah-wah-roo-hoo-*see*-wee *hoo*-moo) (*Animals are not allowed in here.*)

Talkin' the Talk

AUDIO ONLINE

Caitlyn and Trevor are visiting Arusha, Tanzania. They decide to look for an apartment in Njiro. Here is their conversation with the **mwenye nyumba** (*mweh*-nyeh *nyoo*-mbah) (*landlord*).

Mwenye nyumba:	**Hamjambo, karibuni kwenye ghorofa la Njiro Complex!** Hah-mh-*jah*-mboh, kah-ree-*boo*-nee *kweh*-nyeh ghoh-oh-*roh*-fah lah *Njee*-roh Complex. *How are you all doing, welcome to Njiro Complex flats.* *How are you all doing? Welcome to Njiro Complex flats.*
Caitlyn and Trevor:	**Hatujambo,** Hah-too-*jah*-mboh, *We are doing fine.*
Trevor:	**Kodi ya nyumba ni shilingi ngapi?** Koh-dee yah *nyoo*-mbah nee shee-*lee*-ngee *ngah*-pee? *How much is the rent?*
Mwenye nyumba:	**Kodi ya nyumba ni shilingi milioni mbili na elfu thelathini kwa mwezi.** *Koh*-dee yah *nyoo*-mbah nee shee-*lee*-ngee mee-lee-*oh*-nee m-*bee*-lee nah *eh*-lfoo theh-lah-*thee*-nee kwah *mweh*-zee *The rent is 2,030,000 Tanzanian shillings per month.*
Caitlyn:	**Kodi ya nyumba inajumuisha nini?** *koh*-dee yah *nyoo*-mbah ee-nah-joo-moo-*ee*-shah nee-nee? *What does the rent include?*
Mwenye nyumba:	**Kodi ya nyumba inajumuisha umeme, maji, na takataka.** Koh-dee yah nyoo-mbah ee-nah-joo-moo-ee-shah oo-*meh*-meh, *mah*-jee nah tah-kah-*tah*-kah. *The rent includes electricity, water, and trash.*
Caitlyn:	**Tungependa nyumba kubwa kidogo. Je, Nyumba hii ina vyumba vingapi?** Too-ngeh-*peh*-ndah nyoo-mbah *koo*-bwah kee-*doh*-goh. ajaeh, *nyoo*-mbah *hee*-nah *vyoo*-mbah vee-*ngah*-pee? *We would like a big house. How many rooms does this house have?*
Mwenye nyumba:	**Nyumba ina vyumba viwili vya kulala.** *Nyoo*-mbah ee-nah *vyoo*-mbah vee-*wee*-lee vyah koo-*lah*-lah. *The house has two bedrooms.*

Trevor:	**Nyumba ina vyoo vingapi?**
	Nyoo-mbah *ee*-nah *vyoh*-oh vee-*ngah*-pee?
	How many bathrooms are there?

Mwenye nyumba:	**Ina vyoo viwili, na mashine ya kufua inajumuishwa!**
	Ee-nah *vyoh*-oh vee-*wee*-lee, nah mah-*shee*-neh yah koo-*foo*-ah ee-nah-joo-moo-*ee*-shwah
	It has two bathrooms, and the washer and dryer are included.

Caitlyn and Trevor:	**Vizuri sana!**
	Vee-*zoo*-ree *sah*-nah!
	Very nice!

Mwenye nyumba:	**Mngependa kuhamia lini?**
	Mh-ngeh-*peh*-ndah koo-hah-*mee*-ah *lee*-nee?
	When would you all like to move in?

Trevor:	**Tungependa kuhamia Jumatatu! Ahsante sana!! Kwaheri!**
	Too-ngeh-*peh*-ndah koo-hah-*mee*-ah Joo-mah-*tah*-too! Ah-*sah*-nteh *sah*-nah! Kwah-*heh*-ree!
	We would like to move in on Monday! Thank you very much! Goodbye!

• •

FUN & GAMES

Name the following parts of the house.

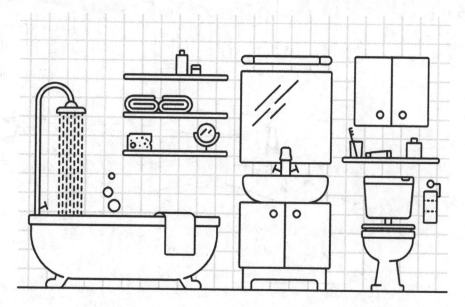

a. _____

littleartvector / Adobe Systems Incorporated

b. _____

c. _____

d. _____

Chapter **16**

Taking Care of Your Health

D o you get health insurance for your travels? That's a smart move if you do, but how else do you prepare in case of a health scare like food poisoning while in a different country? This chapter introduces you to the basics of taking care of your health by talking about your symptoms and understanding a doctor's advice in Swahili.

Parts of the Body

It's impossible to talk about **afya** (*ah*-fyah) (*health*) without mentioning **sehemu za mwili** (seh-*heh*-moo zah m-*wee*-lee) (*parts of the body*). Gestures can only get you so far in explaining to a physician that you have a headache or that your skin tingles, for example. Make a head start when it comes to escaping awkward gesticulations by learning the names of some external and internal body parts.

Identifying the external body parts

Tell a physician where you're experiencing pain by referencing these external parts of your body:

>> **ngozi** (*ngoh*-zee) (*skin*)

>> **kichwa** (*kee*-chwah) (*head*)

>> **shingo** (*shee*-ngoh) (*neck*)

>> **bega/mabega** (*beh*-gah/mah-*beh*-gah) (*shoulder/shoulders*)

>> **mkono/mikono** (m-*koh*-noh/mee-*koh*-noh) (*arm/arms*)

>> **kiganja/viganja** (kee-*gah*-njah/vee-*gah*-njah) *palm/palms*)

>> **kidole/vidole** (kee-*doh*-leh/vee-*doh*-leh) (*finger/fingers*)

>> **kifua** (kee-*foo*-ah) (*chest*)

>> **mgongo** (m-*goh*-ngoh) (*back*)

>> **tumbo** (*too*-mboh) (*belly*)

>> **tako/matako** (*tah*-koh/mah-*tah*-koh) (*buttock/buttocks*)

>> **paja/mapaja** (*pah*-jah/mah-*pah*-jah) (*thigh/thighs*)

>> **mguu/miguu** (m-goo/mee-goo) (*leg/legs*)

>> **goti/magoti** (*goh*-tee/mah-*goh*-tee) (*knee/knees*)

>> **unyayo/nyayo** (oo-*nyah*-yoh/*nyah*-yoh) (*sole of the foot/soles of the feet*)

>> **kidole cha mguu/vidole vya miguu** (kee-*doh*-leh chah m-*goo*-oo/vee-*doh*-leh vyah *mee*-goo) (*toe/toes*)

>> **kwapa** (*kwah*-pah) (*armpit*)

>> **malaika** (mah-lah-*ee*-kah) (*body hair*)

>> **sehemu za siri** (seh-*heh*-moo za *see*-ree) (*private parts*)

>> **kisigino/visigino** (kee-see-*gee*-noh; vee-see-*gee*-noh) (*heel; heels*)

>> **kiuno** (kee-*oo*-noh) (*waist*)

>> **kifundo cha mguu** (kee-*foo*-ndoh chah m-goo) (*ankle*)

>> **kisugudi** (Kee-soo-*goo*-dee) (*elbow*)

Swahili nouns form their plurals by adding (or substituting) various prefixes to the singular form depending on their noun class. Check out Chapter 3 for an in-depth look at plural formation and noun classes in general.

Did you know that Swahili speakers use names of some body parts as insults? For example, saying **matako** (mah-*tah*-koh) (*buttocks*) to someone who has offended you is like dropping an F bomb on someone. To avoid curious looks if you need to refence the buttocks, use the more respectable term **makalio** (mah-kah-*lee*-oh) (*sitting apparatus/buttocks*). **Sehemu za siri** (seh-*heh*-moo za *see*-ree) (*private parts*) is also a less shocking blanket term for male and female genitalia. See Chapter 19 for more insight of how Swahili speakers use body parts as insults.

If you were to take a closer look at your **kichwa** (*kee*-chwah) (*head*), you'd quickly notice the following features:

- » **nywele** (*nyweh*-leh) (*hair*)
- » **sikio/masikio** (see-*kee*-oh/mah-see-*kee*-oh) (*ear/ears*)
- » **jicho/macho** (*jee*-choh/*mah*-cho) (*eye/eyes*)
- » **paji la uso** (*pah*-jee lah *oo*-soh) (*forehead*)
- » **pua** (*poo*-ah) (*nose*)
- » **shavu/mashavu** (*shah*-voo; mah-*shah*-voo) (*cheek/cheeks*)
- » **mdomo/midomo** (m-*doh*-moh; mee-*doh*-moh) (*lip/lips*)
- » **jino/meno** (*jee*-noh; *meh*-noh) (*tooth/teeth*)
- » **ulimi** (oo-*lee*-mee) (*tongue*)
- » **kinywa** (*kee*-nywah) (*mouth*)
- » **kidevu** (kee-*deh*-voo) (*chin*)
- » **masharubu** (mah-shah-*roo*-boo) (*moustache*)
- » **ndevu** (*ndeh*-voo) (*beard*)
- » **taya** (*tah*-yah) (*jaws*)
- » **utosi** (oo-*toh*-see) (*crown*)
- » **kisogo** (kee-*soh*-goh) (*back of the head*)

Master these terms, and you can prove to the world that you have a good **kichwa** (*kee*-chwah) (*head*) on your **mabega** (mah-*beh*-gah) (*shoulders)!*

Listing major internal body parts

Physicians usually refer to internal body parts when carrying out a test or providing a diagnosis. Here are the names of some basic internal parts of the body to help you understand doctor speak.

- **ubavu/mbavu** (u-*bah*-voo/*mbah*-voo) (*rib; ribs*)
- **moyo** (*moh*-yoh) (*heart*)
- **pafu/mapafu** (*pah*-foo; mah-*pah*-foo) (*lung/lungs*)
- **figo** (*fee*-goh) (*kidney*)
- **ini** (*ee*-nee) (*liver*)
- **uti wa mgongo** (*oo*-tee wah m-*goh*-ngoh) (*spine*)
- **utumbo** (oo-*too*-mboh) (*intestine*)
- **kibofu** (kee-*boh*-foo) (*bladder*)
- **nyongo** (*nyoh*-ngoh) (*bile*)
- **kongosho** (koh-*ngoh*-sho) (*pancreas*)
- **kilimi** (kee-*lee*-mee) (*uvula*)
- **koromeo/koo** (koh-roh-*meh*-oh) (*throat*)
- **mishipa** (mee-*shee*-pah) (*veins*)
- **ubongo** (oo-*boh*-ngoh) (*brain*)
- **misuli** (mee-*soo*-lee) (*muscles*)
- **mfupa/mifupa** (m-*foo*-pah/mee-*foo*-pah) (*bones*)
- **tumbo** (*too*-mboh) (*stomach*)
- **kidole tumbo** (kee-*doh*-leh *too*-mboh) (*appendix*)
- **kibofu** (kee-*boh*-foo) (*gallbladder*)
- **damu** (*dah*-moo) (*blood*)
- **wengu** (*weh*-ngoo) (*spleen*)

Describing Different Feelings/States

Have you ever left a medical consultation room convinced you could have done a better job explaining how you feel? We like the 0–10 pain scale question because all we have to do is pick a number and not have to rack our brains for extra adjectives to describe the pain we are experiencing. But discomfort that lands you in hospital isn't always pain, so the pain scale cannot apply in every situation. This section shows you how to talk about various feelings, tells you which questions you can expect when a physician is trying to determine your current state of well- (or ill-)being, and clues you in on how to react appropriately.

Talking about how you feel

To say how you feel, use the phrase **ninahisi** (nee-nah-*hee*-see) (*I feel*) before describing the exact feeling. For example,

» **ninahisi kichefuchefu.** (nee-nah-*hee*-see kee-*cheh*-foo-*cheh*-foo) (*I feel nauseous.*)

» **ninahisi baridi.** (nee-nah-*hee*-see bah-*ree*-dee) (*I feel cold.*)

» **ninahisi kizunguzungu.** (nee-nah-*hee*-see kee-*zoo*-ngoo-*zoo*-ngoo) (*I feel dizzy.*)

» **ninahisi uchovu.** (nee-nah-*hee*-see oo-*choh*-voo) (*I feel exhausted.*)

Another way of expressing your feelings is identifying the part of your body that hurts. Do this using the conjugated form of the verb **kuuma** (koo-*oo*-mah) (*to hurt*):

» **tumbo linaniuma.** (*too*-mboh lee-nah-nee-*oo*-mah) (*My belly hurts.*)

» **kichwa kinaniuma.** (*kee*-chwah kee-nah-nee-*oo*-mah) (*My head hurts.*)

» **sikio linaniuma.** (see-*kee*-oh lee-nah-nee-*oo*-mah) (*My ear hurts.*)

» **macho yananiuma.** (*mah*-choh yah-nah-nee-*oo*-mah) (*My eyes hurt.*)

» **mgongo i unaniuma.** (m-*goh*-ngoh oo-nah-nee-*oo*-mah) (*My back hurts.*)

The subject marker (**li-**, **ki-**, **ya-**, **i-**) is going to change depending on whichever noun class the part of the body described falls in. If noun classes are a new concept to you, check out Chapter 3 for more details.

REMEMBER

Asking about feelings

If someone around you looks unwell and you are inclined to help, you might ask them to describe how they feel before seeking professional help. Use any of these questions:

» **Unajihisi vipi?** (oo-nah-jee-*hee*-see vee-pee) (*How do you feel?*)

» **Unaumwa wapi?** (oo-nah-*oo*-mwah wah-pee) (*Where does it hurt?*)

» **Unajisikiaje?** (oo-nah-*jee*-see-kee-*ah*-jeh) (*How do you feel?*)

» **Ni sehemu gani ya mwili inakuuma?** (nee seh-*heh*-moo *gah*-nee yah *mwee*-lee ee-nah-koo-*oo*--mah) (*Which part of your body hurts?*)

Reacting to other's feelings

How do you react to other people's pain and agony? The Swahili culture appreciates a show of concern and empathy even when you cannot be of any meaningful help. If someone expresses their discomfort to you, you can say:

>> **pole** (*poh*-leh) (*Sorry*) [This in no way implies that you are the cause of the stated discomfort.]

>> **jamani pole!** (jah-*mah*-nee *poh*-leh) (*So sorry!* [with more empathy])

>> **ugua pole** (oo-*goo*-ah *poh*-leh) (*Get well soon.*)

>> **Tulia! Tulia!** (too-*lee*-ah too-*lee*-ah) (*Calm down! calm down!*) [to someone crying in pain]

Seeking Medical Attention

When in a new country, which sites do you view as important to have near your accommodation or easy to get to? The restaurant with glowing online reviews, the neighborhood jazz bar, or perhaps that speakeasy your friends recommended? While you might not plan to visit a hospital in a foreign country, you'll be smart to learn where to look for help if you need medical attention. This section discusses places you're likely to find medical personnel as well as how to communicate with them and understand their directions.

Locating a physician

Most towns and cities have centrally located **hospitali** (hoh-spee-*tah*-lee) (*hospitals*). They're big, prominently labelled, and hard to miss. You can direct your taxi by saying **Nipeleke hospitali ya karibu.** (nee-peh-*leh*-keh hoh-spee-*tah*-lee yah kah-ree-boo) (*Take me to the nearest hospital.*)

In an emergency, call 999 if you're in a Kenyan city; however, you might get a quicker response from private ambulance services. The Tanzanian government advises one to use 112 or 114 in similar situations, but the locals usually arrange their own private means of transportation such as taxis.

You can seek fast medical care in other places as well, including the following:

» **kliniki** (klee-*nee*-kee) (*clinic*)

» **zahanati** (zah-hah-*nah*-tee) (*dispensary*)

» **duka la dawa** (*doo*-kah lah *dah*-wah) (*pharmacy*)

You will find structures marked **kliniki**, **zahanati** and **duka la dawa** in several neighborhoods with staff who offer medical care but will refer you to **hospitali** if need be.

CULTURAL WISDOM

Hospitals in East Africa do not require you to book appointments before seeing a physician as would be the case in the United States and UK. Even in a non-emergency situation, you can walk into a hospital and get attended to on the same day. The trick is to arrive early in the day as queues sometimes get long in the waiting rooms, especially if it's a public hospital.

Explaining your symptoms

Expect the usual triage questions from physicians such as

» **Shida ni nini?** (*shee*-dah nee *nee*-nee) (*What's the problem?*)

» **Unaumwa wapi?** (*oo*-nah-*oo*-mwah *wah*-pee) (*Where does it hurt?*)

» **Tangu lini?** (*tah*-ngoo *lee*-nee) (*Since when?*)

» **Kwa muda gani?** (kwah *moo*-dah *gah*-nee) (*For how long?*)

State your **dalili za ugonjwa** (dah–*lee*–lee zah oo–*goh*–njwah) (*symptoms of illness*) by saying how you feel using **ninahisi** (nee-nah-*hee*-see) (*I feel*) or **kuuma** (koo-oo-mah) (*to hurt*) if a part of your body hurts. Flip back a few pages for some examples.

Other **dalili za ugonjwa** include the following:

» **ninaharisha** (nee-nah-hah-*ree*-shah) (*I have diarrhea.*)

» **ninatapika** (nee-nah-tah-*pee*-kah) (*I am vomiting.*)

» **ninakohoa** (nee-nah-koh-*hoh*-ah) (*I am coughing.*)

» **nina homa** (nee-nah *hoh*-mah) (*I have a fever.*)

» **ninawashwa ngozi** (nee-nah-*wah*-shwah *ngoh*-zee) (*I have itchy skin.*)

Understanding the Doctor's/Pharmacist's Instructions: Using Object Pronouns

Madaktari (mah–dah–*ktah*–ree) (*doctors*) usually take the time to explain what they're doing during a consultation, and they also tell you what to expect. For example, **nitakupima joto** (nee–tah–koo–*pee*–mah *joh*–toh) (*I'll measure your temperature.*). Notice the insertion of **-ku-** into the phrase **nitapima** (nee–tah–*pee*–mah) (*I will measure*). **-ku-** is an object pronoun. Object pronouns refer to the recipient of the action of a verb (**-pima**). These pronouns vary depending on the noun class of the object being referred to. In Swahili, object pronouns are generally placed between the verb and the subject pronoun marker. See examples below.

» **Nitakupa dawa.** (nee–tah–*koo*–pah *dah*–wah) (*I'll give you medicine.*)

» **Ananipima.** (ah–nah–nee–*pee*–mah) (*He/she is diagnosing me.*)

» **Atamchoma sindano.** (ah–tah–m–*choh*–mah see–*ndah*–noh) (*He/she will inject him/her.*)

» **Anawapa chanjo.** (ah–nah–*wah*–pah *chah*–njoh) (*He/she is giving them the vaccine.*)

» **Anakupelekeni hospitalini.** (ah–nah–koo–peh–leh–*keh*–nee hoh–spee–tah–*lee*–nee) (*He/she is taking you all to the hospital.*)

» **Anawapeleka hospitalini.** (ah–nah–wah–peh–leh–*keh*–nee hoh–spee–tah–*lee*–nee) (*He/she is taking you all to the hospital.*)

» **Anajichoma sindano** (ah–nah–jee–*choh*–mah see–*ndah*–noh) (*He/she is injecting himself/herself.*)

Let's break down how a sentence with object pronouns is structured.

Nitakupa dawa.

Ni-	This sentence begins with a first person singular subject pronoun marker **ni-**. That means that the subject pronoun **mimi** has been omitted since you don't necessarily need both the subject pronoun and the pronoun marker. **(Mimi) nitakupa dawa.**
-ta-	This is a tense marker — in this case, the future tense marker **-ta**.
-ku-	An object marker; the second person singular "you" object pronoun marker, to be specific
-pa	The conjugated form of the verb "to give"
dawa	The noun "medicine"

Object markers can be direct or indirect.

>> A *direct object* is the noun that receives/is affected by the action of the verb in a sentence. For example *I saw him*. The word *him* is a direct object of the verb *to see*. In Swahili, **Ananipima** (ah-nah-nee-*pee*-mah) (*He/she is diagnosing me*) breaks down as follows: **-ni-** is a direct object marker referring to the implied object pronoun **mimi**.

>> An *indirect object* receives the direct object. For example, in the sentence *I gave it to him*, *him* is an indirect object receiving *it* — the direct object. In the Swahili sentence **anampa mgonjwa dawa** (ah-nah-*m*-pah m-*goh*-njwah *dah*-wah) (*He/she is giving the patient medicine*); **-m-** is an indirect object marker referring to **mgonjwa**.

REMEMBER

Swahili uses the same object markers for direct and indirect objects. That means you don't have to learn two different sets of object markers; you just have to know when to use them.

Table 16-1 presents the various object pronouns in all their glory.

TABLE 16-1

Object pronouns for people, animals, and all living creatures

Swahili	Pronunciation	English
-ni-	nee	*me (first person singular)*
-ku-	koo	*you (second person singular)*
-m-	m	*he/she (third person singular)*
Swahili	*Pronunciation*	*English*
-tu-	too	*us (first person plural)*
***-wa-(Kenya)**	wah	*you (pl.) (second person plural)*
***ku. . .-eni (Tanzania)**	koo-. . .-eh-nee	*you (pl.) (second person plural)*
-wa-	wah	*them (third person plural)*
-ji-	jee	*self*

TIP

Kenyan and Tanzanian Swahili speakers differ in how they express the second person plural object marker (*you all*). Remember both to communicate seamlessly with speakers from both regions.

Here are a few more examples:

» **Ananisaidia** (ah-nah-nee -sah-ee-*dee*-ah) (*He/she is helping me.*)

» **Tuliwaona** (too-lee-wah-*oh*-nah) (*We saw them.*)

» **Walimkimbiza** (wah-lee-m-kee-*mbee*-zah) (*They chased him/her.*)

» **Alikupikia** (ah-lee-koo-pee-*kee*-aah) (*He/she cooked for you.*)

» **Alikutumieni barua pepe** (ah-lee-koo-too-mee-*eh*-nee bah-*roo*-ah *peh*-peh) (*He sent you all an email.*)

» **Aliwatumia barua pepe** (ah-lee-wah-too-*mee*-ah bah-*roo*-ah *peh*-peh) (*He sent them an email.*)

» **Walijitibu** (wah-lee-jee-*tee*-boo) (*They treated themselves.*)

Talkin' the Talk

Meredith is visiting Mwanza, Tanzania, for the first time. She is not feeling well and decides to go see a **daktari** (dah-*kta*-ree) (*doctor*).

Meredith: **Habari za leo daktari?**
Hah-*bah*-ree zah *leh*-oh dah-*kta*-ree dah–k–*tah*–ree?
How are you doing doctor?

Daktari: **Nzuri sana.Nikusaidieje?**
N-*zoo*-ree *sah*-nah. Nee-koo-sah-ee-dee-*eh*-jeh?
Fine. How can I help you?

Meredith: **Sijisikii vizuri. Nina homa na sina hamu ya kula.**
See-jee-*see*-kee vee-*zoo*-ree. *Nee*-nah *hoh*-mah nah *see*-nah *hah*-moo yah *koo*-lah.
I am not feeling well, and I don't have an appetite.

Daktari: **Pole sana! Tangu lini?**
Poh-leh *sah*-nah. *Tah*-ngoo *lee*-nee?
Very sorry. Since when?

Meredith: **Tangu jana usiku**
Tah-ngoo *jah*-nah oo-*see*-koo.
Since last night

Daktari: **Ulikunywa dawa yoyote?**
Oo-lee-*koo*-nywah *dah*-wah yoh-*yoh*-teh?
Did you take any medicine?

Meredith:	**Ndiyo. Nilikunywa dawa ya kupunguza maumivu.**
	Ndee-yoh yah *koo*-pun-*goo*-zoo *mah*-mee-voo *dah*-wah
	Yes. I took a pain killer.

Daktari:	**Sehemu gani ya mwili inauma?**
	Seh-*heh*-moo *gah*-nee yah *mwee*-lee ee-nah-oo-mah?
	Which part of your body hurts?

Meredith:	**Ninaumwa kichwa, mgongo na miguu.**
	Nee-nah-oo-mwah *kee*-chwah, m-*goh*-ngoh nah mee-*goo*-oo.
	My head, back, and legs ache.

Daktari:	**Pole sana. Nenda maabara wakakupime choo na damu. Halafu urudi kupata majibu yako.**
	Poh-leh *sah*-nah. *Neh*-ndah mah-ah-*bah*-rah wah-kah-koo-pee-meh *choh*-oh nah *dah*-moo. Hah-*lah*-foo oo-*roo*-dee koo-*pah*-tah mah-*jee*-boo *yah*-koh.
	Sorry. Go to the lab; they will take your stool and blood and then come back for your results.

Meredith:	**Sawa daktari. Asante.**
	Sah-wah dah-*kta*-ree dah–k–*tah*–ree. Ah-sah-*nh*-the.
	Okay, doctor. Thanks.

Some time later

Daktari:	**Karibu tena. Nilipata majibu yako. Pole sana una malaria na homa ya matumbo.**
	Kah-*ree*-boo *teh*-nah. Nee-lee-*pah*-tah mah-*jee*-boo *yah*-koh. *Poh*-leh *sah*-nah oo-nah mah-lah-*ree*-ah nah *hoh*-mah yah mah-*too*-mboh.
	Welcome again. I got your results. I am very sorry. You have malaria and typhoid.

Meredith:	**Ahsante daktari. Utanipa dawa?**
	Ah-sah-*n*-teh dah-*kta*-ree dah–*kta*–ree. Oo-tah-*nee*-pah *dah*-wah?
	Thanks doctor. Will you prescribe me medicines?

Daktari:	**Nitakuchoma sindano na nitakupa dawa ya malaria pia.**
	Nee-tah-koo-*choh*-mah see-*ndah*-noh nah nee-tah-*koo*-pah *dah*-wah yah mah-lah-*ree*-ah.
	I will give you an injection, and I will also give you malaria pills.

Meredith:	**Nitameza dawa kwa muda gani?**
	Nee-tah-*meh*-zah *dah*-wah kwah *moo*-dah *gah*-nee?
	How long will I take the medicine?

Daktari:	**Utazimeza kwa wiki moja halafu utarudi kupima tena.**
	Oo-tah-zee-*meh*-zah kwah *wee*-kee *moh*-jah hah-*lah*-foo
	oo-tah-*roo*-dee koo-*pee*-mah *teh*-nah.
	You will take them for one week, and then you will come back
	for another test.
Meredith:	**Sawa daktari.**
	Sah-wah dah-*kta*-ree dak–*tah*–ree.
	Okay, doctor.

● ●

WORDS TO KNOW

dawa ya kupunguza maumivu	*dah*-wah yah koo-poo-*ngoo*-zah mah-oo-*mee*-voo	pain killer (Literally "the medicine for reducing pain"
sindano	see-*ndah*-noh	*injection*
kupima	koo-*pee*-mah	*to test*
majibu	mah-*jee*-boo	*results*
dawa	*dah*-wah	*medicines*
maabara	mah-ah-*bah*-rah	*lab*
hamu ya kula	*hah*-moo yah *koo*-lah	*appetite*
homa ya matumbo	*hoh*-mah yah mah-*too*-mboh	*typhoid*
choo	*choh*-oh	*stool*
damu	*dah*-moo	*blood*
daktari	dah-*kta*-ree	*doctor/physician*

FUN & GAMES

Use the word bank provided to label the following parts of the body.

mkono miguu tumbo shingo

kichwa magoti nywele sikio

mabega pua mdomo

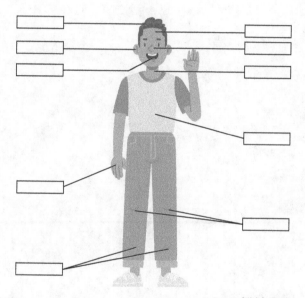

tynyuk/Adobe Stock

Use the word bank provided to label the following parts of the body.

4

The Part of Tens

IN THIS PART . . .

See what Swahili proverbs say about Swahili culture.

Grasp Swahili quickly.

Learn what phrases to avoid.

Chapter **17**

Ten Common Swahili Proverbs and Their Meanings

P roverbs are an essential component of Swahili culture and have been used for ages to impart advice, serve as a warning, ridicule unbecoming behavior, and make jokes among the natives. A lot of Swahili folklore and oral narratives are constructed around proverbs as a way of imparting moral lessons through generations. These proverbs are not hidden in literature only; you will hear them liberally used in everyday conversations as well. As such, they provide insight into the Swahili culture and worldview. Proverbs help Swahili people in making sound decisions and are used to impart cultural values and teachings.

This chapter introduces ten common Swahili proverbs and their meanings.

Haraka Haraka haina baraka/
Polepole ndio mwendo

(hah-*rah*-kah hah-*rah*-kah hah-*ee*-nah bah-*rah*-kah / poh-leh-*poh*-leh *ndee*-oh m-*weh*-ndoh)

(*Hurry hurry has no blessings. / Slowly is the way to go.*)

Rushing through one's duties is likely to result in disasters. The Swahili culture emphasizes the importance of taking one's time to do things well rather than producing shoddy work hastily. These twin proverbs are widely displayed on public transportation vehicles to caution against reckless/high-speed driving. You are likely to hear passengers say one or the other to a driver they consider reckless as a reminder to slow down.

Yaliyopita si ndwele, tugange yajayo

(Yah-lee-yoh-*pee*-tah see *ndweh*-leh too-*gah*-ngeh yah-*jah*-yoh)

(*What has passed is dust; let us look ahead.*)

The past is gone; focus on what the future holds. This saying serves as a gentle reminder to Swahili people to focus on both their immediate present and the most likely future scenarios. People are advised to move on and let go of the past instead of obsessing over past mistakes. It motivates people to take responsibility for their actions and put their futures at the forefront. This proverb is commonly used by people after realizing that they made a mistake in the past and there's nothing they do would change it, so they own up to their wrongdoing and propose to do better in the future. You can use this proverb to reassure a friend that whatever mistake they made was a lesson for a better future; no grudges held.

Mtaka cha mvunguni sharti ainame

(m-*tah*-kah chah m-voo-*ngoo*-nee shah-*r*-tee ah-ee-*nah*-meh)

(*Whoever needs something from under the bed must bend over.*)

For you to succeed in anything, you have to put in disciplined work. Whatever you seek from under the bed does not come to you; you must go to it. This proverb encourages honest work and reminds people that nothing is achieved through sheer luck. A lot of Swahili schoolchildren hear this proverb as advice to work hard for good results.

Maziwa/maji yakimwagika hayazoleki

(mah-*zee*-wah yah-kee-mwah-*gee*-kah hah-yah-zoh-*leh*-kee)

(*When milk spills it cannot be collected back.*)

Have you ever had milk boil over a pot? There's no way to recover the milk lost! This proverb is used in two related instances: One, whatever is damaged cannot be made anew no matter how much effort is put into it; and two, anything will go above and beyond what is anticipated when it reaches its limit. The first meaning serves as a helpful reminder to know when to let go and walk away from situations that damage relationships. The second meaning is a warning to those who tend to take on multiple assignments that they should only accept those duties and obligations they can handle. Otherwise, they might "boil over."

Mficha uchi hazai

(m-*fee*-chah oo-chee hah-*zah*-ee)

(*She who hides her nakedness does not give birth.*)

Exposing your struggles to your community is likely to get you help. This proverb stresses the importance of people being open and addressing what they are struggling with so that they can receive assistance and advice from their family or the community around them. The Swahili culture is big on communal living, and offering a listening ear is one aspect of that culture that still holds true to date. Some midwives use this proverb literally to encourage women in the birthing process not to be shy around medical staff.

Jogoo wa shamba hawiki mjini

(joh-goh-oh wah shah-mbah hah-wee-kee m-jee-nee)

(A village rooster doesn't crow in town.)

A new environment may be disorienting to someone not familiar with it, thus affecting their behavior or performance. This proverb serves as a reminder that everyone comes from a different background and has different experiences, and that when teaching someone anything new, it is crucial to be patient and encouraging. For instance, a person who relocates to the city could find it difficult to get a job or handle some aspects of city life because they are unfamiliar with them, but we can help them succeed in their new surroundings by assisting them in adjusting.

Asiyesikia la mkuu huvunjika guu

(ah-see-yeh-see-kee-ah lah m-koo-o hoo-voo-njee-kah goo-oo)

(One who does not listen to their elders breaks their leg.)

You do not literally break your leg (unless you're very unlucky), but you might encounter a great setback or consequence if you do not listen to your elders. This proverb is rooted in the Swahili culture of revering elder advice and direction. In our earlier years, we often heard this proverb whenever we were about to do or did something contrary to our parents' or teachers' advice. If you hear this proverb said after the recipient has done something contrary to earlier direction, you should understand it as the Swahili version of "I told you so."

Mwenda tezi na omo marejeo ni ngamani

(m-weh-ndah teh-zee nah oh-moh mah-reh-jeh-oh nee ngah-mah-nee)

(One who moves from a ship's bow to the stern must pass through the middle part.)

The Swahili culture emphasizes the importance of knowing and respecting one's roots. Those who busy themselves pursuing new thrills will always long for familiarity — their roots. This maritime proverb implies that no matter how far and wide one travels in pursuit of different dreams, they will always think fondly of home and even eventually return. This proverb is the Swahili equivalent of East or West, home is best.

Mtaka yote hukosa yote

(m-*tah*-kah yoh-teh hoo-*koh*-sah *yoh*-teh)

(*One who wants all misses all.*)

Decisiveness is a virtue, and greed is a vice. One who is faced with multiple enticing choices must make an informed decision or risk losing all of them. We often hear this proverb said to people with multiple love interests; the warning being that if the love interests do not get their undivided attention soon, the person would end up with no partner. Of course, this is not the only applicable area for this proverb: Young people who struggle with decisions on school choices, job offers, or fun events to attend also hear it often.

Mgema akisifiwa tembo hulitia maji

(m-*geh*-mah ah-kee-see-*fee*-wah *teh*-mboh hoo-lee-*tee*-ah *mah*-jee)

(*If the wine tapper is praised, he dilutes the wine with water.*)

Do not let compliments go to your head — in other words, you should be wary of getting too comfortable in your position just because you receive good feedback. Use this proverb to warn someone if they are not working as hard as they used to in the same position because soon enough, the same people who praised their work will notice the slack and conclude they had no talent to begin with. We have seen this proverb used lately to criticize businesses that started out by providing high-quality products or services, thus gaining loyal customers and receiving rave reviews, but a few months down the line, customers start noticing a decline in quality.

Chapter **18**

Ten Ways to Pick Up Swahili Quickly

Even though learning a new language can be a daunting task, you can master Swahili quickly if you use enjoyable and entertaining learning methods alongside learning the more structured language rules. This chapter introduces different techniques that make it easier to learn Swahili.

Watching Swahili Movies and TV Shows

You can improve your Swahili listening and comprehension skills as well as your vocabulary by immersing yourself in Swahili movies and TV. (Rest assured that most have English subtitles to support understanding when you absolutely need it.) Swahili movies and shows can help you pick up new words and phrases more easily, and you get to learn more about Swahili culture while enjoying fantastic narratives. When selecting something to watch, choose something that matches your proficiency level, interest, and engagement. You don't want to watch an incomprehensible movie. There are lots of different Swahili movies and TV series that you can watch on Netflix, YouTube, Amazon Prime, or other streaming services. For a start, check out *Siri ya Mtungi*, *Safari*, *Bahasha*, *Rafiki*, *Binti*, *Tunu*, and *Country Queen*.

Listening to Swahili Songs

Listening to Swahili popular songs is another great way of picking up the language quickly. Add a list of Swahili songs to your playlist, then play them as you take a road trip, go for an evening walk, walk your dog, or are just chilling in the house. Imagine having an earworm after listening to a Swahili song five times. These songs are sure to help you to improve your vocabulary and grammar skills and make the learning entertaining and momentous. Also, they help you brush up your pronunciation and intonation. Many popular individual musicians and musical groups are East African, such as Otile Brown, Diamond Platnumz, Nadia Mukami, Vanessa Mdee, Sanaipei Tande, Eddy Kenzo, Barnaba, Harmonize, Sautisol, Nandy, Zuchu, Alikiba, and Maua Sama, just to mention a few. Go on YouTube or Spotify, search for their names, and check out their music.

Watching the Swahili News

As you study very hard to perfect your Swahili language skills, news channels such as BBC Swahili, VOA Swahili, and DW Swahili are the best additional resources for you to improve your vocabulary, pronunciation, and exposure to different Swahili dialects. These news programs often feature niche topics that might be of interest to you. When you watch Swahili news, opt for subtitles, list down the new words and phrases you hear for the first time, and look for their meanings afterwards. Pay attention to the news headlines and see if you can predict the content of the news-related story.

Reading Swahili Newspapers

Reading Swahili newspapers such as *Taifa Leo, Mwananchi, Tanzania Daima, Jamhuri, Mtanzania, Nipashe,* and *Harakati* can help you to quickly learn the language. These newspapers expose you to a variety of topics and language structures that help you to learn about the culture and the ongoing events in Swahili-speaking countries. As you read these newspapers, scan for specific information, identify the key words and meaningful chunks for grasping complex language structures and for the purpose of understanding the context. Reading these newspapers out loud helps in improving your pronunciation as well. You can access some of these newspapers at `https://taifaleo.nation.co.ke/` and `www.w3newspapers.com/tanzania/`).

Listening to Swahili Radio Stations

If your target is to become fluent in Swahili, listening to radio stations is another exciting and fun way to do it! Tuning into Swahili radio stations helps you become more familiar with Swahili language, people, and their culture. Drawing your attention to a variety of voices, accents, and styles of speaking, Swahili radio stations allow you to pick up the perfect Swahili pronunciation and intonation. Again, listen closely to the words and phrases being used by radio hosts, take notes, and look up new words to help build your vocabulary and understand the context. You can tune into Swahili radio stations online at https://raddio.net/language/swahili/. There you'll find links to *Radio Free Africa, TBC Taifa, Radio One Stereo, EFM Radio, Wapo Radio*, and *Times Fm*, among others.

Watching Swahili Content Creators on Social Media

Numerous incredible Swahili content creators on Facebook, Instagram, YouTube, TikTok, and other social media sites post tutorials, skits, and other types of information in the language. You can learn Swahili more quickly and enjoy it while you watch these videos and interact with the content creators. You may learn more about the culture and the way Swahili is used in daily life by watching what these content creators post. Start by checking out content found on these sites: *Simulizi za Jossy, Simulizi na Sauti, The Storybook, Simulizi za Denis Mpagaze*, and *Bahati Harrison*.

Conversing with Swahili Speakers

If you are already in East Africa, get out and engage the locals in small talk. Regularly communicating with Swahili speakers helps you to pick up new words, phrases, and idiomatic expressions that are used in everyday speech. You can improve your language skills quickly by listening to the accents of native speakers and practicing every day for a few weeks or months. Don't be shy to ask questions or seek clarification when necessary.

Traveling to a Swahili-speaking Country

Embarking on a trip to a Swahili-speaking country and staying there for some time necessitates your speaking Swahili. You must be able to communicate clearly in order to survive in a Swahili-speaking country. Even when you have the option to use your native language, try to speak as much Swahili as you can. Immerse yourself in daily life as a Swahili speaker to better grasp the language's many culturally and contextually specific idioms and slang expressions, which can be understood only by becoming more familiar with the way of life of Swahili speakers. Attempt to interact with locals as well to understand more about their culture and to improve your Swahili.

Reading Swahili Children's Books

You can practice your Swahili language skills by reading children's books in the language. These books have simple vocabulary and grammar, which makes the language learner-friendly. Authors of Swahili children's books craft entertaining and captivating tales that inspire you to hone your communication abilities. The good news is that the stories provide a brief overview of cultural knowledge to help you understand the traditions and customs of the Swahili people. Make sure you read *Mimi ni Mdogo, Nyumbani Kuna Mchele, Nguruwe Hawaruhusiwi, Msichana Mdogo na Simba Watatu, Tom Muuza Ndizi, Adili na Nduguze,* and *Paka Tabibu nk.* You can purchase all of these books on Amazon.

Listening to Swahili Podcasts

You can access a number of free Swahili podcasts online such as *SwahiliPod101, BONGO Classy, LinguaBoost, Africa & Beyond, Kenyan Plug, SBS Swahili, Swahili Audio Lessons,* and *Swahili Talk.* Listening to these podcasts is another useful technique for learning new Swahili words, phrases, and idioms. To assist you in learning the language, these podcasts offer audio lessons, discussions, and cultural insights. You can choose to listen to subjects that you are interested in, like food, clothing, bargaining, and the way of life of the Swahili people in general. Get exposed to various accents and dialects by listening to a variety of podcasts.

Chapter 19

Ten Words You Should Never Say in Swahili

Have you ever tried to learn a new language and a native speaker tricked you into saying a word that elicited uncomfortable laughter or even shock from others? While this prank is harmless in friendly company, it can cause strained relationships for you in East Africa. This chapter explains ten words and phrases that you should never say in Swahili and why they are inappropriate.

Tomba

Tomba (*toh*-mbah) (*the f-word*)

Swahili culture reveres modesty in all forms, including speech. Thus, people view sex and topics related to sex as taboo words. Using the word **tomba** as an insult is seen as highly derogatory and disrespectful toward an individual's dignity. If you ever want to witness pearl clutching by the Swahili, utter this word in a crowded place. Beware that you might be thrown out and banned from said place, too.

Mkundu

Mkundu (m-*koo*-ndoo) (*asshole*)

Mentioning this body part is far from ordinary or casual. It carries the weight of an explosive insult designed to harm. But why does such a word hold such immense power in Swahili culture? The answer lies in the very essence of Swahili values — a deep-rooted reverence for respect of human privates that mentioning them out loud is seen as an obscene act.

Ng'ombe

Ng'ombe (*ng'oh*-mbeh) (*cow*)

Many Swahili-speaking households keep a cow or two in the village for milk and trade later when they need a huge chunk of money. However, calling someone a cow is a negative thing. It means that you view them as stupid, having poor judgement, and being incapable of self-management. A common rebuttal on Kenyan social media is **wazazi wako waliuza ng'ombeh kupeleka ng'ombeh mwingine shuleni** (wah-*zah*-zee *wah*-koh wah-lee-*oo*-zah *ng'o*-mbeh koo-peh-*leh*-kah *ng'oh*-mbeh m-wee-*ngee*-neh shoo-*leh*-nee) (*your parents sold a cow to take another cow through school*) whenever a poster opinion is deemed shallow. This means the parents of the poster sold their prized cow to pay school fees for a stupid child, thus wasting their wealth. However cute or useful you think cows are, do not call a Swahili-speaking person a cow unless you're prepared for a tussle.

Mbwa koko

Mbwa koko (*m*-bwah *koh*-koh) (stray dog)

Family ties and ancestral land ownership/knowledge are important to Swahili-speaking communities. A stray dog has none of these and wanders through different neighborhoods scavenging food from bins and attacking people provoked or unprovoked. Used as an insult, **mbwa koko** refers to an ungovernable person with no hopes for a better future, and generally unwanted by other people in society, or would not be missed if they were to disappear.

Mboro

Mboro (*mboh*-roo) (*penis*)

The term is considered an insult when used to refer to someone. In this context, it is clearly derogatory and disrespectful. In many societies, including the Swahili culture, power dynamics exist between genders, with men often holding dominant positions. Using an insult related to male genitalia may be a way to challenge and undermine a person's masculinity or authority. Another term used similarly is **makende** (mah-*keh*-ndeh) (*balls*), slang for a man's testicles. By likening the person to their reproductive organs, it is intended to degrade their character and belittle their confidence or strength.

Kuma

Kuma (*koo*-mah) (*vagina*)

This is another body part term that can be shockingly crude and offensive to use in public. The reason behind such harsh language being used as an insult is rooted in the strict gender roles and societal norms that surround female sexuality. It's quite unfortunate that many African cultures, including the Swahili culture, often prioritize male dominance and control over women's bodies and behavior. When someone uses **kuma** to insult others, even men, it's essentially their method of humiliating and shaming them if they don't comply with their demands. Generally, using terms for female genitalia in order to insult others is a way of degrading and shaming individuals — particularly women — who don't conform to what society expects of them.

Shenzi

Shenzi (*sheh*-nzee) (*stupid, fool*)

No one likes having their intelligence downplayed, even when it's befitting. Using this word to describe someone is likely to start or escalate an argument — not a smart thing to do in a foreign country! Also beware of its synonyms **jinga**, **pumbavu** (*jee*-ngah, poo-*mbah*-voo) (*stupid, fool*).

Matako yako

Matako (mah-*tah*-koh *yah*-koh) (*your buttocks*)

The Swahili people have a deep appreciation for being modest, polite, and following cultural traditions that encourage appropriate behavior and language. So, if you were to insult someone by talking about their **matako** (mah-*tah*-koh) (*buttocks*) you'd be breaking all of these values! It's not just rude, it's downright disrespectful and hurtful.

Kumamako

Kumamako (koo-mah-*mah*-koh) (*your mother's vagina*)

Kuma (*koo*-mah) (*vagina*) is already a cuttingly rude pronouncement; clarifying it as one's mother's vagina, however, packs an even heavier punch. The Swahili culture may be patriarchal in several ways, but mothers are highly respected for their role in bringing forth and nurturing life. Verbal insults toward someone's mother can lead to severe social consequences, including strained relationships, loss of trust, and even violence.

Malaya

Malaya (mah-*lah*-yah) (*whore*)

People use this term to demean and shame someone, particularly women, by associating them with sex work. In a largely conservative society, women tagged as having loose morals risk being shunned by people around them. Using this word in an insulting manner aims to bring a sense of shame and disgrace upon someone.

5 Appendixes

Appendix A
Swahili Noun Classes

Swahili Noun Class Agreements

Noun Class	Example	Noun Class Marker	Possessive Marker	Subject Marker	Relative Marker	Associative -a	Object Marker
M	mtoto	a-	w-	a-	-ye		-m-
WA	watoto	wa-	w-	wa-	-o	wa	-wa-
M	mlima	u-	w-	u-	-o	wa	-u-
MI	milima	i-	y-	i-	-yo	ya	-i-
JI	jimbo	li-	l-	li-	-lo	la	-li-
MA	majimbo	ya-	y-	ya-	-yo	ya	-ya-
KI	kitabu	ki-	ch-	ki-	-cho	cha	-ki-
VI	vitabu	vi-	vy-	vi-	-vyo	vya	-vi-
CH	chuo						
VY	vyuo						
N	nyumba	i-	y-	i-	-yo	ya	-i-
N	nyumba	zi-	z-	zi-	-zo	za	-zi-

Noun Class	Example	Noun Class Marker	Possessive Marker	Subject Marker	Relative Marker	Associative -a	Object Marker
U	uso	u-	w-	u-	-o	wa	-u-
N	nyuso	zi-	z-	zi-	-zo	za	-zi-
U	upendo	u-	w-	u-	-o	wa	-u-
U	upendo	u-		u-	-o	wa	-u-
PA	nyumbani	pa-	p-	pa-	-po	pa	-pa-
KU	hotelini	ku-	kw-	ku-	-ko	kwa	-ku-
MU	hospitalini	mu-	mw-	mu-	-mo	mwa	-mu-

We cannot stress enough how important noun classes are in Swahili. This is because a noun's classification affects the whole structure of the sentence; all the other words in the sentence will adopt a prefix, infix, or suffix to align with the noun-in-question's class. For example, the words **mtoto** (m-*toh*-toh) (*child*) and **kitabu** (kee-*tah*-boo) (*book*) belong to M-Wa and Ki-Vi noun classes, respectively. If you wanted to show possession, you'd have to add a possessive marker, as in the following examples:

>> **Mtoto wangu** . . . (m-*toh*-toh *wah*-ngoo) (*my child*)

>> **Watoto wangu** . . . (wah-*toh*-toh *wah*-ngoo) (*my children*)

>> **Kitabu changu** . . . (kee-*tah*-boo *chah*-ngoo) (*my book*)

>> **Vitabu vyangu** . . . (vee-*tah*-boo *vyah*-ngoo) (*my books*)

Chapter 3 discusses the noun class markers and subject markers in more detail. In this Noun Class table, we have included three new elements: the relative marker, the associative a- marker, and the object marker.

A relative marker introduces a relative clause in Swahili. In English, for example, the following sentences all have relative clauses:

>> The girl <u>whom you saw yesterday</u> has been arrested.

>> The elephant <u>that was injured</u> is receiving treatment.

>> The lady <u>whose bag was stolen</u> has reported to the police.

As you can see, relative clauses are extra information added to a noun phrase using relative pronouns — in English, the pronouns *who, whom, that, which,* and *whose*. In Swahili, we use one relative pronoun **amba-** (*ah*-mbah) and attach an appropriate relative pronoun marker according to the noun class of the word we're adding extra information for. For example,

» **Mlima ambao unachosha sana ni mlima Kilimanjaro.** (m-*lee*-mah ah-*mbah*-oh oo-na-*choh*-shah *sah*-nah nee m-*lee*-mah Kilimanjaro) (*The mountain that tires you out most is Mt. Kilimajaro.*)

» **Milima ambayo inachosha sana ni milima Kilimanjaro na Kenya.** (m-*lee*-mah ah-*mbah*-yoh ee-na-*choh*-shah *sah*-nah nee mee-*lee*-mah Kilimanjaro nah Kenya) (*The mountains that tire you out most are Mt. Kilimajaro and Mt. Kenya.*)

» **Nyumba ambayo ilijengwa karibu na mto imeporomoka.** (*nyoo*-mbah ah-*mbah*-yoh ee-lee-*jeh*-ngwah kah-*ree*-boo nah *m*-toh ee-lee-poh-roh-*moh*-kah) (*The house that was built close to the river collapsed.*)

» **Nyumba ambazo zilijengwa karibu na mto zimeporomoka.** (*nyoo*-mbah ah-*mbah*-zoh zee-lee-*jeh*-ngwah kah-*ree*-boo nah *m*-toh zee-lee-poh-roh-*moh*-kah) (*The houses that were built close to the river collapsed.*)

Sometimes it's necessary to show the relationship between one noun and another in a sentence. To do this, Swahili uses the associative marker **-a**. For example,

» **Chuo _cha_ sanaa mtandaoni kimezinduliwa.** (*choo*-oh chah sah-*nah*-ah m-tah-ndah-*oh*-nee kee-meh-zee-ndoo-*lee*-wah) (*An online art school has been launched.*) [literally, *An online school of art has been launched.*]

» **Vyuo vya sanaa vimezinduliwa** (*vyoo*-oh vyah sah-*nah*-ah m-tah-ndah-*oh*-nee vee-meh-zee-ndoo-*lee*-wah) (*Online art schools have been launched.*) [literally, *Online schools of art have been launched.*]

The word **cha** links the two nouns **chuo** (*school*) and **sanaa** (*art*), while **vya** links the two nouns **vyuo** (*schools*) and **sanaa** (*art*), Other examples include the following:

» **Mwalimu _wa_ sayansi** (m-wah-*lee*-moo wah sah-*yah*-nsee) (*science teacher*) [literally, *teacher of science*]

» **Walimu _wa_ sayansi** (wah-*lee*-moo wah sah-*yah*-nsee) (*science teachers*) [literally, *teachers of science*]

» **Uso _wa_ Mariamu** (*oo*-soh wah Mariamu) (*Mariamu's face*) [literally, *the face of Mariamu*]

» **Nyuso _za_ Mariamu na Hawa** (nyoo-soh zah Mariamu nah Hawa) (*Mariamu and Hawa's faces*) [literally, *the faces of Mariamu and Hawa*]

An *object* in a sentence refers to a person or thing that is affected by the action in that sentence. For example, in the sentence **Mtoto alikamua mbuzi** (m-*toh*-toh ah-lee-kah-*moo*-ah m-*boo*-zee) (*The child milked a goat.*), **mbuzi** is the object.

Swahili speakers can choose to add an object marker to the noun subject to make sentences like the following:

» **M**toto alimkamua mbuzi (m-*toh*-toh ah-lee-m-kah-*moo*-ah m-*boo*-zee) (*The child milked the goat*),

» **Wa**toto waliwakamua mbuzi (wa-*toh*-toh wah-lee-wah-kah-*moo*-ah m-*boo*-zee) (*The children milked the goats.*)

The **-m-** and **-wa-** here make definite reference to **mbuzi**.

Appendix B
Swahili Verbs

Past Tense

Regular Swahili verbs ending with "a" in the past tense

Aliagiza	ah-lee-ah-*gee*-zah	*He/she ordered.*
Uliamka	oo-lee-ah-*m*-kah	*You woke up.*
Niliamua	nee-lee-ah-*moo*-ah	*I decided.*
Mliandika	m-lee-ah-*ndee*-kah	*You all wrote.*
Tuliangalia	too-lee-ah-ngah-*lee*-ah	*We watched.*
Walitembea	wah-lee-teh-*mbeh*-ah	*They walked.*
Ulianza	oo-lee-ah-*n*-zah	*You started.*
Alichanganya	ah-lee-chah-*ngah*-nyah	*He/she mixed.*
Tulichelewa	too-lee-cheh-*leh*-wah	*We were late.*
Mlicheza	m-lee-*cheh*-zah	*You (plural) played.*
Walichoka	wah-lee-*choh*-kah	*They were tired.*

Monosyllabic Swahili verbs in the past tense

Nilikula	nee-lee-*koo*-lah	*I ate.*
Ulikunywa	oo-lee-*koo*-nywah	*You drank.*
Mlikuja	m-lee-*koo*-jah	*You all came.*
Walikufa	wah-lee-*koo*-fah	*They died.*

Borrowed Swahili verbs ending with "e, i, u" in the past tense

Alifikiri	ah-lee-fee-*kee*-ree	*He thought.*
Ulijaribu	oo-lee-jah-*ree*-boo	*You tried.*
Nilihesabu	nee-lee-heh-*sah*-boo	*I counted.*

Present Tense

Regular Swahili verbs ending with "a" in the present tense

Anaagiza	ah-nah-ah-*gee*-zah	*He/she is ordering.*
Unaamka	oo-nah-ah-*m*-kah	*You are waking up.*
Ninaamua	nee-nah-ah-*moo*-ah	*I am deciding.*
Mnaandika	m-nah-ah-*ndee*-kah	*You all are writing.*
Tunaangalia	too-nah-ah-ngah-*lee*-ah	*We are watching.*
Walitembea	wah-lee-teh-*mbeh*-ah	*They are walking.*
Unaanza	oo-nah-ah-*n*-zah	*You are starting.*
Anachanganya	ah-nah-chah-*ngah*-nyah	*He/she is mixing.*
Tunachelewa	too-nah-cheh-*leh*-wah	*We are running late.*
Mnacheza	m-nah-*cheh*-zah	*You (plural) are playing.*
Wanachoka	wah-nah-*choh*-kah	*They are tired.*

Monosyllabic Swahili verbs in the present tense

Ninakula	nee-nah-*koo*-lah	I am eating.
Unakunywa	oo-nah-*koo*-nywah	You are drinking.
Mnakuja	m-nah-*koo*-jah	You all are coming.
Wanakufa	wah-nah-*koo*-fah	They are dying.

Borrowed Swahili verbs ending with "e, i, u" in the present tense

Anafikiri	ah-nah-fee-*kee*-ree	He is thinking.
Unajaribu	oo-nah-jah-*ree*-boo	You are trying.
Ninahesabu	nee-nah-heh-*sah*-boo	I am counting.

Future Tense

Regular Swahili verbs ending with "a" in the future tense

Ataagiza	ah-tah-ah-*gee*-zah	He/she will order.
Utaamka	oo-tah-ah-*m*-kah	You will wake up.
Nitaamua	nee-tah-ah-*moo*-ah	I will decide.
Mtaandika	m-tah-ah-*ndee*-kah	You all will write.
Tutaangalia	too-tah-ah-ngah-*lee*-ah	We will watch.
Walitembea	wah-lee-teh-*mbeh*-ah	They will walk.
Utaanza	oo-tah-ah-*n*-zah	You will start.
Atachanganya	ah-tah-chah-*ngah*-nyah	He/she will mix.
Tutachelewa	too-tah-cheh-*leh*-wah	We will run late.
Mtacheza	m-tah-*cheh*-zah	You (plural) will play.
Watachoka	wah-tah-*choh*-kah	They will be tired.

Monosyllabic Swahili verbs in the future tense

Nitakula	nee-tah-*koo*-lah	*I will eat.*
Utakunywa	oo-tah-*koo*-nywah	*You will drink.*
Mtakuja	m-tah-*koo*-jah	*You all will come.*
Watakufa	wah-tah-*koo*-fah	*They will die.*

Borrowed Swahili verbs ending with "e, i, u" in the future tense

Atafikiri	ah-tah-fee-*kee*-ree	*He will think.*
Utajaribu	oo-tah-jah-*ree*-boo	*You will try.*
Nitahesabu	nee-tah-heh-*sah*-boo	*I will count.*

Perfect Tense

Regular Swahili verbs ending with "a" in the perfect tense

Ameagiza	ah-meh-ah-*gee*-zah	*He/she has ordered.*
Umeamka	oo-meh-ah-*m*-kah	*You have woken up.*
Nimeamua	nee-me-ah-*moo*-ah	*I have decided.*
Mmeandika	m-meh-ah-*ndee*-kah	*You all have written.*
Tumeangalia	too-meh-ah-ngah-*lee*-ah	*We have watched.*
Walitembea	wah-lee-teh-*mbeh*-ah	*They have walked.*
Umeanza	oo-meh-ah-*n*-zah	*You have started.*
Amechanganya	ah-meh-chah-*ngah*-nyah	*He/she has mixed.*
Tumechelewa	too-mh-cheh-*leh*-wah	*We are late.*
Mmecheza	m-meh-*cheh*-zah	*You (plural) have played.*
Wamechoka	wah-meh-*choh*-kah	*They are tired.*

Monosyllabic Swahili verbs in the perfect tense

Nimekula	nee-lee-*koo*-lah	*I have eaten.*
Umekunywa	oo-lee-*koo*-nywah	*You have drunk.*
Mmekuja	m-lee-*koo*-jah	*You all have come.*
Wamekufa	wah-lee-*koo*-fah	*They have died.*

Borrowed Swahili verbs ending with "e, i, u" in the perfect tense

Amefikiri	ah-lee-fee-*kee*-ree	*He has thought.*
Umejaribu	oo-lee-jah-*ree*-boo	*You have tried.*
Nimehesabu	nee-lee-heh-*sah*-boo	*I have counted.*

Habitual Tense

Regular Swahili verbs ending with "a" in the habitual tense

Yeye huagiza	Yeh-yeh hoo-ah-*gee*-zah	*He/she normally orders.*
Wewe huamka	Weh-we hoo-ah-*m*-kah	*You normally wake up.*
Mimi huamua	mee-mee hoo-ah-*moo*-ah	*I decide.*
Ninyi huandika	Nee-nyee hoo-ah-*ndee*-kah	*You all write.*
Sisi huangalia	see-see hoo-ah-ngah-*lee*-ah	*We normally watch.*
Wao hutembea	wah-oh hoo-teh-*mbeh*-ah	*They always walk.*
Wewe huanza	weh-weh hoo-ah-*n*-zah	*You normally start.*
Yeye huchanganya	yeh-yeh hoo-chah-*ngah*-nyah	*He/she normally mixes.*
Sisi huchelewa	see-see hoo-cheh-*leh*-wah	*We are always late.*
Ninyi hucheza	nee-nyee hoo-*cheh*-zah	*You (plural) normally play.*
Wao huchoka	wah-oh hoo-*choh*-kah	*They are always tired.*

Monosyllabic Swahili verbs in the habitual tense

Mimi hula	mee-mee *hoo*-lah	*I always eat.*
Wewe hunywa	weh-weh *hoo*-nywah	*You always drink.*
Ninyi huja	nee-nyee *hoo*-jah	*You all always come.*
Wao hufa	wah-oh *hoo*-fah	*They always die.*

Borrowed Swahili verbs ending with "e, i, u" in the habitual tense

Yeye hufikiri	yeh-yeh hoo-fee-*kee*-ree	*He always thinks.*
Wewe hujaribu	weh-weh hoo-jah-*ree*-boo	*You always try.*
Mimi huhesabu	mee-mee hoo-heh-*sah*-boo	*I always count.*

The Verb "Kuwa" (To Be)

Present tense

Mimi ni mwalimu	*mee*-mee ne mwah-*lee*-moo	*I am a teacher.*
Yeye ni daktari	*yeh*-yeh nee dah-*ktah*-ree	*He/she is a doctor.*
Wao ni walimu	*wah*-oh nee wah-*lee*-moo	*They are teachers.*
Ninyi ni Wamarekani	*nee*-nyee nee wah-mah-reh-*kah*-nee	*You (plural) are Americans.*
Mtoto ni mkubwa	m-*toh*-toh nee m-*koo*-bwah	*The baby is big.*

Past tense

Mimi nilikuwa mwalimu	*mee*-mee nee-lee-*koo*-ah mwah-*lee*-moo	*I was a teacher.*
Yeye nilikuwa daktari	*yeh*-yeh ah-lee-*koo*-ah dah-*ktah*-ree	*He/she was a doctor.*
Wao walikuwa walimu	*wah*-oh wah-lee-*koo*-ah wah-*lee*-moo	*They were teachers.*

| Ninyi mlikuwa Wamarekani | *nee*-nyee m-lee-*koo*-ah wah-mah-reh-*kah*-nee | You (plural) were Americans. |
| Mtoto alikuwa mkubwa | m-*toh*-toh ah-lee-*koo*-ah m-*koo*-bwah | The baby was big. |

Future tense

Mimi nitakuwa mwalimu	*mee*-mee nee-tah-*koo*-ah mwah-*lee*-moo	I will be a teacher.
Yeye nitakuwa daktari	*yeh*-yeh nee-tah-*koo*-ah dah-*ktah*-ree	He/she will be a doctor.
Wao watakuwa walimu	*wah*-oh wah-tah-*koo*-ah wah-*lee*-moo	They will become teachers.
Ninyi mtakuwa Wamarekani	*nee*-nyee m-tah-*koo*-ah wah-mah-reh-*kah*-nee	You (plural) will be Americans.
Mtoto atakuwa mkubwa	m-*toh*-toh ah-tah-*koo*-ah m-*koo*-bwah	The baby will be big.

Present tense

Nina kaka	*nee*-nah *kah*-kah	I have a brother.
Una gari	*oo*-nah *gah*-ree	You have a car.
Wana nyumba	*wah*-nah *nyoo*-mbah	They have a house.
Mna paka	*m*-nah *pah*-kah	You all have a cat.
Tuna pesa	*too*-nah *peh*-sah	We have money.

Past tense

Nilikuwa na paka	nee-lee-*koo*-wah nah *pah*-kah	I had a cat.
Ulikuwa na gari	oo-lee-*koo*-wah nah *gah*-ree	You had a car.
Walikuwa na nyumba	wah-lee-*koo*-wah nah *nyoo*-mbah	They had a house.
Mlikuwa na paka	m-lee-*koo*-wah nah *pah*-kah	You all had a cat.
Tulikuwa na pesa	too-lee-*koo*-wah nah *peh*-sah	We had money.

Future tense

Nitakuwa na paka	nee-tah-*koo*-wah nah *pah*-kah	I will have a cat.
Utakuwa na gari	oo-tah-*koo*-wah nah *gah*-ree	You will have a car.
Watakuwa na nyumba	wah-tah-*koo*-wah nah *nyoo*-mbah	They will have a house.
Mtakuwa na paka	m-tah-*koo*-wah nah *pah*-kah	You all will have a cat.
Tutakuwa na pesa	too-tah-*koo*-wah nah *peh*-sah	We will have money.

Tense Negation: Past Tense

Regular Swahili verbs ending with "a"

Hakuagiza	hah-koo-ah-*gee*-zah	He/she didn't order.
Hukuamka	hoo-koo-ah-*m*-kah	You didn't wake up.
Sikuamua	see-koo-ah-*moo*-ah	I didn't decide.
Hamkuandika	hah-m-koo-ah-*ndee*-kah	You all didn't write.
Hamkuangalia	hah-m-koo-ah-ngah-*lee*-ah	You all didn't watch.
Hawakutembea	hah-wah-koo-teh-*mbeh*-ah	They didn't walk.
Hakuchanganya	hah-koo-chah-*ngah*-nyah	He/she didn't mix.
Hatukuchelewa	hah-too-koo-cheh-*leh*-wah	We weren't late.
Hamkucheza	hah-m-koo-*cheh*-zah	You (plural) didn't play.
Hawakuchoka	hah-wah-koo-*choh*-kah	They weren't tired.

Monosyllabic Swahili verbs

Sikula	see-*koo*-lah	I didn't eat.
Hukunywa	hoo-*koo*-nywah	You didn't drink.
Hamkuja	hah-m-*koo*-jah	You all didn't come.
Hawakufa	hah-wah-*koo*-fah	They didn't die.

Borrowed Swahili verbs ending with "e, i, u"

Hakufikiri	hah-koo-fee-*kee*-ree	*He didn't think.*
Hukujaribu	hoo-koo-jah-*ree*-boo	*You didn't try.*
Sikuhesabu	nee-lee-heh-*sah*-boo	*I didn't count.*

Tense Negation: Present Tense

Regular Swahili verbs ending with "a"

Haagizi	hah-ah-*gee*-zee	He/she doesn't order.
Huamki	hoo-*ah*-mkee	You don't wake up.
Siamui	see-ah-*moo*-ee	I don't decide.
Hamuandiki	hah-moo-ah-*ndee*-kee	You all don't write.
Hamwangalii	hah-moo-ah-ngah-*lee*-ee	You all don't watch.
Hawatembei	hah-wah-teh-*mbeh*-ee	They don't walk.
Hachanganyi	hah-chah-*ngah*-nyii	He/she doesn't mix.
Hatuchelewi	hah-too-cheh-*leh*-wee	We aren't late.
Hamchezi	hah-m-*cheh*-zee	You (plural) don't play.
Hawachoki	hah-wah-*choh*-kee	They don't get tired.

Monosyllabic Swahili verbs

Sili	*see*-lee	*I don't eat.*
Hunywi	*hoo*-nywee	*You don't drink.*
Haji	*hah*-jee	*You all don't come.*

Borrowed Swahili verbs ending with "e, i, u"

Hafikiri	hah-koo-fee-*kee*-ree	*He/she doesn't think.*
Hujaribu	hoo-koo-jah-*ree*-boo	*You don't try.*
Sihesabu	see-heh-*sah*-boo	*I don't count.*

Tense Negation: Future Tense

Regular Swahili verbs ending with "a"

Hataagiza	hah-tah-ah-*gee*-zah	*He/she won't order.*
Hutaamka	hoo-tah-*ah*-mkah	*You won't wake up.*
Sitaamua	see-tah-ah-*moo*-ah	*I won't decide.*
Hamtaandika	hah-m-tah-ah-*ndee*-kah	*You all won't write.*
Hamtaangalia	hah-m-tah-ah-ngah-*lee*-ah	*You all won't watch.*
Hawatatembea	hah-wah-tah-teh-*mbeh*-ah	*They won't walk.*
Hatachanganya	hah-tah-chah-*ngah*-nyah	*He/she won't mix.*
Hatutachelewa	hah-too-tah-cheh-*leh*-wah	*We won't be late.*
Hamtacheza	hah-m-tah-*cheh*-zah	*You (plural) won't play.*
Hawatachoka	hah-wah-tah-*choh*-kah	*They won't be tired.*

Monosyllabic Swahili verbs

Sitakula	see-tah-*koo*-lah	*I won't eat.*
Hutakunywa	hoo-tah-*koo*-nywah	*You won't drink.*
Hamtakuja	hah-m-tah-*koo*-jah	*You all won't come.*
Hawatakufa	hah-wah-tah-*koo*-fah	*They won't die.*

Borrowed Swahili verbs ending with "e, i, u"

Hatafikiri	hah-koo-fee-*kee*-ree	*He won't think.*
Hutajaribu	hoo-koo-jah-*ree*-boo	*You won't try.*
Sitahesabu	see-tah-heh-*sah*-boo	*I won't count.*

Tense Negation: Present Perfect Tense

Regular Swahili verbs ending with "a"

Hajaagiza	hah-jah-ah-*gee*-zah	*He/she hasn't ordered.*
Hujaamka	hoo-jah-ah-*m*-kah	*You haven't woken up.*
Sijaamua	see-k-jah-ah-*moo*-ah	*I haven't decided.*
Hamjaandika	hah-m- jah-ah-*ndee*-kah	*You all haven't written.*
Hamjaangalia	hah-m-jah-ah-ngah-*lee*-ah	*You all haven't watched.*
Hawajatembea	hah-wah-jah-teh-*mbeh*-ah	*They haven't walked.*
Hajachanganya	hah-jah-chah-*ngah*-nyah	*He/she hasn't mixed.*
Hatujachelewa	hah-too-jah-cheh-*leh*-wah	*We aren't late.*
Hamjacheza	hah-m-jah-*cheh*-zah	*You (plural) haven't played.*
Hawajachoka	hah-wah-jah-*choh*-kah	*They aren't tired.*

Monosyllabic Swahili verbs

Sijala	see-*jah*-lah	*I haven't eaten.*
Hujanywa	hoo-*jah*-nywah	*You haven't drink.*
Hamjaja	hah-m-*jah*-jah	*You all haven't come.*
Hawajafa	hah- wah-lee-*koo*-fah	*They aren't dead.*

Borrowed Swahili verbs ending with "e, i, u"

Hajafikiri	hah-jah-fee-*kee*-ree	*He hasn't thought.*
Hujajaribu	hoo-jah-jah-*ree*-boo	*You haven't tried.*
Sijahesabu	see-ja-heh-*sah*-boo	*I haven't counted.*

Tense Negation: Habitual Tense

Regular Swahili verbs ending with "a"

Yeye haagizi	*yeh*-yeh hah-ah-*gee*-zee	*He/she doesn't order.*
Wewe huamki	*weh*-weh hoo-ah-*m*-kee	*You don't wake up.*
Mimi siamui	*mee*-mee see-ah-*moo*-ee	*I don't decide.*
Ninyi hamuandiki	*nee*-nyee hah-m-ah-*ndee*-kee	*You all don't write.*
Ninyi hamwangalii	*nee*-nyee hah-m-ah-ngah-*lee*-ee	*You all don't watch.*
Wao hawatembei	*wah*-oh hah-wah-teh-*mbeh*-ee	*They don't walk.*
Yeye hachanganyi	*yeh*-yeh hah-chah-*ngah*-nyii	*He/she doesn't mix.*
Sisi hatuchelewi	*see*-see hah-too-cheh-*leh*-wee	*We don't get late.*
Ninyi hamchezi	*nee*-nyee hah-m-*cheh*-zee	*You (plural) don't play.*
Wao hawachoki	*wah*-oh hah-wah-*choh*-kee	*They don't get tired.*

Monosyllabic Swahili verbs

Mimi sili	*mee*-mee *see*-lee	*I don't eat.*
Wewe hunywi	*weh*-weh *hoo*-nywee	*You don't drink.*
Yeye haji	*yeh*-yeh *hah*-jee	*He doesn't come.*

Borrowed Swahili verbs ending with "e, i, u"

Yeye hafikiri	*yeh*-yeh hah-fee-*kee*-ree	*He doesn't think.*
Wewe hujaribu	*weh*-weh hoo-jah-*ree*-boo	*You don't try.*
Mimi sihesabu	*mee*-mee see-heh-*sah*-boo	*I don't count.*

The Verb "Kuwa" (To Be)

Present negation

Mimi si mwalimu	*mee*-mee see mwah-*lee*-moo	I am not a teacher.
Yeye si daktari	*yeh*-yeh see dah-*ktah*-ree	He/she is not a doctor.
Wao si walimu	*wah*-oh see wah-*lee*-moo	They are not teachers.

Past negation

Sikuwa mwalimu	see-*koo*-wah mwah-*lee*-moo	I was not a teacher.
Hakuwa daktari	hah-*koo*-wah dah-*ktah*-ree	He/she was not a doctor.
Hawakuwa walimu	hah-wah-*koo*-wah wah-*lee*-moo	They were not teachers.

Future negation

Mimi sitakuwa mwalimu	*mee*-mee see-tah-*koo*-wah mwah-*lee*-moo	I won't be a teacher.
Yeye hatakuwa daktari	*yeh*-yeh hah-tah-*koo*-wah dah-*ktah*-ree	He/she won't be a doctor.
Wao hawatakuwa walimu	*wah*-oh hah-wah-tah-*koo*-wah wah-*lee*-moo	They won't become teachers.

The Verb "Kuwa na" (To Have)

Present negation

Sina kaka	*see*-nah *pah*-kah	I don't have a brother.
Huna gari	*hoo*-nah *gah*-ree	You don't have a car.
Hawana nyumba	hah-*wah*-nah *nyoo*-mbah	They don't have a house.

Past negation

Sikuwa na paka	see-*koo*-wah nah *pah*-kah	*I didn't have a cat.*
Hukuwa na gari	hoo-*koo*-wah nah *gah*-ree	*You didn't have a car.*
Hawakuwa na nyumba	hah-wah-*koo*-wah nah *nyoo*-mbah	*They didn't have a house.*

Future negation

Sitakuwa na paka	see-tah-*koo*-wah nah *pah*-kah	*I won't have a cat.*
Hutakuwa na gari	hoo-tah-*koo*-wah nah *gah*-ree	*You won't have a car.*
Hawatakuwa na nyumba	hah-wah-tah-*koo*-wah nah *nyoo*-mbah	*They won't have a house.*

Appendix C
Swahili-English Mini-Dictionary

A

ada (*ah*-dah): fee

adhibu (ah-*dhee*-boo): to punish

agiza (ah-*gee*-zah): to order (food, etc.)

aibu (ah-*ee*-boo): shame

akiba (ah-*kee*-bah): savings

akili (ah-*kee*-lee): brain

alika (ah-*lee*-kah): to invite

amani (ah-*mah*-nee): peace

ambia (ah-*mbee*-ah): to tell (someone)

amini (ah-*mee*-nee): to believe

amka (*ah*-mkah): to wake up

amsha (*ah*-m-shah) to wake [someone] up

amua (ah-*moo*-ah): to decide

andaa (ah-*ndah*-ah): to prepare, get ready

andamana (ah-ndah-*mah*-nah): to protest

anga (*ah*-ngah): sky

angalia (ah-ngah-*lee*-ah): to look

anika (ah-*nee*-kah): to hang/lay out to dry

anua (ah-*noo*-ah): to unhang clothes from the drying rack

anza (*ah*-nzah): to begin/start

apisha (ah-*pee*-shah): to swear (somebody) in

arifu (ah-*ree*-foo): to inform

B

baba (*bah*-bah): dad

babu (*bah*-boo): grandfather

bahari (bah-*hah*-ree): ocean

bahasha (bah-*hah*-shah): envelope

bahati (bah-*hah*-tee): lucky

baisikeli (bah-ee-see-*keh*-lee): bicycle

baki (*bah*-kee): to remain

bakuli (bah-*koo*-lee): bowl

bamia (bah-*mee*-ah): okra

bandia (bah-*ndee*-ah): fake

bandika (bah-*ndee*-kah): to stick on/ paste

barafu (bah-*rah*-foo): ice

baraka (bah- *rah*-kah): blessing

baridi (bah-*ree*-dee): cold

bariki (bah-*ree*-kee): to bless

bata (*bah*-tah): duck n.

bembea (beh-*mbeh*-ah): a swing

bembeleza (beh-mbeh-*leh*-zah): to coddle/appease (like you do to a baby to stop fussing)

bibi (*bee*-bee): grandmother (Tz); wife (Ke)

binamu (bee-*nah*-moo): cousin

binti (bee-ntee): daughter

birika (bee-*ree*-kah): kettle

biskuti (bee-*skoo*-tee): biscuit

boma (*boh*-mah): homestead

bomba (*boh*-mbah): faucet; tap

bomoa (boh-*moh*-ah): to demolish [a structure]

bomu (*boh*-moo): bomb

bonde (*boh*-ndeh): valley

bonde la ufa (*boh*-ndeh lah *oo*-fah): rift valley

bondia (boh-*ndee*-ah): a boxer

bonyeza (boh-*nyeh*-zah): dial

bora (*boh*-rah): better/fine/best

bubu (*boo*-boo): mute person

bunduki (boo-*ndoo*-kee): gun

busara (boo-*sah*-rah): wisdom; tact

bwana (*bwah*-nah): mister; sir

bwawa (*bwah*-wah): pool

CH

chachu (*chah*-choo): tangy

chafua (chah-*foo*-ah): to make dirty

chai (*chah*-ee): tea

chakula (chah-*koo*-lah): food

chapa (*chah*-pah): to flog

chapati (chah-*pah*-tee): chapati

chatu (*chah*-too): a python

chawa (*chah*-wah): lice

chechemea (cheh-cheh-*meh*-ah): to limp [as if hurt]

cheka (*cheh*-kah): to laugh

chenga (*cheh*-ngah): to evade

chenza (*cheh*-nzah): tangerine

cheza (*cheh*-zah): to play

chimba (*chee*-mbah): to dig [a hole]

chini (*chee*-nee): down/below/under

chombo (*choh*-mboh): utensil; instrument

choo (*choh*-oh): toilet

chora (*choh*-rah): to draw

chota (*choh*-tah): to fetch [a liquid; e.g., water]

chubua (choo-*boo*-ah): to bleach (the skin)

chui (*choo*-ee): leopard

chuki (*choo*-kee): hatred

chuma (*choo*-mah): to pick v./iron n.

chumvi (*choo*-mvee): salt

chungwa (*choo*-ngwah): orange

chuo (*choo*-oh): university

chupa (*choo*-pah): bottle
chupi (*choo*-pee): underwear
chura (*choo*-rah): frog

D

dada (*dah*-dah): sister
dai (*dah*-ee): to allege/claim; demand
daima (dah-*ee*-mah): forever
dakika (dah-*kee*-kah): minute(s)
daktari (dah-*ktah*-ree): doctor
dalali (dah-*lah*-lee): agent; broker
dalili (dah-*lee*-lee): sign/indication/
 trace
damu (*dah*-moo): blood
daraja (dah-*rah*-jah): bridge
darasa (dah-*rah*-sah): classroom
dawa (*dah*-wah): medicine
dini (*dee*-nee): religion; faith
divai (dee-*vah*-ee): wine
doa (*doh*-ah): stain
-dogo (*doh*-goh): small; young
dola (*doh*-lah): dollar
dua (*doo*-ah): prayer; plea
duara (doo-*ah*-rah): circle n.
duka (*doo*-kah): shop n.
dunia (doo-*nee*-ah): world

E

egesha (eh-*geh*-shah): to park [a car]
ekari (eh-*kah*-ree): acre
elewa (eh-*leh*-wa): to understand
eleza (eh-*leh*-zah): to explain
elfu (*ehl*-foo): thousand
elimu (eh-*lee*-moo): education
-embamba (eh-*mbah*-mbah): thin;
 narrow
embe (*eh*-mbeh): mango

endelea (eh-ndeh-*leh*-ah):
 to continue; to progress
endesha (eh-*ndeh*-shah): to drive
enea (eh-*neh*-ah): to spread
eneo (eh-*neh*-oh): area
enzi (*eh*-nzee): era
-epesi (eh-*peh*-see): light [in terms
 of weight]
epuka (eh-*poo*-kah): to escape;
 to avoid

F

faa (*fah*-ah): to be useful
fagia (fah-*gee*-ah): to sweep
fahamu (fah-*hah*-moo): know v. ;
 consciousness n.
faida (fah-*ee*-dah): profit n.
familia (fah-mee-*lee*-ah): family
fanya (*fah*-nyah): to do
fanya kazi (*fah*-nyah *kah*-zee):
 to work
faragha (fah-*rah*-ghah): privacy
ficha (*fee*-chah): to hide
fichua (fee-*choo*-ah): to reveal
fikiri (fee-*kee*-ree): to think
filimbi (fee-*lee*-mbee): whistle n.;
 flute n.
fimbo (*fee*-mboh): cane; stick
finya (*fee*-nyah): to squeeze; to pinch
fomu (*foh*-moo): form n.
fua (*foo*-ah): to wash clothes
fuata (foo-*ah*-tah): to follow
funga (*foo*-ngah): to close; to tie up;
 to fast.
funguo (foo-*ngoo*-ah): key
funika (foo-*nee*-kah): to cover
funua (foo-*noo*-ah): to uncover
fununu (foo-*noo*-noo): rumor
-fupi (*foo*-pee): short adj.

fupisha (foo-*pee*-shah): to shorten
furaha (foo-*rah*-hah): happiness
furahi (foo-*rah*-hee): to be happy
futa (*foo*-tah): to erase; to delete

G

ganda (*gah*-ndah): to coagulate
gani (*gah*-nee): what?
gari (*gah*-ree): car
gauni (gah-*oo*-nee): a dress n.
gereza (geh-*reh*-zah): jail
ghafla (*ghah*-flah): suddenly; abruptly adv.
ghali (*ghah*-lee): expensive
gharama (ghah-*rah*-mah): cost n.
gharimu (ghah-*ree*-moo): to cost
gitaa (gee-*tah*-ah): guitar
giza (*gee*-zah): darkness
glavu (*glah*-voo): gloves
godoro (goh-*doh*-ro): mattress
goma (*goh*-mah): to strike [workers' strike]
gombana (goh-*mbah*-nah): to quarrel
gonga (*goh*-ngah): to hit/strike/knock
goti (*goh*-tee): knee
gulio (goo-*lee*-oh): market
gumba (*goo*-mbah): thumb

H

haba (*hah*-bah): scarce; few adj.
habari (hah-*bah*-ree): news
hali ya hewa (*hah*-lee yah *heh*-wah): weather
halisi (hah-*lee*-see): original; genuine
hama (*hah*-mah): to move out
hamia (hah-*mee*-ah): to move to
hapa (*hah*-pah): here

haribu (hah-*ree*-boo): to destroy
harusi (hah-*roo*-see): wedding
hebu (*heh*-boo): well [interjection]
hedhi (*heh*-dhee): menstruation
hesabu (heh-*sah*-boo): math; calculation
heshima (heh-*shee*-mah): respect; dignity
hewa (*heh*-wah): air
hodari (hoh-*dah*-ree): skillful adj.
hofu (*hoh*-foo): fear n.
hoho (*hoh*-hoh): bell pepper
homa (*hoh*-mah): fever
honga (*hoh*-ngah): to bribe
hongera (hoh-*ngeh*-rah): congratulations
hongo (*hoh*-ngoh): bribe n.
hubiri (hoo-*bee*-ree): to preach
huyo (*hoo*-yo): that person
huyu (*hoo*-yoo): this person
huzuni (hoo-*zoo*-nee): sadness

I

iba (*ee*-bah): to steal
ibada (ee-*bah*-dah): religous sermon/service
ibilisi (ee-bee-*lee*-see): devil; Satan
ibuka (ee-*boo*-kah): to appear, to surface
idadi (ee-*dah*-dee): number [of people, things etc.]
idara (ee-*dah*-rah): department; ministry
idhaa (ee-*dhah*-ah): channel
iga (*ee*-gah): to imitate; to copy
igiza (ee-*gee*-zah): to act
Ijumaa (ee-joo-*mah*-ah): Friday
ikiwa (ee-*kee*-wah): if; supposing that, conj.

ikulu (ee-*koo*-loo): palace; state house

ilani (ee-*lah*-nee): warning; notice

imamu (ee-*mah*-moo): Imam

imara (ee-*mah*-rah): stable adv.

Imba (*ee*-mbah): to sing

ingia (ee-*ngee*-ah): to enter

ini (*ee*-nee): liver

-ishi (*ee*-shee): live

ita (*ee*-tah): to call

itwa (*ee*-twah): to be called

iva (*ee*-vah): ripe adj; ripen v; mature v; ready to eat [for food]

J

jaa (*jah*-ah): full

jahazi (jah-*hah*-zee): dhow (a sailboat common in the Indian Ocean)

jalala (jah-*lah*-lah): dump; rubbish pit

jali (*jah*-lee): to care

jamaa (jah-*mah*-ah): relative/family; community

jamba (*jah*-mbah): to fart/pass wind

jambo (*jah*-mboh): issue; matter

jana (*jah*-nah): yesterday

jaribio (jah-ree-*bee*-oh): quiz n.

jaribu (jah-*ree*-boo): to try

jarida (jah-*ree*-dah): magazine; journal

jaza (*jah*-zah): to fill

jicho (*jee*-choh): eye

jiko (*jee*-koh): stove/kitchen

jimbo (*jee*-mboh): state n.

jina (*jee*-nah): name

jinamizi (jee-nah-*mee*-zee): nightmare

jini (*jee*-nee): ghost

jioni (jee-*oh*-nee): evening

jipu (*jee*-poo): boil; abscess n.

jitihada (jee-tee-*hah*-dah): effort

jitu (*jee*-too): giant

jogoo (joh-*goh*-oh): rooster

jokofu (joh-*koh*-foo): refrigerator

joto (*joh*-toh): heat n.

jua (*joo*-ah): know v; sun n

juisi (joo-*ee*-see): juice

juma (*joo*-mah): week

jumanne (joo-mah-*n*-neh): Tuesday

jumapili (joo-mah-*pee*-lee): Sunday

jumatano (joo-mah-*tah*-noh): Wednesday

jumatatu (joo-mah-*tah*-too): Monday

juzi (*joo*-zee): the day before yesterday

K

kaa (*kah*-ah): to sit

kabisa (kah-*bee*-sah): absolutely; completely adv.

kabla (*kah*-blah): before

kahawa (kah-*hah*-wah): coffee

kahawia (kah-hah-*wee*-ah): brown

kaka (*kah*-kah): brother

kalamu (kah-*lah*-moo): pen

kali (*kah*-lee): (of taste) bitter; (of a person) mean; (of an animal); fierce

kama (*kah*-mah): like/as

kamusi (kah-*moo*-see): dictionary

kamwe (*kah*-mweh): never; not at all adv.

kana (*kah*-nah): to deny

kawaida (kah-wah-*ee*-dah): normal

kawia (kah-*wee*-ah): to delay

kera (*keh*-rah): to irritate

kero (*keh*-roh): irritation; eye sore n.

kikapu (kee-*kah*-poo): basket

kikombe (kee-*koh*-mbeh): cup

kilo (*kee*-loh): kilogram

kioo (kee-*oh*-oh): mirror/glass

kisima (ke-*see*-mah): well

kitabu (kee-*tah*-boo): book

kiti (*kee*-tee): chair; seat

kobe (*koh*-beh): tortoise

kondoo (koh-*ndoh*-oh): sheep

koo (*koh*-oh): throat

kufa (*koo*-fah): to die

kuku (*koo*-koo): chicken

kumi (*koo*-mee): ten

kura (*koo*-rah): to vote

kutu (*koo*-too): rust n.

kwa sababu (kwah sah-*bah*-boo): because

L

la (lah): no

la hasha (lah *hah*-shah): absolutely not; no never

lala (*lah*-lah): to sleep

lalamika (lah-lah-*mee*-kah): to complain

lamba (*lah*-mbah): to lick

lango (*lah*-ngoh): gate

laumu (lah-*oo*-moo): to blame

lawama (lah-*wah*-mah): blame n. ; complaint

lengo (*leh*-ngoh): to target; to aim

leseni (leh-*seh*-nee): license; permit

leta (*leh*-tah): to bring

lia (*lee*-ah): to cry

lima (*lee*-mah): to dig

limao (lee-*mah*-oh): lemon

linda (*lee*-ndah): to protect, to guard

lingana (lee-*ngah*-nah): similar to

linganisha (lee-ngah-*nee*-shah): to compare

lini (*lee*-nee): when?

lipa (*lee*-pah): to pay

lipua (lee-*poo*-ah): to blow up [with a bomb for example]

lori (*loh*-ree): lorry

lowa (*loh*-wah): wet/soaked [from the rain, a swim, etc.]

M

maabara (ma-ah-*bah*-rah): laboratory

mada (*mah*-dah): title; topic of debate

maji (*mah*-jee): water

mali (*mah*-lee): wealth

maliza (mah-*lee*-zah): to finish

mama (*mah*-mah): mother

maridadi (mah-ree-*dah*-dee): stylish adj.

mbali (*mbah*-lee): far

mbona (*m-boh*-nah): why; how come?

mbuzi (m-*boo*-zee): goat

mchele (m-*cheh*-lee): uncooked rice

mechi (*meh*-chee): match/game

medali (meh-*dah*-lee): medal

meli (*meh*-lee): ship

meneja (meh-*neh*-jah): manager

meno (*meh*-noh): teeth

meza (*meh*-zah): table; to swallow (something)

mkulima (m-koo-*lee*-mah): farmer

mkurugenzi (m-koo-roo-*geh*-nzee): director

mlima (m-*lee*-mah): mountain

mnyama (m-*nyah*-mah): animal

Mola (*moh*-lah): God

moto (*moh*-toh): fire

mpunga (m-*poo*-ngah): rice in the farm

mti (*m*-tee): tree

mto (*m*-toh): river/pillow

mtoto (m-*toh*-toh): baby

mua (*moo*-ah): sugarcane

Mungu (*moo*-ngoo): God

mwalimu (mwah-*lee*-moo): teacher

mwindaji (m-wee-*ndah*-jee): hunter

mwindaji haramu (m-wee-*ndah*-jee hah-*rah*-moo): poacher

mwizi (m-*wee*-zee): thief

mzee (m-*zeh*-eh): elder; old man

mzio (m-*zee*-oh): allergy

N

na kadhalika (nah kah-dhah-*lee*-kah): et cetera

nabii (nah-*bee*-ee): prophet

nafasi (nah-*fah*-see): spot/space; vacancy

nafsi (*nah*-fsee): soul

nahodha (nah-*hoh*-dhah): captain [of a boat/ship]

naibu (nah-*ee*-boo): deputy

nambari (nah-*mbah*-ree): number

nanasi (nah-*nah*-see): pineapple

nasa (*nah*-sah): to trap, to capture

nawa (*nah*-wah): to wash one's hands/face

nazi (*nah*-zee): coconut

ndizi (*ndee*-zee): banana

ndoa (*ndoh*-ah): marriage

nembo (neh-*mboh*): logo; coat of arms

nene (*neh*-neh): fat; thick

nia (*nee*-ah): intention

noa (*noh*-ah): to sharpen

noti (*noh*-tee): banknote

nta (*n*-tah): wax

nuka (*noo*-kah): to stink/ to smell bad adj.

nukia (noo-*kee*-ah): to smell good adj.

nunua (noo-*noo*-ah): to buy

nusa (*noo*-sah): to smell something

nusu (*noo*-soo): half

O

oa (*oh*-ah): to marry (for men)

oga (*oh*-gah): to shower, to bathe

ogopa (oh-*goh*-pah): scared

oka (*oh*-kah): to bake

okoa (oh-*koh*-ah): to save

okota (oh-*koh*-tah): to pick up [something from the ground]

olewa (oh-*leh*-wah): to get married (for women)

ona (*oh*-nah): to see

onana (oh-*nah*-nah): to meet, to see each other

ondoa (oh-*ndoh*-ah): to remove

ondoka (oh-*ndoh*-kah): to leave

ongea (oh-*ngeh*-ah): to talk

osha (*oh*-shah): to wash

ota (*oh*-tah): to sprout; to dream

oza (*oh*-zah): to rot; to give away in marriage

P

paa (*pah*-ah): roof; gazelle

paka (*pah*-kah): cat/paint

pakia (pah-*kee*-ah): to pack

pakua (pah-*koo*-ah): to serve food

panga (*pah*-ngah): to organize v.; machete n.

pangusa (pah-*ngoo*-sah): to wipe, to clean

pasi (*pah*-see): to iron

pata (*pah*-tah): to get, to find

pesa (*peh*-sah): money

piga (*pee*-gah): to hit

pinda (*pee*-ndah): to turn

pingu (*pee*-ngoo): handcuffs

pini (*pee*-nee): pin n.

pipa (*pee*-pah): barrel

pipi (*pee*-pee): candy/sweet

pochi (*poh*-chee): handbag

pombe (*poh*-mbeh): alcohol

pooza (poh-*oh*-zah): to cool

potea (poh-*teh*-ah): lost

pua (*poo*-ah): nose

punda (*poo*-ndah): donkey

punguza (poo-*ngoo*-zah): to reduce

puuza (poo-*oo*-zah): to ignore, to trivialize

R

radi (*rah*-dee): lightning

rafiki (rah-*fee*-kee): friend

rafu (*rah*-foo): shelf

ramani (rah-*mah*-nee): map

rangi (*rah*-ngee): color

rarua (rah-*roo*-ah): to tear [something]

ratiba (rah-*tee*-bah): schedule; routine

rauka (rah-*oo*-kah): to wake up early; to set off early

redio (reh-*dee*-oh): radio

-refu (*reh*-foo): tall

riadha (ree-*ah*-dhah): athletics

rika (*ree*-kah): agemate/person of the same age

rinda (*ree*-ndah): dress n.

ringa (*ree*-ngah): to show off, to boast

risasi (ree-*sah*-see): bullet

robo fainali (*ro*-boh fah-ee-*nah*-lee): quarterfinals

robota (roh-*boh*-tah): bundle/bale n.

roho (*roh*-hoh): spirit; soul

rubani (roo-*bah*-nee): pilot n.

rudi (*roo*-dee): to return

rudia (roo-*dee*-ah): *to* repeat

ruhusa (roo-*hoo*-sah): permission

ruka (*roo*-kah): to jump

runinga (roo-*nee*-ngah): television

S

saa (*sah*-ah): watch/time/clock

sahihi (sah-*hee*-hee): correct; true; right; signature

sajili (sah-*jee*-lee): to register

salama (sah-*lah*-mah): peace; safe

salamu (sah-*lah*-moo): greetings

samaki (sah-*mah*-kee): fish n.

sanifu (sah-*nee*-foo): accurate/ grammatical adj.

sasa (*sah*-sah): now

sauti (sah-*oo*-tee): voice

sehemu (she-*heh*-moo): part

seremala (seh-reh-*mah*-lah): carpenter

sikiliza (see-kee-*lee*-zah): to listen

sikio (see-*kee*-oh): ear

siku (*see*-koo): day

simama (see-*mah*-mah): to stand

simu (*see*-moo): telephone

sketi (*skeh*-tee): skirt

soko (*soh*-koh): market

soma (*soh*-mah): to read, to study

suala (soo-*ah*-lah): issue/ matter

subira (soo-*bee*-rah): patience

subiri (soo-*bee*-ree): to wait

sukuma (soo-*koo*-mah): to push

sumbua (soo-*mboo*-ah): to disturb

sumu (*soo*-moo): to poison

sungura (soo-*ngoo*-rah): rabbit

supu (*soo*-poo): soup

suti (*soo*-tee): suit

T

taa (*tah*-ah): light/lamp

tabasamu (tah-bah-*sah*-moo): smile n. v.

tabia (tah-*bee*-ah): character; behavior

tabianchi (tah-bee-ah-*n*-chee): climate

tabibu (tah-*bee*-boo): physician

tabiri (tah-*bee*-ree): to predict

tabu (*tah*-boo): difficulty; trouble

tafsiri (tah-*fsee*-ree): to translate

tafuta (tah-*foo*-tah): to find, to search

tai (*tah*-ee): necktie

taka (*tah*-kah): to want

takataka (tah-kah-*tah*-kah): trash/ rubbish

talaka (tah-*lah*-kah): divorce n.

tamaa (tah-*mah*-ah): desire/lust/ greed n.

tamani (tah-*mah*-nee): to envy

tambi (*tah*-mbee): spaghetti

taratibu (tah-rah-*tee*-boo): rules; slowly

tatua (tah-*too*-ah): to solve

televisheni (teh-leh-vee-*sheh*-nee): television

tema (*teh*-mah): to spit out

tema mate (*teh*-mah *mah*-teh): to spit saliva

tembea (teh-*mbeh*-ah): to walk

tia (*tee*-ah): to put

tia sahihi (*tee*-ah sah-*hee*-hee): to sign

tisa (*tee*-sah): nine

titi (*tee*-tee): breast

toa (*toh*-ah): to remove

toka (*toh*-kah): from

U

ua (*oo*-ah): flower; hedge; to kill

uawa (oo-*ah*-wah): to be killed

ubagizi wa rangi (oo-bah-*goo*-zee wah *rah*-ngee): racism

ubaguzi (oo-bah-*goo*-zee): discrimination

ubahili (oo-bah-*hee*-lee): stinginess; miserliness

ubinafsi (oo-bee-*nah*-fsee): selfishness

uchaguzi (oo-chah-*goo*-zee): election

udhaifu (oo-dhah-*ee*-foo): weakness; infirmity

udongo (oo-*doh*-ngoh): soil

ufisadi (oo-fee-*sah*-dee): corruption

ugali (oo-*gah*-lee): ugali [maize meal mush]

ujasiri (oo-jah-*see*-ree): bravery; courage

uji (*oo*-jee): porridge

ukali (oo-*kah*-lee): sternness/ harshness

ukatili (oo-kah-*tee*-lee): cruelty

ukeketaji (oo-keh-keh-*tah*-jee): female genital mutilation

ukimwi (oo-*kee*-mwee): AIDS

ukoo (oo-*koh*-oh): clan

ukweli (oo-*kweh*-lee): truth

ulimwengu (oo-lee-*mweh*-ngoo): world

uma (*oo*-mah): fork; bite

umbea (oo-*mbeh*-ah): gossip n.
umoja (oo-*moh*-jah): unity
upendo (oo-*peh*-ndoh): love
upole (oo-*poh*-leh): gentleness
ushuru (oo-*shoo*-roo): tax n.
uso (*oo*-soh): face
utabiri (oo-tah-*bee*-ree): forecast; prediction
utu (*oo*-too): humanity; kindness
uwezo (oo-*weh*-zoh): ability
uwongo (oo-*woh*-ngoh): false/a lie
uzoefu (oo-zoh-*eh*-foo): experience

V

vaa (*va*-ah): wear
vamia (vah-*mee*-ah): to attack
vamiwa (vah-*mee*-wah): to be attacked
vazi (*vah*-zee): cloth; garment
viatu (vee-*ah*-too): shoes
vifaa (vee-*fah*-ah): tools; items
vigezo (vee-*geh*-zoh): criteria
vijana (vee-*jah*-nah): youth; young people
vimba (*vee*-mbah): swell; bulge
vimbe (*vee*-mbeh): wound
vita (*vee*-tah): war/fight/conflict n.
vitisho (vee-*tee*-shoh): threats
vitu (*vee*-too): things
voliboli (voh-lee-*boh*-lee): volleyball
vua (*voo*-ah): to undress, to fish
vuguvugu (voo-goo-*voo*-goo): to warm [water, milk, etc.]
vuka (*voo*-kah): to cross; to cross over
vuli (*voo*-lee): fall/autumn season; shade
vumbua (voo-*mboo*-ah): to invent
vuna (*voo*-nah): to harvest

vunja (*voo*-njah): to break
vuruga (voo-*roo*-gah): to disorganize
vuta (*voo*-tah): to pull

W

wadudu (wah-*doo*-doo): insects
wali (*wah*-lee): cooked rice
wanyama (wah-*nyah*-mah): animals
wao (*wah*-oh): they/them
wapi (*wah*-pee): where
wavu (*wah*-voo): net
waya (*wah*-yah): cable
waziri (wah-*zee*-ree): minister
waziri mkuu (wah-*zee*-ree *m*-koo): prime minister
wazo (*wah*-zoh): idea; thought
wema (*weh*-mah): kindness
wembe (*weh*-mbeh): razor
wengi (*weh*-ngee): many
wengu (*weh*-ngoo): spleen
wifi (*wee*-fee): sister-in-law
wiki (*wee*-kee): week
wimbo (*wee*-mboh): song
wingu (*wee*-ngoo): cloud
wino (*wee*-noh): ink
wito (*wee*-too): to call (to action)
wokovu (woh-*koh*-voo): salvation
wosia (woh-*see*-ah): will [written to bequeath property]

Y

yai (*yah*-ee): an egg
yaya (*yah*-yah): babysitter
Yesu (*yeh*-soo): Jesus
yeye (*yeh*-yeh): he/she

Z

zaa (*zah*-ah): to give birth

zabibu (zah-*bee*-boo): grapes

zawadi (zah-*wah*-dee): gift/present

zeituni (zeh-ee-*too*-nee): olives

ziada (zee-*ah*-dah): extra

ziara (zee-*ah*-rah): visit n.

ziba (*zee*-bah): to block [an opening]; to clog up

zibua (zee-*boo*-ah): to unclog

zidi (*zee*-dee): to exceed

zika (*zee*-kah): to bury

zima (*zee*-mah): to switch off

zimia (zee-*mee*-ah): to faint, to pass out

-zito (*zee*-toh): heavy adj.

ziwa (zee-wah): lake

zizi (*zee*-zee): animal pen

zoezi (zoh-*eh*-zee): to exercise, to practice

zuhura (zoo-*hoo*-rah): Venus

zuia (zoo-*ee*-ah): to prevent

zulia (zoo-*lee*-ah): carpet

English-Swahili Mini-Dictionary

A

about: **kuhusu** (koo-*hoo*-soo)

to accuse: **shtaki** (sh-*tah*-kee)

ache: **maumivu** (mah-oo-*mee*-voo) n.

to anger: **hasira** (hah-*see*-rah)

to annoy: **kera** (*keh*-rah)

apple: **tofaa** (toh-*fah*-ah)

art: **sanaa** (sah-*nah*-ah)

to ask: **uliza** (oo-*lee*-zah)

at: **kwa** (kwah)

to attack: **shambulia** (shah-mboo-*lee*-ah)

to attempt: **jaribu** (jah-*ree*-boo)

August: **agosti/mwezi wa nane** (ah-*goh*-stee/m-*weh*-zee wah *nah*-neh)

average: **wastani** (wah-*stah*-nee)

axe: **shoka** (*shoh*-kah)

B

To bake: **oka** (*oh*-kah)

To ban: **piga marufuku** (*pee*-gah mah-roo-*foo*-koo)

bank: **benki** (*beh*-nkee)

to beat: **piga** (*pee*-gah)

bed: **kitanda** (kee-*tah*-ndah)

bedbug: **kunguni** (koo-*ngoo*-nee)

beer: **bia** (*bee*-ah)

before: **kabla** (*kah*-blah)

to bend down: **inama** (ee-*nah*-mah)

to bend: **kunja** (*koo*-njah)

bin: **jaa la taka** (*jah*-ah lah *tah*-kah)

to blame: **laumu** (lah-*oo*-moo)

to bless: **bariki** (bah-*ree*-kee)

to boast: **ringa** (*ree*-ngah)

bone: **mfupa** (m-*foo*-pah)

book: **kitabu** (kee-*tah*-boo)

to borrow: **kopa** (*koh*-pah) [of money]; **azima** (ah-*zee*-mah) [other items]

bowl: **bakuli** (bah-*koo*-lee)

C

cat: **paka** (*pah*-kah)

to chase: **kimbiza** (kee-*mbee*-zah)

choice: **chaguo** (chah-*goo*-oh)

to choose: **chagua** (chah-*goo*-ah)

to chop: **katakata** (kah-tah-*kah*-tah)

church: **kanisa** (kah-*nee*-sah)

to clap: **piga makofi** (*pee*-gah mah-*koh*-fee)

clean: **safi** (*sah*-fee) adj;

to clean: **safisha** (sah-*fee*-shah)

client: **mteja** (m-*teh*-jah)

to copy: **iga** (*ee*-gah)

country: **nchi** (*n*-chee)

court: **mahakama** (mah-hah-*kah*-mah) n.

crawl: **tambaa** (tah-*mbah*-ah)

crazy: **kichaa** (kee-*chah*-ah); **wazimu** (wah-*zee*-moo)

to create: **umba** (*oo*-mbah)

creature: **mnyama** (m-*nyah*-mah)

to cry: **lia** (*lee*-ah)

to cut: **kata** (*kah*-tah)

D

damp: **unyevu** (oo-*nyeh*-voo)

dance: **densi** (*deh*-nsee) n.

December: **disemba/mwezi wa kumi na mbili** (dee-*seh*-mbah/m-*weh*-zee wah *koo*-mee nah m-*bee*-lee)

To defeat: **shinda** (*shee*-ndah)

demon: **shetani** (sheh-*tah*-nee)

to deny: **kataa** (kah-*tah*-ah)

desire: **tamaa** (tah-*mah*-ah) n.

to destroy: **haribu** (hah-*ree*-boo)

difficult: **ngumu** (*ngoo*-moo)

to dig: **chimba** (*chee*-mbah)

dog: **mbwa** (*m*-bwah)

dove: **njiwa** (n-*jee*-wah)

down: **chini** (*chee*-nee)

downpour: **mvua kubwa** (m-*voo*-ah *koo*-bwah)

drizzle: **manyunyu** (mah-*nyoo*-nyoo)/ **rasharasha** (rah-shah-*rah*-shah) n.

to drop: **dondosha** (doh-*ndoh*-shah)/ **angusha** (ah-*ngoo*-shah)

to drown: **zama** (*zah*-mah)

drum: **ngoma** (*ngoh*-mah)

E

eagle: **mwewe** (m-*weh*-weh)

ear: **sikio** (see-*kee*-oh)

east: **mashariki** (mah-shah-*ree*-kee)

to eat: **kula** (*koo*-lah)

egg: **yai** (*yah*-ee)

eight: **nane** (*nah*-neh)

elephant: **ndovu/tembo** (n-*doh*-voo/*teh*-mboh)

email: **barua pepe** (bah-*roo*-ah *peh*-peh) n.

end: **mwisho** (m-*wee*-shoh)/**tamati** (tah-*mah*-tee) n.

to enter: **ingia** (ee-*ngee*-ah)

exactly: **hasa** (*hah*-sah) / **kabisa** (kah-*bee*-sah)

to exaggerate: **tia chumvi** (*tee*-ah *choo*-mvee)

exam: **mtihani** (m-tee-*hah*-nee)

to examine: **pima** (*pee*-mah)

to exit: **ondoka** (oh-*ndoh*-kah)

to export: **kuuza nje** (koo-*oo*-zah
  n-jeh)
eye: **jicho** (*jee*-choh)

F

fake: **bandia** (bah-*ndee*-ah)
false: **uongo** (oo-*oh*-ngoh)
far: **mbali** (m-*bah*-lee)
farm: **shamba** (*shah*-mbah) n.
farmer: **mkulima** (m-koo-*lee*-mah)
farming: **kilimo** (kee-*lee*-moh)
fat: **mafuta** (mah-*foo*-tah) n. ; **nene**
  (*neh*-neh) adj.
father: **baba** (*bah*-bah)
fear: **ogopa** (oh-*goh*-pah)
February: **februari/ mwezi wa pili**
  (feb-roo-*ah*-ree/ m-*weh*-zee wah
  pee-lee)
to feel: **hisi** (*hee*-see)
feet: **miguu** (mee-*goo*-oo)
to fight: **piga** (*pee*-gah)
to find: **pata** (*pah*-tah)
five: **tano** (*tah*-noh)
to flee: **toroka** (toh-*roh*-kah)
flowers: **maua** (mah-*oo*-ah)
fly: **nzi** (*n*-zee)
to fly: **ruka** (*roo*-kah)
foam: **povu** (*poh*-voo)
foolish: **-jinga** (*jee*-ngah)
foot: **mguu** (m-*goo*-oo)
four: **nne** (*n*-neh)
friend: **rafiki** (rah-*fee*-kee)
to fry: **kaanga** (kah-*ah*-ngah)
full: **shiba** (*shee*-bah) [of food]; **jaa**
  (*jah*-ah)
fun: **raha** (*rah*-hah)

G

gate: **lango** (*lah*-ngoh)
to gather: **kusanya** (koo-*sah*-nyah)
gender: **jinsia** (jee-*nsee*-ah)
to get: **pata** (*pah*-tah)
girl: **msichana** (m-see-*chah*-nah)
goat: **mbuzi** (m-*boo*-zee)
God: **Mungu** (*moo*-ngoo)
good: **-zuri** (*zoo*-ree); **-ema** (*eh*-mah)
gospel: **injili** (ee-*njee*-lee)
to gossip: **sengenya** (seh-*ngeh*-nyah)
to grind: **saga** (*sah*-gah)
guard: **mlinzi** (m-*lee*-nzee) / **askari**
  (ah-*skah*-ree) n.
guava: **pera** (*peh*-rah)
guide: **mwongozo** (m-who-*ngoh*-zoh)
  [eg. guide book]; **kiongozi** (kee-oh-
  ngoh-zee) [eg. tour guide]
guinea fowl: **kanga** (*kah*-ngah)
gun: **bunduki** (boo-*ndoo*-kee)

H

habit: **mazoea** (mah-zoh-*eh*-ah)/
  tabia (tah-*bee*-ah)
to harvest: **vuna** (*voo*-nah)
he/him: **yeye** (*yeh*-yeh)
head: **kichwa** (*kee*-chwah)
to heal: **pona** (*poh*-nah)
to hear: **sikia** (see-*kee*-ah)
heart: **moyo** (*moh*-yoh)
heat: **joto** (*joh*-toh) n.
help: **usaidizi** (oo-sah-ee-*dee*-zee)
to help: **saidia** (sah-ee-*dee*-ah)
to hide: **ficha** (*fee*-chah)
to hold: **shika** (*shee*-kah)
to hop: **rukaruka** (roo-kah-*roo*-kah)

hope: **matumaini** (mah-too-mah-*ee*-nee) n.

hot: **moto** (*moh*-toh)

human: **binadamu** (bee-nah-*dah*-moo)

humane: **utu** (*oo*-too)

to hurry: **haraka** (hah-*rah*-kah)/ **kasi** (*kah*-see)

husband: **mume** (*moo*-meh)

I

ice cream: **aisikrimu** (ah-ee-see-*kree*-moo)

ice: **barafu** (bah-*rah*-foo)

ill: **-gonjwah** (*goh*-njwah)

immediately: **sasa hivi** (*sah*-sah *hee*-vee); **mara moja** (*mah*-rah *moh*-jah)

to increase: **ongeza** (oh-*ngeh*-zah)

inside: **ndani** (*ndah*-nee)

interesting: **ya kupendeza** (yah koo-peh-*ndeh*-zah)

is: **ni** (nee)

island: **kisiwa** (kee-*see*-wah)

to itch: **washa** (*wah*-shah)

itinerary: **mpango** (m-*pah*-ngoh)

J

January: **Januari/mwezi wa kwanza** (jah-noo-*ah*-ree/m-*weh*-zee wah *kwah*-nzah)

jeans: **jinsi** (*jee*-nsee)

job: **kazi** (*kah*-zee)

to join in: **ungana** (oo-*ngah*-nah)

joke: **mzaha** (m-*zah*-hah) / **masihara** (mah-see-*hah*-rah) n.

judge: **hakimu** (hah-*kee*-moo) n.

jug: **jagi** (*jah*-gee) / **dumu** (*doo*-moo)

juice: **juisi/sharubati** (joo-*ee*-see/ shah-roo-*bah*-tee)

July: **julai/ mwezi wa saba** (joo-*lah*-ee/ m-*weh*-zee wah *sah*-bah)

jump: **ruka** (*roo*-kah)

junction: **njia panda** (n-*jee*-ah *pah*-ndah)

June: **juni/mwezi wa sita** (joo-nee/ m-*weh*-zee wah *see*-tah)

justice: **haki** (*hah*-kee)

K

to keep: **weka** (*weh*-kah)

kettle: **birika** (bee-*ree*-kah)

key: **ufunguo** (oo-foo-*ngoo*-oh)

kidney: **figo** (*fee*-goh)

to kill: **ua** (*oo*-ah)

kindergarten: **shule ya chekechea** (*shoo*-leh yah cheh-keh-*cheh*-ah)

king: **mfalme** (m-*fah*-lmeh)

kiosk: **kibanda** (kee-*bah*-ndah)

kiss: **busu** (*boo*-soo) n. v.

kitchen: **jiko** (*jee*-koh)

kitten: **mtoto wa paka** (m-*toh*-toh wah *pah*-kah)

to knead: **kanda** (*kah*-ndah)

knife: **kisu** (*kee*-soo)

knife: **kisu** (*kee*-soo)

to knit: **fuma** (*foo*-mah)

to knock: **bisha** (*bee*-shah) [at the door]

to know: **jua** (*joo*-ah)

knowledge: **maarifa** (mah-ah-*ree*-fah)

L

lake: **ziwa** (*zee*-wah)

lamp: **taa** (*tah*-ah)

land: **ardhi** (ah-*r*-dhee)

language: **lugha** (*loo*-gah)

last: **mwisho** (m-*wee*-shoh)

late: **chelewa** (cheh-*leh*-wah)

leaf: **jani** (*jah*-nee)

to leave: **ondoka** (oh-*ndoh*-kah)

left hand: **mkono wa kushoto** (m-*koh*-noh wah koo-*shoh*-toh)

left: **kushoto** (koo-*shoh*-toh)

to lend: **azima** (ah-*zee*-mah); **kopesha** (koh-*peh*-shah) [of money]

lesson: **somo** (*soh*-moh)

to lie: **danganya/sema uwongo** (dah-*ngah*-nyah/*seh*-mah oo-*woh*-ngoh)

to lift: **inua** (ee-*noo*-ah)

light: **-epesi** (eh-*peh*-see) adj. [weight] ; **mwanga** (m-*wah*-ngah) n.

lightning: **radi** (*rah*-dee)

little: **-dogo** (*doh*-goh) /**chache** (*chah*-cheh) / **haba** (*hah*-bah)

loan: **mkopo** (m-*koh*-poh) n.

to loan: **mkopo** (m-*koh*-poh)

long: **refu** (*reh*-foo)

love: **mapenzi** (mah-*peh*-nzee) n.

man: **mwanaume** (m-wah-nah-*oo*-meh)

March: **machi/mwezi wa tatu** (*ma-chee*/ m-*weh*-zee wah *tah*-too)

market: **soko** (*soh*-koh)

marriage: **ndoa** (n-*doh*-ah)

to marry: **oa** (*oh*-ah) [of a man]; **olewa** (oh-*leh*-wah) [of a woman]

May: **mei**/ **mwezi wa tano** (*meh*-ee/ m-*weh*-zee wah *tah*-noh)

meat: **nyama** (*nyah*-mah)

to meet: **kutana** (koo-*tah*-nah)

meeting: **mkutano** (m-koo-*tah*-noh)

to mend: **rekebisha** (reh-keh-*bee*-shah) / **tengeneza** (teh-ngeh-*neh*-zah)

menu: **menyu** (*meh*-nyoo); **orodha ya vyakula** (oh-*roh*-dhah yah vyah-*koo*-lah)

message: **ujumbe** (oo-*joo*-mbeh) / **taarifa** (tah-ah-*ree*-fah) / **habari** (hah-*bah*-ree)

metal: **chuma** (*choo*-mah)

middle: **katikati** (kah-tee-*kah*-tee)

mom: **mama** (*mah*-mah)

money: **pesa** (*peh*-sah)

month: **mwezi** (m-*weh*-zee)

moon: **mwezi** (m-*weh*-zee)

morning: **asubuhi** (ah-soo-*boo*-hee)

mountain: **mlima** (m-*lee*-mah)

museum: **jumba la makumbusho** (*joo*-mbah lah mah-koo-*mboo*-shoh)

naked: **uchi** (*oo*-chee)

name: **jina** (*jee*-nah)

near: **karibu** (kah-*ree*-boo)

necessary: **sharti** (shah-*r*-tee)/ **lazima** (lah-*zee*-mah)

neck: **shingo** (*shee*-ngoh)

to need: **hitaji** (hee-*tah*-jee)

net: **neti** (*neh*-tee) n.

news: **habari** (hah-*bah*-ree)

nice: **-zuri** (*zoo*-ree)

nine: **tisa** (*tee*-sah)

no: **hapana/la** (hah-*pah*-nah/lah)

noise: **kelele** (keh-*leh*-leh)

nor: **wala** (*wah*-lah)

north: **kaskazini** (kas-kah-*zee*-nee)

nose: **pua** (*poo*-ah)

not: **sio** (*see*-oh)

noun: **nomino** (noh-*mee*-noh)

November: **novemba/mwezi wa kumi na moja** (noh-*veh*-mbah/m-*weh*-zee wah *koo*-mee nah *moh*-jah)

nutrition: **lishe** (*lee*-sheh)

O

obey: **tii** (*tee*-ee)

October: **oktoba/ mwezi wa kumi** (oh-*ktoh*-bah/m-*weh*-zee wah *koo*-mee)

office: **ofisi** (oh-*fee*-see)

oil: **mafuta** (mah-*foo*-tah)

okay: **sawa** (*sah*-wah)

old: **-zee** (*zeh*-eh)

olive: **zeituni** (zeh-ee-*too*-nee)

on: **juu ya** (*joo*-oo yah)

one: **moja** (*moh*-jah)

opportunity: **fursa** (foo-*r*-sah)/ **nafasi** (nah-*fah*-see)

or: **au** (*ah*-oo)

orange: **chungwa** (*choo*-ngwah) [fruit]

orange: **rangi ya chungwa** (*rah*-ngee yah *choo*-ngwah) [the color]

P

To pack: **funga virago** (*foo*-ngah vee-*rah*-goh)

pain: **maumivu** (mah-oo-*mee*-voo)

to panic: **shikwa na hofu** (*shee*-kwah nah *hoh*-foo)

to pass: **pita** (*pee*-tah)

passport: **pasipoti** (pah-see-*poh*-tee)

to pay: **lipa** (*lee*-pah)

pin: **pini** (*pee*-nee) n.

To point: **nyoosha kidole** (nyo-*oh*-shah kee-*doh*-leh)

To praise: **sifu** (*see*-foo)

to pray: **omba** (*oh*-mbah)

priest: **padri/ kasisi** (*pah*-dree/ kah-*see*-see)

Q

quarter: **robo** (*roh*-boh)

queen: **malkia** (mahl-*kee*-ah)

queue: **laini** (lah-*ee*-nee)

quick: **haraka** (hah-*rah*-kah)

R

rabbit: **sungura** (soo-*ngoo*-rah)

radio: **radio** (reh-*dee*-oh)

to rape: **najisi** (nah-*jee*-see)

rat: **panya** (*pah*-nyah)

raw: **-bichi** (*bee*-chee)

red: **-ekundu** (eh-*koo*-ndoo)

religion: **dini** (*dee*-nee)

to repeat: **rudia** (roo-*dee*-ah)

riot: **fujo** (*foo*-joh)

to riot: **fanya fujoh** (*fah*-nyah *foo*-joh)

to roam: **randaranda** (rah-ndah-*rah*-ndah)

to rot: **oza** (*oh*-zah)

S

safe: **salama** (sah-*lah*-mah) adj

save: **weka akiba** (*weh*-kah ah-*kee*-bah) [of money]

September: **septemba/ mwezi wa tisa** (sep-*teh*-mbah/ m-*weh*-zee wah *tee*-sah)

to serve: **pakua** (pah-*koo*-ah) [of food]

seven: **saba** (*sah*-bah)

shirt: **shati** (*shah*-tee)

sin: **dhambi** (*dhah*-mbee)

six: **sita** (*see*-tah)

skin: **ngozi** (*ngoh*-zee)

skirt: **sketi** (*skeh*-tee)

socks: **soksi** (*soh*-ksee)

song: **wimbo** (*wee*-mboh)

to start: **anza** (*ah*-nzah)

station: **stesheni** (steh-*sheh*-nee)/**kituo** (kee-*too*-oh)

to stop: **acha** (*ah*-chah)

sweater: **sweta** (*sweh*-tah)

T

team: **timu** (*tee*-moo)

teeth: **meno** (*meh*-noh)

ten: **kumi** (*koo*-mee)

three: **tatu** (*tah*-too)

too: **pia** (*pee*-ah)

tooth: **jino** (*jee*-noh)

top: **kilele** (kee-*leh*-leh)

train: **treni** (*treh*-nee); **gari moshi** (*gah*-ree *moh*-shee)

traffic jam: **msongamano wa magari** (m-soh-ngah-*mah*-noh wah mah-*gah*-ree)

trap: **mtego** (m-*teh*-goh)

to trap: **tega** (*teh*-gah)

true: **ukweli** (oo-*kweh*-lee)

to turn: **pinda/geuka** (*pee*-ndah/ geh-*oo*-kah)

two: **mbili** (m-*bee*-lee)

U

umbrella: **mwavuli** (m-wah-*voo*-lee)

uncle: **mjomba** (m-*joh*-mbah)

union: **muungano** (moo-oo-*ngah*-noh)

unity: **umoja** (oo-*moh*-jah)

university: **chuo kikuu** (*choo*-oh *kee*-koo)

unstoppable: **isio epukika** (ee-*see*-oh eh-poo-*kee*-kah)

V

vanish: **potea** (poh-*teh*-ah)

vein: **mshipa** (m-*shee*-pah)

Venus: **zuhura** (zoo-*hoo*-rah)

video: **video** (vee-*deh*-oh)

virus: **virusi** (vee-*roo*-see)

voice: **sauti** (sah-*oo*-tee)

vomit: **matapishi** (mah-tah-*pee*-shee)

to vomit: **tapika** (tah-*pee*-kah)

to vote: **piga kura** (*pee*-gah koo-rah)

W

wait: **subiri** (soo-*bee*-ree)

walk: **tembea** (teh-*mbeh*-ah)

wall: **ukuta** (oo-*koo*-tah)

west: **magharibi** (mah-gah-*ree*-bee)

wife: **mke** (*m*-keh)

win: **shinda** (*shee*-ndah)

winner: **mshindi** (m-*shee*-ndee)

work: **kazi** (*kah*-zee)

to work: **fanya kazi** (*fah*-nyah *kah*-zee)

to worry: **waza** (*wah*-zah)

to write: **andika** (ah-*ndee*-kah)

writer: **mwandishi** (m-wah-*ndee*-shee)

Y

to yawn: **piga miayo** (*pee*-gah mee-*ah*-yoh)

yeast: **hamira** (hah-*mee*-rah)

to yell: **piga mayowe** (*pee*-gah mah-*yoh*-weh)

yellow: **rangi ya manjano** (*rah*-ngee yah mah-*njah*-noh)

yes: **ndio** (n-*dee*-oh)

yet: **bado** (*bah*-doh)

young: **changa** (*chah*-ngah)

Z

zebra: **punda milia** (*poo*-ndah mee-*lee*-ah)

zero: **sufuri/sifuri** (soo-*foo*-ree/ see-*foo*-ree)

to zigzag: **zigizaga** (zee-gee-*zah*-gah)

zoo: **bustani la wanyama** (boo-*stah*-nee lah wah-*nyah*-mah)

zucchini: **zukini** (zoo-*kee*-nee)

Appendix D
Answer Key

Chapter 2

1.

A	B
Habari za safari?	Salama
Hujambo	Sijambo.
Mambo vipi?	Poa.Salama.
Shikamoo	Marahaba.
Kwema?	Kwema.

2. a.HA**BA**RI; b. **SALAMA**; c. SI**JAM**BO

Chapter 3

M/WA: Mwalimu, watoto, simba, mama, daktari

M/MI: miti, milimao,

JI/MA: parachichi, jimbo

KI/VI: kiatu, kioo, chama, chakula, kitabu, vikombe, kiti

N/N simu, kompyuta, shati, nyumba, meza, sahani, karoti,

U/N: uso, wimbo,

U/U: uzuri, upendo

PA/KU/MU nyumbani, chuoni, hospitalini

Chapter 4

✓ kuoga   ✓ kupiga mswaki   ✓ kuimba

✓ kulala   ✓ kusoma   ✓ kuchora

Chapter 5

1.

9	tisa
18	kumi na nane
177	mia moja sabini na saba
1888	elfu moja mia nane themanini na nane
16,000	elfu kumi na sita
150,000	elfu mia moja na Hamsini/ laki moja na nusu
3,330,000	milioni tatu, elfu mia thelathini na tatu

2.

saa tatu na nusu	d.
saa kumi na moja kasoro dakika ishirini	e.
saa tano na dakika kumi	b.
saa moja na dakika arobaini na tano	f.
saa mbili kamili	a.
saa mbili kasorobo	f.
saa kumi na dakika arobaini	e.
saa tisa na robo	c.

Chapter 6

   a. mama

   b. mama wa kambo

   c. mume

   d. mke

   e. bibi/nyanya

Chapter 7

1.

   a. chini ya kiti

   b. nyuma ya kiti

   c. mbele ya kiti

   d. juu ya kiti

2.

Nenda moja kwa moja, pinda kulia na uendelee kwenda moja kwa moja kwa mita chahche. Pinda kushoto halafu kulia. Tena pinda kulia na uendee moja kwa moja hadi mwisho kisha pinda kushoto. Utafika nje.

3.

a, c, d, e

Chapter 8

sukari	image of sugar
mayai	image of eggs
samaki	image of fish
nyama	image of meat
asali	honey

Chapter 9

<table>
<tr><td>

B: <u>Your spouse</u>

Mambo!

Mpenzi wangu

Mpenzi wako daima,

</td><td>

C: <u>Your new business partner</u>

Shikamoo!

Bw. Otieno

Wako mwaminifu,

</td></tr>
</table>

Chapter 10

1. b
2. e
3. d
4. c
5. a
6.

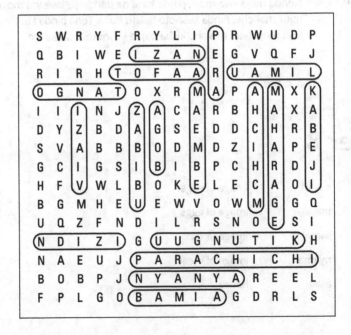

Chapter 12

People at the office	Things at the office
mkurugenzi	kalamu
katibu	ripoti
mwajiri	rafu

Chapter 13

(from left to right)

kifaru, nyati, ndovu/tembo, simba, chui

Chapter 14

1. pikipiki/bodaboda
2. basi
3. treni/gari la moshi
4. bajaji/tuktuk

Chapter 15

a. bafu
b. sebule
c. chumba cha kulala
d. jikoni

Chapter 16

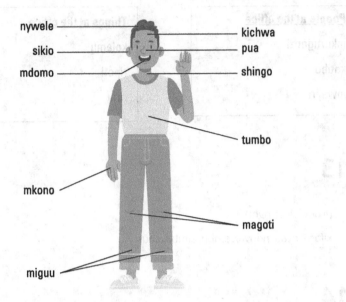

nywele — kichwa

sikio — pua

mdomo — shingo

tumbo

mkono

magoti

miguu

Index

A

accommodations
  about, 243
  bathroom, 246–247
  bedroom, 245
  dining room, 245
  finding, 247–254
  Fun & Games, 259–260
  kitchen, 245–246
  renting apartments, 254–256
  sitting room, 244–245
  spaces in apartment/home, 243–247
  Talkin' the Talk, 252–253, 257–258
activities, daily, 124–125
addresses, requesting and giving, 91–94
adjectives
  comparative, 185
  using numbers as, 118–119
adverbs, sequence, 126
afya (health), 261
age, asking "how old are you" and stating your, 94
ahsante (thank you), 152
Airtel Money, 182
allergies, food, 150–151
alphabet
  consonants, 15–17
  sounds, 13–14
amani (peace), 10
amenities, asking about, 247
answer key, 329–334
anuani (address), 93
apartments, renting, 254–256
apatiment (apartment), 142

asiyesikia la mkuu huvunjika guu
    proverb, 280
askari (guard), 10
Audio Online icon, 5

B

baadaye (later), 24
baba (father), 22
bado (not yet), 114
bahati (luck), 227
bajeti (budget), 255
baraka (blessing), 10
barua pepe (email), 160, 251
basi (bus), 233–234
bathroom, 246–247
beaches, 218
bedroom, 245
bei (price), 182, 184
bei rahisi (cheap), 184
beseni (bucket), 244
beverages, 148–149
Bi (Mrs/Ms.), 200
bicycles, 236–237
bili (bill), 152
bill, paying at a restaurant, 152–153
birthdays, 100
boats, 237–238
bodaboda (motorcycle taxi), 236
bodaboda ya baisikeli (bicycle taxi), 236
body parts, 261–264
bomba (faucets), 32
breakfast, 146
brokoli (broccoli), 54
buchani (butcher shop), 176

bucket showers, 244
bus travel, 233–234
business dinners, 208–210
Bwana (Mister/Mr.), 200
bweni (dormitory/hostel), 121, 248

C

calendar
  days of the week, 96–97
  months, 97–99
cardinal numbers
  counting 0-10, 82–83
  counting 11-100, 83
  counting 101-1,000,00, 83–85
casual clothing, 191
cellphones
  about, 157–158
  asking someone to call you, 158
  asking to speak with someone, 161
  leaving messages, 161–162
  texting, 162
chai (tea), 146
chakula cha kubeba (take away food), 155
chakula cha mchana/chamcha (lunch), 145
chakula cha usika/chakula cha jioni/chajio
    (supper), 146
Cheat Sheet (website), 5
checking in, to hotels, 251
checking out, of hotels, 253–254
children's books, 286
choo (stool/toilet), 133, 272
chores, 124–125
chumba (single room), 243
chuo (school/university), 132, 295
clothing
  about, 187
  casual, 191
  cultural, 189–190
  describing, 193–195

formal, 192–193
for occasions, 187–189
Talkin' the Talk, 195–197
types of, 191–193
for weather, 187–189
Words to Know, 197
Coca-Cola Company, 149
colleagues, interacting with, 200–202
comparative adjectives, 185
consonants, 13–14, 15–17
content creators, on social media, 285
conversations, with Swahili speakers, 285
counting
  11-100, 83
  101-1,000,00, 83–85
  ordinal numbers, 86
  0-10, 82–83
cultural clothing, 189–190
Cultural Wisdom icon, 4
currencies, 181

D

dada (sister), 116
daily activities, 124–125
dakika (minutes), 104–105
daktari (doctor/physician), 272
daladala, 232–233
dalili za ugonjwa (symptoms of illness), 267
damu (blood), 272
dates. See numbers and dates
dawa (medicines), 272
dawa ya kupunguza maumivu (pain
    killer), 272
days of the week, 96–97
dazeni (dozen), 179
dereva (driver), 232, 234
dereva wa teksi (taxi driver), 236
dh consonant cluster, 15
digrii (degree), 222

O

P

R

weather
  clothing for, 187–189
  for travel, 220–222
wenyeji (locals), 160
wewe (you), 22
what/where do you study, 29–30
where questions, asking, 133–134
where you come from/live, 25–27
wike tatu (three weeks ago), 62
wiki ijayo (next week), 63, 100
wiki iliyopita (last week), 62
wiki kumi zijazo (ten weeks from now), 63
wiki kumi zilizopita (ten weeks ago), 62
wiki tatu zijazo (three weeks from now), 63
woman, revealing marital status as a,
      114–115
words, to avoid, 287–290
Words to Know
  clothing, 197
  directions, 142
  eating in and dining out, 155
  expressions, 22
  health, 272
  nouns, 54–55
  numbers and dates, 93, 99, 105
  safaris, 227
  shopping, 184
  small talk, 121, 129
  technology, 160, 164, 167

transportation, 240
  verbs, 62, 63, 65
  workplace, 205
workplace
  about, 199–200
  attending meetings, 205–206
  business dinners, 208–210
  finding people/things at the office, 202–203
  Fun & Games, 211
  interacting with colleagues, 200–202
  making introductions, 206–207
  Talkin' the Talk, 203–205
  talking in meetings, 207–208
  Words to Know, 205
writing dates, 99

Y

yaliyopita si ndwele, tugange yajayo
      proverb, 278
yangu (my), 123
years, 96
yeye (he/she), 22
yourself, introducing, 24–25

Z

zawadi (gift), 10
zuri (beautiful/good), 10

About the Authors

Seline Ayugi Okeno was born and raised in Siaya, Kenya. She holds a B.Ed. Arts from Maseno University in Kenya and an M.A. in Applied Linguistics from Ohio University. Before moving to the United States, she taught English at various high schools in East Africa. Seline taught Swahili as a Fulbright Foreign Language Teaching Assistant at Northwestern University before proceeding to Ohio University as course coordinator of the Swahili language program. She is currently a Swahili and English Teaching Fellow at The University of Edinburgh in Scotland. In her spare time, she enjoys discovering new walking trails, sampling the music scene in Edinburgh, and reading.

Asmaha Heddi hails from Arusha, Tanzania. She is a Kiswahili lecturer at the University of Kansas. She holds a B.A. from the University of Dar es Salaam in Tanzania and an M.A. in Applied Linguistics from Ohio University. Asmaha was a Fulbright Foreign Language Teaching Assistant at Michigan State University where she taught Kiswahili. Her research interests include Second Language Teaching, Second Language Acquisition, and Computer Assisted Language Learning. She has taught Kiswahili at different universities both in Tanzania and the United States, such as MS TCDC–Tanzania, The University of Virginia, The University of Illinois–Urbana Champaign, The International Centre for Language Studies, Ohio University, and Michigan State University. She enjoys reading, dancing, cooking, and spending time with her family and friends.

Dedication

To my parents, Mr. Gilbert Okeno and Mrs. Florence Okeno, who cannot wait to receive a physical copy of this book, although they have no use for it. [**Seline**]

and

To my husband, Denis Waswa, for his steady support and understanding throughout the journey of writing this book. To my son Amani Waswa, this book is dedicated to you, my little Swahili explorer, in the hopes that it will inspire you to embrace our language and culture. [**Asmaha**]

Authors' Acknowledgments

We would like to extend our gratitude to the individuals whose contributions and support made this project a reality. Our sincere appreciation goes to our voice actors, Janet Ochieng' and Abbie Abuya for bringing our characters to life in the audio files. Their voices added depth to our work and widened the scope of this book beyond reading.

To our diligent technical editor, Jossy Mutisya, your expertise in this language and keen eye were instrumental in carving this book into its final form. Your commitment to excellence and making Swahili accessible made all the difference, and we thank you for your contributions.

We also extend our thanks to John Wiley & Sons Inc., our publisher, for believing in our vision and supporting us throughout the journey. To the team at Wiley, thank you for your professionalism, patience, and firm guidance through the tight deadlines and time difference logistics.

Our deepest gratitude goes to our family and friends for their unwavering encouragement and understanding as we poured countless hours into writing this book.

Publisher's Acknowledgments

Acquisitions Editor: Jennifer Yee
Senior Project Editor: Paul Levesque
Copy Editor: Kelly D. Henthorne
Technical Editor: Jossy Mutisya

Production Editor: Saikarthick Kumarasamy
Cover Image: © ac productions/Getty Images

Take dummies with you everywhere you go!

Whether you are excited about e-books, want more from the web, must have your mobile apps, or are swept up in social media, dummies makes everything easier.

Leverage the power

Dummies is the global leader in the reference category and one of the most trusted and highly regarded brands in the world. No longer just focused on books, customers now have access to the dummies content they need in the format they want. Together we'll craft a solution that engages your customers, stands out from the competition, and helps you meet your goals.

Advertising & Sponsorships

Connect with an engaged audience on a powerful multimedia site, and position your message alongside expert how-to content. Dummies.com is a one-stop shop for free, online information and know-how curated by a team of experts.

- Targeted ads
- Video
- Email Marketing

- Microsites
- Sweepstakes sponsorship

20 MILLION
PAGE VIEWS
EVERY SINGLE MONTH

15 MILLION
UNIQUE
VISITORS PER MONTH

43%
OF ALL VISITORS
ACCESS THE SITE
VIA THEIR MOBILE DEVICES

700,000 NEWSLET
SUBSCRIPTI
TO THE INBOXES OF
300,000 UNIQUE INDIVIDUALS
EVERY WEEK

# of dummies

Custom Publishing

Reach a global audience in any language by creating a solution that will differentiate you from competitors, amplify your message, and encourage customers to make a buying decision.

- Apps
- Books
- eBooks
- Video
- Audio
- Webinars

Brand Licensing & Content

Leverage the strength of the world's most popular reference brand to reach new audiences and channels of distribution.

For more information, visit dummies.com/biz

PERSONAL ENRICHMENT

9781119187790	9781119179030	9781119293354	9781119293347	9781119310068	9781119235606
USA $26.00	USA $21.99	USA $24.99	USA $22.99	USA $24.99	USA $24.99
CAN $31.99	CAN $25.99	CAN $29.99	CAN $27.99	CAN $27.99	CAN $29.99
UK £19.99	UK £16.99	UK £17.99	UK £16.99	UK £16.99	UK £17.99

9781119251163	9781119235491	9781119279952	9781119283133	9781119287117	9781119130246
USA $24.99	USA $26.99	USA $24.99	USA $24.99	USA $24.99	USA $22.99
CAN $29.99	CAN $31.99	CAN $29.99	CAN $29.99	CAN $29.99	CAN $27.99
UK £17.99	UK £19.99	UK £17.99	UK £17.99	UK £16.99	UK £16.99

PROFESSIONAL DEVELOPMENT

9781119311041	9781119255796	9781119293439	9781119281467	9781119280651	9781119251132	9781119310563
USA $24.99	USA $39.99	USA $26.99	USA $26.99	USA $29.99	USA $24.99	USA $34.00
CAN $29.99	CAN $47.99	CAN $31.99	CAN $31.99	CAN $35.99	CAN $29.99	CAN $41.99
UK £17.99	UK £27.99	UK £19.99	UK £19.99	UK £21.99	UK £17.99	UK £24.99

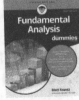

9781119181705	9781119263593	9781119257769	9781119293477	9781119265313	9781119239314	9781119293323
USA $29.99	USA $26.99	USA $29.99	USA $26.99	USA $24.99	USA $29.99	USA $29.99
CAN $35.99	CAN $31.99	CAN $35.99	CAN $31.99	CAN $29.99	CAN $35.99	CAN $35.99
UK £21.99	UK £19.99	UK £21.99	UK £19.99	UK £17.99	UK £21.99	UK £21.99